All Change at Work?

British employment relations
1980–1998, as portrayed by the
Workplace Industrial Relations
Survey series

**Neil Millward, Alex Bryson
and John Forth**

London and New York

First published 2000 by Routledge
11 New Fetter Lane, London EC4P 4EE

Simultaneously published in the USA and Canada
by Routledge
29 West 35th Street, New York, NY 10001

Routledge is an imprint of the Taylor & Francis Group

Transferred to Digital Printing 2003

Typeset in Garamond by
Keystroke, Jacaranda Lodge, Wolverhampton

British Library Cataloguing in Publication Data
A catalogue record for this book is available from the British Library

Library of Congress Cataloging in Publication Data
Millward, Neil.
    All change at work? : British employment relations 1980–1998, as
portrayed by the workplace industrial relations survey series / Neil Millward,
Alex Bryson, and John Forth.
        p.   cm.
Includes bibliographical references and index.
    1. Industrial relations–Great Britain. I. Title: British employment
relations 1980–1998. II. Title: Workplace industrial relations survey series.
III. Bryson, Alex. IV. Forth, John (John Andrew) V. Title.

HD8391 .M548 2000
331'.0941'09048–dc21   99–089145

ISBN 0-415-20634-0 (hbk)
ISBN 0-415-20635-9 (pbk)

Contents

Figures

Tables

Foreword

This book is the second volume of findings arising from the 1998 Workplace Employee Relations Survey (WERS98). It is appropriate that it should focus on change. WERS98 was the fourth in a series of workplace surveys, the first of which was conducted as long ago as 1980. The last two decades have seen extensive change in the economic, social and political landscape of Britain including – as this book amply demonstrates – employment relations policies and practices. But the extent of change – and the factors behind it – have been the subject of continuing debate among academics, practitioners and policy makers.

The purpose of the survey series has always been to contribute to public discussion on employment relations by providing an extensive and authoritative body of factual information on practice in British workplaces. On each successive survey this has been achieved through the publication of at least one volume by the primary research team and a plethora of journal articles and research papers by academics in Britain and abroad. The surveys have thus gained an international reputation and formed the model for similar ones in several other countries.

The design and content of the survey evolved to meet changing requirements and changing circumstances. For example, compared with the 1980 Workplace Industrial Relations Survey, WERS98 placed less emphasis on formal institutions and more emphasis on management practice. The main 1998 survey, for the first time, included workplaces with between ten and twenty-four employees. And even more of a departure was the introduction of an employee element through self-completion questionnaires passed on to randomly selected workers in the sampled workplaces.

In deciding to make these major changes to survey design and content, the WERS steering committee was acutely conscious of the need to retain an element of continuity with earlier surveys. Hence the panel element to the survey was expanded considerably and given more focus than the earlier ones. A special interview schedule was used for these workplaces, retaining many questions from the 1990 survey and probing, where appropriate, for the reasons why change had taken place.

Survey fieldwork finished in June 1998 for the main survey and a month later for the panel. A booklet of first findings was published in October 1998. The first volume of survey findings, *Britain at Work*, was published in September 1999. Both these publications concentrated on providing an overview of results from the 1998 cross-section element of the survey. Chapter 10 of *Britain at Work* presented key time-series results from the survey series, but only a little material from the panel survey. In a sense, it provided the appetizer to the main course provided by this book.

The survey itself remains a collaborative enterprise between the four sponsors: the Department of Trade and Industry (DTI), which in 1995 took over from the former Employment Department responsibility within government for employment relations; the Economic and Social Research Council (ESRC); the Advisory, Conciliation and Arbitration Service (ACAS) and the Policy Studies Institute (PSI), supported in part with funds from the Leverhulme Trust. Not only does co-sponsorship spread the costs, it also ensures that the surveys reflect a variety of interests – including those of policy makers, practitioners and academics. And it safeguards the independence and credibility of the survey findings.

This survey has been overseen from inception to completion by a steering committee of the four sponsors. Zmira Hornstein chaired the committee until her retirement in spring 1998. On behalf of the entire steering committee, I wish to record my thanks for her unique and valuable contribution. Other members of the steering committee have been: Bernard Carter, representing DTI policy interests; W. R. Hawes and, lately, Peter Syson, representing ACAS; Pam Meadows, Margaret Blunden and Jim Skea who successively represented PSI; and Christine McCullough, Jeremy Neathey and Paul Marginson representing ESRC. Their constructive approach has contributed greatly to the success of the project.

The committee has been supported by an able research team. The team was headed, from DTI, by Mark Cully who, along with Stephen Woodland and Andrew O'Reilly (both DTI) and Gill Dix (ACAS), took primary responsibility for the cross-section element of the survey and for writing *Britain at Work*. The authors of this volume, led by Neil Millward, took primary responsibility for the panel survey and the analysis of change over time.

Fieldwork for the survey was contracted, after competitive tendering, to Social and Community Planning Research (SCPR) – now the National Centre for Social Research. Particular recognition must go to Colin Airey and Rosemary Hamilton of SCPR, who have worked on all four surveys to date, together with Anthony McKernan. They were backed up by a first-rate team of interviewers and data processors.

The steering committee has always taken great pride in achieving a high response rate for the survey, and in this respect the outcome of the fourth survey is again a source of satisfaction. Credit must go to both the research team and SCPR; but the response rate also says much about the importance of the subject to those at the sharp end of employment relations.

The authors write in their professional capacity as social scientists. Hence the views expressed in this volume do not necessarily represent the position of any of the four survey sponsors or the authors' employing organizations. No doubt some will disagree with the authors' interpretation of the data. This is to be welcomed. Indeed, we hope this volume, like its companion, will act as a spur to further analysis and reflection. That is why the data have been lodged at the ESRC Data Archive. The impact that the survey results have on policy and academic debate, together with the feedback that we receive from readers and users of the data, will be important factors in determining the future course of workplace surveys in Britain.

Mark Beatson
Chair, WERS98 Steering Committee
October 1999

Acknowledgements

Our thanks go, first and foremost, to the Leverhulme Trust for providing generous support for the research that culminated in the writing of this book. The Trust has supported PSI's involvement in the survey series since the beginning; it helpfully agreed to continue supporting the current enterprise when two of us moved to the National Institute of Economic and Social Research. Both institutes generously provided additional and continuing support for the work.

We are also grateful for the personal and professional contributions made by our colleagues on the wider WERS98 research team. Members of the team and of the steering committee provided us with valuable comments on the manuscript, for which we thank them. We particularly acknowledge the work done by Stephen Woodland at the DTI in initially preparing many of the time-series variables used in our analysis. Ultimate responsibility for the contents of the book, however, rests with us.

Finally, we wish to thank the thousands of managers and other employees who gave freely of their time to provide the data for WERS98 and its three predecessors. We and readers of this volume will always be in their debt.

Conventions used in tables and text

General conventions used in tables

\#   Unweighted base is fewer than 20 and therefore too low for percentages to be presented.

( ) Unweighted base is between 20 and 49; percentages should be treated with caution.

. . Data not available, either because the question was not asked or because it was asked in a sufficiently different form to make strict comparisons difficult.

*   Fewer than 0.5 per cent.

0   Zero.

General conventions used in text

Branch sites: All workplaces that are part of larger organizations, excluding head offices.

Closures: Workplaces with twenty-five or more employees in 1990 that had ceased their operations by 1998.

Continuing workplaces: Workplaces that remained in continuous operation between 1990 and 1998 and employed at least twenty-five employees at the time of both the 1990 and 1998 surveys.

Establishment: See Workplace.

Establishments that form part of larger organizations: Workplaces that belong to a larger organization with additional sites, either in Britain or elsewhere.

Independent establishments: Workplaces that do not belong to any larger organization.

Industry and commerce: Private sector workplaces, together with those workplaces in the public sector that form part of trading public corporations or nationalized industries.

Joiners: Combination of **New workplaces** and **Workplaces that grew into the scope of the survey.**

Leavers: Combination of **Closures** and **Workplaces that fell out of the scope of the survey.**

New workplaces: Workplaces that came into being between 1990 and 1998 and employed twenty-five or more employees at the time of the 1998 survey.

Private manufacturing establishments: All private sector establishments in which the main activity lies within Division 2 (Extraction and manufacture of metals, minerals and chemicals), 3 (Manufacture of metal goods and engineering) or 4 (Other manufacturing) of the 1980 *Standard Industrial Classification.*

Private service sector establishments: All private sector establishments in which the main activity lies within Division 1 (Energy and water supply), 5 (Construction), 6 (Distribution; hotels and catering; and repairs), 7 (Transport and communication), 8 (Banking; finance; insurance; business services; and leasing) or 9 (Other services) of the 1980 *Standard Industrial Classification.*

Public sector establishments: All establishments within the public sector, irrespective of their main industrial activity.

Stand-alone sites: See **Independent establishments.**

Trading sector: See **Industry and commerce.**

WERS: Workplace Employee Relations Survey. Used to refer to the 1998 survey only.

WIRS: Workplace Industrial Relations Survey. Used to refer to the 1980, 1984 and 1990 surveys and to the survey series as a whole.

Workplace: The activities of a single employer at a single set of premises (for example, a single branch of a bank, a car factory, a department store or a school).

Workplaces that fell out of the scope of the survey: Workplaces with twenty-five or more employees at the time of the 1990 survey that, although still in operation, employed less than twenty-five employees at the time of the 1998 survey.

Workplaces that grew into the scope of the survey: Workplaces that employed less than twenty-five employees at the time of the 1990 survey, but twenty-five or more at the time of the 1998 survey.

1 Introduction

Eighteen years spanned the successive Conservative governments that started with Mrs Thatcher's election victory in 1979. Eighteen years span the successive Workplace Industrial Relations Surveys that started with our first survey in 1980.

This happy coincidence of timing allows us – almost compels us – to use the full range of information from the survey series to assess the impact of the Conservatives' policies and initiatives upon employment relations in Britain. The first survey was undertaken before the incoming government's initial 'reforms' in 1980. Our fourth survey was completed before the first wave of primary legislation enacted by the incoming Labour government of Mr Blair. The intervening eighteen years saw a host of changes affecting people at work. Successive Acts of Parliament sought to weaken trade unions and give employers and managers more power in the labour market and in the workplace. Tripartite national institutions were progressively abolished and new bodies created with employers and consumers the dominant interests. Developments in the world economy impinged greatly upon the structure and operations of industry and commerce. Privatization shifted whole sectors of the economy from public to private ownership as part of a broader programme of economic liberalization. 'Flexibility' became a goal and a guiding principle of government labour market policy. Social and demographic trends brought about changes in the composition of the labour force and in the types of jobs on offer and taken up. 'Human resource management' began to replace 'personnel management' and 'industrial relations' in the discourse of management and employee relations practitioners as well as among academics. Job insecurity became a dominant concern of many in employment; 'employability' the panacea for those who lost their jobs.

Did all this signal a transformation in British employment relations? Were the changes that took place so widespread and fundamental that to characterize them as a transformation is justified? Was it really 'All Change at Work?'

Our aim in this volume is to set out as much empirical evidence as we can from the Workplace Industrial Relations Survey (WIRS) series to answer this broad question. The WIRS series comprises a set of four national surveys of British workplaces, in which key role-holders at each workplace (most notably, the senior person dealing with industrial relations, employee relations or personnel matters) provide information on the nature of employment relations at their place of work. The surveys themselves took place in 1980, 1984, 1990 and 1998.

Many of the changes evident from the first three surveys in the series have been documented to some degree in our earlier reports (Millward *et al.*, 1992; Millward, 1994a) and in further explorations of the data by other analysts.[1] Commentators, teachers and researchers appreciated the great advantages of having results from a consistently designed series of surveys upon which to base those analyses. Yet in contemplating a fourth survey, many thought that so much of the landscape had changed that surveying it with the same instruments would provide a partial or misleading picture. Hence, when the four organizations that had been responsible for mounting the 1990 WIRS came together to discuss collaborating on a new survey, a radical rethink of its focus and design was high on the agenda. The four organizations were the Department of Trade and Industry (having taken over responsibility for industrial relations matters from the Department of Employment), the Economic and Social Research Council, the Advisory, Conciliation and Arbitration Service, and the Policy Studies Institute. Each of the four sponsors supported the discussions that led to the refocusing and redesign of the survey; those discussions are well documented elsewhere (Cully, 1998). One outcome was the renaming of the 1998 survey as the Workplace Employee Relations Survey (WERS), although we still use the original title (WIRS) to refer to the first three surveys and when referring to the series as a whole. However, the more crucial outcomes, in terms of our focus in this volume, were decisions as to how new elements could be added to the design and content of the latest survey without detracting from the essential comparability with the earlier surveys in the series.

We believe that, given the inevitable constraints of time and money, the updating of the survey instruments has been achieved with considerable success. Core topics have been retained, providing invaluable consistency, but important new elements have also been introduced into the survey.[2] The research team's companion volume (Cully *et al.*, 1999) draws on the wealth of data available from the 1998 WERS to provide an initial exploration of the state of employment relations at the end of the 1990s. Yet it contains only a brief overview of the changes that can be observed over the eighteen years since the first survey took place in 1980 (Millward *et al.*, 1999a).

Change, however, forms the sole focus of this book. Having achieved a balance of old and new in the 1998 survey, we are now able to compile a substantial bank of reliable data on workplace employment relations that stretches back over nearly two decades. The aim of this book is to present and interpret those data and, in so doing, provide an informed assessment of the changes that have taken place in workplace employment relations in Britain between 1980 and 1998.

The essential features of the WIRS design

Before providing some detail on the data and methods that will be employed in our analysis, it is necessary to say a little about the design of the Workplace Industrial Relations Surveys. Further detail may be found in the Technical Appendix.

In each of the surveys in the series, the establishment or workplace constitutes the principal unit of analysis. A workplace is defined as comprising the activities of a single employer at a single set of premises; examples might include a single branch of a bank, a car factory, a department store or a school. The central focus of the survey series has been the formal and structured relations that take place between management and employees at the workplace, although this focus softened in WERS98.

The geographical scope of each survey in the series extends to cover Great Britain, namely England, Scotland and Wales. The surveys cover workplaces in the private and public sectors and span all sectors of industry with only limited exceptions. The significant omissions are agriculture, forestry, fishing and deep coal mining.

Very small workplaces are also excluded for practical reasons. The 1980, 1984 and 1990 surveys limited their scope to workplaces with twenty-five or more employees, this being seen as the threshold below which it would be difficult to administer a survey of structured relations. After a fresh investigation of the practicalities, the 1998 survey dropped the threshold from twenty-five employees to ten. However, to retain consistency with earlier years we use only those workplaces from the 1998 survey employing twenty-five or more workers. Overall, the workplaces represented by each of the surveys are estimated to account for around 70 per cent of all employees in Britain in each of the survey years.

Each of the four cross-section surveys in the WIRS series is based on rigorous sampling methods, designed to ensure that results from the survey are representative of the total population of workplaces from which the sample is drawn. The samples themselves have been taken from frames considered to be the best available at the time, namely the Censuses of Employment of 1977, 1981 and 1987 and the Inter Departmental Business Register (IDBR) of 1997. Differential sampling by employment size has been used throughout the series to permit separate analysis of larger workplaces, which employ the majority of workers. Some modest differential sampling by industry was also introduced in 1990 and the principle extended in 1998. In each case, weights have been used in analysis to compensate for unequal probabilities of selection.

The representativeness of the results and quality of the data are further promoted by the investment of considerable time, energy and financial resources into the conduct of fieldwork. Carefully thought-out contact procedures, the deployment of professional, trained interviewers and meticulous data verification have been central features throughout the series. The high response rates that have been achieved – at least 75 per cent for each survey – are a testament to the efforts of the fieldwork organization (Social and Community Planning Research) and give a clear indication of the quality of the resultant data.[3]

The surveys themselves obtain information about the workplace through face-to-face interviews with key role-holders, using a standardized questionnaire. The main respondent at each establishment is the senior person dealing with industrial relations, employee relations or personnel matters, based on the principle that they are the most informed and reliable single source of information about employment relations at that workplace.[4] In some cases, particularly small establishments, this person is not a personnel specialist but may be a general manager, senior administrator or head teacher. Each survey has also included interviews with worker representatives, where present, though these data are not utilized in this volume, since changes in the selection procedures used in successive surveys mean that the samples are not comparable over time. Individual surveys have also included interviews with production managers (1984), financial managers (1990) and a survey of employees (1998) but, in the absence of time-series data, this information has also been largely ignored for the purposes of our analysis of change.

Thus, whilst there have been variations in peripheral elements from one survey to another, the principal features of the WIRS design have remained constant throughout the survey series. This consistency, when allied to a significant degree of continuity in questioning, means that the WIRS series represents the largest, most comprehensive and authoritative research resource available to those wishing to chart developments in workplace employment relations in Britain over the past twenty years.

Elements of the survey series employed in this volume

Having outlined the broad nature of the surveys, we now give some detail about those particular elements that will be employed in our analyses and explain how each can assist us to chart and explain recent changes in British employment relations. Figure 1.1 provides an illustration of the various components of the WIRS series, with the shaded cells representing those elements of the series that will be focused upon in this volume. Our analyses are based on what is, potentially, a very powerful combination of time-series and panel data.

WIRS time series 1980–98

The time series is formed from the interviews with the main management respondent in each of the four cross-section surveys. In Figure 1.1 these are represented by the four large cells labelled 'Senior person dealing with employee relations'. In each case, the cell also contains the total number of achieved interviews. As noted above, little of the information obtained from interviews

Figure 1.1 Elements of the survey series employed in our analysis

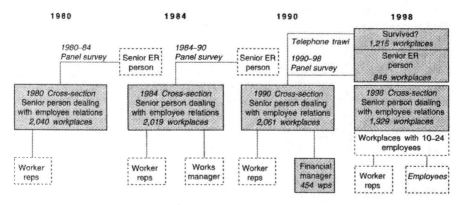

Notes

a In each year information was obtained from each of the specified role-holders via face-to-face interviews, with two exceptions. One exception was the interview that established the survival status of those 1,215 workplaces from 1990 that were excluded from the 1998 panel survey, where a telephone interview was conducted with the first informed contact at the establishment. The second exception was the 1998 survey of employees, conducted by means of a self-completion questionnaire.

b In 1990, we only use that part of the interview with the finance manager in which the respondent answered questions on behalf of the personnel manager. Data concerning the financial status of the establishment, obtained only from financial managers, is not used in this book.

with other role-holders is used, except for those elements of the 1990 survey of financial managers in which selected questions from the main interview were asked of this respondent instead of the personnel manager.[5]

This time-series dataset makes the most of the continuity present within the survey series by providing direct comparisons of employment relations practice at four specific points in time over the past two decades. It is therefore possible to investigate the degree of change or stability in the incidence of specific practices over time, both in aggregate and within particular sectors of the economy or types of workplace. One can also assess the extent to which historical relationships – such as that between workplace size and union presence, for example – have changed over the period of observation.

However, whilst comparisons between cross-sections can reveal interesting patterns of change, these represent the combined, 'net' outcome of what may amount to many different processes acting concurrently. Being simple 'snapshots' of practice at a particular point in time, cross-section data are unable to identify the means by which such 'net' changes have occurred. One possible explanation is that workplaces forming part of the population at both time-points have altered their behaviour in some way, derecognizing their unions for example. This may or may not be linked to a change in some other feature of the workplace that is known to be associated with the matter in question, such as a change in its size. A second possible explanation for 'net' changes over time is that, as workplaces leave a particular sector of the economy and are replaced by new establishments in that sector, the incidence of the practice in question may change as a result of differences in behaviour between the two groups. For example, large manufacturing plants that have closed down between the two time-points may have been more likely to recognize trade unions than new ones that were set up during the same period. The third, remaining explanation may be that 'net' change has arisen purely as a result of changes in the composition of the population. If, for example, trade union recognition is more prevalent in manufacturing than in services, and service-sector workplaces are becoming numerically more dominant in the population, this shift in the structure of industry could, all other things being equal, bring about a net change in the aggregate level of union recognition.

Of course, it is also the case that, where time-series results show stability between two points in time, there may none the less be considerable change beneath the surface. Any or all of the three types of change may be taking place within the population. The stability seen in the time series then merely reflects the fact that they have, in combination, served to cancel each other out at the aggregate level.

Whilst it is true that changes of the types mentioned above can be revealed to some extent within cross-section surveys through the use of retrospective questions, these are unlikely to be reliable when one is concerned with matters of detail or when lengthy periods of recall are required. In addition, the usual practice of drawing fresh samples for each cross-section means that information is not collected about the survival of different types of establishment over time. Hence, the role played by workplace closures, for example, in bringing about 'net' change remains obscure. These problems can be overcome by survey designs that separately identify three categories of workplace within the changing population:

1   Workplaces that are present within the survey population at both t_1 and t_2 (here termed 'continuing workplaces');
2   Workplaces that are present in the survey population at t_1 but not at t_2 ('leavers'); and
3   Workplaces that are not present in the survey population at t_1 but which are present at t_2 ('joiners').

Such a design exists within the WIRS series for the period 1990–98. The design and its uses are explained below, first considering the 1998 WERS Panel Survey of continuing workplaces.

The 1998 WERS panel survey

A panel survey allows one to measure 'within unit' change – that is, change which occurs within workplaces that continue in operation over the period of observation. The 1998 WERS panel survey traced a random selection of workplaces that responded to the cross-section survey of 1990 for re-interview in 1998. The survey, with a response rate of 82 per cent, yielded a sample of 846 continuing workplaces, as shown in Figure 1.1. Such a high response rate, and the measures taken to correct for non-response bias, minimize the biggest source of error in panel studies – attrition.

For the purposes of the panel survey, a continuing workplace was defined as one that employed twenty-five or more employees at the time of both the 1990 and 1998 interviews and had continued to operate throughout the intervening period. Changes of activity, ownership or location were not considered to critically impair this concept of continuity, but meticulous checks were made to ensure that the history of the 1998 unit could be clearly traced back to that surveyed in 1990.[6] The coverage of the panel survey was equivalent to that of the cross-section surveys which comprise our time series, namely workplaces from almost all types of industry across Britain, in both private and public sectors. However, the survey only sought interviews with managers and did not attempt to interview worker representatives or survey individual employees.

The panel survey interview repeated many of the questions that had been asked at the same workplace eight years earlier in the 1990 cross-section, covering a variety of workplace characteristics as well as many features of employment relations. In addition, through the use of Computer Assisted Personal Interviewing (CAPI) technology, it was possible to feed information from the 1990 survey directly into the 1998 interview. Changes in practice between 1990 and 1998 could then be automatically identified during the interview and questions triggered to enquire about the circumstances surrounding a particular change. The collection of such data allows one to look not only at the ways in which employment relations have developed within continuing workplaces during the 1990s, but also at the extent to which changes in practice are associated with other developments at the establishment or beyond it.

The use of a specially designed panel questionnaire was a new development in the WIRS series. Panel surveys conducted at earlier points of the series had simply used the questionnaire being employed in the main cross-section survey at the time. One added advantage of using a customized panel questionnaire in 1998 was that it allowed for a greater degree of freedom in the design of the 1998 cross-section questionnaire, by providing a fall-back for measuring change over the period since 1990. The previous panel surveys were either largely experimental, as in the case of the 1980–84 panel, or restricted to workplaces in industry and commerce, as in 1984–90, and so have not been utilized in this volume.[7]

The 1998 panel survey was accompanied by a short telephone survey of all remaining workplaces from the 1990 cross-section not included within the panel sample. The purpose of this short interview was purely to establish whether the establishment had survived over the period and, if so, in what form. Hence, information was sought on the size of the workforce and whether the workplace had moved, changed ownership, amalgamated with or split from another establishment since the time of the 1990 interview. These data were added to the information on the survival status of all workplaces selected into the panel sample. Such data enable one to look at the role played in 'net' change by workplaces leaving the survey population over the period of observation.

Workplaces leaving the survey population between 1990 and 1998

What we hereafter refer to as 'leavers' comprise those establishments that closed down in the period between the 1990 and 1998 surveys and those that fell out of the scope of the survey. Workplaces that fell out of scope are essentially those in which the size of the workforce was below the twenty-five employee threshold at the time of the 1998 survey.[8] Each workplace in the sample of 'leavers' formed part of the 1990 cross-section survey, and so our dataset contains full information on the nature of each workplace in 1990, together with an indicator of why it left the population (whether through closure or through falling outside the scope of the survey).

When we place the information about the two types of 'leaver' together with information about the nature of continuing workplaces in 1990, we are able to trace the whole of the 1990 survey sample through to 1998. Figure 1.2 shows that continuing workplaces accounted for 72 per cent of the 1990 population of workplaces with twenty-five or more employees, closures for 15 per cent and workplaces that fell out of scope for 13 per cent. By comparing 'leavers' with continuing workplaces in 1990, we are able to investigate whether those workplaces that left the survey population were in some way distinct from those that remained. If 'leavers' were behaving differently from continuing

Figure 1.2 Panel survey, leavers and joiners data structure

Percentage of 1990 population (weighted)		1990	1998		Percentage of 1998 population (weighted)
72%	A	Continuing workplaces (1990 interview) *846 workplaces (unweighted)*	Continuing workplaces (1998 interview) *846 workplaces (unweighted)*	D	64%
15%	B	Workplaces that closed down *259 workplaces (unweighted)*	New workplaces *286 workplaces (unweighted)*	E	19%
13%	C	Workplaces that fell out of scope *123 workplaces (unweighted)*	Workplaces that grew into scope *104 workplaces (unweighted)*	F	17%
	25+ emps			25+ emps	
	1–24 emps			1–24 emps	

Key:
A, D: Continuing workplaces
B, C: Leavers (i.e. establishments that moved outside the survey population between 1990 and 1998)
E, F: Joiners (i.e. establishments that moved into the survey population between 1990 and 1998)

workplaces, we are then able to assess the extent to which such differences were important in bringing about change at the aggregate level.

Workplaces that joined the survey population between 1990 and 1998

In the same way that the 1990 population consists of continuing workplaces and 'leavers', the 1998 population constitutes the combination of continuing workplaces from 1990 and establishments that have joined the population since that time, here termed 'joiners'. 'Joiners' are of two types and, to compile the two datasets, we turned to the 1998 cross-section survey. In keeping with our definition of the WIRS population, both types necessarily employed at least twenty-five employees in 1998. The first group of 'joiners' consisted of workplaces that had been in operation for less than eight years at the time of the 1998 survey. These were identified by means of a set of questions in the 1998 cross-section giving the age of the workplace.[9] The second group consisted of workplaces that had less than twenty-five employees in 1990 but had grown to employ twenty-five or more by 1998. Unfortunately, the 1998 cross-section questionnaire did not include a retrospective question asking the respondent to state the number of workers employed eight years ago. In the absence of more suitable data, members of this group were therefore identified by a retrospective question giving the number of workers employed five years before (hence at some point between October 1992 and July 1993, depending upon the date of the interview).[10] We believe this approximation does not invalidate the results presented from the sample of 'joiners'.

Since our dataset of 'joiners' was compiled from cases in the 1998 cross-section survey, it contains full information on the characteristics of each workplace in 1998, together with an indicator of why it joined the population (namely, whether a new workplace or one which grew into scope between 1990 and 1998). When we place the information about the two types of 'joiner' with information about the nature of continuing workplaces in 1998, obtained from the 1998 panel interview, we are able to trace the origins of the whole of the 1998 survey population. Figure 1.2 shows that continuing workplaces accounted for 64 per cent of the 1998 population of workplaces with twenty-five or more employees, new workplaces for 19 per cent and workplaces that grew into scope for 17 per cent. By comparing the characteristics of 'joiners' with those of our continuing workplaces in 1998, we are able to investigate whether those workplaces that joined the survey population were in some way distinct from those that had remained in operation since 1990. If they were found to be distinct in some way, this would clearly be important since the proportion of the 1998 population accounted for by 'joiners' (36 per cent) was considerable, certainly being larger than the proportion of the 1990 population accounted for by 'leavers' (28 per cent).

Combined analysis of continuing workplaces, 'leavers' and 'joiners' provides us with a valuable means of investigating any patterns that are apparent within the second half of our time series between 1990 and 1998. In particular, we are able to examine the extent to which change (or stability) on a particular item has arisen through change in behaviour at workplace level, change in the composition of industry or a mixture of the two. It will be seen that this provides us with many notable and interesting findings about the sources of change in British employment relations over the most recent period covered by our survey series.

The changing landscape, 1980–98

Before outlining more about the nature and contents of the book, it is useful to consider the backdrop against which the developments that can be charted by the WIRS series have taken place. Notable changes have occurred in the political, legal and social spheres over the past eighteen years. Substantial developments have also taken place in the economy and labour market. All are relevant to our discussion of developments in the conduct of workplace employment relations.

The political, legal and social contexts

The political context to the survey series is of undoubted significance, as the series neatly spans what is arguably the most distinctive political era in recent British history. As stated earlier in the chapter, our 1980 survey took place before the incoming Conservative administration had brought in any of their initial legislative reforms, whilst our 1998 survey was carried out before the new Labour government had begun to implement their own legislative programme. The intervening eighteen years of Conservative rule constituted a period of policy reform that was to change the face of the British labour market. Our time series enables us to look back over the full length of this period. The series also provides a suitable benchmark against which to assess subsequent eras of a different complexion.

The election of Mrs Thatcher's Conservative government in 1979 represented a turning point in British politics, as the arrival of the new administration signalled the end of the post-war consensus. In its place, the government embarked upon a broad social programme aimed at the promotion of individualism, self-reliance and private enterprise. Entrepreneurship and the rule of the market were the new mantras of business, pushed along by what one commentator has termed a wave of 'acquisitive individualism' (Phelps Brown, 1990: 1).

Such a programme required freedom of action, both for individuals and the market. A large part of the Conservatives' deregulatory programme focused on the operations of the labour market. The principal aim was to bolster employers' 'right to manage' and promote greater flexibility in the labour market, in the hope that this would improve the competitiveness of British business and encourage employment growth. To this end, there was a progressive weakening of the framework of statutory employment protection and a gradual tightening of restrictions on the activities of trade unions throughout the period covered by our survey series (Dickens and Hall, 1995; Brown *et al.*, 1997).

The process began in the period between our first and second surveys. Between 1980 and 1984, the government repealed provisions for the statutory recognition of unions and the extension of negotiated terms to other workers, placed restrictions on secondary industrial action and the enforceability of the closed shop, and also made unions liable for unlawful industrial action. Employees' protection against unfair dismissal was weakened and they also became more vulnerable to selective dismissal when on strike. The period leading up to our third survey in 1990 then saw a further weakening of the law on unfair dismissal and a reduction in the scope and functions of Wages Councils which provided statutory minima in many low-paid sectors. The right to time off for trade union duties was also narrowed, the enforceability of the closed shop further restricted and unions prohibited from taking disciplinary action against members who refused to participate in industrial action. All forms of industrial action became unlawful unless preceded by a secret ballot.

The programme of change did not stop there. The period between our third survey in 1990 and the Conservatives' departure from power in 1997 saw an increase in the balloting and notice requirements over lawful industrial action and the extension of union liability to cover unlawful industrial action called by union officials, including shop stewards. All forms of secondary industrial action were finally outlawed, the closed shop was made legally unenforceable, and additional administrative requirements were placed on check-off procedures for paying union subscriptions. The abolition of the Wages Councils in 1993 also removed the last vestiges of minimum wage protection (except in agriculture). Labour's National Minimum Wage only came into force after fieldwork for our 1998 survey was complete.

However, then, as now, the British government did not have a completely free hand in changing the legal context of the employment relationship. There were also countervailing influences from Europe that led to an extension in the coverage of sex discrimination legislation, the introduction of the principle of equal pay for equal value, enhanced protection and consultation during business transfers and the extension of regulations governing health and safety consultation. None the less, when one considers the overall picture, these hardly undermined the Conservatives' programme that was targeted, particularly, at the restriction of union power and the reassertion of managerial prerogative.

The government's willingness to promote the discipline of the market was clearly apparent in its approach to the public sector. A wave of privatizations, beginning around the time of our second survey, injected new competitive pressures into many companies and industries, forcing a greater concentration on efficiency and profitability. In other parts of the public sector, market disciplines were introduced by encouraging existing employees to bid with the private sector for the opportunity to deliver services such as hospital cleaning and refuse disposal. Centralized control of local and central government was also relaxed by the movement of many functions from core departments to agencies, whilst a similar process of decentralization saw the creation of self-managing trusts in the National Health Service and the development of grant-maintained status in education.

In its transformation of the public sector, the government was arguably seeking both to emulate and influence practice in the private sector of the economy. Much academic debate in the 1980s focused on the extent to which the 'macho-management' and anti-union strategies seen in many state enterprises during their preparation for privatization had subsequently percolated through to the private sector. However, over the course of the 1980s and 1990s, attention in management and academic circles was also directed towards practices that embodied the new spirit of individualism: methods of direct communication and employee involvement, systems of individual appraisal and performance-related pay.

Observers noted that managers were, to some extent, moving away from the pluralism of the post-war decades towards a more unitarist approach (Poole and Mansfield, 1993) and that many were beginning to reject long-held assumptions of joint regulation (Kessler and Bayliss, 1998: 130). Opinions were none the less divided upon the precise direction of any movement. Some argued that a new style of management was emerging which, in some cases, amounted to a more integrated, strategic and people-centred version of personnel management labelled 'human resource management' or HRM (Guest, 1987). Others said that, in practice, developments were more in keeping with the cost-reduction or 'macho-management' approach of the early 1980s (Sisson, 1994a: 15).

Whatever the outcome, it is clear that developments in the economy and labour market had provided employers with a major incentive to re-examine the way that workplaces were managed.

The economic and labour market context

Increasing competition within product markets was a key feature of the economy in the 1980s and 1990s. In many sectors, such as financial services, transportation, telecommunications and broadcasting, competitive pressures were intensified by domestic deregulation. Conditions in many industries were also radically changed by the promotion of free and fair competition between states of the European Union and by liberalization on a global scale. At the same time, the changing economics of production, transportation and communication prompted many to reassess their means of competing in an increasingly international market-place.

The British economy moved through what amounted to two full cycles over the period covered by the WIRS series. The economy experienced a short period of growth during the late 1970s in the period leading up to the first survey, having made a brief recovery from the effect of the oil price shocks of 1973–74

Figure 1.3 Gross domestic product, inflation and unemployment over the WIRS series

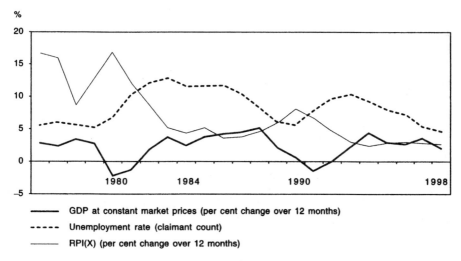

——— GDP at constant market prices (per cent change over 12 months)

- - - - Unemployment rate (claimant count)

——— RPI(X) (per cent change over 12 months)

Source: Economic Trends.

(Figure 1.3). The rate of unemployment, although giving some cause for concern, stood at around 5 per cent. However, inflation was high by both domestic and international standards, having reached record levels in 1975. The economy fell into recession in the final quarter of 1979, six to eight months before the fieldwork for the 1980 survey began. Production industries were badly hit, with the economy as a whole coming out of recession in only the second quarter of 1981. Unemployment rose substantially over this period, reaching its peak of 13 per cent shortly before our second survey in 1984, but inflation had fallen swiftly and remained low until the boom of 1989.

Continued growth in output after our 1984 survey was accompanied by a gradual fall in the unemployment rate. However, the rate of growth in GDP finally began to tail off in both manufacturing and service industries after 1988, with the economy finally entering a deep recession in the second quarter of 1990, just after fieldwork for the third survey in the series had begun. The third survey therefore came slightly earlier in the cycle than our first survey in 1980. Conditions for the fourth survey in 1998 were much closer to those seen for the second survey in the series. In 1998, as in 1984, fieldwork took place against the backdrop of a period of steady growth in the economy, although there were concerns about future prospects, particularly among production industries. Inflation and unemployment were at some of their lowest levels since 1980.

The effects of the two recessions on the composition of industry are examined in Chapter 2. There, we also explore the effects of the changing composition of the labour force, as seen in our survey data. However, it is pertinent to briefly outline some of the principal changes in the nature of the labour market as part of this more general discussion. The growth in female employment has been one of the most obvious developments, with the proportion of female employees rising from 42 per cent to 47 per cent over the course of our survey series.[11] Women also moved into occupations and positions of authority where their presence had previously been uncommon. At the same time, the extent of labour market participation among young people declined, particularly during the 1990s, as the expansion of further and higher education persuaded many to delay their entry into paid work.

These changes have been accompanied by a significant shift towards non-standard forms of employment. Self-employment rose rapidly during the 1980s. Accounting for 7 per cent of all workers in 1980, the proportion stood at 12 per cent in 1998.[12] However, the more significant developments at workplace level concern the increased use of part-time and temporary workers. The proportion of all employees working part-time (defined as 30 hours or less per week) rose from 21 per cent in 1981 to 25 per cent in 1998.[13] The proportion in temporary jobs, which stood at 4 per cent in 1984, had doubled by the time of our fourth survey in 1998.[14]

Changes in the composition of the labour force often form part of our analysis in the remainder of the book. More generally, however, it is hoped that the preceding discussion has served to provide the essence of the context into which our survey data can be located. The context of British employment relations has changed rapidly over the course of the past eighteen years and many of the developments that have taken place are relevant to the interpretation of our results.

The nature of our analyses and contents of the book

Before beginning to present results from our survey series, it is necessary to say a little about the nature of the analyses that have been conducted in preparing this volume as well as outlining the contents of the remainder of the book.

The nature of our analyses

In the main, we have used detailed tabular analysis to explore the data contained within the surveys at our disposal. Ideally suited to the identification of patterns and trends within survey data, this form of analysis also provides results that can be presented in a manner that is easily comprehensible to most readers. In a selected number of instances, however, this tabular analysis has been extended by the use of multivariate statistical techniques. Such techniques are designed to separate out the impact of different characteristics upon the issue under investigation. Because the techniques are not universally understood, we have attempted to present the results in as straightforward a manner as possible. Inevitably, this may have resulted in the loss of some detail that is of interest to the more statistically sophisticated reader.

When studying the results of any survey one must, of course, bear in mind the implications of the survey design. In common with all sample surveys, the WIRS series can only provide estimates of the occurrence of a particular phenomenon within the population that each sample is intended to represent – in this case, workplaces in Britain with twenty-five or more employees. Such estimates may deviate from the true population value if, by either chance or fault, the process of selection arrives at a sample that does not precisely capture the variation in behaviour present within the population as a whole. However, the degree of precision inherent in any survey estimate can itself be gauged by statistical procedures. Given a particular survey design, these procedures specify a range around the estimated value within which the actual population value is likely to fall, known as the 'confidence interval'.

Our prime interest is in examining changes over time. Therefore, when analysing our results, we are most often concerned to know whether an estimate arising from Survey 1 (for example, the proportion of all workplaces in 1990 with a joint consultative committee) is sufficiently different from the same estimate within Survey 2 (which, in this case, could be the 1998 survey) to suggest that a difference also exists within the population as a whole. This is the same as asking whether the value of zero falls within the confidence interval around the absolute difference between the two estimates. If it does not, meaning that the difference itself is unlikely to be zero within the population, we can be confident in saying that there has been a rise (or fall) in the prevalence of joint consultative committees over the period between the two surveys.

For the purposes of our analyses, we have constructed tables that allow the reader to calculate the approximate confidence intervals for differences between estimates from each of the surveys. Separate tables cover estimates from the 1990–98 panel survey. These tables are contained within the Technical Appendix to this volume. However, the convention adopted in the remainder of the volume is to comment only upon those trends or differences that pass a 95 per cent test of statistical significance. In such cases there is, at most, only a 5 per cent chance that the difference identified by our surveys does not exist, to some degree, within the population as a whole. This is the most common criterion to be used when comparing results from large-scale social surveys.

Sampling error is, nevertheless, only one of the possible sources of error that arises within survey research. Measurement error can also occur as a result of a variety of factors, including imprecision in question wording, misinterpretation of questions by respondents and coding errors by interviewers or coders. The implications are often difficult to quantify. However, consistency of survey design and administration helps to reduce the risk of such errors appearing within the data. Where our data are thought to suffer from imprecision arising from measurement error, such as a change in question wording between surveys, we have alerted the reader in the text and through the judicious use of endnotes.

The contents of the book

The remainder of the book is divided into six substantive chapters. Each is intended to address a particular theme in employment relations.

Chapter 2 discusses changes in the characteristics of workplaces over the period covered by the WIRS series. The chapter covers a wide range of features but looks, in particular, at commonly cited developments such as the increasing dominance of the service sector and the changing composition of the labour force. It also provides much of the background for later investigations of the role played by 'compositional change' in the development of employment relations.

Chapter 3 looks in detail at the management of employees. After examining the development of more specialist management of personnel, it goes on to look at particular phenomena such as the rise of the human resource manager and the increasingly prominent role of women. The management of personnel within complex organizations provides the focus for the second half of the chapter.

The extent of 'employee voice' at work forms the focus for Chapter 4, which looks at the prevalence of structures that enable employees to influence the actions of their employer. The changing fortunes of trade unions are explored, along with other forms of indirect or representative participation in managerial decisions. One aim is to assess the degree to which non-union forms of 'voice' have filled the gap in representation left by the decline of workplace trade unionism.

Chapter 5 pursues a different, but related, theme by examining how the nature of union representation has changed among workplaces that still contain the basic structure of joint regulation. A number of measures of union 'power' are used to assess the extent to which unions still retain an influential presence where they are formally recognized by management.

Chapter 6 focuses on what, for many, is the most central aspect of the employment contract: pay and rewards. Attention is principally focused on the structures and procedures through which pay is determined in both union and non-union workplaces. However, other forms of reward systems, such as profit sharing and share ownership schemes, are also considered.

The final chapter builds upon the evidence compiled within the rest of the book in examining the extent to which one can identify particular trajectories of change throughout the survey series: the decline of joint regulation or the development of a non-union 'model', for example. The chapter also assesses the prospects for the future in the light of the current policy environment.

2 The dynamic context of workplace employment relations

Changes in workplace employment relations do not take place within a vacuum. The discussion in the latter half of Chapter 1 served to outline some of the principal changes that have taken place in the economic, legal, political and social spheres in Britain over the past twenty years. These included significant shifts in the fortunes of the economy, the character of public policy and the nature of the labour market. However, these wider dynamics were observed and discussed at a level of abstraction from the workplace. Here we seek to explore changes in the population of workplaces – the canvas on which our analysis of change in employment relations is to be portrayed.

The population of workplaces is extremely heterogeneous, exhibiting wide variety across a range of characteristics: the types of goods produced or services delivered, patterns of ownership and the size and composition of workforces are notable examples. Such characteristics do much to aid our understanding of the patterns of employment relations. The size of the workforce at an establishment, or in the wider organization of which it is part, may have important implications for the character of relations between management and employees (Marginson, 1984). Similarly, the identity of the owner may also affect key features of this relationship (Enderwick, 1985; Sisson and Marginson, 1995: 101–4). It is natural, then, that knowledge of the patterns of change or stability in the characteristics of workplaces can also greatly enhance our understanding of developments in employment relations.

When debating the trends in employment relations over the past two decades, attention has frequently been drawn to the apparent developments that have occurred in the population of workplaces. The decline of manufacturing and increasing dominance of service industries, the contraction and reorganization of the public sector, the shift towards smaller workplaces, the rise of foreign ownership and the increased use of non-standard employment contracts are among the most commonly cited.[1] The WIRS series contains numerous items of data that can be used to examine such trends among workplaces with twenty-five or more employees, thereby enabling us to investigate the true nature and degree of change that has occurred in the characteristics of our population over this period.

The purpose of this chapter is to map out changes in the population so that the linkages with behaviour at workplace level might be more ably explored and discussed throughout the remainder of the book. This is not to suggest a deterministic or unidirectional train of causality between changes in the population of workplaces and changes in the character of employment relations at establishment level. Rather, it is recognized that developments in employment relations may be both the product and the architect of change in other spheres. None the less, where links are apparent between the changing composition of the population and developments in behaviour, the trends evident in this chapter may also go some way to assisting us in an assessment of possible developments in British employment relations in the future.

The discussion begins by examining trends in the types of activity undertaken within workplaces and the nature of their ownership. This is followed by a discussion of the size of workforces across the population, the proportion of workplaces that form part of wider organizations, the size of such organizations and the degree of foreign ownership. Trends in the age and location of the population of workplaces are also considered, as is the spread of micro-technology. The chapter ends by looking at changes in the composition of workforces. The discussion shows that there have been many important changes in the characteristics of the population of workplaces since the beginning of the WIRS series, as well as notable patterns of stability.

Industry and ownership

Many features of employment relations are seen to vary according to the type of goods produced or services delivered at a workplace and according to whether the establishment is under private or public ownership. Traditionally, the stereotype has been of heavy industry as the bastion of institutionalized, collective industrial relations, with certain private services – hotel and catering, for example – seen as direct opposites in this respect (Lucas, 1995: 4). The public sector has also had a stereotype of its own: that of the 'good employer', characterized by joint regulation and procedural formality, together with highly centralized bargaining structures (Winchester and Bach, 1995: 308).

These are, of course, simplifications. The degree of diversity in employment relations within sectors, and the extent to which there have been changes in these relations over time, will be examined in later chapters. However, to the extent that these stereotypes have substance, changes in the composition of the population of workplaces by activity and ownership represent important contextual variables in our analysis of change at the aggregate level.[2] Looking back over the period covered by the WIRS series, the changing fortunes of manufacturing and service industries and the contraction of the public sector in particular are both clearly evident within our survey population.

At the beginning of our survey series in 1980, one quarter of all workplaces were engaged in private sector manufacturing activities (see Table 2.1a).[3] A further two fifths (43 per cent) were engaged in private sector services, whilst one third (32 per cent) were located within the public sector.[4] Despite their numerical inferiority, manufacturing workplaces employed almost two fifths (38 per cent) of all employees, reflecting their larger than average size (Table 2.1b). Private sector services accounted for a further 26 per cent of all employees, the public sector for 36 per cent.

The recession of the early 1980s bit hard into Britain's manufacturing base, contributing to a fall in the proportion of all workplaces engaged in production industries. By the time of our second survey in 1984, the proportion of

Table 2.1 Industry and ownership, 1980 to 1998

(a) Establishments

	Column percentages[a]			
	1980	1984	1990	1998
Private sector manufacturing and extraction	25	21	21	18
Extraction of minerals/ores; manufacture of metals, minerals and chemicals	3	4	3	2
Metal goods, engineering and vehicle industries	10	7	8	9
Other private sector manufacturing	12	10	10	6
Private sector services	43	42	49	54
Energy and water supply	1	*	1	*
Construction	4	4	4	3
Distribution, hotels and catering, repairs	22	18	21	23
Transport and communications	2	3	4	4
Banking, finance, insurance, business services and leasing	8	11	13	10
Other private sector services	6	6	7	13
Public sector	32	37	30	28
Energy and water supply	1	2	*	*
Transport and communications	3	3	2	1
Central and local government	8	8	7	6
Education	11	13	11	13
Health	3	2	2	2
Other public sector services	6	7	7	7
Weighted base	2,000	2,000	2,000	2,000
Unweighted base	2,040	2,019	2,061	1,929

Base: all establishments with 25 or more employees.

Notes
Table compiled with reference to the divisions and classes of the Standard Industrial Classification (SIC) 1980. For 1998, data have been recoded from SIC 1992.

a Subtotals in italics.

Table 2.1 continued

(b) Employees				
	Column percentages[a]			
	1980	*1984*	*1990*	*1998*
Private sector manufacturing and extraction	38	27	27	25
Extraction of minerals/ores; manufacture of metals, minerals and chemicals	5	6	4	6
Metal goods, engineering and vehicle industries	17	11	11	11
Other manufacturing	16	11	11	8
Private sector services	26	29	38	44
Energy and water supply	1	*	2	1
Construction	3	2	3	2
Distribution, hotels and catering, repairs	12	12	15	17
Transport and communications	2	2	4	4
Banking, finance, insurance, business services and leasing	4	7	10	11
Other private sector services	5	5	5	9
Public sector	36	43	35	32
Energy and water supply	2	3	*	*
Transport and communications	4	5	3	2
Central and local government	11	10	11	9
Education	7	10	8	9
Health	6	8	7	8
Other public sector services	7	7	7	5
Weighted base	*2,000*	*2,000*	*2,000*	*2,000*
Unweighted base	*2,040*	*2,019*	*2,061*	*1,929*

Base: all establishments with 25 or more employees.

Notes
Table compiled with reference to the divisions and classes of the Standard Industrial Classification (SIC) 1980. For 1998, data have been recoded from SIC 1992.

a Subtotals in italics.

workplaces engaged in manufacturing had fallen from 25 per cent to 21 per cent. The proportion of the total workforce employed there had dropped from 38 per cent to 27 per cent. Falls were apparent in both heavy industry and other manufacturing. Service industries, in contrast, were left relatively unscathed by this recession, although they were to suffer in the recession of the early 1990s. The proportion of all workplaces engaged in private sector service activities held steady between 1980 and 1984, whereas the proportion of all employees working in such establishments rose from 26 per cent to 29 per cent.

Workplaces engaged in distribution, hotels and catering and repairs fell as a proportion of all establishments from 22 per cent to 18 per cent, but retained their share of all employees (12 per cent). In contrast, private sector workplaces engaged in finance and business services rose as a proportion of all establishments (from 8 per cent to 11 per cent) and as a proportion of total employment (from 4 per cent to 7 per cent). The proportion employed in finance and business services was to continue to rise throughout the period covered by our surveys.

The privatization of nationalized industries did not begin in earnest until the mid-1980s and the period between 1980 and 1984 saw some relative expansion in the public sector, no doubt partially reflecting the effects of recession on the private sector. The proportion of workplaces located in the public sector rose from 32 to 37 per cent between the first and second surveys; the proportion of employees rose from 36 to 43 per cent. At this time, in 1984, one seventh (14 per cent) of public sector workplaces and one fifth (20 per cent) of public sector employees formed part of public sector trading corporations or nationalized industries. Across the whole economy, these accounted for one in every twenty workplaces (5 per cent) and one in every ten employees (9 per cent).

Between 1984 and 1990, many of these workplaces moved from public to private ownership. British Telecom, British Airways, British Steel, British Gas and the water supply industry were among the most prominent privatizations.[5] As a result, in our survey the proportion of all workplaces engaged in energy and water supply that were under public ownership fell dramatically from around four fifths (78 per cent) to less than one fifth (14 per cent); in the area of post and telecommunications the proportion fell from 100 per cent to just three fifths (58 per cent). The overall impact of the privatization programme was to reduce the proportion of all workplaces that were part of public trading corporations or nationalized industries from 5 per cent in 1984 to 2 per cent in 1990. The proportion of all employees working in such establishments fell from 9 per cent to just 3 per cent over the same period.

The privatization programme was accompanied by a host of initiatives intended to commercialize public sector services such as local government and health. Detailed analysis shows that the proportion of all workplaces engaged in medical services that were part of the public sector fell between 1984 and 1990, from exactly three quarters to around one half (52 per cent). We also know from other sources that many activities within both local government and health were subject to competitive tendering over this period (and beyond) and were subsequently provided by the private sector, often using the same employees on new terms and conditions (Winchester and Bach, 1995: 306–7, 314–15).

The recession of the early 1990s affected both manufacturing and service industries, although manufacturing was hardest hit. Between our third and fourth surveys, in 1990 and 1998, the proportion of all workplaces engaged in private sector manufacturing and extraction activities fell from 21 per cent to

18 per cent.[6] The proportion of establishments in the public sector also continued to fall, although at a much slower rate than in the previous period. In contrast, private sector services enhanced their dominance of the population of workplaces, rising from 49 per cent in 1990 to 54 per cent in 1998. Their share of employment rose from 38 per cent to 44 per cent over the period. The biggest rises were apparent under the heading of 'Other private sector services', including private education establishments, health and social work activities.

Only a small part of this recent rise in private services came as a result of changes among continuing workplaces. Our panel survey shows that 2 per cent of continuing establishments, mostly engaged in rail transport and social services activities, moved from the public sector into private sector services between 1990 and 1998. However, a further 1 per cent moved, within the private sector, away from the delivery of services into the production of goods. Less than 1 per cent moved in the other direction. The net result was that the proportion of continuing establishments engaged in private sector services remained stable (45 per cent in 1990; 46 per cent in 1998).

The rise in private services therefore arose as a result of differences between establishments leaving the population between 1990 and 1998 and those joining the population over the same period. It is notable that there was actually a higher representation of private sector services among 'leavers' (55 per cent) than there was among continuing establishments (45 per cent, as noted above). However, the influx of such establishments into the population over the period more than compensated for this outflow. Two thirds (65 per cent) of workplaces that joined the population between 1990 and 1998 were engaged in private sector service activities. The dominance of private services among 'joiners', together with the fact that joiners, were, as a whole, numerically more prevalent than leavers over the period, lay at the heart of the growth in private sector services during the 1990s.

Turning to look at survival rates among the three different sectors, we see that a high proportion of workplaces within private sector manufacturing (37 per cent) left the survey population between 1990 and 1998. This is partly a reflection of the economic trends discussed in Chapter 1. One quarter (25 per cent) of those private sector manufacturing workplaces in existence at the time of the 1990 survey had closed down by 1998. A further 12 per cent had reduced the size of their workforce to below twenty-five employees, thereby falling out of the scope of the survey. Of those workplaces engaged in private sector services in 1990, 31 per cent had left the population by 1998: 15 per cent had closed down and 16 per cent had shrunk to below twenty-five employees. The overall figure in the public sector was lower at just 17 per cent: 7 per cent had closed down and 10 per cent had fallen out of scope.

Unsurprisingly, it was the relatively buoyant private services sector that, in 1998, had the highest proportion of joiners. Over two fifths (43 per cent) of establishments within private sector services in 1998 had joined the population since 1990. One quarter (24 per cent) of establishments in this sector had been newly established in this time; one fifth (19 per cent) had grown from having a workforce of less than twenty-five employees. The total proportion of joiners was lower within both private sector manufacturing and the public sector in 1998, standing at 27 per cent in either sector. Of the two, private sector manufacturing had the higher proportion of new workplaces (18 per cent of all workplaces in 1998, compared with 11 per cent in the public sector).

Changes in ownership within the private and public sectors

In the previous discussion it was noted that only a very small proportion of establishments were found to have moved from public to private ownership between 1990 and 1998. However, changes of ownership *within* the private and public sectors were more prevalent. In the private sector these include takeovers, mergers and demergers, in the public sector the creation of self-managing units such as health trusts. Such changes of ownership may have profound implications for employment relations if, for example, they are associated with either a restructuring of the activities at the workplace or a change of management style or philosophy.

Our panel survey shows that three tenths (29 per cent) of those workplaces that were located in the private sector in both 1990 and 1998 had undergone a change of ownership over that period. This proportion stood at two fifths (39 per cent) within private sector manufacturing and one quarter (25 per cent) within private sector services. Just under a half (46 per cent) of all changes of ownership within the private sector came about through a takeover or merger, although this route was much more common in services (58 per cent) than in manufacturing (25 per cent). A further third (34 per cent) of all changes of ownership had arisen as a result of the establishment being sold by the parent organization, with little difference in incidence evident between the two sectors. One in seven ownership changes (14 per cent) arose through a management buy-out. Management buy-outs accounted for 29 per cent of all changes of ownership in private sector manufacturing but only 5 per cent in private sector services.

Around one fifth (18 per cent) of workplaces that were located in the public sector in both 1990 and 1998 reported some change in the ownership of the establishment during this period. Ownership changes were reported by around half of all public sector health establishments, one quarter of local government workplaces and one fifth of primary and secondary schools.[7] Here we see the effects of the creation of self-managing trusts in the National Health Service, the reorganization of local government and moves to grant-maintained status within state education.

Many establishments that had experienced changes of ownership between 1990 and 1998 had also either amalgamated with, or split away from, another workplace over that period. Our data do not tell us whether the amalgamation or split was directly linked to the change of ownership, but one might expect this to be so in many cases. Among private manufacturing plants and private service sector establishments alike, just over half of all workplaces that had experienced a change of ownership had also amalgamated with, or split away from, another establishment in the preceding eight years. Where no change of ownership had taken place, the proportion with such changes stood at around one in ten. Around one half of public sector workplaces that experienced changes of ownership also amalgamated with, or split from, other establishments between 1990 and 1998; among workplaces with no ownership change the proportion was slightly higher than in the private sector, at around one third.

Overall, 16 per cent of continuing private sector workplaces within our panel survey experienced both a change of ownership and an amalgamation with, or split from, another workplace between 1990 and 1998. A further 13 per cent experienced only a change of ownership whilst 7 per cent experienced only an amalgamation or a split. Within the public sector, where changes of ownership were less common, 10 per cent saw only a change of ownership and 8 per cent saw both an ownership change and an amalgamation with, or split from, another workplace. A substantial proportion (25 per cent) amalgamated with, or split from, another workplace whilst remaining under the same ownership.

Our panel survey respondents were asked, in a simple closed question, whether any of these developments – changes of ownership, amalgamations or workplace splits – had any effect on management's approach to employee relations at the establishment. Much has been written about the effects of the reorganization of the public sector on employment relations.[8] However, private sector respondents were more likely than those from the public sector to report some consequential effect on management's approach to employee relations. Changes in management's approach were most common in establishments that had experienced both a change of ownership and an amalgamation or split.[9] Fifty per cent of such private sector establishments reported a subsequent change in the approach of management, compared with 30 per cent within the public sector. Where only a change of ownership had occurred, changes of approach were slightly less common (42 per cent in the private sector; 22 per cent in the public sector). Changes in management's approach were least common among workplaces that had merely amalgamated with, or split from, another establishment. One quarter (26 per cent) of private sector cases led to a change in management's approach to employee relations; in the public sector the proportion was one sixth (17 per cent).

Our closed question about changes in management's approach gives only a broad indication of the effects of workplace reorganization on employment relations at the establishment. However, by identifying that such reorganization has occurred, we are able to examine associations with changes in a number of specific features of employment relations. The nature of these associations will be explored in later chapters.

Size of workforce

The size of the workforce at an establishment is another important variable along which many features of the employment relationship are seen to vary. The way that managers organize themselves to deal with employment relations, the structure of their relations with trade unions and the incidence of particular employment practices, such as formal procedures for resolving disputes, are all generally associated with the number of workers employed at an establishment (Millward *et al.*, 1992). Within the WIRS series, the size of the workforce is taken as the total number of employees at the workplace; that is, all those who have a contract of employment with the employer at the named establishment and who work at, or from, that site. This includes representatives, salespersons and similar employees who principally report to the establishment. It excludes any freelance workers, homeworkers or outworkers and casual workers who do not have a contract of employment.[10]

The population of workplaces covered by our survey series is dominated by small establishments such as bank branches, shops and small workshops or offices. However, despite being much fewer in number, large workplaces employ by far the greater proportion of all employees. Our series of cross-section surveys shows that, overall, there has been little change in the size of workplaces between 1980 and 1998. If there has been a decrease in workplace size over the course of the 1980s and 1990s, as many suggest, this phenomenon must have been restricted to that part of the population with less than twenty-five employees, who are outside the scope of the survey series. Within our survey population, there have been changes in the size of the typical workplace within different sectors of industry, but such changes have balanced themselves out at the aggregate level.

Establishments employing between twenty-five and forty-nine employees dominate the population of workplaces covered by our surveys, accounting for one half of all workplaces with twenty-five or more employees. Those with between fifty and ninety-nine employees account for a further quarter of the population. One eighth of all workplaces (around 12 per cent) employ between 100 and 199 employees, one twelfth (around 8 per cent) employ between 200 and 499 employees and just 3 per cent have workforces numbering 500 or more.

The distribution of employees across workplaces of different sizes stands in stark contrast. In each of the surveys, workplaces with twenty-five to forty-nine employees, fifty to ninety-nine employees and 100 to 199 employees have each employed one sixth (around 17 per cent) of all employees covered by the survey series. A further fifth have been employed in workplaces with between 200 and 499 employees, whilst a substantial proportion of all employees – three tenths – have been accounted for by those few establishments having workforces of 500 or more.

Patterns of growth and decline amongst individual workplaces

Of course, the stability seen at the aggregate level in our time series masks considerable change among individual workplaces. New establishments are set up, others close down, whilst continuing establishments may also change in size dramatically over the course of their lifetime. In the most recent period (1990 to 1998), survival rates varied little between workplaces of different sizes. Fifteen per cent of small workplaces from our 1990 survey (those employing between twenty-five and 100 employees in 1990) were found to have closed down by 1998. This compared with 10 per cent of large workplaces employing 500 or more. However, a substantial proportion of small workplaces in 1990 (16 per cent) dropped below the twenty-five employee threshold and so fell out of the scope of the survey. This was rare among establishments with large workforces of 500 or more (1 per cent).

New workplaces featured prominently throughout the size distribution of workplaces in 1998. One fifth (20 per cent) of small workplaces in 1998 had been newly established in the preceding eight years, compared with 18 per cent of medium-sized establishments and 11 per cent of large ones. Hence, even among workplaces of considerable size, the incidence of new establishments was substantial, providing much potential for change. A further fifth (20 per cent) of small workplaces had grown into scope over the course of the eight-year period, having employed less than twenty-five employees in 1990, yet this was rare among large workplaces (1 per cent).

To add to this information about the changing elements of the population, our panel survey allows us to also look at changes in the size of continuing workplaces between 1990 and 1998.[11] Comparing the size of the workforce in each establishment in 1998 with its size in the same establishment in 1990, we find that one tenth (8 per cent) of all continuing establishments had at least doubled in size over the period. A further quarter (24 per cent) had increased the size of their 1990 workforce by between 20 and 99 per cent between the two surveys. Just under half (45 per cent) of all continuing workplaces had remained relatively stable in size, their 1998 workforce deviating no more than 20 per cent in size from that in 1990. A small proportion (5 per cent) had shrunk by between 20 and 49 per cent. This left almost one fifth (18 per cent) that had decreased the size of their 1990 workforce by at least half over the eight-year period (that is, without dropping below the twenty-five employee threshold for the survey).

We asked respondents in continuing workplaces exhibiting substantial growth or decline (taken as a change of 20 per cent or more from their 1990 employment level) to account for the changes in the size of their workforce; interviewers recorded up to five reasons. The clear majority (68 per cent) of workplaces exhibiting substantial growth were said to have done so in response to an increase in demand for their products or services. This proportion was similar in both the private and public sectors. In three fifths (60 per cent) of all cases exhibiting substantial growth, increased demand was given as the only reason why the workforce had grown. One quarter of respondents (24 per cent) in growing establishments reported that growth was associated with either a change in the ownership of the establishment or some reorganization of activities within the wider organization. In many of these cases (around two thirds) the establishment had amalgamated with another over the period. The two other specific reasons given for growth in the size of workforces were, first, the internalization of work previously done by freelance workers or subcontractors (3 per cent) and, second, the increasing use of part-time workers (3 per cent).[12]

The reasons given for substantial proportionate decline in employment numbers over the 1990s were more varied. Just over one third of respondents (36 per cent) cited a decrease in demand for the establishment's products or services, 30 per cent citing this reason alone. A similar proportion (35 per cent) mentioned a change in the ownership of the establishment or some reorganization of activities within the wider organization. Only one third of these workplaces had actually split from another since 1990, however. Almost one quarter (23 per cent) of respondents reported that the shrinkage in employment at the workplace was due to redundancies or the non-replacement of employees leaving the establishment. One sixth (17 per cent) cited the use of improved methods of working. A small proportion (5 per cent) mentioned the outsourcing or subcontracting of work previously carried out by employees; 2 per cent cited the increasing use of full-time employees rather than part-timers.

Changes in the relationship between size and industry

Turning back to the aggregate distribution of workplaces shown by our time series, there are clear differences between the size of workplaces in different sectors of the economy. Workplaces in private sector service industries tend to be the smallest, although their typical size has increased gradually over the series. In 1980, almost nine in every ten establishments (86 per cent) in private sector services had workforces numbering less than 100 employees. By 1998 this had fallen to 81 per cent. The proportion of private sector service workplaces with large numbers of employees (500 or more) has remained steady, however, at around 1 per cent. In contrast, private sector manufacturing now has a higher percentage of small workplaces with less than 100 employees (68 per cent in 1998, compared with 64 per cent in 1980) and a lower percentage of large establishments employing 500 or more (4 per cent, compared with 7 per cent in 1980). Within the public sector, the percentage of small workplaces has also risen over the series, from 70 per cent in 1980 to 77 per cent in 1998, whilst the percentage of large workplaces has remained almost unchanged at around 4 per cent.

These trends do not mean, however, that the population of workplaces is now any less dominated by small service sector establishments, since the growth in the number of service sector workplaces (evident from Table 2.1a) has occurred throughout the size distribution. In 1998, small service sector workplaces (i.e. those with less than 100 employees) accounted for 44 per cent of the population, compared with the low of 35 per cent in 1984 (Table 2.2a). There is also now a greater percentage of medium-sized private service establishments (i.e. those with between 100 and 499 employees), their incidence having doubled from 5 per cent in 1980 to 10 per cent in 1998. The proportion of all employees working in medium-sized private service establishments has also doubled over the same period, from 9 per cent to 18 per cent (Table 2.2b). And whilst we cannot state with confidence that there has been an increase in the proportion of large private service sector workplaces (i.e. those with 500 or more employees), the proportion of all employees that are working in such establishments has clearly grown, rising almost by a factor of three from 3 per cent in 1980 to 8 per cent in 1998.

The proportion of workplaces engaged in private sector manufacturing is shown by size band in Table 2.2a. The fall has been greatest amongst small manufacturing plants with less than 100 employees: these accounted for 16 per cent of the population in 1980, 12 per cent in 1998. The decline in manufacturing employment was most apparent among large plants, however (Table 2.2b). In 1980, manufacturing plants with 500 or more workers employed one in every six employees (17 per cent). By 1990, this proportion had more than halved, to around one in every fourteen (7 per cent). A small reversal was apparent in the latest period, the 1998 figure standing at 10 per cent. However, the proportion of all employees working in large manufacturing plants is now only just over half its level at the beginning of the series.

Some analysts have argued that much of the fall in union membership and the scope of collective bargaining reflects the decline of large workplaces in manufacturing (Sisson and Marginson, 1995: 100). We will examine this and alternative explanations in Chapter 4. However, since the importance of such workplaces stems, primarily, from the organization of their manual labour it is interesting to note that the incidence of medium-sized or large manual-dominated manufacturing plants has changed little since the mid-1980s. In 1980, at the start of our series, 4 per cent of all workplaces were engaged in either private sector manufacturing or extraction, had at least 100 workers and employed at least three quarters of these workers in manual occupations. The proportion of all workplaces meeting this definition fell slightly in the early 1980s, from 4 per cent in 1980 to 2 per cent in 1984. However, there has been no further fall since then, even through the severe recession of the early 1990s, and such workplaces accounted for 3 per cent of all establishments in 1998. Similarly, the proportion of all employees working in such establishments, despite falling by one third in the early 1980s, from 13 per cent in 1980 to 7 per cent in 1984, has remained steady since that time, and in 1998 stood at just under one tenth (8 per cent). None of these figures change to any substantial degree if one widens the definition to include manufacturing activities located within the public sector. Clearly, there may have been significant changes over time in the nature of employment relations within sizeable manual-dominated

Table 2.2 Distribution of all workplaces by size and sector, 1980 to 1998

(a) Establishments

	Column percentages			
	1980	1984	1990	1998
25–99 employees				
Private sector manufacturing and extraction	16	15	15	12
Private sector services	37	35	41	44
Public sector	22	27	23	22
100–499 employees				
Private sector manufacturing and extraction	7	6	6	5
Private sector services	5	6	8	10
Public sector	8	8	6	6
500 or more employees				
Private sector manufacturing and extraction	2	1	1	1
Private sector services	*	*	1	1
Public sector	1	2	1	1
Weighted base	2,000	2,000	2,000	2,000
Unweighted base	2,040	2,019	2,061	1,929

Base: all establishments with 25 or more employees.

(b) Employees

	Column percentages			
	1980	1984	1990	1998
25–99 employees				
Private sector manufacturing and extraction	7	7	8	6
Private sector services	14	15	18	18
Public sector	9	11	10	9
100–499 employees				
Private sector manufacturing and extraction	13	10	12	9
Private sector services	9	10	14	18
Public sector	14	16	11	10
500 or more employees				
Private sector manufacturing and extraction	17	10	7	10
Private sector services	3	4	5	8
Public sector	14	17	15	12
Weighted base	2,000	2,000	2,000	2,000
Unweighted base	2,040	2,019	2,061	1,929

Base: all establishments with 25 or more employees.

manufacturing plants, but our data show that, although their prevalence within the population dipped somewhat between 1980 and 1984, there has been no such decline since then.

Location within larger organizations

Being part of a larger organization, rather than existing as an independent establishment, can have a critical impact on the character of employment relations at workplace level. So too can the size of the wider organization of which the workplace is part. In the simplest terms, it can be expected that the management of employee relations across multiple sites and large numbers of employees is a more complex task, precipitating a greater degree of formality than may be required at a single site. Yet there may also be considerable variation between organizations. Some exert a great deal of control over processes and outcomes across the organization. Others give their establishments a great deal of autonomy.[13] We explore some of these issues in Chapter 3 when we discuss the degree of autonomy afforded to the personnel function at establishment level. The effect of the wider organization on outcomes is covered in Chapter 6 which looks at pay determination and reward systems. Here however, as a prelude to those discussions, we look at the extent to which workplaces form part of wider organizations, at the size of the organizations themselves and at how these two features may have changed over the past two decades.

Our time series shows that the percentage of workplaces that form part of a larger organization has fallen since 1984, having risen slightly between the first and second surveys (Table 2.3). In 1980, four fifths (78 per cent)

Table 2.3 Incidence of head offices, branch establishments and independent establishments, 1980 to 1998

	Column percentages[a]			
	1980	*1984*	*1990*[b]	*1998*
Head office of a larger organization	8	9	4	8
Branch establishment of a larger organization	70	73	76	65
All workplaces that form part of a larger organization	*78*	*82*	*80*	*73*
Independent establishment	22	18	21	27
Weighted base	*1,955*	*2,000*	*2,000*	*1,981*
Unweighted base	*1,998*	*2,019*	*2,061*	*1,925*

Base: all establishments with 25 or more employees.

Notes
a Subtotals in italics.
b See endnote 14.

of all establishments were part of larger organizations. This figure rose slightly in 1984 to just over four fifths (82 per cent), partly as a result of the rising proportion of public sector workplaces (see Table 2.1a). The proportion of workplaces that are part of larger organizations has fallen since then, with the rate of fall accelerating slightly in the most recent period. In 1990 the figure stood at four fifths (80 per cent); by 1998 it was less than three quarters (73 per cent). Within this final period, falls have been seen among workplaces of all sizes and in each of the three broad divisions of the economy categorized in Table 2.1.

Analysis of our panel survey, and of leavers and joiners, shows that the recent rise in the proportion of independent establishments is chiefly due to their relatively high incidence among establishments that have joined the population. Establishments leaving the population between 1990 and 1998 were quite similar to continuing workplaces, around one fifth of each comprising independent establishments. However, joiners were quite different, with one third (34 per cent) being independent. The principal cause lay in the high proportion of independent establishments (42 per cent) among workplaces joining private sector services, compared with establishments from this sector that left the population (19 per cent).

Since 1980, the proportion of all workplaces that accommodate the head office function of multi-site organizations has remained steady at around 8 per cent (Table 2.3); the lower figure of 4 per cent in 1990 is thought to be the result of a change in question wording.[14] Instead, it is the smaller proportion of all workplaces that operate as branch establishments which has fallen. The comparison between 1984 and 1998 shows that the proportion of branch sites dropped from almost three quarters (73 per cent) to two thirds (65 per cent) between the second and fourth surveys.[15]

Since organizations comprising a single site (independent establishments) are generally smaller than multi-site organizations, it is to be expected that workplaces are now less likely to belong to very large enterprises than was the case at the beginning of our survey series. However, the change over the course of the series has been slight. Since there are concerns about the comparability of our 1984 and 1990 data, we focus here on data from the first and last of our surveys.[16] In 1980, 28 per cent of all workplaces were located within small organizations having less than 100 employees, whilst 30 per cent were located within very large organizations having 10,000 employees or more. In 1998, the figures stood at 30 per cent and 26 per cent respectively.

In the private sector, the link with very large organizations has most clearly declined within manufacturing. In 1980, around one in every six private sector manufacturing plants (16 per cent) belonged to very large organizations employing 10,000 or more workers. By 1998, the proportion had fallen to fewer than one in twenty (4 per cent). There was an increase in the proportion of workplaces belonging to medium-sized and large enterprises, however, with the proportion belonging to small concerns (those with less than 100 employees) being the same (44 per cent) in both surveys. Within private sector services, the fall in the proportion of establishments that belong to very large enterprises has been less dramatic (28 per cent in 1980; 23 per cent in 1998), but the proportion belonging to small organizations has risen (from 33 per cent to 39 per cent). Within the public sector, there has been less change in the distribution. In both the 1980 and 1998 surveys, around half of all public sector workplaces were found to belong to very large organizations (51 per cent in 1980; 49 per cent in 1998) whilst only a small minority (3 per cent in 1980; 2 per cent in 1998) were part of small ones.

The decline in the proportion of private sector workplaces that form part of a larger organization would appear to add weight to suggestions that a greater part of the economy is now accounted for by small firms. Indeed, our survey series shows that, among the population of workplaces employing twenty-five or more employees, the incidence of small independent establishments under private ownership has clearly risen since the mid-1980s. In 1980 and 1984, one tenth (11 per cent) of all workplaces were accounted for by independent private sector establishments employing between twenty-five and forty-nine employees. This rose to one in seven (14 per cent) in 1990 and one in six (16 per cent) in 1998.

Internationalization

Remaining with the characteristics of the wider organization to which a workplace belongs, we now examine the trends in internationalization over the course of the 1980s and 1990s. The UK economy has a distinctly international flavour. This is evident through the significant amounts of foreign investment that flow into the UK and also in the degree to which investment flows out as part of the activities of multinational corporations and financial institutions abroad (UNCTAD, 1998). We look here at one aspect of inward investment, the extent of foreign ownership among British workplaces.[17] Previous reports in the WIRS series have shown foreign ownership to be associated with such diverse matters as the presence of specialist personnel management at the establishment, the structure of collective bargaining and the degree of information sharing between management and employees (Millward *et al.*, 1992: 33, 88, 175).

In examining the trend in foreign ownership, the most secure comparison is between data from the 1980 and 1998 surveys. Both questions asked the respondent whether the establishment, or the organization to which it belonged, was under UK or foreign ownership or control. The two observations showed that the proportion of all private sector workplaces that were wholly or majority owned or controlled by foreign (non-UK) organizations more than doubled over the course of the survey series, from 6 per cent in 1980 to 13 per cent in 1998 (Table 2.4).

The intervening surveys, in 1984 and 1990, contained a slightly different question that asked the respondent about the ownership of the establishment or its ultimate controlling company. The ultimate controlling company may be a broader entity than the organization which directly owns the establishment and so the data are not strictly comparable with those collected in 1980 and 1998.[18] The nature of the incomparability means that the 1984 and 1990 questions can be expected to indicate a higher degree of foreign ownership since they focus on a higher level unit in some cases. It is notable, then, that the estimates for 1984 and 1990 – 7 per cent and 8 per cent respectively – are closer to the 1980 estimate than they are to the figure that we have for 1998. This suggests that most of the growth in foreign ownership that took place over the course of our survey series actually occurred during the 1990s.

In order to look in more detail at the changing degree of foreign ownership of British workplaces, we return to the secure comparison between our 1980 and 1998 questions. These show that, between 1980 and 1998, the degree of foreign ownership increased among workplaces of all sizes and within each of the nine divisions of the 1980 *Standard Industrial Classification* (Table 2.4). The steepest rise occurred within Division 7 covering transport and communications. In 1980, less than 1 per cent of all private sector workplaces in this sector of industry were owned or controlled by non-UK organizations. By 1998, however, the proportion stood at around one quarter. Steep increases were also evident in miscellaneous manufacturing (Division 4), where foreign ownership rose from 3 per cent of all workplaces in 1980 to 20 per cent in 1998, and in financial and business services (Division 8), where its incidence rose from 5 per cent to 17 per cent. Across the whole of private sector manufacturing, the incidence of foreign ownership almost trebled, from one

Table 2.4 Foreign ownership by industry within the private sector, 1980 and 1998

	Cell percentages	
	1980	*1998*
All private sector establishments	6	13
Private sector manufacturing and extraction	7	19
Extraction of minerals/ores; manufacture of metals, minerals and chemicals	11	(25)
Metal goods, engineering and vehicle industries	9	17
Other private sector manufacturing	3	20
Private sector services	5	11
Energy and water supply	#	17
Construction	1	4
Distribution, hotels and catering, repairs	7	10
Transport and communications	(*)	26
Banking, finance, insurance, business services and leasing	5	17
Other private sector services	*	3

Base: all private sector establishments with 25 or more employees.

in every fourteen workplaces (7 per cent) in 1980 to one in every five (19 per cent) in the most recent survey. The incidence doubled, from 5 per cent to 11 per cent, within private sector services. Across the whole population of workplaces with twenty-five or more employees, including the public sector, the proportion of workplaces that are foreign owned or controlled rose from one in twenty (4 per cent) to one in ten (9 per cent) over the period covered by our survey series.

Analysis of the different components of the changing population of workplaces between 1990 and 1998 – leavers, continuing workplaces and joiners – shows that each contributed to the rise in foreign ownership. Foreign-owned private sector workplaces were less likely to leave the population than domestically owned ones. Twelve per cent of foreign-owned workplaces in the private sector closed down between 1990 and 1998, whilst a further 10 per cent shrank below the twenty-five employee threshold. Among domestically owned establishments, 19 per cent closed down and 15 per cent fell out of scope. As a consequence, only 5 per cent of workplaces leaving the population were under foreign ownership or control, compared with 10 per cent of continuing workplaces in 1990. The degree of foreign ownership increased among continuing workplaces between 1990 and 1998, from 10 per cent to 15 per cent, whilst the fact that joiners were more likely to be under foreign ownership or control than leavers (11 per cent, compared with the aforementioned 5 per cent) only served to consolidate this rise.[19]

Age and relocation

Age is another important structural characteristic of the workplace that is associated with particular features of employment relations. One notable example comes from the analysis of younger workplaces within the 1990 survey, which were shown, among other things, to be less likely to recognize trade unions than older establishments (Millward, 1994a: 21). Care must be taken, however, in seeking to attribute patterns of behaviour to age effects. The distinctiveness of young workplaces may indeed be related to their age, with maturity yielding change in the way that employment relations are managed at an establishment. Alternatively, age may act as a proxy for cohort effects (also termed generation effects), with the year in which the establishment was set up being the key variable. Disney *et al.* (1995) suggested that cohort effects had some role to play in explaining the decline in union recognition during the 1980s. A third possibility is that patterns observed within the population are due, not to age or cohort effects, but instead reflect the date of measurement – so-called period effects. In other words, there may be something particular about 1998 which means that certain patterns emerge within a survey conducted in that year. Whilst it may be possible to discount any one of the three factors – age, cohort or period – most survey designs (including WIRS) do not permit the analyst to adjudicate between the remaining two (Plewis, 1985: 7–8). One must accept this limitation. Associations between our measure of workplace age and key features of employment relations can, none the less, be both striking and informative.

Within the WIRS series, there is a break in the continuity of our measure of establishment age. In the first and second surveys, respondents were asked to state how long the establishment had been engaged in its main activity. There was little change in the distribution of responses between the two surveys, with around one fifth (19 per cent) of establishments having been engaged in their main activity for less than ten years, around three tenths (28 per cent in 1980; 30 per cent in 1984) for between ten and twenty-four years and around half (53 per cent in 1980; 51 per cent in 1984) for twenty-five years or more (Table 2.5). The age profiles of workplaces in private manufacturing, private services and the public sector were also relatively uniform and stable. In 1990, the question was changed and respondents to the latter two surveys in the series were asked, instead, to state how long the establishment had been at its current address. This question yielded a younger age profile and although the population appears to have become more youthful over the course of the 1990s, which may represent the continuation of a trend from the late 1980s, it is possible that at least some of the difference between the age profiles depicted in 1984 and 1990 is due to the change in question wording.

In 1990, using the revised question, 28 per cent of workplaces were found to have been at their current address for less than ten years (Table 2.5). A further quarter (24 per cent) had been there for between ten and twenty years, whilst the remaining half (48 per cent) had existed on the same site for more than twenty years.[20] The 1998 survey found that one third (34 per cent) of workplaces were young establishments (i.e. had been at their current address for less than ten years) and 24 per cent were middle-aged (i.e. had been there for between

Table 2.5 Age of establishment, 1980 to 1998

	Column percentages			*Column percentages*	
	1980	*1984*		*1990*	*1998*
Less than 5 years	6	7	Less than 5 years	14	16
5–9 years	13	12	5–9 years	14	18
10–24 years	28	30	10–20 years	24	24
25 years or more	53	51	21 years or more	48	42
Weighted base	*1,930*	*1,944*	*Weighted base*	*1,951*	*1,983*
Unweighted base	*1,986*	*1,965*	*Unweighted base*	*2,009*	*1,902*

Base: all establishments with 25 or more employees.

Note: in 1980 and 1984, age is measured as the number of years over which the establishment has been engaged in its current activity. In 1990 and 1998, age is measured as the time spent at the current address.

ten and twenty years). Only two fifths (42 per cent) were mature establishments (i.e. had been on the same site for more than twenty years).

Under the measure of age used in the 1990 and 1998 surveys, the increasing youthfulness of the age profile suggests that, compared with the late 1980s, the 1990s either saw the creation of a greater proportion of entirely new workplaces or a greater degree of relocation among existing workplaces. In fact, our data suggest that it was the former rather than the latter. The proportion of all workplaces in the 1990 population that had been established anew on their current site within the nine years prior to the survey was 8 per cent, the remaining young workplaces comprising the 18 per cent that had relocated to the current site from elsewhere within this period. In 1998, the proportion of all workplaces that had been set up afresh on their current site in the previous nine years was double that seen in the previous survey, at 16 per cent. The proportion that had relocated to a new site was, however, the same as in 1990: 17 per cent.

The increasing incidence of new, young workplaces within the population may prove to be an important cause of change during the 1990s if such establishments are found to have adopted approaches to employment relations that are distinct from those pursued by more mature workplaces within the population. In particular, if the low rates of recognition among young workplaces in the 1980s have been repeated in the 1990s, notwithstanding the different measures of age, then the trends depicted here clearly bode ill for the union movement.[21]

In many ways, this echoes one of the principal messages to arise from the chapter so far. The rising prevalence of private sector service workplaces, the increase in small firms and the progressive youthfulness of workplaces (at least during the 1990s) in particular each suggest that the population of workplaces is becoming more and more dominated by the types of workplace that have, traditionally, been characterized by less formal and more unilateral forms of management. Later chapters will show how important these compositional developments have been in changing the character of employment relations over the past eighteen years.

In the remainder of this chapter, we continue to investigate the ways in which the population of workplaces has changed over the course of our survey series. However, the focus begins to turn from what might be termed 'structural characteristics' to features that say something more about how the nature of work and the workforce has changed within workplaces since 1980. We look first, albeit briefly, at the spread of technology. This is followed by a more substantial discussion of the many changes in the composition of workforces over the period. Changes along these lines may be equally as important as structural developments in bringing about change in the commonly studied features of employment relations. However, this represents only part of their interest. They also tell us something more direct about changes in the way that workplaces themselves have been managed and, as such, provide a lead for the discussion of employee relations management contained within the following chapter.

Changes in technology

The spread of microtechnology has been one of the most revolutionary developments within British industry over the past twenty years. Indeed, it is often easy to forget that microelectronic technology only became generally available in the second half of the 1970s, just prior to the beginning of our survey series (Daniel, 1987: 2). The incidence of particular forms of microtechnology was not investigated in the first survey in our series or the last. However, our second and third surveys did investigate this issue, as did our panel survey. These provide us with two indicators, the first concerning the automation of production and the second concerning the computerization of office work.

For our first measure, respondents who had indicated that their establishment was engaged in manufacturing were asked if they were using microelectronics in a list of specified applications, including machine control and automated handling or storage.[22] In 1984, under half (44 per cent) of all such establishments were using microelectronics in these applications. A substantial degree of automation clearly followed since, by 1990, the proportion had risen to two thirds (66 per cent). Between 1984 and 1990, there was a notable spread of microelectronics into smaller manufacturing workplaces, perhaps reflecting a decline in cost. In 1984, one third (35 per cent) of establishments with less than 100 employees were using such applications, but by 1990 the proportion stood at over half (57 per cent). Among large establishments with 500 or more employees, microelectronic applications became almost universally available with 94 per cent using them (compared with 85 per cent in 1984).

Notably, we find that those manufacturing workplaces that closed down between 1990 and 1998 were relatively unlikely to be using microelectronic technology: only half were doing so (51 per cent). Among workplaces that fell below the twenty-five employee threshold for the survey, the proportion was 69 per cent, whilst among continuing workplaces it was 81 per cent. By 1998, the proportion of continuing workplaces in manufacturing that made use of microtechnology had risen to 87 per cent.

Our second indicator of the spread of microtechnology covers all workplaces in the population and shows the proportion of establishments with what are now one of the most common forms of office equipment: word processors. In 1984, only one quarter (25 per cent) of all workplaces had word processors on site. They were present in almost one third (31 per cent) of establishments in private manufacturing, one quarter (24 per cent) of establishments in private sector services and one fifth (21 per cent) of public sector workplaces. Smaller workplaces were much less likely to have word processors than larger ones.

By 1990, significant growth had occurred in both the availability and use of such applications, and word processors were to be found in over three fifths (62 per cent) of all establishments. Almost three quarters (71 per cent) of workplaces in private manufacturing now had them, as did three fifths (62 per cent) of those in private services and a similar proportion (57 per cent) of workplaces in the public sector. Among small workplaces with less than

100 employees the proportion had risen from one fifth (19 per cent) to almost three fifths (57 per cent), whilst among large establishments with workforces of 100 or more the availability of such equipment had risen from over two thirds of all workplaces (69 per cent) to become almost universal (95 per cent).

As with the analysis of manufacturing technology just discussed, we can only bring the story up to date through analysis of continuing workplaces in our panel survey; a comparable question was not present in the 1998 cross-section. However, the pattern of use among continuing workplaces, which comprise around two thirds of the population for the 1998 cross-section, shows that the proportion of all workplaces in 1998 with word-processing technology will have risen significantly from the 1990 figure of 62 per cent. Among the continuing workplaces in our panel, the proportion with this technology rose from 62 per cent in 1990 to 90 per cent in 1998. Since our time-series data from 1984 and 1990 show that new workplaces have always been more likely to have word processors than older ones, one might expect the cross-section estimate to be at least as high as that obtained from our panel.

These are only two crude indicators of the extent to which automation and computerization have moved into the workplace during the past two decades. However, the contrast between the situation in the early 1980s and the late 1990s could not be more striking.

Changes in the composition of the workforce

The composition of the workforce in Britain has also changed in many notable ways over the past twenty years. On the supply side, the continual increase in female employment rates has been one of the most pivotal developments. However, in the 1990s, this has been accompanied by a decrease in employment rates among young people as larger numbers delay their entry into paid work in favour of further and higher education. On the demand side, the sectoral shift from manufacturing to services has been a critical development, as discussed earlier in the chapter. The use of non-standard employment contracts has also been a central theme, with much debate focusing on the increasing proportion of jobs that are now either part-time, temporary or provided through employment agencies.

Changes in both person-specific and job-specific characteristics are examined here. At the individual level, trends in the characteristics of employees and of jobs over the past twenty years are ably quantified by a variety of other data sources.[23] However, the WIRS series makes a unique contribution by providing information on the incidence and concentration of employee-related and job-related characteristics across the population of workplaces. Such data enable us to see the degree to which developments in the composition of the labour force have either been concentrated in particular types of workplace or have spanned the whole economy. In subsequent chapters, we will then be able to investigate the extent to which trends in the composition of the workforce have interacted with changes in the nature of employment relations over time.

Women's employment

The Labour Force Survey shows that the employment rate among women of working age in Britain increased from 59 per cent to 68 per cent between 1980 and 1998, helping to raise women's share of all employment from 42 per cent to 47 per cent over the course of our survey series. This increase in female employment is relevant to our discussion because women differ from men along certain dimensions of work-related behaviour. Women are less likely than men to be union members, for example, although the difference has become much smaller in recent years (Cully and Woodland, 1998). The concentration of women in a workplace has been shown to be associated with higher quit rates and absence, whilst there is also a link with the activities of management since the collection and distribution of data on the gender mix of the workforce is more common in workplaces with high concentrations of female employees (Millward *et al.*, 1992: 175, 327–9).

The WIRS series shows that women's share of employment in workplaces with twenty-five or more employees increased from 38 per cent in 1980 to 48 per cent in 1998. In keeping with trends evident amongst the working population as a whole, this rise was almost exclusively driven by an expansion in part-time working amongst women. The proportion of all employees accounted for by women working full-time rose from 26 per cent in 1980 to 28 per cent in 1984 but has remained steady since then. In contrast, the proportion accounted for by women working part-time increased from 14 per cent in 1980 to 20 per cent in 1998. The association between women's employment and part-time work will be returned to in the discussion of non-standard employment. First, we explore the changing patterns of women's employment as a whole.

Table 2.6 shows that the proportion of all workplaces with low concentrations of female employees (less than 25 per cent) has fallen by one quarter over the series, from 36 per cent in 1980 to 27 per cent in 1998. This decline in the proportion of male-dominated workplaces has occurred principally as a result of a fall in the proportion of workplaces with very low concentrations of female employees (less than 10 per cent). Such workplaces accounted for 17 per cent of the population in 1984 but only 10 per cent in 1998.

The proportion of all workplaces with a high proportion of women workers (75 per cent or more) has risen by one third between 1980 and 1998, from 22 per cent to 29 per cent (Table 2.6). There was little change during the early 1980s, however. Most of the change has taken place in the period since 1984, with the pace of change appearing to accelerate during the 1990s. An important element of this trend has been a rise in the proportion of establishments with very high concentrations of women (at least 90 per cent). These workplaces accounted for 8 per cent of the population in 1984 but 13 per cent in 1998.

One important question that might be asked in response to these trends is whether they have primarily arisen because workplaces in general are now employing greater numbers of women, or whether the trends might simply be

Table 2.6 Composition of the workforce, 1980 to 1998

	Column percentages			
	1980	*1984*	*1990*	*1998*
Proportion of employees that are female				
Less than 25 per cent	36	35	33	27
25–74 per cent	42	44	43	44
75 per cent or more	22	22	24	29
Proportion of employees from ethnic minority groups				
None	64	63	60	52
Less than 5 per cent	23	25	25	28
5–10 per cent	5	7	7	9
11–19 per cent	4	3	2	5
20 per cent or more	4	2	5	7
Proportion of employees that work part-time				
None	13	18	14	16
Less than 25 per cent	55	51	54	40
25 per cent or more	32	31	32	44
Any employees on fixed-term contracts of less than 12 months	19	20	22	35
Any agency temps	20	..	..	28
Any freelance workers[a]	24	14	16	13
Any homeworkers or outworkers	8	4	5	..

Base: all establishments with 25 or more employees.

Note

a In 1980, 1984 and 1990 figures give the percentage of workplaces employing any freelance workers in the 12 months prior to the survey date. The 1998 figure gives the percentage of workplaces employing freelancers at the time of the survey.

the result of changes in the composition of industry, with those sectors that have always employed more women now being more dominant than ones that have traditionally relied more on male labour. Further investigation of our time-series data shows that both effects have been important, at least in bringing about the rise in female-dominated workplaces.[24] Basing our analysis on the fine division of industry and ownership categorized in Table 2.1, it can be shown that four sectors have driven most of the rise in female-dominated workplaces. First, private sector distribution, hotels and catering and repairs, where the proportion of female-dominated workplaces has risen during the 1990s from 16 per cent to 20 per cent, and where the aggregate effect of the rise has been amplified by a slight increase in the prevalence of such workplaces (see Table 2.1a). Second, private sector finance and business services, where the increase in female-dominated workplaces (15 per cent in 1990; 34 per cent in 1998) has more than outweighed the slight fall in the proportion of workplaces in the sector. Third, miscellaneous private services, where the proportion of female-dominated workplaces has remained steadily high (at around 55 per cent) but which has grown considerably in size. And fourth, public sector education, where the proportion of female-dominated workplaces has grown slightly (from 63 per cent to 66 per cent) along with the size of the sector as a whole.

However, if women's presence in the workplace is now greater than ever, there still remains the question of their relative standing in the occupational hierarchy. Following our companion volume (Cully *et al.*, 1999), we develop a measure of vertical segregation that can be used to examine changes in the representation of women in middle or senior managerial positions through a major part of our survey series. This measure takes the proportion of middle or senior managers in each workplace that are female and compares it with the proportion of all female employees at that workplace. A ratio of one would represent precise numerical equality. This situation is extremely rare and so we create some leeway by defining equality as a ratio of between 0.95 and 1.05. If the ratio is less than 0.95, women are considered to be under-represented in managerial positions when compared with their share of all employment at that establishment. If the ratio is greater than 1.05, women are considered to be over-represented in such positions. In fact, a wider band of 0.90 to 1.10, whilst changing the estimates, produces the same overall patterns of change.

To look at vertical segregation, we focus on those workplaces in which there was a mixture of male and female employees and at least some individuals in middle or senior management positions.[25] Figure 2.1 clearly shows that since 1984, when we were first able to compile our measure, women have accompanied their increasing share of employment by making considerable

Figure 2.1 Representation of women among managerial positions, 1984 to 1998

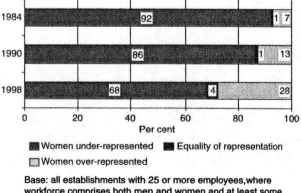

Base: all establishments with 25 or more employees, where workforce comprises both men and women and at least some middle or senior managers.

inroads into middle and senior management. In 1984, women were under-represented among the managerial ranks in some 92 per cent of workplaces. At the same time, women were over-represented amongst managers in only 7 per cent of all workplaces, with only 1 per cent of establishments having equality. The pattern had begun to change by 1990, when the proportion of workplaces in which women were under-represented had fallen to 86 per cent. A much larger change has occurred in the 1990s, however. In 1998, women were under-represented amongst managers in 68 per cent of workplaces. One in every twenty-five workplaces (4 per cent) had equality whilst three in ten (28 per cent) had an over-representation of women.

In the 1990s, the proportion of workplaces in which women are under-represented amongst middle and senior managers has fallen within the private and public sectors and in each division of industry. It has fallen amongst workplaces of all sizes, amongst single independent workplaces and those that form part of larger organizations, amongst head offices and branch establishments, amongst those that are domestically owned and those under foreign ownership, and amongst workplaces of all ages. Our panel of continuing workplaces shows that behavioural change within workplaces has had an important part to play in this development. Between 1990 and 1998, one in seven continuing workplaces (14 per cent) moved from a position where women were under-represented among managers to a position of equality or over-representation. Half as many (7 per cent) moved in the opposite direction. The overall result was that, in 1990, 86 per cent of continuing workplaces had a disproportionate number of men among managerial positions, but by 1998 this had fallen to 79 per cent.

Clearly much has changed in terms of the gender breakdown of roles and responsibilities amongst workplaces throughout the 1980s and 1990s. We return to this theme again in Chapter 3 when we look at women's penetration of one particular management function: the management of employment relations.

Employment of ethnic minorities

It was noted above that previous surveys in the WIRS series have shown the proportion of women among the workforce at an establishment to be associated with certain features of employment relations, and so it is with the proportion of employees from ethnic minorities. Workplaces with high concentrations of employees from ethnic minorities were found to have experienced a significant decline in the incidence of trade union recognition during the second half of the 1980s (Millward *et al.*, 1992: 73). Early work also showed a negative association with levels of pay (Blanchflower, 1984). The association with union recognition, in particular, will be examined again in Chapter 4 in order to see if it has persisted into the 1990s.

In contrast to the continual increase in the employment rate among women, that of ethnic minorities has fluctuated over the course of the 1980s and 1990s.

Figures for the period 1984–97 from the Labour Force Survey show that the employment rate among ethnic minorities rose from 54 per cent in 1984 to a high of 62 per cent in 1989; the rate then fell back to 51 per cent in 1994, following the recession of the early 1990s, but has since recovered to 57 per cent (Sly *et al.*, 1998: 612). The ethnic minority share of the working age population has risen continually though, from around 4.6 per cent in 1984 to 6.4 per cent in 1997 (*Employment Gazette*, 1988: 166; Sly *et al.*, 1998: 602).

At workplace level, significant changes are apparent across the period covered by the WIRS series. In 1980, ethnic minorities were employed in one third (36 per cent) of all establishments (Table 2.6). This figure rose to two fifths (40 per cent) in 1990 and has since risen further to reach almost one half (48 per cent) in 1998. Analysis of our panel survey shows a substantial 'spreading out' of ethnic minority employment among continuing workplaces between 1990 and 1998. In 1990, two fifths (40 per cent) of all continuing workplaces employed at least some ethnic minorities among their staff, yet in 1998 the figure had risen to three fifths (60 per cent). Twenty-three per cent of continuing workplaces moved from the position of employing no ethnic minorities in 1990 to having some ethnic minority representation among their workforce in 1998, whereas only 3 per cent of workplaces moved in the other direction. Two fifths of workplaces leaving the survey population between 1990 and 1998 employed at least some ethnic minority employees, whilst this was true for exactly one half of those workplaces joining the population over the period.

Our time-series data show that, between 1990 and 1998, workplaces of almost all sizes became more likely to employ at least some ethnic minorities. The exception was establishments with 500 or more employees, where the proportion employing ethnic minorities has remained relatively high at around nine in every ten. The likelihood of employing at least some ethnic minorities rose between 1990 and 1998 among both UK and foreign-owned establishments and in each of the three broad sectors of the economy: private manufacturing, private services and the public sector.

At the other end of the scale, the proportion of workplaces in which ethnic minorities made up more than one fifth of those employed stood at 7 per cent in 1998, having trebled since 1984 when the figure stood at just 2 per cent. Increases have been particularly notable in the public sector (rising from 1 per cent in 1984 to 9 per cent in 1998), among small workplaces (less than one per cent in 1984; 7 per cent in 1998) and among foreign-owned workplaces (4 per cent in 1984; 14 per cent in 1998).

Non-standard employment

We have examined trends in two of the most notable person-specific characteristics of workforces in the economy – gender and ethnicity – but there have also been important developments in the nature of jobs over the period since 1980. Among the most significant of these, at least in terms of the level of debate generated among practitioners, researchers and policy-makers alike, is the growth of so-called flexible forms of employment. Here we shall employ the less value-laden term 'non-standard employment', using it to refer to working arrangements that differ from the traditional full-time, open-ended employment contract. This includes part-time work, short fixed-term contracts, temporary employment via agencies, freelance work and homework or outwork. Some in-depth analysis of relevant data from the 1984 and 1990 surveys has already been reported elsewhere (see Casey *et al.*, 1997). We shall draw on some parts of that analysis here, extending our discussion to incorporate new data from the 1998 survey as well as from the first survey in 1980, wherever it proves practicable to do so.

Part-time work

Part-time work is the most established and widely used form of non-standard employment. The WIRS series defines part-time employees as those working less than 30 hours per week. Using this definition, our first survey in 1980 found that only one in every eight workplaces (13 per cent) did not have any part-time workers amongst their labour force (Table 2.6). This figure has fluctuated slightly over the series and, in 1998, stood at the marginally higher level of around one in every six (16 per cent). Still, it is clear that the vast majority of employers do make use of part-time workers. Indeed, the survey series shows that the proportion of establishments making substantial use of part-timers, whilst remaining stable throughout the 1980s, has increased markedly over the most recent decade. The proportion of workplaces in which part-timers made up at least one quarter of the workforce remained at around one third throughout each of the first three surveys, but had increased to more than two fifths (44 per cent) by the time of the fourth survey in 1998 (Table 2.6). This increase was wholly due to a rise in the proportion of workplaces with very high proportions of part-timers (i.e. 50 per cent or more), whose incidence within the population doubled from 13 per cent in 1990 to 27 per cent in 1998.

In total, one quarter (25 per cent) of all employees covered by our 1998 survey were working part-time hours. This represented a substantial increase on the figure of 18 per cent from our 1990 survey. However, there was only a small increase in part-time employment among continuing workplaces (19 per cent in 1990; 21 per cent in 1998). The primary impetus came, therefore, from a greater provision of part-time work among workplaces that joined the population when compared with those establishments that either closed down or fell out of scope. One sixth (16 per cent) of those employed in workplaces that left the population worked part-time, compared with 27 per cent among establishments that joined it. Further analysis showed that the origins of this difference were partly compositional and partly behavioural. Around two fifths of the difference between leavers and joiners was due to private service industries being more prevalent among joiners. Part-time employment is particularly common in private services, as shown later in this section. However around three fifths was due to the fact that workplaces joining the private services sector between 1990 and 1998 employed greater proportions of part-time workers than establishments that left the sector over the period.

The recent trend towards a greater use of part-time workers may have important implications for some of the key institutions of employment relations. For instance, part-timers are known to have considerably lower levels of union membership than full-time employees (Cully and Woodland, 1998). In addition, previous analysis of WIRS data has shown that the likelihood of a workplace having recognized trade unions declines as the proportion of part-time workers increases, even after controlling for the influence of other workplace characteristics (Disney *et al.*, 1995). Such issues will be examined in Chapter 4. Here, however, we explore some of the aggregate trends in more detail.

As suggested above, the use of part-time workers rose substantially among private service sector workplaces between 1990 and 1998. The percentage of private service sector workplaces in which part-timers accounted for at least one quarter of the workforce rose from 33 per cent to 49 per cent over the period. In the public sector it rose from 53 per cent to 60 per cent. The large rise in private services was particularly evident among workplaces engaged in distribution, hotels and catering and repairs (1980 SIC Division 6), where the percentage of workplaces with high concentrations of part-time workers rose from 43 per cent in 1990 to 61 per cent in 1998. More broadly, the incidence of high concentrations of part-time workers rose among workplaces of all sizes, among independent establishments as well as those that form a part of larger organizations, among UK-owned and foreign-owned workplaces and among those with mixed and female-dominated workforces.

In contrast to the general trend, however, the percentage of all private sector manufacturing plants in which part-timers accounted for at least one quarter of the workforce remained low (2 per cent in 1990; 4 per cent in 1998). Furthermore, the proportion that did not employ any part-timers actually doubled, from 18 per cent in 1990 to 36 per cent in 1998. Increases were apparent in all three areas: extraction, heavy industry and light manufacturing. This contrasts with the situation in private services, where the proportion of workplaces without any part-timers remained stable at 15 per cent, and the public sector, where it fell from 9 per cent in 1990 to just 5 per cent in 1998. There are numerous reasons why the use of part-time labour may be less prevalent in manufacturing than in services: greater capital intensity and higher levels of male employment are two. Yet it is less clear why the use of part-time labour in manufacturing should have become less common between 1990 and 1998.

Finally, it has long been known that the majority of part-time workers are women. In our first three surveys, the association between the employment of women and the provision of part-time work at workplace level was a strong one. In 1980, 1984 and 1990, part-time workers made up the majority of the workforce in over two fifths (43 per cent) of female-dominated workplaces (those in which women accounted for 75 per cent or more of all employees). The association grew even stronger in the 1990s, however, with our fourth survey finding that, in 1998, part-time workers made up the majority of the workforce in almost three fifths (59 per cent) of female-dominated workplaces. These workplaces with high concentrations of women and part-time workers accounted for one sixth (17 per cent) of the population in 1998, compared with just one tenth (9 per cent) in 1990.

Short fixed-term contracts

In the first three surveys in the series, respondents were asked if any employees at the establishment were 'currently working on the basis of a short fixed-term contract for 12 months or less'.[26] There was a marginal increase in the percentage of workplaces using such contracts, from 19 per cent in 1980 to 22 per cent in 1990 (Table 2.6). In 1998, the question wording was altered slightly and respondents were asked if there were 'any employees at this workplace who are working on a temporary basis or have fixed-term contracts for less than one year'. A much larger increase was registered between the 1990 and 1998 surveys, the proportion of respondents answering affirmatively rising to 35 per cent. Some small part of this increase might be attributed to the change in question wording between the third and fourth surveys which may have resulted in some respondents including agency temps. However, the question followed a bank of detailed questioning specifically devoted to agency temps and so it is likely that most respondents did not include them again here. As a result, much of the increase in the incidence of short-term contracts between 1990 and 1998 is thought to be real. Further support for this view emerges from our panel survey of continuing workplaces, which retained the 1990 question wording within its 1998 interviews. The panel survey shows a substantial rise in the proportion of continuing workplaces that use short fixed-term contracts, from one quarter (25 per cent) in 1990 to over two fifths (44 per cent) in 1998. Alone, these continuing workplaces that were using short-term contracts accounted for 28 per cent of the whole population of workplaces in 1998 – itself a greater proportion than was evident among the whole sample in 1990.

Returning to the time-series data, previous analysis of short-term contracts using the 1984 and 1990 survey data found that this form of non-standard employment was more common in the public sector than the private sector, more common in larger workplaces than in smaller ones and more prevalent among foreign-owned workplaces than domestically owned establishments (Casey *et al.*, 1997: 46–50, 69). However, the same source showed that employees on short-term contracts usually accounted for only a small proportion of the workforce, the median in 1990 being 5 per cent. The 1998 survey does not permit us to examine the concentration of short-term contract workers within an establishment, but the data do show that the workplace characteristics associated with a greater likelihood of employing any workers on short-term contracts were the same in 1998 as in 1990. Substantial increases in the incidence of short-term contracts were evident within particular industries between the two surveys. Referring back to the categories listed in Table 2.1, large increases were apparent in all three areas of private sector manufacturing and, within private sector services, among workplaces engaged in transport and communications, construction and finance and business services. The proportion of public sector workplaces employing workers on fixed-term contracts rose sharply among workplaces engaged in transport and communications, but declined among establishments in central and local government, education and health.

Temporary workers from employment agencies

Many of our survey questions about the employed workforce at an establishment exclude workers on a temporary assignment from an employment agency, since such workers are employees of the agency and not the sampled establishment. However, specific questions have been asked about agency temps in all but the 1990 survey. The first and fourth surveys, from 1980 and 1998, provide the most comparable questions. The 1980 survey asked if any persons had been working at the establishment on a temporary assignment from an employment agency *during the last month*; one fifth (20 per cent) of respondents answered positively (Table 2.6). The 1998 survey was somewhat more restrictive, asking if there were any temporary agency employees *presently* working at the workplace; yet more than one quarter (28 per cent) of respondents said that there were. Under either measure, the use of agency temps has clearly increased by at least 8 percentage points over the course of the series. Referring back to the categories of industry listed in Table 2.1, the incidence of agency temps had risen within each of the three areas of private manufacturing and each part of the public sector. However, within the private services sector, the only statistically significant increase was among workplaces engaged in transport and communications. This may partly reflect the timing of our interviews. The median interview date for our 1980 survey was June, whilst in our 1998 survey it was February. One would expect certain service industries such as hotels and catering and construction to have a greater demand for additional short-term labour in the summer months, and so increases may have been registered in those industries too if the 1998 survey had taken place a little later in the year.

Freelance workers, homeworkers and outworkers

In the final part of our discussion on non-standard employment, and workforce composition more generally, we take a brief look at the use of freelancers, homeworkers and outworkers. In each case, respondents were given specific instructions to exclude such workers from the data given about the employees of the establishment. Freelancers are not considered to be employees, being engaged on contracts for services rather than contracts of service, although the legal status of homeworkers and outworkers is somewhat less clear. One of the rationales for using such workers, however, is to create flexibility by limiting the term of engagement solely to the period for which a particular form of labour is required. It is notable, then, that in the context of an increasingly flexible labour market, the proportion of workplaces making use of these forms of labour contract has actually changed little over the course of our survey series.

In our first three surveys, we asked respondents if any freelancers had been used by the establishment in the twelve months prior to the survey. The proportion responding affirmatively fell between 1980 and 1984, from 24 per cent to 14 per cent, but remained steady between 1984 and 1990 (Table 2.6). In 1998, the question referred only to the time of the survey and gave a figure of 13 per cent. In the 1990s, as in the 1980s, freelance workers remained more common in private manufacturing and private services than in the public sector.

Given the change in question wording between our third and fourth surveys, it is unlikely that the use of freelancers fell during the 1990s and it is possible that it, in fact, rose somewhat. Evidence from our panel survey lends some weight to this hypothesis. Our panel survey is free from the uncertainties present within the time series since it used the same question wording in both years. It shows that, among continuing workplaces, the overall incidence of freelancers rose from 16 per cent of workplaces in 1990 to 21 per cent in 1998. It was notable, however, that few workplaces were using freelance workers at both points in time (6 per cent).

We also asked respondents to our first three cross-section surveys if their establishment had used any homeworkers or outworkers in the twelve months prior to the survey. Over the course of the 1980s, the proportion that had used this type of worker in the previous twelve months stood at around one in twenty (8 per cent in 1980; 4 per cent in 1984 and 5 per cent in 1990) (Table 2.6). In 1998, the question was amended and is not thought to provide comparable results.[27] However, our panel survey did retain the previous question wording from the 1990 survey. The data provide a different picture from that relating to freelancers, with the proportion of continuing workplaces that used homeworkers or outworkers changing little between 1990 and 1998 (4 per cent in 1990; 5 per cent in 1998). Yet, again, few workplaces were using this type of worker in both years (1 per cent).

Clearly, problems of comparability impair the precision with which we are able to gauge changes in the use of some types of non-standard employment over the course of our survey series. However, although some of the estimates may be subject to a degree of uncertainty, the patterns of change are generally apparent. In particular, the increased use of part-time workers and short fixed-term contracts during the 1990s, together with the increased use of agency temps over the series as a whole, all ably illustrate how the character of jobs and, more particularly, workplaces has developed in recent years.

Summary and conclusions

This chapter has attempted to show how the population of workplaces has changed over the past eighteen years. In some respects, change has been substantial. In the private sector, the domination of service industries over manufacturing has clearly increased. This has been accompanied by a rise in the incidence of small firms, greater degrees of foreign ownership and the development of a more youthful population in general. Workforces are now somewhat less segregated by either gender or ethnicity, whilst in the 1990s in particular, the use of certain non-standard forms of employment such as part-time work and short fixed-term contracts has become much more commonplace. In most cases, these changes clearly seem to be secular rather than cyclical. There are some elements of stability: in the overall size of workplaces, for example. Yet even here, the aggregate picture masks changes in particular sectors. On balance then, the character of the population – and hence, the context of workplace employment relations – is clearly quite different to that present at the beginning of our survey series.

Since many of the workplace characteristics discussed here are associated with patterns of employment relations practice, our analysis will go some way in helping us to uncover how change has occurred in the incidence of some of the key institutions and practices of employment relations over the past eighteen years. The rising prevalence of service industries and the greater use of part-time work are shown to be particularly important in relation to the changing patterns of employee representation, for example. As later chapters will show, aggregate compositional change in the population can play a key role in bringing about changes in the overall incidence of particular practices within the economy.

However, this chapter has also pointed to many notable patterns of change that occur at the micro-level, whether in continuing workplaces or as a result of transitions in and out of the population. Within continuing workplaces, we have been able to point to the high degree of ownership change and also to changes in workforce size, both of which are seen, in subsequent chapters, to have associations with changes in employment relations within establishments. In examining the characteristics of leavers and joiners, we showed that small service sector workplaces were a common feature of both groups. Yet we also identified differences, such as the higher incidence of independent establishments and greater degree of foreign ownership, which suggest that joiners may have brought a particular brand of employment relations into the population in the 1990s. The substantial use of part-time workers among joiners is one indication of this. More of their distinguishing features will become apparent in the remainder of the book.

3 The management of employee relations

It is commonly accepted that the management of employee relations has undergone unprecedented change since 1980, when our survey series began. Although a large management literature has focused on the role of employee relations managers as initiators of change, they have also been the subject of change as organizations have sought to respond to new competitive pressures in product and labour markets (see Bach and Sisson, 1999, for a discussion). Changes in corporate structure and strategy create new demands of employee relations managers, as well as shaping the function itself. Often, developments in employee relations management represent 'not so much a new departure within personnel, as a set of movements from outside it' (Storey, 1992: 274). Continually seeking to reorient itself to these changing circumstances, employee relations management has been variously characterized as in crisis, in transition, and increasingly on the periphery of corporate decision-making, which is now dominated by financial rather than employment considerations. As long ago as 1987, Tyson warned of the 'balkanization of the personnel role':

> The territory which could once have been delineated as personnel country, is being invaded, sold-off, subdivided and put under lease to consultants, sub-specialist and line managers, whose cross-cutting alliances do not correspond to a coherent separate function.
>
> (Tyson, 1987: 530)

It is against this backdrop that personnel management has been fashioning a new future for itself, often seeking to justify its role in terms of the financial contribution it can make to organizations through the introduction and development of so-called 'high performance' or 'innovative' practices.

This chapter considers the management of employee relations over the last two decades, concentrating on the way in which workplace-level employee relations management has developed over time. Business strategies, structures and styles of management organization are all important in shaping management industrial relations practice (Sisson and Marginson, 1995: 106), but here the focus is on management structures and procedures, areas of inquiry which have featured heavily in the WIRS series.[1] Other chapters say more about the substance of management practices, including approaches to the utilization of labour and employee involvement.

We begin with the issue of who manages employee relations, identifying the incidence of employee relations specialists and a new breed, the human resources manager. Then we consider whether employee relations management is emerging as a profession, looking at trends in qualifications, job tenure and experience, and time spent on employee relations matters. A growing proportion of employee relations managers are women: we track this development from the beginning of our series in 1980 and consider how they differ from men doing the same job. In the second half of the chapter, we tackle some broader issues facing employee relations. First, we consider the changing role of employee relations managers, looking at the responsibilities they have, their role as managers of information, and the advice they seek in performing their jobs. Finally, we look at the status and influence of employee relations managers before concluding.

Much of the analysis is based on information provided by managers interviewed on site, thus excluding information on a small minority of workplaces where the interview was conducted with informants elsewhere in the organization, generally at a higher level.[2] This improves the reliability of data on the internal workings of the establishment, and provides a workplace-level perspective on issues such as the relationship with the wider organization, rather than relying on the views of more senior managers. In addition, data relating to individual respondents, such as gender, time in the job, and job title, cannot be related to workplace characteristics where the informant is employed elsewhere. Where these considerations are not relevant, analyses are based on all respondents.

Who manages employee relations?

We begin our analysis by asking: 'Who manages employee relations?' In each survey our management respondents, whom we refer to generally as employee relations managers, have been asked to give their job title. Their responses have been coded into a number of categories and from them we have distinguished three broad types of employee relations manager. First, there are those whose dedicated function is the management of employee relations, identified by having any of the terms 'personnel, human resources or industrial, employee or staff relations' in their job title. We refer to them hereafter as ER specialists. The second group are managers who have a specialist responsibility for a function other than employee relations, but whose job also includes responsibility for employee relations at the workplace. These include marketing and sales managers, accountants and other professional and technical managers. We refer to them as 'line managers'. Finally, there are those managers who have overall responsibility for the workplace, including the management of employee relations. These include general managers and site managers, with titles such as branch, office or depot manager in service industries and works or plant manager in manufacturing. We refer to this group as 'generalists'.

A growth in the number of specialists

Trends in the job titles held by employee relations managers indicate that there has been significant change in who manages workplace employee relations in the last two decades (Table 3.1). The big switch since 1980 has been the transfer of responsibility away from generalists towards line managers and ER specialists. Whereas generalists accounted for three quarters (75 per cent) of employee relations managers in 1980, this had fallen to under one half (46 per cent) by 1998.

In the 1980s, responsibility for employee relations was being shifted to line managers responsible for individual functional departments other than personnel. A high proportion of these was involved in the finance or accounting function in the workplace. By 1990, they made up 28 per cent of managers

Table 3.1 Job titles of workplace employee relations managers, 1980 to 1998

	Column percentages[a]			
	1980	*1984*	*1990*	*1998*
Employee relations specialists	15	16	17	23
Personnel manager[b]	14	14	16	22
Employee/industrial/staff relations manager	1	2	1	1
Line managers	10	14	28	28
Accountant/finance function	6	7	11	10
Marketing/commercial/sales function	2	1	2	2
Professional/technical	2	6	15	16
Generalists	75	64	51	46
General management	49	49	24	34
Production/works/factory/plant manager	5	5	5	2
Branch/depot/establishment manager	21	11	22	10
Other	0	6	3	3
Don't know/not answered	*	*	1	0
Weighted base	*1,830*	*1,779*	*1,644*	*1,821*
Unweighted base	*1,868*	*1,794*	*1,697*	*1,740*

Base: all establishments with 25 or more employees where the survey interview was conducted on site.

Notes
a Subtotals in italics.
b Includes human resources managers in 1990 and 1998.

responsible for employee relations – nearly a threefold increase since 1980 when they made up one tenth.

A different trend emerged in the 1990s with the rise of ER specialists. Generalist involvement in employee relations management continued to decline, but the management of workplace employee relations was increasingly undertaken by those with designated employee relations job titles rather than line managers. During the 1980s, around one sixth of managers responsible for employee relations were ER specialists, but between 1990 and 1998 this rose to nearly one quarter. The increase was apparent across the economy, in the public and private sectors, in manufacturing and services,[3] in UK and foreign-owned workplaces, among those recognizing unions and those that did not, in independent workplaces and branches of larger organizations, and in all but the largest workplaces (where ER specialists were already almost universal).[4]

If it is assumed that workplaces yielding proxy interviews did not have ER specialists (this being the reason for referring the interview to a higher level), the proportion of all sampled workplaces with an ER specialist rose by half between 1990 and 1998 to 21 per cent, having remained static at 14 per cent since 1980. The recent increase is accounted for by the particularly low incidence of ER specialists among establishments leaving the survey population between 1990 and 1998. One tenth (11 per cent) of employee relations managers employed by 'leavers' in 1990 were ER specialists, compared with 17 per cent in the 1990 cross-section as a whole. On the other hand, one sixth (18 per cent) of the establishments entering the survey population in 1998 were employing ER specialists.[5]

The incidence of ER specialists among continuing workplaces remained constant at 19 per cent, so these establishments did not contribute to the aggregate increase in ER specialists between 1990 and 1998.[6] This is not to say that all those employing ER specialists in 1990 continued to do so, while all those employing non-specialists remained without. Between 1990 and 1998, 7 per cent of continuing workplaces started to employ an ER specialist, while a further 7 per cent ceased to do so.

The significance of the growth in ER specialists depends, in part, on how they differ from other managers responsible for employee relations. This issue is explored below. However, they still constitute a relatively small proportion of employee relations managers. Generalists continue to account for almost half of all employee relations managers, and line managers outnumber ER specialists. Furthermore, ER specialists feature in only one in eight of the workplaces employing fewer than 100 people, which make up three quarters of the workplaces in our sample.

The rise of human resource managers

Commentators have pointed to the increasing involvement of line managers in personnel matters as a possible indicator of human resource management

(HRM) principles taking root (Sisson, 1993). However, the fact that fewer than 1 per cent of respondents in 1990 bore a 'human resources' job title confirmed the suspicions of others that 'human resource management has found a very modest existence in some head offices but at establishment level is scarcely breathing' (Guest and Hoque, 1993: 40). This is no longer the case.

By 1998, 7 per cent of managers responsible for workplace employee relations were human resource managers or officers, making up nearly one third (30 per cent) of all ER specialists.[7] Of course, the growing incidence of the HRM job title is not, in itself, sufficient to indicate that principles of human resource management were being applied in practice. It may be that employee relations managers have simply been relabelled as 'human resource managers'. We briefly consider this issue later when we compare the responsibilities of human resource managers with personnel managers.

The increase in human resource managers wholly accounts for the increase in specialists between 1990 and 1998. If there had been no rise in their numbers, specialists would have continued to be present in roughly 16 per cent of workplaces. Nor were human resource managers confined to head offices, 'a strategic phenomenon at the strategic apex of the organization' (Guest and Hoque, 1993: 41). Twelve per cent of head offices had human resource managers in 1998.

The incidence of human resource managers increased with workplace size, but there was no simple relationship between size of workplace and the proportion of ER specialists with human resource job titles. Perhaps surprisingly, 40 per cent of ER specialists in the smallest workplaces with fewer than fifty employees were human resource managers, a higher proportion than for any other size-band.

The human resource manager job title was particularly in evidence in the electricity, gas and water supply industries, large parts of which have been privatized since the mid-1980s. Two fifths (43 per cent) of employee relations managers in these industries had human resource job titles. It was the only sector in which human resource managers made up the majority (61 per cent) of ER specialists.

One factor contributing to the growth in human resource managers between 1990 and 1998 is the increased penetration of foreign-owned workplaces. As well as relying more heavily on ER specialists to manage employee relations, foreign-owned workplaces had a higher incidence of human resource managers among their ER specialists than UK-owned workplaces. Human resource managers accounted for two thirds (64 per cent) of ER specialists in foreign-owned workplaces, compared with one quarter (26 per cent) in UK-owned workplaces. Human resource managers constituted 30 per cent of all employee relations managers in foreign-owned workplaces, compared with 6 per cent among UK-owned workplaces.

Human resource managers were less common in the public sector: 20 per cent of ER specialists in the public sector were human resource managers, compared with 35 per cent of the ER specialists in the private sector.

It is difficult to judge from cross-sectional data whether the increase in the number of human resource managers has resulted from a change in practice among continuing workplaces, or whether it reflects an innovation by relatively new workplaces. However, the cross-sectional data do indicate that human resource managers were by no means confined to new workplaces. Thirty-two per cent of the ER specialists in workplaces aged ten years or more were human resource managers, compared with 29 per cent in workplaces aged under ten years. In fact, our panel data show that the increased incidence of human resource managers is accounted for both by changes within continuing establishments and by the practices of newer workplaces.

Whereas less than 1 per cent of continuing workplaces had employed a human resource manager in 1990, 5 per cent were doing so by 1998. In almost two thirds (63 per cent) of these cases employee relations had been managed by a personnel manager in 1990, and in a further 8 per cent by ER specialists with other titles. In the remainder of cases the manager had not been an ER specialist in 1990. Similarly, less than 1 per cent of workplaces leaving the survey population between 1990 and 1998 employed a human resource manager, while 6 per cent of workplaces joining the survey population in 1998 employed human resource managers, accounting for one third of all ER specialists. The human resource managers among 'joiners' were almost wholly confined to new workplaces, rather than those that had grown above the twenty-five employee threshold since 1990. Human resource managers made up 11 per cent of all employee relations managers among the new 'joiners'. It seems likely that human resource managers will become more prevalent if more continuing workplaces change the type of ER specialist they employ and new workplaces continue to introduce them.

If, as is often suggested, the introduction and successful development of human resource management is frequently associated with fundamental change to management practices and organizational cultures, one might expect it to accompany organizational change. We address this issue with our panel of continuing establishments. Where continuing workplaces had merged, amalgamated, split or changed ownership since 1990, respondents were asked: 'Has the change of ownership/merger/split/demerger you mentioned had any effect on the following: the type of products made or services provided here? . . . the number of employees here? . . . the way work is done here? . . . the management structure here? . . . management's approach to employee relations here?' In fact, human resource managers were no more prevalent in workplaces that had split, merged, amalgamated or changed ownership since 1990 than they were in workplaces which had not undergone any of these changes. Nor were they any more in evidence where organizational change was perceived to have affected management structures, the managerial approach to employee relations or 'the way work is done here'. These findings also held among the subset of continuing establishments employing ER specialists in 1998. So there is little evidence of an association between changes in management practice or structural organizational change and the adoption of the 'human resource manager' job title for workplace employee relations managers.

The emergence of a profession?

The qualifications of employee relations managers

Since the beginning of the series our main managerial respondents have been asked an identical question: 'Apart from your experience, do you have any formal qualifications in personnel management or a closely related subject?' The proportion answering 'yes' has risen by a half over the period, from 31 per cent in 1980 to 45 per cent in 1998, most of the increase coming since 1990 (Figure 3.1).[8] Since the mid-1980s there has been an increase in the level of qualifications required for jobs across all occupational classes (Gallie *et al.*, 1998), so this finding alone may not tell us very much about developments in employee relations management. However, the aggregate figure hides a big divide between ER specialists and other employee relations managers. Over the period since 1980, ER specialists have been two to three times more likely to hold formal qualifications than other employee relations managers, but the gap grew during the 1990s. In fact, the increase in qualified employee relations managers in the 1990s was almost wholly accounted for by ER specialists. Between 1990 and 1998 the proportion of ER specialists with personnel qualifications rose from 57 per cent to nearly three quarters (72 per cent), whereas the proportion of other employee relations managers with personnel qualifications remained at around one quarter (Figure 3.1). So there has been a growing polarization between those who are not ER specialists on the one hand, most of whom have no personnel qualifications, and ER specialists for whom

Figure 3.1 Formal qualifications in personnel management, 1980 to 1998

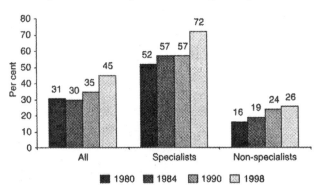

Base: all establishments with 25 or more employees where survey interview was conducted on-site, and respondent spent 25 per cent or more of time on employee relations matters, or a major part of their time in 1980.

employee relations management has become a profession, underpinned by professional credentials. This trend suggests that the growth in ER specialists in the 1990s was not simply a re-labelling exercise, as mentioned in the previous section. Rather, it signifies a shift in the approach adopted by employers in the conduct of employee relations management.

If the growth in qualified practitioners was simply an attempt to 'professionalize' the occupation, or a new entry barrier erected by employers keen to screen applicants for high-quality candidates, one might expect most of the growth in qualifications to be accounted for by new entrants as they replace an older cohort of non-qualified managers. In fact, although there has been a big increase in the number of new entrants with qualifications, the trend is also evident among those with substantial experience. Furthermore, the proportion of employee relations managers with formal personnel qualifications increases with the length of experience in employee relations. In 1990, one quarter (27 per cent) of those with less than five years' experience of employee relations had personnel qualifications. This had risen to 38 per cent in 1998. Over the same period, the proportion of those with at least ten years' experience who had personnel qualifications rose from 38 per cent to almost half (49 per cent). Increasing demand for professional credentials from newcomers and experienced managers alike may be a response to the demise of the managerial career and of internal career ladders, motivated by a belief that qualifications may improve 'employability' (McGovern *et al.*, 1998).

The job tenure and experience of employee relations managers

Organizational restructuring, particularly 'delayering' the managerial hierarchy, has resulted in fewer opportunities for managerial promotion within the same employing organization (McGovern *et al.*, 1998). As a consequence, inter-organizational mobility, which has been a growing trend during the post-war period (Mansfield and Poole, 1991), may increase in prevalence as managers construct their own careers. This would tend to reduce managerial job tenure. However, job tenure may lengthen for those less able to compete for the diminishing number of promotion opportunities internally if they also lack the skills or experience to compete in the external labour market.

Over the course of the WIRS series, there has been a modest decline in the job tenure of employee relations managers. Between 1980 and 1998 the proportion spending under two years in post rose from one fifth (20 per cent) to one quarter (25 per cent), while the proportion spending five or more years in post dropped from over half (52 per cent) to 41 per cent. Most of this change was concentrated in the private sector, and in private services in particular. The trend affected ER specialists and other employee relations managers alike.

Although employee relations managers move jobs more than they used to, there has been no change in the amount of experience they have in the management of employee relations. Throughout the series respondents have been asked: 'How many years' experience do you have in personnel or employee relations management either in this establishment or elsewhere?'[9] In 1984, nearly two thirds (64 per cent) had spent ten years or more in employee relations, while 4 per cent had spent less than two years in it. In 1998, the equivalent figures were 65 per cent and 3 per cent respectively.

Time spent on employee relations

The designation of a manager as an ER specialist through a job title may be a good indicator of the priority a workplace attaches to employee relations management, and the resources it devotes to it, but the time managers devote to the employee relations function is a more direct measure.

Since 1984, respondents have been asked what proportion of their time they spend on employee relations matters.[10] The time spent on employee relations has remained roughly constant over that period: in 1998 managers responsible for employee relations spent the same proportion of their time on employee relations as they had in 1984 (35 per cent on average). Generalists and line managers have continued to spend around one quarter of their time on employee relations since 1984.[11] However, the average amount of time devoted to employee relations by ER specialists has fallen from over four fifths (83 per cent) in 1984 to under two thirds (63 per cent) in 1998 (Table 3.2). This is due to a substantial fall in the proportion spending all of their time on employee relations matters.

Table 3.2 Time spent on employee relations matters, 1984 to 1998

	Column percentages					
	Specialists			*Non-specialists*		
	1984	*1990*	*1998*	*1984*	*1990*	*1998*
Percentage of time spent on employee relations						
1–9 per cent	*	1	2	20	19	18
10–24	4	8	8	36	39	35
25–49	2	10	16	22	22	23
50–74	17	17	29	15	9	18
75–89	16	12	16	3	2	3
90–99	7	8	13	1	1	1
100	51	40	15	2	2	*
Don't know	3	5	*	2	5	2
Mean percentage of time	83	74	63	26	23	26
Weighted base	*273*	*271*	*410*	*1,501*	*1,366*	*1,411*
Unweighted base	*797*	*841*	*799*	*995*	*848*	*941*

Base: all establishments with 25 or more employees where the survey interview was conducted on site.

There may be various reasons for this trend. There could be real diversification in the workload of ER specialists, with the push for lean management structures resulting in managers 'doubling up' on functions. This is an issue discussed further below. Alternatively, the growth in ER specialists noted earlier could be a 're-labelling exercise', conferring ER specialist job titles on people who would not have merited them previously, so blurring the distinction between ER specialists and other managers responsible for employee relations. However, this is unlikely to account for much of the change. The fall in the proportion of time ER specialists spend on employee relations matters began in the 1980s, prior to the growth in ER specialists, and ER specialists remain distinctive in many ways (see below). In 1998, 90 per cent of ER specialists were still spending at least one quarter of their time on employee relations matters, compared with about half (47 per cent) of generalists and line managers.

The gender issue: women managing employee relations

In 1980 and 1998 the gender of our management respondents was coded by interviewers from observation, providing an opportunity to assess differences and similarities between men and women managing employee relations at workplace level. This section is confined to respondents interviewed on site.

Increasingly, it is women who manage workplace employee relations. Two fifths (39 per cent) of employee relations managers were women in 1998, compared with one eighth (12 per cent) in 1980. Although women's share of jobs in higher occupations generally has risen with their share of employment since the 1970s (Hakim, 1996), the increase is very marked. By 1998 women were particularly well represented in employee relations management relative to other managerial roles. It seems that, at least as far as employee relations management is concerned, women are breaking through the 'glass ceiling' which has prevented them from attaining higher occupational status. However, some observers have noted that within employee relations women managers continue to be disproportionately represented in more junior jobs (Gooch and Ledwith, 1996: 112). This possibility cannot be tested directly with WIRS data: we do not know the gender of subordinates to our employee relations managers within the workplace. Nor do we have data on the representation of women among board-level employee relations managers. However, we do have data on the relative incidence of women managers working at head offices. This may be a rough indicator of their seniority within multi-site organizations. Around one in ten of those managing employee relations in multi-site organizations in 1998 were working in head offices. They accounted for 12 per cent of our male survey respondents, and 10 per cent of our female respondents, indicating no significant gender difference. But, whereas a similar proportion of men had been working at head office in 1980 (10 per cent), the proportion of women doing so had been much higher, at 18 per cent. The fact that the proportion of women managing employee relations at head offices fell without a commensurate rise in the proportion of men managing at head offices suggests that the trend is simply due to the increased penetration of women into branch-level employee relations management.[12]

The female managers of 1998 differed markedly from those managing in 1980. Whereas the incidence of ER specialists among male employee relations managers remained static over the period at 14 per cent, the percentage of female managers who were ER specialists rose from one quarter (25 per cent) in 1980 to over one third (36 per cent) in 1998. Women made up almost two thirds (63 per cent) of all ER specialists in 1998, compared with one fifth (19 per cent) in 1980.

In some respects, the last two decades have witnessed a convergence in the attributes and experiences of men and women managing employee relations. In 1980, male managers were almost twice as likely as female managers to have formal personnel qualifications (31 per cent compared with 18 per cent). But by 1998, women were just as likely to hold qualifications as men (44 per cent did so, compared with 45 per cent of men). By 1998, women were just as likely as men to have acquired at least two years' experience in employee relations. And, whereas men were more likely to identify training employees and handling grievances in their portfolio of responsibilities in 1980, there was no significant difference between men and women by 1998. Nevertheless, differences remained. Men were still more likely to have responsibility for pay and conditions of employment, and systems of payment, for example. And, although job tenures shortened for men and women, a job tenure 'gap' opened up over the period: by 1998, women were spending significantly less time in their current jobs than men, whereas this had not been the case in 1980.[13]

The increased number of women managing employee relations is accounted for by their concentration in the expanding service sector of the economy, rather than an increased propensity to employ female employee relations managers in any particular sector. In 1998, male and female employee relations managers were distributed across industries in broadly the same way as they were in 1980. As in 1980, women were over-represented in the public sector and private services in 1998, and under-represented in manufacturing. In both 1980 and 1998 'other services' accounted for half (50 per cent) of all women managing employee relations. In 1980 the distribution of employee relations managers by workplace size was almost identical for men and women, and the situation remained virtually unchanged in 1998.

In 1980, men were more likely than women to manage employee relations in unionized workplaces (62 per cent of male employee relations managers were doing so, compared with 56 per cent of female employee relations managers). By 1998, women were more likely to manage employee relations in unionized workplaces (45 per cent did so, compared with 42 per cent of male managers), although the difference was not statistically significant. The shift is accounted for by the relative concentration of men in manufacturing, where recognition rates fell dramatically over the period, and the greater incidence of women in the public sector, where recognition declined less sharply.

A changing role for employee relations managers?

The responsibilities of ER specialists and other employee relations managers

Throughout the survey series, our main management respondents have been shown a list of job responsibilities and asked: 'Can you tell me for each one whether or not it forms part of your job or the job of someone responsible to you?'[14] The list has varied across the years, reflecting contemporary interest, but a subset has been ever present, allowing us to map change over time.[15]

ER specialists perform different roles from those undertaken by other employee relations managers (Table 3.3). In 1998, they were significantly less likely than other employee relations managers to have responsibility for training, staffing and manpower planning, and health and safety.[16] This may reflect a greater division of labour among those with responsibility for various employee relations tasks in establishments where the employee relations function is separately identified. ER specialists were more likely to be responsible for pay and conditions and payment systems than other employee relations managers.

Table 3.3 Job responsibilities of employee relations managers, 1984 to 1998

	Cell percentages		
	1984	*1990*	*1998*
Personnel specialists			
Pay or conditions of employment	91	90	89
Recruitment or selection	91	94	93
Training of employees	77	69	78
Systems of payment	66	63	61
Handling grievances	95	92	95
Staffing or manpower planning	87	80	80
Weighted base	*273*	*273*	*410*
Unweighted base	*797*	*845*	*799*
Non-specialists			
Pay or conditions of employment	64	69	73
Recruitment or selection	88	91	92
Training of employees	84	82	88
Systems of payment	50	59	54
Handling grievances	82	87	92
Staffing or manpower planning	85	84	90
Weighted base	*1,506*	*1,371*	*1,411*
Unweighted base	*997*	*852*	*941*

Base: all establishments with 25 or more employees where the survey interview was conducted on site.

There has been little change in the functions performed by ER specialists since 1984, at least for the six responsibilities for which we have time-series data. The only enduring change was the reduced responsibility for staffing and manpower planning between 1984 and 1990. This is perhaps surprising given the amount of academic and practitioner speculation about the changing role of ER specialists (Storey, 1992; Gennard and Kelly, 1997).

In contrast, the portfolio of employee relations responsibilities falling to other managers has been growing. Since 1984 generalists and line managers have been increasingly responsible for pay and conditions of employment and the handling of grievances and, since 1990, a growing proportion have cited the training of employees and staffing and manpower planning among their tasks.

Whereas employee relations management has been making increasing demands on generalists and line managers, the average number of tasks performed by ER specialists has been falling since 1984. Although ER specialists were still performing marginally more employee relations tasks than other employee relations managers in 1998, the difference was no longer statistically significant.[17] This is consistent with the finding that ER specialists were spending less time on employee relations matters.

Ever since the start of the survey series in 1980, nine tenths of ER specialists and other employee relations managers have identified recruitment and selection as one of their responsibilities. In 1998, two other tasks were performed by at least 90 per cent of ER specialists, generalists and line managers, namely the handling of grievances and equal opportunities. Together, these might be viewed as the 'core' of the workplace-level employee relations function.

What of the role played by the new human resource managers? One way to establish whether the growth in the 'human resource' title is simply a re-labelling exercise is to see if human resource managers differ from personnel managers in what they actually do. On the face of it, they appear to differ very little (Table 3.4), at least in terms of the nine job responsibilities for which we have data in 1998. However, although we have data on a number of the tasks thought important in human resource management (such as selection, performance appraisal and training), we do not have data on the degree to which these were integrated with one another, or with business objectives, integration being the key distinguishing feature of HRM according to some commentators (Storey, 1992).

The public sector

Over the series the role of employee relations managers in the public sector has changed radically, with workplace-level managers taking on more responsibility across the board.

Changes in the public sector are particularly marked with respect to pay and conditions, which in the 1980s were largely set by national collective agreements and, more recently in some industries, by government on the advice

Table 3.4 Job responsibilities of personnel and human resource managers in 1998

	Cell percentages	
	Human resource managers	Personnel managers
Pay or conditions of employment	88	90
Recruitment or selection	93	94
Training of employees	76	80
Systems of payment	62	61
Handling grievances	96	95
Staffing or manpower planning	80	80
Equal opportunities	85	93
Health and safety	65	68
Performance appraisals	79	81
None of the above	1	0
Weighted base	*123*	*273*
Unweighted base	*236*	*529*

Base: all establishments with 25 or more employees where the survey interview was conducted on site.

of review bodies, so that establishment-level managers were less involved in the process than was the case in the private sector. This changed dramatically in the 1990s, reflecting innovations such as local budget holding in schools and general medical practices, moves to local bargaining arrangements (for instance, in some NHS Trusts), and provisions within national agreements and review body recommendations for local discretion in setting pay and conditions. So, whereas only a little over one third (36 per cent) of public sector employee relations managers cited pay or conditions of employment among their job responsibilities in 1990, this had risen to 60 per cent by 1998 (Table 3.5).

These trends have also meant that public sector employee relations managers have become increasingly responsible for systems of payment, that is, the procedures and processes by which pay is determined. Four in every ten (41 per cent) cited it as their responsibility in 1998, compared with one quarter (24 per cent) in 1990. It is likely that these changes reflect the devolution of responsibilities to local level in the public sector and the increasing adoption of performance-related pay. Time pressures did not permit us to ask about job responsibilities in our panel survey, so we cannot discount the possibility that some of the change is due to change in the composition of the public sector as a result of privatization. (If the privatized parts of the public sector were less likely than the rest of the public sector to have devolved pay responsibility in 1990, and the position had remained constant among the 'surviving' public sector, this would show up as an increase in public sector devolution of pay responsibility.) However, only 2 per cent of continuing workplaces switched

Table 3.5　Job responsibilities of employee relations managers, by broad sector, 1984 to 1998

	Cell percentages								
	Private sector manufacturing			Private sector services			Public sector		
	1984	1990	1998	1984	1990	1998	1984	1990	1998
Pay or conditions of employment	90	92	92	77	83	79	43	36	60
Recruitment or selection	92	87	92	88	93	91	88	92	94
Training of employees	76	76	82	81	77	84	89	90	94
Systems of payment	80	78	74	63	71	56	23	24	41
Handling grievances	92	90	89	84	89	93	80	84	93
Staffing or manpower planning	86	84	83	89	84	86	79	83	95
Weighted base	*400*	*404*	*349*	*767*	*800*	*983*	*612*	*440*	*490*
Unweighted base	*566*	*583*	*278*	*535*	*617*	*927*	*693*	*497*	*535*

Base: all establishments with 25 or more employees where the survey interview was conducted on site.

from public to private ownership between 1990 and 1998, a proportion which is far too small to account for the amount of change apparent from the cross-sectional data.

The private sector

By comparison with the public sector, changes in the responsibilities of employee relations managers in private sector manufacturing and services have generally been small (Table 3.5). The exception was the substantial fall between 1990 and 1998 in the proportion of employee relations managers in private services responsible for systems of payment. However, within the private service sector, there were marked differences between the patterns of change in union and non-union workplaces during the 1990s, with employee relations managers in unionized establishments gradually taking on more responsibilities. In the non-union sector, the only major change has been a decline in the proportion of managers citing payment systems as their responsibility, from 73 per cent in 1990 to 58 per cent in 1998. This decline was also apparent in unionized establishments where the percentage citing it as their responsibility fell from 65 per cent to 50 per cent. But increased responsibility for training employees, handling grievances and staffing and manpower planning, were much more apparent in unionized establishments. For example, 97 per cent of employee relations managers in unionized private service establishments were responsible for handling grievances in 1998, compared with 86 per cent in 1990. The equivalent figures for non-unionized establishments in the sector were 92 per cent and 89 per cent respectively.

In private manufacturing, there were also marked differences in the pattern of change between unionized and non-unionized workplaces. The employee relations managers in the unionized sector were taking on more responsibilities during the 1990s, with substantial increases in the proportions that cited training and the handling of grievances as their responsibilities. In non-unionized manufacturing establishments there was very little change, although there was a noticeable decline in the proportion citing payment systems as their responsibility (down from 81 per cent in 1990 to 75 per cent in 1998).

Managers of information

Information collection

The collection and interpretation of information is one of the basic tasks of management, who can be expected to collect a range of information about the nature and behaviour of the employees within their workplace. This information may be used for a variety of reasons, such as monitoring group and individual performance, tracking the effects of recruitment and retention policies, redesigning work processes, feeding into management decision-making at workplace or corporate level, or complying with legislation.

In the 1990 survey managers were asked whether certain items of information were 'collected and used by management, here or at a higher level, to review performance and policies on an annual or more frequent basis?' In 1998 respondents were asked a less specific question in relation to many of the same items: 'Are any of the following records kept for this establishment?' Even accounting for the fact that the less specific 1998 question may have elicited more positive responses, there appears to have been an increase in information collection by workplace managers on the six items common to both surveys (Table 3.6). The mean number of items for which information was collected rose substantially from 3 to 3.7 and, whereas one tenth (11 per cent) of managers said none of the items were collected in 1990, only 2 per cent did so in 1998.

While there must remain doubts about how much the apparent increase in information collected by management is an artefact of the change in question wording, the comparability problem is less acute when assessing the relative prominence of the various items over time.

Wage costs are one of the few 'knowns' which managers can have some control over, so it is not surprising that, in the competitive environment of the 1990s, more private sector establishments have been collecting wage cost information. But it is among public sector establishments, where influence over pay, conditions and staffing is a relatively new experience, that the collection of wage-cost information has grown most rapidly. Between 1990 and 1998 the proportion of public sector workplaces collecting wage-cost information rose

Table 3.6 Information collected by management, 1990 and 1998

	Cell percentages							
	Private manufacturing		Private services		Public sector		All	
	1990	1998	1990	1998	1990	1998	1990	1998
Information collected on:								
Wage/salary costs	83	89	73	94	48	79	69	89
Labour productivity	70	76	43	57	23	30	44	53
Staff sickness and other absences	71	87	70	82	75	89	71	85
Training received	57	81	60	83	66	86	61	83
Ethnic mix of workforce	12	18	18	31	43	49	24	33
Gender mix of workforce	18	17	21	20	41	58	26	20
None of the above	10	7	12	1	11	1	11	2
Weighted base	404	349	800	983	440	490	1,644	1,821
Unweighted base	583	278	617	927	497	535	1,697	1,740

Base: all establishments with 25 or more employees where the survey interview was conducted on site.

from around a half (48 per cent) to four fifths (79 per cent), compared to increases from 83 to 89 per cent in private manufacturing and 73 to 94 per cent in private services.

Labour productivity has traditionally been the concern largely of the manufacturing and extraction sector of the economy, partly because of the difficulties of accurately measuring productivity in services (O'Mahony *et al.*, 1998). However, the collection of labour productivity information in the private service sector shifted from a minority to a majority pursuit during the 1990s (rising from 43 per cent to 57 per cent). Although public sector establishments were increasingly likely to collect information on productivity, less than a third (30 per cent) were doing so by 1998.

Although the increased propensity to collect labour productivity information was apparent across the broad sectors of the economy, it was confined to workplaces without recognized unions; whereas 42 per cent had been collecting this information in 1990, 59 per cent were doing so in 1998. Workplaces with recognized unions were more likely to collect labour productivity information in 1990 (47 per cent did so), but by 1998 this was no longer the case, with 46 per cent of unionized workplaces collecting this information.

Managers were much more likely to be monitoring absence and training received by employees by the late 1990s, perhaps in an attempt to improve productivity or keep costs under review. The collection of information on absence may also be prompted by changes in arrangements for statutory sick pay, which may have given management a greater incentive to manage absence. This trend was apparent across the private services and manufacturing, and public sector, and throughout the unionized and non-unionized sectors.

More workplaces were also collecting information on the gender and ethnic composition of their workforces, information that is often used in monitoring recruitment, retention and equal opportunities policies. Increased interest in the gender mix of workforces was largely confined to the public sector and to private sector workplaces with union recognition, where equal opportunities policies were more prevalent in 1998.[18] However, establishments with a relatively small percentage of female workers (25 per cent or less) were increasingly likely to collect information on the gender mix of their workforce, irrespective of the broad sector they operated in, or their union recognition status (the exception being non-unionized private manufacturers). Where at least three quarters of the workforce were women, the proportion of workplaces where management collected data on the gender composition of the workforce actually fell in all but public sector unionized workplaces. These findings suggest that in the 1990s managers began to keep a watchful eye on gender composition where there was a substantial male bias in the workforce, or where they were responding to the concerns of recognized unions.

Increases in the collection of information on the ethnic composition of the workforce were apparent across the public and private sectors, but the pattern varied when controlling for the proportion of ethnic minority workers at the workplace. Only among those workplaces reporting no ethnic minority workers was there an unequivocal increase in the collection of information on ethnicity across all three broad sectors.

During the 1990s, managers in establishments belonging to larger organizations collected more information on their workforces than managers in single independent establishments, irrespective of workplace size, perhaps because they were required to do so by managers higher up in the organization. But the increase in the mean number of items collected by single independent establishments (from 2.2 to 3.2) was just as marked as the increase in information collection by branches of larger organizations (from 3.2 to 4.0 items), indicating that this change in practice cannot be explained purely by the requirements of large organizations. The explanation may lie in increased competitive pressures motivating the collection of more information to assess labour requirements and utilization, or a greater tendency to monitor workforce composition to avoid challenges of unfair treatment.

For the 1998 panel interview we replicated the 1990 question on the collection of information across eleven specified items, so we can be confident that they give us a firm basis for establishing whether there had been a change in behaviour among continuing workplaces. The results show a substantial increase in the range of information that continuing workplaces collected to review performance and policies. The increase was apparent across all eleven items, with the mean number of items collected rising from 5 to 7.7 between 1990 and 1998 (Table 3.7). Those collecting none of the items fell from 10 per

Table 3.7 Information collected by management in continuing establishments, 1990 and 1998

	Cell percentages	
	1990	*1998*
Information collected on:		
Levels of wages/salary costs	64	86
Labour productivity	40	61
Staff sickness and other absences	68	90
Training received	61	85
Ethnic mix of workforce	27	55
Gender mix of workforce	28	57
Age structure of workforce	26	53
Accidents and injuries	56	82
Occupational health matters	36	64
Skills and qualifications	52	77
Number of resignations	44	64
None of the above	10	3
Weighted base	730	802
Unweighted base	700	782

Base: all continuing establishments with 25 or more employees in the relevant year, where the survey interview was conducted on site.

cent in 1990 to 3 per cent in 1998, while those collecting all eleven items rose from 7 per cent to 25 per cent.

These panel data include the six core items that appeared in the 1990 and 1998 cross-section questionnaires, allowing us to compare the practices of continuing establishments with 'joiners' and 'leavers'. Workplaces leaving the survey in 1990 were no different from continuing workplaces in the amount of information they were collecting in 1990: the mean number of items collected by leavers was 2.8, compared with 2.9 by continuing workplaces. The joiners in 1998 were similar in their behaviour to the leavers in 1990, collecting an average of 2.8 items. However, by 1998, continuing workplaces were collecting an average of 4.3 items. So the increase in the collection of information over the 1990s was accounted for by a change in behaviour among continuing establishments.

Information dissemination

Making employees aware of the financial and market imperatives facing employers and, by extension, the workforce, is widely believed to be a prerequisite for maintaining employee commitment to an organization's objectives and for successful organizational change. Our survey series captures something of the extent to which management inform employees or their representatives about matters that might be expected to be of general interest and concern.

Workplace managers appear to have heeded the advice of commentators who have advocated increased efforts to inform employees, at least in the service sector of the economy, because there has been a marked increase in the number of items of information they disseminated to employees or their representatives during the 1990s. Increases in the amount of information provided were most apparent in the public sector (Table 3.8). In private sector manufacturing the figures suggest a reduction in the amount of information disseminated to employees, but the difference between 1990 and 1998 was not statistically significant.

There have been some changes in the items inquired about, but four items have consistently featured in our management interviews. Three concern financial matters; the fourth concerns employment levels.[19] The first of the questions asked managers if they gave employees or their representatives any information about the financial position of the workplace. In 1998 the question included the word 'regularly'. Despite this change, which would tend to produce fewer positive responses, the proportion of workplaces where management provided this information rose from 56 per cent in 1990 to 67 per

Table 3.8 Provision of information by management to employees or their representatives, 1990 and 1998

	Cell percentages							
	Private manufacturing		*Private services*		*Public sector*		*All*	
	1990	*1998*	*1990*	*1998*	*1990*	*1998*	*1990*	*1998*
Information about:								
Financial position of the establishment	55	58	51	61	67	83	56	67
Financial position of the organization[a]	55	56	58	64	51	62	55	62
Investment plans	48	53	38	50	33	65	39	54
Staffing and manpower plans	52	36	49	58	77	84	57	61
None of the above	23	27	28	19	12	4	22	16
Weighted base	396	347	789	984	414	487	1,598	1,818
Unweighted base	570	275	609	929	464	529	1,643	1,733

Base: all establishments with 25 or more employees where the survey interview was conducted on site, unless otherwise specified.

Note
a Establishments that formed part of multi-site organizations only.

cent in 1998. An increase was discernible across all three broad sectors (although it was not statistically significant in private manufacturing), perhaps reflecting the devolution of financial management structures and responsibility to establishment level throughout the economy. But it was in the public sector, where many establishments in the health and education sectors have become cost or profit centres for the first time in the 1990s, that the increase in the provision of financial information on the establishment was most marked. Whereas two thirds (67 per cent) of public sector workplaces were giving this information to their employees in 1990, this had risen to over four fifths (83 per cent) in 1998.

A similar picture emerged from the second question (not asked in stand-alone sites) which related to the financial position of the organization to which the workplace belonged. There was a substantial increase in the provision of this information to public sector employees, whereas the rise in the private sector was smaller and only significant in private service establishments. Further analysis of all workplaces revealed that the significant increase in the dissemination of this information during the 1990s was confined to those with recognized unions. Among this unionized sector, the proportion of establishments giving organizational financial information to their employees rose from 56 per cent in 1990 to 71 per cent in 1998. In the non-unionized sector the proportion remained at 53 per cent.

The third question asked whether employees or their representatives were given information about internal investment plans. Despite the insertion of the word 'regularly' in 1998 this practice became more common in the service sector, actually rising twofold in the public sector. This shift in the public sector may reflect changes such as moves to agency operation in much of central government, to trust status in the health services and the devolution of budgeting in many spheres, all of which would have involved more transparent financial planning.

Taken together, these three measures indicate a clear increase in the information provided to employees by managers on financial matters, though significant increases were confined to the service sector of the economy. In contrast, the aggregate figures on the fourth question about information given to employees on management's staffing plans suggest no change in the 1990s, with roughly six in ten establishments providing this information to their employees. (Once again, the word 'regularly' was inserted in 1998, reducing the proportion of affirmative responses in 1998.) However, this aggregate picture of no change hides marked differences across sectors, with rises in public and private services being offset by a dramatic decline in private manufacturing. Further analysis indicates that this dramatic decline in the dissemination of information on staffing levels in manufacturing was only significant in workplaces without union representation.

A comprehensive assessment of the provision of information by management to employees would cover further topics besides the ones discussed above. However, an overall impression can be gained by combining the three topics covered by our four questions (two on financial performance, one on investment and one on staffing plans) into a single measure that counts the number of topics on which management gave their employees information. This summary measure suggests an increase in the flow of information from management to employees. The proportion of workplaces where management gave employees no information fell from 22 per cent in 1990 to 16 per cent in 1998, while the proportion providing information on all three topics rose from 25 per cent to 36 per cent. So while there remained a substantial minority of employers divulging little information to their workforces, an increasing number gave out information over a range of issues. This increase was more rapid in the public sector than in the private sector, as is apparent from Table 3.8. The increase was also more rapid among unionized workplaces. By 1998, they were almost twice as likely as non-union workplaces to provide employees with all three types of information (49 per cent against 27 per cent), and four times less likely to provide them with none (6 per cent as against 23 per cent).

There was a strong association between the number of items management collected information on and the amount of information they divulged to employees. In 1990 and 1998, those disseminating none of the three types of information discussed above collected a mean of 2.0 of the six information items reported on in the previous section, whereas those disseminating all three types of information were collecting a mean of 3.5 items.

Is the increase in the provision of information due to a behavioural change among continuing establishments, or is it accounted for by the changing composition of workplaces? To answer this question, we turn to our panel survey, which contains data on the provision of financial information to employees and their representatives in 1998. It replicates the 1990 questions on information relating to the financial performance of the establishment, internal investment plans and, in the case of establishments belonging to larger organizations, the financial performance of the organization.

Between 1990 and 1998 the proportion of continuing establishments providing information on all three items rose substantially. Over this period, the proportion of continuing establishments saying that they provided employees or their representatives with information on the financial performance of the establishment rose from 59 per cent to 77 per cent. The proportion reporting dissemination on internal investment plans rose from 42 per cent to 60 per cent. And the proportion of establishments belonging to larger organizations reporting provision of information on the organization's financial performance rose from 53 per cent to 76 per cent.

Since continuing establishments made up the majority of workplaces operating in 1998, this change in their behaviour accounts for most of the increase in information provision to employees in the 1990s. However, compositional changes in the population of workplaces also played a part. Leavers were not very different from continuing establishments in the information they provided to employees in 1990: 53 per cent provided information on establishment financial performance; 38 per cent provided information on internal investment plans; and 56 per cent of those belonging to larger organizations provided information on organizational performance. Although joiners did not provide as much information as continuing establishments in 1998, they did provide more information than leavers (the respective figures being 63 per cent, 48 per cent and 63 per cent). Since joiners gave their employees more information than leavers, this compositional shift played some part in the increase in information provided which is apparent in the cross-sectional data.

External sources of advice for employee relations managers (including employers' association membership)

No manager operates in a vacuum. All require some input from others in approaching issues and coming to decisions. Previous WIRS source books have identified the resources available to employee relations managers at their workplace, the availability of assistance higher up in the organization, and sources of advice beyond the organization. Here we focus on two aspects of support where data collected during the course of the series are most clearly comparable: sources of external advice and membership of employers' associations.[20]

In 1980, 1990 and 1998 respondents were asked whether management at their establishment had sought advice on any employee relations issues during the previous twelve months from an outside person or body.[21] Over the period there was a very substantial increase in the use of all sources of external advice (Table 3.9).[22] The proportion seeking some external advice rose from around one third (31 per cent) at the start of the 1980s to over a half (56 per cent) in 1998. The mean number of advice sources used rose from 0.5 in 1980 to 1.2 in 1998. However, among those using advice, there was little change in the number of advice sources used. Whereas 56 per cent of advice users relied on only one source of external advice in 1980, this remained true for 48 per cent in 1998.

During the 1990s, the number of workplaces seeking advice from the Advisory, Conciliation and Arbitration Service (ACAS) and other government agencies doubled. This reflects an increase in the number of government agencies offering assistance to employers, and the growing willingness of employers to involve ACAS in conciliation and dispute resolution (ACAS, 1998).

The proportion using lawyers also doubled in the 1990s. By 1998, one third (32 per cent) of establishments were using them, making them the most common provider of external advice on employee relations issues, perhaps reflecting the increasingly legalistic nature of employee relations. Concerned at the rate and volume of legislative change, the increased complexity of the law, and the increasing litigiousness of employees and their representatives,[23] employers may perceive greater risks in failing to keep abreast of legal matters, and prefer to take expert advice to minimize those risks.

Table 3.9 External sources of advice for employee relations managers, 1980, 1990 and 1998

Sources of advice	Cell percentages		
	1980	*1990*	*1998*
ACAS and other government agencies	10	12	23
Management consultants	4	6	16
External lawyers	1	16	32
External accountants	2	2	14
Employers' associations	12	6	10
Other professional bodies	*	1	19
Other answers	12	13	6
None of these	69	68	44
Weighted base	*1,830*	*1,644*	*1,821*
Unweighted base	*1,868*	*1,697*	*1,740*

Base: all establishments with 25 or more employees where the survey interview was conducted on site.

The surge in demand for outside advice may be linked to the changing nature of the employee relations function. Many organizations have been scaling down their personnel resources, so that there are fewer colleagues to turn to for advice, either within the workplace or higher up in the organization. The WIRS panel data reveal that, over the period 1990 to 1998, the percentage of employee relations managers with non-clerical staff to assist them at the workplace fell from 52 per cent to 44 per cent among continuing establishments. At the extreme, organizations are retaining no internal personnel capacity, resorting instead to external consultants (Adams, 1991). This may partly explain the rapid growth since 1990 in the use by workplace ER managers of management consultants and accountants.

The percentage of workplaces using employers' associations for advice fell in the 1980s, reflecting a decline in membership (see below). Although the latest figures show an increase in the use of employers' associations as a source of advice in the 1990s, as anticipated by some commentators (Sisson, 1993: 205), their relative importance as an advice source remained low. In 1980 they were the most cited source of external advice whereas, by 1998, they were the least cited of the six main categories identified.

For the first time in 1998, 'other professional bodies' were explicitly identified as a possible source of advice on the showcard accompanying the question. To obtain time-series information on advice provided by professional bodies we inspected the 'other, please specify' answers in 1980 and 1990 for references to such bodies. In fact, there were very few such cases, which may be another indicator of the extent to which employee relations management has become a profession in the last decade. Although respondents' failure to spontaneously refer to professional bodies may account for some of the increase in the use of professional bodies, it seems likely that most of the increase represents a real change.

These increases in the use of external advice on employee relations matters were evident across all types of workplace, large and small, in the public and private sectors, and in manufacturing and services. Nor were they confined to particular types of employee relations manager: ER specialists, generalists and line managers alike were using more external advice.

If, as some commentators maintain, there has been devolution of responsibilities on a range of employee relations matters to workplace level, this may help explain why managers have felt an increasing need to resort to external advisers. We tested this hypothesis by looking for an association between the number of employee relations tasks undertaken by workplace managers and the number of external advice sources they used. In fact, the relationship was curvilinear, the mean number of sources used being greatest among those with either a very high or very low number of employee relations tasks to perform. Most of those with a small number of employee relations tasks were generalists and line managers who, perhaps, resorted to external advice because employee relations matters were fairly unfamiliar to them. However, the curvilinear relationship also held for ER specialists, suggesting that it cannot be explained simply by the degree to which workplace ER managers specialized in employee relations. It may be that some ER specialists undertaking relatively few employee relations tasks routinely involve external advisers, either because they have no internal advisers to go to, or because the nature of their work is so specialized that it requires frequent expert input.

Single independent establishments have always been greater users of external advice on employee relations matters than branch sites, partly because branches can tap expertise elsewhere in their organization, or at their head office. But the difference between independent workplaces and branches has grown since 1980. For example, by 1998, independent establishments were five times more likely than branches of multi-site organizations to use external lawyers (30 per cent against 6 per cent), and twice as likely to use ACAS and other government organizations (31 per cent against 16 per cent). For the first time, they were more likely than branches to use management consultants.

Head offices are big users of external advice, perhaps because of the nature of the issues they deal with, such as strategic decision-taking, devising organization-wide systems and policies, and tackling the most difficult disputes in an organization. Their reliance on external advice rose in the 1990s, probably reflecting reductions in resources devoted to the central personnel function in multi-site organizations.

Membership of employers' associations

Traditionally, workplaces belonging to employers' associations have used them for a range of information and advice, while those covered by multi-employer bargaining have also relied on them to negotiate with unions or staff associations to regulate pay and other terms of employment. In both these roles, employers' associations diminished in importance during the 1980s, indicating that 'more and more managements seem to be assuming responsibility for their own industrial relations' (Sisson, 1993: 205). Comparable data for 1984 and 1990 indicate that employers' association membership in industry and commerce fell after 1984, from 22 per cent of establishments to 13 per cent in 1990. The latest results are little different from 1990, with 18 per cent of workplaces reporting membership in 1998. However, the 1998 measure is broader than the measure used in earlier surveys because the 1998 question about employers' associations omits reference to their negotiating on behalf of their members to regulate pay or terms of employment. One might therefore expect to see some increase in the measured level of employers' association membership arising from the changed wording. In addition, the positive answers to the 1984 and 1990 questions were only retained if the association mentioned by name was listed by the Certification Officer; no such restriction was made on the 1998 data. For these two reasons, it seems unlikely that there was any increase in membership between 1990 and 1998.

No such difficulty arises in interpreting the results from our panel survey. Panel respondents were asked an identical question in 1990 and 1998: 'Is this establishment (either directly or through the parent organization) a member of an employers' association that negotiates on behalf of its members with unions or staff associations to regulate pay or terms of employment?' One in ten (11 per cent) of continuing workplaces in industry and commerce belonged to an employers' association which negotiated on their behalf in 1990, compared with 8 per cent in 1998. In only 10 per cent of cases did an employers' association cease (6 per cent) or begin (4 per cent) to negotiate on behalf of a continuing establishment. It seems that conscious decisions to either join or leave employers' associations engaged in multi-employer bargaining were made by few established workplaces in the 1990s, but those ceasing membership predominated.

The employers' association membership rate among workplaces leaving the survey population from 1990 onwards was 15 per cent, slightly higher than the rate for continuing establishments. This small population difference, coupled with the small drop in membership among continuing establishments during the 1990s, indicates that employers' associations now negotiate on behalf of fewer workplaces than in 1990 – unless, of course, joiners are more likely to use employers' associations for this purpose. Although we have no comparable data for joiners, this seems unlikely, since they are much less likely to negotiate with unions over pay and conditions in any event (see Chapter 4). On balance, then, we interpret the results as indicating static or slightly falling membership of employers' associations between 1990 and 1998.

The status and influence of employee relations managers

In this section we consider what Purcell and Ahlstrand (1989: 404) have described as 'critical choices' facing multi-site organizations when making strategic decisions about employee relations management, namely 'the deployment of personnel management resources and levels of decision-making within personnel and industrial relations'. We focus on board-level representation of employee relations and the extent of workplace-level managerial autonomy.

A seat on the board?

Employee relations considerations are more likely to feature in the formulation of business strategy in multi-site organizations where the function is represented at board level (Marginson *et al.*, 1993; Sisson, 1994b) and where ER specialists are located in head offices. Earlier research also suggests that the presence of a personnel director at board level is associated with the personnel function having greater influence over organizational decision-making more generally (Guest and Peccei, 1994). Yet the WIRS series indicates that fewer head offices were employing such ER specialists in 1998 than before: the proportion doing so fell sharply between 1990 and 1998, from nearly half (47 per cent) to just over one third (36 per cent).

Personnel representation at board level fell in the private sector from 1984 onwards, from 76 per cent in 1984 to 71 per cent in 1990 and 64 per cent in 1998 (Figure 3.2).[24] This trend accelerated in the 1990s. It was particularly marked in smaller organizations with fewer than 2,000 employees and in private

Figure 3.2 Representation of the personnel function on the board of directors of the organization, by broad industry within the private sector, 1980 to 1998

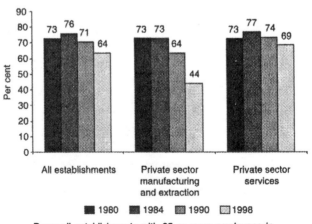

Base: all establishments with 25 or more employees in private sector multi-site organizations with a UK head office.

manufacturing generally. By 1998, two thirds (69 per cent) of private sector service workplaces reported board-level representation for employee relations, but in manufacturing the figure was only two fifths (44 per cent).

The fall in board-level representation raises questions about the weight attached to employee relations issues by senior managers. Commentators have been arguing for some time that some firms no longer view industrial relations and personnel issues as major influences on performance, but instead treat employment concerns as subordinate to financial concerns. If firms are increasingly likely to treat employment concerns as operational matters, rather than of strategic concern (Purcell and Ahlstrand, 1989), this may explain the decline in board-level personnel representation.[25] However, board-level representation did not decline in all parts of the economy. During the 1990s, board-level personnel representation remained constant in UK-based multinational companies at 70 per cent, while in workplaces recognizing trade unions it rose from 71 per cent to 77 per cent (compared with 79 per cent in 1984). It also rose among establishments belonging to the largest organizations with over 10,000 employees, from 76 per cent in 1990 to 88 per cent in 1998 (compared with 87 per cent in 1984). The fall was thus concentrated in smaller, 'local' firms and those without union representation.

We turn to the panel data once more to untangle the effects of compositional and behavioural change on the fall in board-level representation. We find substantial change in board-level personnel representation within continuing workplaces during the 1990s.[26] However, the net effect was one of little aggregate change: one eighth (16 per cent) of workplaces operating throughout the period ceased to have board-level personnel representation, while another eighth (16 per cent) acquired a board-level personnel representative. Seventy-two per cent reported board-level employee relations representation in 1990, compared with 74 per cent in 1998.[27] So, although there is evidence of substantial behavioural change among the organizations owning continuing establishments, the fact that it was balanced means that it cannot account for the decline in board-level personnel representation identified in the time-series data between 1990 and 1998. Rather, that decline from 71 per cent to 64 per cent of establishments is explained by the changing composition of workplaces. Those workplaces leaving the sample after 1990 were similar to continuing workplaces, with around two thirds (68 per cent) reporting board-level representation. But workplaces joining the sample after 1990 were less likely to have board-level personnel representatives: 58 per cent did so. It is new workplaces, rather than established ones, which remained to be convinced of the value of board-level personnel representation in organizational decision-making.

The nature and extent of workplace autonomy

Since the 1980s, there has been a consensus in the management literature that the devolution of management responsibilities to the business unit is both desirable and expedient (Colling and Ferner, 1992). According to Sisson and Marginson (1995: 105), 'the conventional wisdom is that management should devolve operational and financial responsibility to the lowest possible unit so that business-level managements are in a position to determine their own costs'. Gallie and colleagues argued that 'the second half of the 1980s and early 1990s saw a marked decentralization of decision-making within organizations', linking this trend with 'significant delayering in which employers were reducing the number of middle-level managers, and devolving responsibilities' (Gallie *et al.*, 1998: 38–9).

However, decentralization does not necessarily entail increased autonomy for workplace managers. Corporations have evolved forms of central control within which devolved managerial powers operate with a view to maintaining what has been described as 'the co-existence of firm central direction and maximum individual autonomy' (Peters and Waterman, 1982: 318). Consequently, strict budgetary controls severely limit the power of local managers to act unilaterally, even in highly decentralized management structures (Purcell and Gray, 1986; Marginson *et al.*, 1993). This has led some to conclude that 'much of the decentralization that has taken place is an "illusion". Things may "happen" at local level, but they are not decided there' (Storey and Sisson, 1993).

In fact, Gallie and colleagues (Gallie *et al.*, 1998: 38) find that, over the period 1986–92, in contrast to other social classes, professionals and managers 'appear to have seen increased constraints on their ability to take everyday decisions', owing to the intensification of bureaucratic control through performance management systems.

The WIRS panel provides unequivocal evidence of a substantial reduction in the decision-making capacity of workplace managers during the 1990s. In 1990 and 1998 respondents in multi-site organizations were asked how decisions were made on three major issues. Respondents were asked an identical question in 1990 and 1998: 'Which of the statements on this card best describes how decisions about this workplace are made in your organization? Firstly in relation to the appointment of a new senior manager at this workplace; and in relation to a decision to recognize or derecognize a trade union or unions; and in relation to the use of any financial or budgetary surplus?'[28] Here we distinguish between decisions at the workplace, workplace recommendations approved elsewhere, and decisions made elsewhere without workplace recommendations.

In 1990, two fifths (39 per cent) of branches in trading sector organizations had been able to make the decision to appoint a new senior manager at their workplace, but by 1998 only one quarter (24 per cent) could do so (Table 3.10). In nearly a half (47 per cent) of cases the decision was made higher up in the organization without even a recommendation from workplace managers even though, as shown earlier, recruitment is one of the core activities carried out by workplace employee relations managers.

Although it is often assumed that union recognition and derecognition decisions are matters determined centrally, nearly one third (31 per cent) of

Table 3.10 Workplace involvement in decision-making among continuing establishments, 1990 and 1998

	Column percentages					
	Senior manager appointment		Union recognition or derecognition		Use of financial or budgetary surplus	
	1990	*1998*	*1990*	*1998*	*1990*	*1998*
Workplace decision	39	24	31	23	34	14
Workplace recommendation, approved elsewhere	27	28	16	17	23	31
Decided elsewhere	29	47	47	57	39	52
Don't know/unsure	4	1	6	4	5	4
Weighted base	296	328	296	328	296	328
Unweighted base	366	407	366	407	366	407

Base: all continuing establishments with 25 or more employees belonging to trading-sector multi-site organizations where survey interview was conducted on site. Excludes all head offices, and establishments that represented the sole UK establishment of foreign parent organizations.

continuing workplaces belonging to larger organizations were empowered to make this decision for themselves in 1990. By 1998, however, only one quarter (23 per cent) were able to do so.

Perhaps most significantly of all, the proportion of workplaces able to decide upon the use of any financial surplus fell from one third (34 per cent) in 1990 to 14 per cent in 1998. In over half (52 per cent) of cases this decision was made elsewhere without reference to the workplace concerned. This finding is consistent with the view that there has been a centralization of budgetary control in multi-site organizations during the 1990s.

A simple measure of the extent to which decision-making has been centralized during the 1990s can be obtained by summing the number of decisions workplaces were able to take. Whereas half (53 per cent) of continuing establishments took at least one of the three decisions in 1990, this had fallen to one third (35 per cent) by 1998. One fifth (20 per cent) had been free to make all three decisions in 1990, but this had fallen to only 6 per cent in 1998. This aggregate change occurred because, whereas three quarters of those unable to make any of the decisions in 1990 were still unable to do so in 1998, only 7 per cent of those able to take all three decisions in 1990 were still able to make all three decisions in 1998.

Changes in decision-making processes often accompanied structural organizational change. Ownership change was associated with a significant reduction in the decision-making powers of the workplace, whereas there was virtually no change among continuing establishments with stable ownership.

Among those experiencing ownership change, the mean number of decisions made at the workplace fell from 1.03 to 0.54 between 1990 and 1998, compared with an insignificant drop from 0.72 to 0.69 among those without ownership change.[29]

Other forms of structural change, such as workplace amalgamations and splits, were not significantly associated with change in the number of decisions made at workplace level. However, where any structural change was identified respondents were asked: 'Has the [change] you mentioned had any effect on the following: the type of products made or services provided here; the number of employees here; the way work is done here; the management structure here; management's approach to employee relations here; the way pay and conditions are determined here?' Where managers perceived such an effect, there was a strong link between structural change and a decline in workplace managers' autonomy. The link was strongest where the change resulted in what managerial respondents perceived to be a change in the workplace's management structure, number of employees, management approach to employee relations, or 'the way work is done here'.

It appears that trading sector organizations in the 1990s have responded to competitive pressures by centralizing control over decision-making, often taking advantage of structural organizational shifts to effect the change.

Conclusions

There has been considerable speculation about what may have happened to the management of employee relations in the wake of the legal, political and economic changes that occurred during the 1990s, many of which we outlined in Chapters 1 and 2. Prior to WERS98, most of the empirical evidence shedding light on the subject for the current decade emanated from case studies and small surveys, with notable contributions from some larger surveys focusing on complex multi-site organizations. It is only now, with the help of cross-section and panel data from WERS98, that we can map the extent of change during the 1990s, extending the changing picture of the 1980s that our first three surveys documented. What emerge from this analysis are trends which amount to a marked shift in the way employers manage employee relations in Britain, a shift that gathered pace during the 1990s.

One of the most significant changes is that the people responsible for managing employee relations in 1998 were quite different from those who were managing it at the beginning of the 1980s. The rise of women within the ranks of employee relations management is perhaps the most striking example of this, and further research will need to explore its ramifications for the conduct of employee relations. But perhaps the most important change has been the degree to which the management of employee relations has shifted from generalist managers to ER specialists and line managers.

The rise of the ER specialist is a 1990s phenomenon, and has resulted from compositional change within the population of workplaces, with joiners more likely to employ them than leavers, rather than from behavioural change within continuing establishments. The rise of the ER specialist, and the increased likelihood that they will hold employee relations qualifications, mark a significant departure in the way that a growing minority of workplaces manage employee relations. Among these establishments, the conduct of employee relations is treated as a professional pursuit requiring formal credentials.

ER specialists continue to operate in a distinctive fashion, marking them out from other employee relations managers in terms of the functions they perform and how they perform them. However, the content of their work appears to have changed little in the 1990s, which is surprising in the light of speculation about the way in which their role has changed. What we do find, however, is something that needs further examination. ER specialists are spending less and less time on the ER functions we identify in the survey series, and the number of those tasks they are performing has dropped. This is in stark contrast to other employee relations managers, whose employee relations responsibilities have grown, as measured by the number of ER tasks they perform. If ER specialists are spending less time on ER, what are they doing? One possible explanation is that they are engaged in the sort of strategic management decision-making that some HRM commentators have advocated for some time. Another possible cause is the 'multi-tasking' of managers. However, both these suggestions are speculation.

In the 1990s we have also witnessed what some anticipated in the late 1980s, namely the growth in human resource management. An increasing proportion of ER specialists carry the HRM title, partly because HR managers are more prevalent among workplaces joining the population than among leavers, but mainly because more continuing establishments are referring to their ER specialists as 'human resource managers'. In this chapter we have not tackled the implications of this trend for the conduct of employee relations, other than to note that HR managers did not differ significantly from personnel managers in terms of the tasks they performed in 1998.

The survey offers evidence of a reappraisal of the role performed by employee relations managers in multi-site private sector organizations. Since 1984 board-level representation of employee relations has fallen: our panel analysis reveals that, during the 1990s, this was due to the lower propensity of joiners to have board-level employee relations representatives. Also during the 1990s, fewer head offices were employing ER specialists. These findings, which are consistent with a 'downgrading' of the employee relations function within multi-site organizations, were most apparent in smaller organizations. The seeming paradox of a rise in ER specialists at the workplace and the decline of employee relations at board level may be explained by the decentralization of responsibilities.

The job of the workplace employee relations manager working in a multi-site organization appears to have become more difficult over time. First, as anticipated by commentators, the decision-making capacity of workplace managers in multi-site organizations has been curtailed, although many workplace managers have nominal responsibility for a wider range of employee relations matters than in the 1980s. Second, the facilities devoted to employee relations management have been streamlined, as evidenced by the reduction in the number of non-clerical staff assisting employee relations managers in our panel establishments. It is not surprising, then, to find that employee relations managers are increasingly resorting to external sources of advice.

One commentator, reflecting on the development of management in Britain, refers to:

> a series of organizational initiatives . . . which aim to systematically deconstruct management by emphasising worker empowerment, delayering, downsizing, and the redistribution of managerial functions . . . Managerial groups are subject to intensification and polarization, while managerial practices are diffused throughout the work process.
>
> (Scarborough, 1998: 691)

There is evidence in this chapter of intensification of the work undertaken by employee relations managers, polarization within the ranks of employee relations management, and the diffusion of employee relations managerial tasks across various functions in the workplace. Whether the processes of worker empowerment, delayering and downsizing are driving these developments is an issue worthy of further investigation. It is not clear from the evidence collected from workplace employee relations managers that there is anything 'systematic' about the initiatives that have led to these changes. What we have observed is that the rate of change differs across and within sectors. During the 1990s, the biggest changes have come in the public sector and, within the private sector, in unionized workplaces – not, as commentators in the early 1990s had been anticipating, from within the non-unionized private sector.

4 Have employees lost their voice?

The ability of employees to influence the actions of their employer has been a contested area of working life since the beginnings of the modern industrialized economy. Where the size and nature of organizations are such that direct and frequent contact between employee and employer ceases to be commonplace, employees often seek a mechanism for putting their collective views and interests to their employer or manager. The most established mechanism for voicing the common concerns and opinions of workers to management or employer is representation by trade unions.[1] However, our attention in this chapter is not solely on trade unions. We consider other forms of indirect or representative 'participation' by employees in managerial decisions, forms which some commentators have regarded as substitutes for the role which unions have traditionally played in the employment relationship. We also consider forms of 'direct participation' where no intermediaries between employees and management are involved. We then look at how the various combinations of direct and indirect participation have varied through time and across different types of workplace. At the end of the chapter we see how the various arrangements for employee voice are currently associated with employees' perceptions of how responsive management is to their views and suggestions and how successful managers are in creating a climate of fairness at work.

The WIRS series has provided some of the most widely used evidence for the decline in employee 'voice' since 1980. In previous reports (Millward *et al.*, 1992; Millward, 1994a) we saw the withering of trade union representation as being at the core of this decline, with all of the surveys' indicators of union presence and strength falling by 1990. Most notably the proportion of workplaces that had recognized trade unions fell by nearly a fifth.[2] Generally the falls in the various indicators were more apparent in the second half of the decade than in the first half. In addition, the incidence of the other main channel of collective representation – consultative committees or works councils – also declined markedly in the late 1980s after a plateau in the earlier half of the decade. These results led many observers to believe that the decline in employee 'voice' would continue, perhaps with even greater rapidity, given that many of the causes of the decline appeared to be unabated (Purcell, 1993; Brown, 1993).

The reaction of the trade union movement was to reconsider its policies on representation at work and subsequently to renew its advocacy of legislation to underpin union representation. Legislation providing for a statutory recognition procedure is under debate at the time we write.

We begin the chapter by using the evidence from the WIRS series to describe and analyse the changes in the main indicators of employee representation at work. Our five principal indicators are: union presence, union membership density, union recognition, the presence of workplace representatives (union or non-union), and the presence of a consultative committee or works council. For each of these we use data from the management interviews of the four main surveys to describe the overall picture and the more detailed changes within sectors and types of workplace. This is supplemented by a more searching analysis of particular recent changes using the 1990–98 panel survey. We begin by looking at union presence at the workplace.

Union presence

The presence of one or more union members is a crude indicator of whether a workplace has employee representation based on trade unions. A lone member among a sea of non-members is unlikely to be a channel for representing employees' collective views to management. But the lone member is the exceptional case: in most workplaces with union members there are substantial numbers of them. For the moment we ignore these differences in membership numbers and examine briefly the simple indicator: whether or not a workplace has any union members. The basic indicator of union presence shows us the extent of some degree of unionization across different types of workplace. It also shows the degree to which workplaces have one or more employees who are linked to the resources and facilities of the wider trade union movement. We examine union presence by using the reports of managers, these being the only respondents from whom we have consistent data throughout the survey series.

Union presence at workplace level remained stable in the early 1980s, then dropped sharply from 1984 to 1990 and continued to do so until 1998. From 73 per cent of workplaces in 1984, the proportion fell to 64 per cent in 1990 (Table 4.1). Slight changes in question format between 1984 and 1990 qualified the precise amount of the decline for that period,[3] but there is no such difficulty with the 1990–98 comparison. A further fall of nearly a sixth occurred in the most recent interval, from 64 to 54 per cent. It brought the proportion of workplaces with a union presence from nearly three quarters in 1980 to just over one half in 1998, a fall of almost one third.

Our panel survey showed that between 1990 and 1998 this decline did not come about because of the widespread disappearance of unionism from among continuing workplaces. The proportion of continuing workplaces with at least some union presence remained unchanged at two thirds (67 per cent). In only a small proportion of continuing workplaces did union membership completely

Table 4.1 Union presence by broad sector and by workplace female proportion, 1980 to 1998

	Cell percentages			
	1980	1984	1990	1998
All establishments	73	73	64	54
Broad sector				
Private manufacturing	77	67	58	42
Private services	50	53	46	35
Public sector	99	100	99	97
Proportion of employees female				
0–24 per cent	81	79	66	47
25–74 per cent	66	68	55	46
75 per cent or more	72	78	72	72
Private sector only				
Proportion of employees female				
0–24 per cent	76	72	60	39
25–74 per cent	52	51	41	30
75 per cent or more	46	42	40	49

Base: all establishments with 25 or more employees, where reported whether any union members or not.

disappear (4 per cent), and these were counterbalanced by a similar proportion of continuing workplaces (5 per cent) in which unions achieved a new presence. Therefore, the aggregate fall in union presence between 1990 and 1998 arose wholly through the lesser penetration of workplaces that joined the population when compared with those that left it. Unions had a presence in three fifths (59 per cent) of workplaces that left the population between 1990 and 1998, but in only two fifths (42 per cent) of those that joined it over the same period.

Union presence has always differed markedly across the broad sectors of the economy and, in our time series, these differences have become more pronounced since 1980. Of the three broad sectors that we have distinguished throughout the WIRS series, the public sector has always had union members in virtually every workplace, with private manufacturing industry having high proportions and private services industries having the lowest proportions. This ordering persisted in 1998. However, while union presence in the public sector remained almost ubiquitous over the period 1980 to 1998, it dropped in private manufacturing from 77 per cent of workplaces in 1980 to 42 per cent in 1998. In private services it fell from 50 per cent of workplaces in 1980 to 35 per cent in 1998. In both parts of the private sector the fall accelerated over the most recent period, 1990–98.

In the private sector, both manufacturing and services, the recent drop was more substantial in small workplaces, but it was not confined to them. Similarly, the recent drop was apparent amongst workplaces of all ages, but it was most pronounced amongst young workplaces. The most notable change in the private sector was among male-dominated workplaces. In the early 1980s, when trade unions largely reflected a male-dominated labour market and work culture, male-dominated private sector workplaces were much more likely to have union members than female-dominated workplaces: 76 per cent, compared with 46 per cent (Table 4.1). But union presence in male-dominated workplaces plummeted during the course of our surveys – from 76 per cent down to 39 per cent – while in female-dominated workplaces it stayed more or less constant. So by 1998 the difference between them had reversed in the private sector. In the new era of greatly reduced union membership, female-dominated workplaces had become the ones most likely to have members in the private sector and, indeed, in the economy as a whole. Workplaces that had formed the bedrock for union membership in earlier decades, male-dominated workplaces, had not just become less common (as we saw in Chapter 2) – they had also lost their appetite for unionism.

Was this pattern of change with respect to union presence at the workplace also manifested in relation to union membership density?

Union membership density

Our initial analysis of the changing pattern of union density in *Britain at Work* (Millward *et al.*, 1999a) revealed a number of features of interest. We highlighted the continuation of the fall in membership density since 1980, amounting to a drop from 47 per cent down to 36 per cent between 1990 and 1998. We showed that the recent fall was most rapid in private sector services and we drew attention to the large fall in workplaces with very high membership density, especially those with 100 per cent membership in 1990. In the private sector, the fall in the extent of trade union recognition was a major source of the accelerating decline in union density, but even within workplaces with recognized unions there was a substantial fall in membership, as we discuss further in Chapter 5. We also noted in our initial analysis the greater propensity than in earlier periods for new private sector workplaces to have low membership levels or no members at all.

In developing that analysis we first describe the overall picture of aggregate membership density by industry sectors.[4] We then examine two general sources of change that might have affected all sectors of the economy: the successive legislative restrictions on the practice of the closed shop; and management attitudes to union membership. We then probe in more detail the public and private sectors separately, on the grounds that a number of other influences might have affected the two sectors differently.

The changing pattern of aggregate membership density by industry is given in the first section of Table 4.2. It shows substantial declines in aggregate

Table 4.2 Aggregate union membership density in relation to workplace characteristics, 1980 to 1998

	Cell percentages				Percentages	
	Aggregate union membership density (%)				Average annual change (%)	
	1980[a]	1984	1990	1998	1984–90	1990–98
All workplaces	65	58	47	36	−3.1	−3.2
Industry (SIC 1980)						
Energy and water supply	91	88	75	68	−2.5	−1.1
Extraction of minerals/ores; manufacture of metals, minerals and chemicals	64	64	56	47	−2.3	−2.1
Metal goods, engineering and vehicles industries	67	60	46	45	−3.8	−0.3
Other manufacturing industries	68	53	47	33	−1.6	−4.0
Construction	54	36	46	30	4.4	−4.5
Distribution, hotels and catering, repairs	34	31	19	12	−6.3	−4.7
Transport and communications	88	90	73	54	−3.2	−3.4
Banking, finance, insurance, business services and leasing	36	29	28	15	−0.4	−6.0
Other services	75	68	61	46	−1.9	−3.0
Size of establishment						
25–49 employees	47	43	34	23	−3.7	−4.0
50–99	51	46	37	27	−3.2	−3.5
100–199	60	54	44	32	−3.2	−3.6
200–499	70	64	56	38	−2.0	−4.0
500 or more	78	74	61	48	−2.9	−2.9
Proportion of employees that work part-time						
None	70	62	54	36	−2.2	−4.4
1–24 per cent	65	59	47	39	−3.4	−2.2
25 per cent or more	62	53	44	32	−3.0	−3.6
Proportion of employees that are female						
0–24 per cent	72	68	56	47	−3.1	−2.0
25–74 per cent	59	51	38	29	−4.1	−3.3
75 per cent or more	62	54	50	37	−1.3	−3.3
Proportion of employees that are non-manual						
0–24 per cent	72	63	49	40	−3.8	−2.5
25–74 per cent	64	60	47	37	−3.7	−2.8
75 per cent or more	58	50	47	32	−1.0	−4.1

Table 4.2 continued

	Cell percentages				Percentages	
	Aggregate union membership density (%)				Average annual change (%)	
	1980[a]	1984	1990	1998	1984–90	1990–98
Sector						
Private	56	43	36	26	–2.7	–3.5
Public	84	81	72	57	–1.9	–2.6

Base: all establishments with 25 or more employees, where number of union members reported.

Note
a In 1980, figures refer to full-time employees only.

density over the period of the survey series in each of the nine industry divisions of the economy.[5] In the recent period, 1990 to 1998, falls were recorded in every industry division, although only in the service industries and 'other manufacturing' were they statistically significant. Taking the figures at face value, the falls generally amounted to over 1 percentage point per year and most industries exceeded 3 percentage points per year. Industries apparently showing an accelerating annual rate of loss of membership in 1990–98, when compared with the period 1984 to 1990, were miscellaneous manufacturing, construction, banking, financial and other business services, and other services. Only metal goods and engineering, and to a lesser extent the energy and water supply industries, appeared to be slowing the rate of decline in union membership. However, the rank order of industries in terms of their aggregate membership density hardly changed between 1990 and 1998, as indeed has been the case over the whole period since 1980. Despite wholesale privatization and reorganization, the energy and water supply industries remained the sector with the highest levels of membership; and distribution, hotels and catering remained the sector with the lowest levels.

Numerous explanations are available for the pervasive falls in membership density and for the persistent tendency for some industries to have higher densities than others. Structural factors are natural candidates for the latter. The lower sections of Table 4.2 show how density has changed in relation to some of these factors, often cited as relevant to explaining union membership patterns (Waddington and Whitson, 1995; Green, 1992). Workplace size is the first. Smaller workplaces have always exhibited substantially lower levels of membership than larger ones, but this tendency appears to have increased somewhat. Workplaces with between twenty-five and forty-nine employees now have less than half the membership levels of larger workplaces with 500 or more employees, compared with around three fifths in the early 1980s.

On the next three structural factors for which results are given in Table 4.2, the indications are less clear. While it is historically clear that part-time, female and non-manual employees have each been less likely to be union members than their opposites (Waddington and Whitson, 1995), two of our workplace measures reflecting these aspects of workforce composition (the proportion of part-timers and the proportion of females) do not exhibit clear linear relationships with aggregate union density in 1998, probably because of interactions between them and because of the influence of occupational and ownership sector differences.[6] Nevertheless, workplaces with high proportions of females and non-manuals continued to have lower density than those with low proportions of such workers. While there has been a shift towards the use of large numbers of part-time employees (as noted in Chapter 2) there has also recently been a narrowing in the union membership differences between workplaces with high and low proportions of part-time employees. This is likely to underlie some of the changes in the relative unionization rates of different industries.[7]

The final section of Table 4.2 shows a clear and continuing relationship between ownership sector and aggregate membership density. Employees in the private sector showed substantially lower rates of unionization throughout the period from 1980. Falls in membership were more rapid in the private sector so that the differential between the two sectors increased. By 1998, private sector union density was less than half the density in the public sector.

The weight of the above analysis is that the origins of the falls in union membership were themselves widespread, rather than confined to particular industries or types of workforce or of employer. One of the general factors that bore upon the density of union membership in the economy as a whole was the succession of restrictions upon the practice of the closed shop that was imposed by statute during the course of the 1980s, culminating in the 1990 Employment Act that made the closed shop unlawful in 1991. By 1990, when many employers appeared to have anticipated the forthcoming legislation, a mere 4 per cent of all workplaces had a closed shop for some employees (compared with 23 per cent in 1980). By 1998 the figure had fallen still further, but a few (1 per cent of all workplaces) still reported that some employees had to be members of a trade union in order to get or keep their jobs. Among these few remaining closed shops, membership densities were very much lower than was the case in the 1980s. However, workplaces with closed shops were not the only workplaces where there had been very high levels of union membership density; there were others where management strongly encouraged union membership. These became rarer and also suffered declines in membership density, as we discuss in more detail in Chapter 5. Thus declining union membership can be attributed not only to fewer managements encouraging employees to be members, but also to a decreased willingness of employees to be members where their employer encouraged unionism.

Part of the foregoing discussion noted that the differential between the rates of unionization in the private and public sectors had increased over the course of the survey series. We now present a more in-depth analysis of the changes in density within the two sectors in order to illuminate the different contours of change. We begin by looking at the private sector.

Union density in the private sector

Aggregate union density in the private sector fell from 56 per cent in 1980 to 36 per cent in 1990 and still further to 26 per cent in 1998. Those results are from our cross-section surveys, which also revealed the virtual disappearance of workplaces with very high membership densities in this sector. In 1998 no private sector workplaces had 100 per cent union membership. Only 2 per cent had densities of 90 per cent or more, compared with 7 per cent in 1990 and 17 per cent in 1980.

Membership density continued to be strongly associated with union recognition. From 1990 onwards, density in private sector workplaces without union recognition remained constant at 4 per cent, while density in workplaces with union recognition fell from 66 to 53 per cent. As we shall see later in this chapter, recognition in the private sector had dropped from 38 to 25 per cent of workplaces. This added a further twist to the downward spiral of membership decline.

The decline in density within private sector workplaces could have occurred through two main routes. Did it arise because membership levels fell generally among workplaces that continued in operation between 1990 and 1998 or because changes in the population of workplaces resulted in the replacement of workplaces with high levels of membership by others where membership levels were low or non-existent? To assess the first possibility we turned to our panel dataset.

The first way in which we used the panel data was to see how aggregate union density had changed between 1990 and 1998. This showed us that the fall in continuing workplaces in the private sector was from 36 down to 27 per cent, very close to the cross-section results, which were 36 and 26 per cent respectively.[8] Since continuing workplaces account for most of the private sector population, this is clear evidence that the fall in density was largely because membership declined sharply among them.

The second way we used the panel data was to compare membership density in 1998 with what it was in the same establishment in 1990 and construct a measure of change. This variable shows whether membership density increased by 10 or more percentage points during the period, remain roughly stable, or decreased by 10 or more percentage points. On this measure, 69 per cent of continuing private sector workplaces had roughly stable membership density between 1990 and 1998, 9 per cent had increasing density and 21 per cent had falling density (Table 4.3).

Table 4.3 Changes in workplace union density in continuing private sector workplaces, 1990 to 1998

	Row percentages				
	Increase 10 percentage points or more	*Stable + or −10%*	*Decrease 10 percentage points or more*	*Weighted base*	*Unweighted base*
All private sector	9	69	21	*512*	*508*
Trade union recognition					
Recognition in 1990 and 1998	17	40	43	*140*	*262*
No recognition in either 1990 or 1998	4	89	8	*326*	*200*
Newly recognized between 1990 and 1998	#	#	#	*19*	*14*
Derecognized between 1990 and 1998	(0)	(23)	(77)	*26*	*32*
Private sector with recognition in both years					
Employment size					
Grew by 20 per cent or more	(4)	(59)	(37)	*20*	*34*
Stable size	16	39	45	*65*	*93*
Shrank by 20 per cent or more	23	35	42	*55*	*135*
Management endorsement of unionism					
No change	19	46	36	*87*	*151*
Less favourable in 1998 than in 1990	19	40	41	*39*	*92*

Base: all continuing workplaces remaining in the private sector, 1990 to 1998.

Among workplaces with union recognition in both 1990 and 1998, nearly a half (43 per cent) recorded falls in density of at least 10 percentage points. In the larger number of workplaces without recognized unions in either year, the great majority had stable density.[9] Unsurprisingly, in the small number of workplaces where unions were completely derecognized between 1990 and 1998, membership generally fell substantially. Cases where recognition was granted between 1990 and 1998 were too few to give reliable results on density changes, but indications were that it increased. The most significant part of the picture, as far as the effect on aggregate membership density in continuing workplaces in the private sector was concerned, was the preponderance of substantial falls in membership in workplaces with recognized unions in both 1990 and 1998.

We examined a number of variables characterizing panel workplaces in 1990 and the changes in them between 1990 and 1998. No clear relationships were found between static or change measures of workforce composition and the changes in union membership density in continuing workplaces. There was a weak indication that workplaces that grew during the period were less likely to have increased membership density than those with stable or shrinking workforces (Table 4.3), perhaps because existing union representatives experienced greater difficulties in recruiting members among types of employee that were new to the workplace. More striking was the lack of association between changes in density and changes in management attitudes towards union membership. We classified workplaces as having a less favourable management attitude to union membership if they had moved from having a closed shop in 1990 to not having one in 1998 or reported that management strongly recommended union membership in 1990 but did not do so in 1998.[10] Table 4.3 shows no significant difference in the proportion of workplaces with membership declines between those where management support for unionism had reduced and those where it had remained unchanged. Withdrawal of management support can hardly have been a primary reason for the falls in membership in continuing workplaces in the private sector.

What, then, were the reasons for the widespread falls in membership? We asked managers in panel workplaces where their estimates of union density had changed by 10 percentage points or more since 1990, 'How did this change come about?'[11] Table 4.4 gives the results for the private sector, showing reasons for falls in density first. A third of managers attributed the fall in membership density at their workplace to a decline in employee support for their union or unions, including non-renewal of subscriptions (possibly a consequence of the more stringent legal requirements for check-off arrangements). A quarter cited changes in the structure of the workforce and a quarter saw the fall as the natural product of staff turnover. Both these reasons clearly have assumptions behind them, such as new employees being less likely to join than existing employees, or perhaps being in different occupations or on less permanent employment conditions that would predispose them to be less likely to join a union. A fifth of managers explained that management had become less supportive of unions at their workplace. These included 5 per cent who cited derecognition of the union or unions. Similarly small proportions mentioned that management had set up alternative channels of communication and that the unions were less active in recruiting members than formerly.

The broad tenor of these results, albeit depending on managers' accounts, is that management hostility was not the main reason for falls in union membership among continuing workplaces in the private sector. Rather, a withering of support for membership among the existing workforce, plus a lack of recruitment as the workforce evolved, were more common causes. This is not

Table 4.4 Managers' explanations for changes in workplace union density in continuing workplaces, 1990 to 1998

	Percentages	
	Private sector	Public sector
Reasons for fall in density of 10 percentage points or more		
Decline in employee support for union	34	(14)
Natural product of staff turnover	29	(50)
Change in structure of workforce	25	(47)
Management less supportive of unions	18	(8)
Employees treated better by employer	9	(*)
Alternative channels of communication set up by management	5	(*)
Union less active in recruiting members	4	(0)
Other answers	16	(*)
Weighted base	*84*	*48*
Unweighted base	*112*	*42*
Reasons for increase in density of 10 percentage points or more		
Change in structure of workforce	(32)	(27)
Recruitment activity by union	(25)	(12)
Increase in employee support for union	(14)	(29)
Natural product of staff turnover	(11)	(14)
Worsening terms and conditions of employment	(11)	(18)
Management more supportive of unions	(11)	(17)
Other answers	(9)	(22)
Weighted base	*30*	*53*
Unweighted base	*38*	*29*

Base: continuing workplaces remaining in the specified sector, 1990 to 1998, where union density had changed by 10 percentage points or more and where managers gave a codeable answer to the question.

to say that managers were dismissive of employee support for union membership or union recruitment activity where it occurred. In workplaces where there had been increases in membership between 1990 and 1998 these were two of the three most common explanations given by private sector managers (Table 4.4, lower half). But, as noted above, increases in membership were outnumbered by decreases by a factor of more than two to one.

We showed earlier that the fall in union membership in continuing workplaces was responsible for most of the fall in density between 1990 and 1998 in the private sector. But a possible minor cause may have been that workplaces that left the population from 1990 onwards had different levels of membership from workplaces that joined the population in the same period. This was indeed the case.

Aggregate density among 'leavers' in the private sector was 36 per cent, precisely the same as the figure for private sector workplaces in 1990. (Closures, with a figure of 39 per cent, were not greatly different from workplaces that dropped below our twenty-five employee threshold, with 30 per cent aggregate density.) Workplaces joining the population were, however, clearly different from the generality of private sector workplaces in 1998. Among 'joiners' aggregate density was only 14 per cent, compared with 26 per cent in continuing private sector workplaces in 1998. However, with joiners being generally smaller and accounting for a quarter of private sector employment, their impact on the overall change was much less than the decline in density among continuing workplaces.

Union density in the public sector

Results from our cross-section surveys showed that aggregate density in the public sector fell from 84 per cent in 1980 to 72 per cent in 1990 and then more rapidly to 57 per cent in 1998. These also revealed changes in the way union density was distributed across public sector workplaces. In contrast with the private sector, where cases of high density had virtually disappeared by 1998, the public sector continued to have many workplaces where membership of a trade union was very much the norm. Nevertheless, the norm had weakened. In 1980, well over a half (63 per cent) of public sector workplaces had densities of 90 per cent or more; by 1998 only 17 per cent did so. The picture had changed noticeably in relation to the gender composition of the workforce. In 1980, female-dominated workplaces (those with three quarters or more of their staff being women) were nearly as likely to have high union density as male-dominated workplaces (correspondingly defined). By 1998, female-dominated workplaces were less than half as likely to have high density as male-dominated ones. In addition, female-dominated workplaces had become a larger portion of the public sector, thus compounding the change. Both these sources of change had occurred throughout the period, but appeared to be more marked from 1990 onwards.

The change in union density in the public sector was less apparent among continuing workplaces than was the case in the private sector. Here, aggregate density among panel workplaces fell only moderately, from 72 to 66 per cent between 1990 and 1998, compared with 72 to 57 per cent given by the cross-section results. Thus the fall in continuing workplaces was an important factor in the public sector, but not the dominant one. To examine this further we looked at changes in union density within workplaces on a case-by-case basis. Surprisingly, there were just as many public sector workplaces in our panel that registered an increase in union density between 1990 and 1998 as there were that registered a decrease: 26 per cent had increases; 24 per cent had decreases; and 50 per cent had stable membership. However, the increases were generally in smaller workplaces, whereas the decreases were commonly in larger ones, so there is no real paradox with the overall decline in aggregate density. A preponderance of increases in central and local government was matched by falls in higher education and health. In primary and secondary education, increases and decreases balanced out.

In public sector continuing workplaces, management attitudes to union membership moderated the falls in membership, compared with the private sector. Workplaces with more favourable attitudes in 1998 than in 1990 were only a little less common in the public sector than cases where management attitudes had moved against the unions, and more favourable management attitudes were associated with membership increases.

Managers' explanations of changes in union membership density between 1990 and 1998 in continuing public sector workplaces are shown in Table 4.4. Those explaining decreases in density gave prominence to workforce changes that imply a lower propensity to join among recruits or particular categories of employee. Less than one in five managers cited a decline in support for union membership among employees; less than one in ten cited less supportive attitudes among management as a reason for falling membership. Among the similar number of managers explaining increased union density in the public sector, increased support by employees was given by nearly a third and worsening terms and conditions (a traditional stimulus for union recruitment) was the reason given by a fifth. Workforce changes were also cited as reasons for increases, but less commonly than as reasons for decreases.

If, as was the case, continuing workplaces in the public sector showed only a modest fall in aggregate union density between 1990 and 1998, then the fall in the time-series results must have arisen partly through differences between leavers and joiners. In fact, aggregate density among leavers, at 77 per cent, was a little higher than the generality of public sector workplaces in 1990. Public sector workplaces that were privatized or otherwise moved to private owner- ship after 1990 had much higher 1990 density, at 91 per cent, while the great majority that remained in the public sector were very close to the overall figure at 71 per cent. So privatization and the contracting out of some public sector services did contribute to the fall in union density in the public sector.[12] More important were public sector workplaces that joined the population after 1990. These had substantially lower aggregate density of 52 per cent. In short, changes in the population of public sector workplaces, and the lower unionization of new workplaces in particular, appear to account for as much of the decline in public sector union density as the fall in density among continuing workplaces.

Trade union recognition

Our third and most telling indicator of employee 'voice' is management's recognition of a union for collective bargaining over pay, either at the workplace or a higher level. There was no dispute that this was a fundamental element of the institutional structure of industrial relations when the first of the WIRS surveys was being designed at the end of the 1970s. In the mid to late 1990s, when so much evidence was accumulating about the decline of collective bargaining in Britain, there was at least some suggestion that trade union recognition was an out-moded concept and could be dropped from the survey instruments in favour of more contemporary ideas. On the other hand, leading writers in the field still regarded union recognition for pay bargaining as of fundamental importance: 'The employment relationship is formed around the payment of labour; payment is the most conspicuous focus of collective concern for labour' (Brown *et al.*, 1995: 123). More recently, the decline in joint regulation by collective bargaining has been called 'the most fundamental change in the practice of personnel management' (Bach and Sisson, 2000: 20). And both the Trades Union Congress and the Labour Party had, by the time we were designing WERS98, clarified their enthusiasm for legislation that would support trade union recognition. Union recognition was again a topic of serious debate and there was no doubt that questions on it should be included. As before, having ascertained which unions, if any, had members at the workplace, our question to management respondents was, 'Are any of these unions recognized for negotiating pay and conditions of employment for any section of the workforce at this establishment?' As in previous surveys, if negotiations took place at a higher level in an organization, but applied to employees in the sampled establishment, the union was regarded as being recognized.

Despite the reversal of government policy from 1979 onwards – and the removal in 1980 of the statutory procedure for obtaining union recognition – our first two surveys showed no overall decline in the extent of recognition between 1980 and 1984. Roughly 65 per cent of workplaces had recognized unions in both years (Table 4.5). By 1990 this figure had fallen to 53 per cent of workplaces, a change that we interpreted as the strongest evidence of the decline in collective bargaining – a fall that was 'stark, substantial and incontrovertible' (Millward *et al.*, 1992). Many commentators viewed it similarly, including one who entitled his article, 'The end of institutional industrial

Table 4.5 Trade union recognition, by broad sector, 1980 to 1998

	Cell percentages			
	1980	*1984*	*1990*	*1998*
All establishments	64	66	53	42
Public sector	94	99	87	87
Private sector	50	48	38	25
Private manufacturing and extraction	65	56	44	29
Private services	41	44	36	23
Weighted base	2,000	2,000	2,000	2,000
Unweighted base	2,040	2,019	2,061	1,929

Base: all establishments with 25 or more employees.

relations' (Purcell, 1993). While such an obituary smacked of hyperbole, it might be more aptly applied to the most recent results: by 1998 only 42 per cent of workplaces had recognized trade unions.[13]

Looked at in absolute terms, the fall from 1990 onwards of 1.5 percentage points per year represented a slowing down from the 1984–90 period, when it was 2.2 percentage points per year. In relative terms, the difference in the rate of decline as a proportion of the initial level was hardly significant, being around 3 per cent per year for each period. Either way, the results leave no room for doubt about the continuing decline in the extent of recognition.

The WIRS survey results constitute the longest time series of systematic evidence on trade union recognition in Britain. Since the beginning of our surveys in 1980, and probably long before, union recognition has been almost ubiquitous in the public sector and concentrated among larger employers and workplaces in the private sector. These generalities still hold. But each is becoming increasingly qualified.

In the public sector, the recognition of at least one union with employees at a given workplace has fallen over the period of the series, but the change was confined to the period 1984 to 1990. That change largely came about through the government's dismantling of the national pay-negotiating machinery for schoolteachers in England and Wales in 1987 and its replacement by a pay review body. Other changes have affected the public sector since then. Recent legislation has allowed some state schools to become more autonomous from their local authority and to determine their own pay and grading policies. In the health sector local autonomy has reportedly increased through the transfers from regional health authorities to local health trusts (Thornley, 1998: 414–18). However, neither of these developments showed through as significant changes in union status at workplace level, if we take the simple indicator of some, as against no, unions being recognized for pay bargaining. Our results show union recognition at 87 per cent of public sector workplaces in both 1990 and 1998. If such changes did impinge on union recognition, it must have impacted upon more subtle indicators such as the levels of pay negotiations for particular occupational groups, in the first case, and the numbers of recognized unions at workplace level in the second case. These matters are addressed in later chapters. But the fall in our broad measure of union recognition in the public sector was small and confined to the late 1980s.

The decline in the incidence of union recognition from 1980 onwards was thus almost wholly a private sector phenomenon. From 1990 onwards it was entirely so. Recognition in the private sector fell progressively from 50 per cent in 1980 to 25 per cent in 1998 (Table 4.5).

From 1984 onwards the rate of decline of recognition in the private sector, relative to the starting level, was steady at between 3 and 4 per cent per year. Manufacturing and service industries were equally affected. Almost all of the broad industrial sectors experienced a substantial fall in union recognition between 1990 and 1998. The principal exception was the energy and water supply sector, where former public utilities predominated (Table 4.6).

Table 4.6 Trade union recognition in the private sector, 1980 to 1998, by industry and other workplace and organization characteristics

	Cell percentages			
	1980	*1984*	*1990*	*1998*
All private sector establishments	50	48	38	25
Industry (SIC 1980)				
Energy and water supply	#	#	(95)	98
Extraction of minerals/ores; manufacture of metals, minerals and chemicals	67	52	64	(34)
Metal goods, engineering and vehicles industries	65	53	37	19
Other manufacturing industries	64	59	45	40
Construction	51	(47)	36	28
Distribution, hotels and catering, repairs	35	40	27	17
Transport and communications	(59)	(74)	58	39
Banking, finance, insurance, business services and leasing	54	48	42	27
Other services	26	28	28	25
Size of establishment				
25–49 employees	41	40	30	16
50–99	49	49	40	23
100–199	65	62	48	39
200–499	75	66	69	54
500 or more	92	86	75	64
Size of organization				
25–99 employees	32	30	18	13
100–999	65	51	35	28
1,000–9,999	70	74	46	54
10,000 or more	80	85	67	69
Ownership				
Single independent establishment	32	34	21	19
Part of a larger organization	72	73	61	51
UK owned	50	47	38	26
Foreign owned	49	54	39	19
Organization has employee relations director on the board	55	62	49	38
No employee relations director on the board	51	48	51	20
Proportion of employees that are female				
0–24 per cent	63	59	43	27
25–74 per cent	42	44	32	22
75 per cent or more	37	35	36	28

Table 4.6 continued

	Cell percentages			
	1980	1984	1990	1998
Proportion of employees that work part-time				
None	54	54	36	24
1–24 per cent	56	50	43	25
25 per cent or more	34	35	25	25
Proportion of employees that are non-manual				
0–24 per cent	55	52	40	29
25–74 per cent	50	50	36	23
75 per cent or more	41	39	39	22
Proportion of employees from ethnic minority groups				
None	46	47	34	24
1–10 per cent	56	49	41	26
11 per cent or more	48	45	20	25
Age of workplace				
Less than 5 years	37	46	..	18
5–9 years	46	38	..	18
10–24 years	47	42	..	22
25 years or more	53	52	..	32
Years at current address				
Less than 5 years	..	..	30	14
5–9 years	..	..	17	21
10–20 years	..	..	31	24
21 years or more	..	..	52	33

Base: all private sector establishments with 25 or more employees.

Engineering and metal goods showed a particularly sharp fall from 37 to 19 per cent of workplaces having recognized unions, continuing an earlier trend that was accentuated by the collapse of the industry-wide negotiating machinery in 1990. And so the engineering industry has turned from being the model of collective bargaining in the 1960s and 1970s (witness its importance to the Donovan Commission and a host of academic writers at the time) to having nearly the lowest rate of recognition of any industry in 1998.

The declining incidence of union recognition affected all sizes of workplace in the private sector from 1984 onwards, but from 1990 the smallest workplaces had a greater rate of fall than larger ones. In workplaces with 25 to 49 employees recognition fell by a half between 1990 and 1998, from 30 to 16 per cent, whereas for workplaces with 500 or more employees it fell from 75 to 64 per cent. Over the whole period of the series, the gap between the largest and the smallest workplaces widened in terms of their incidence of recognition.

The picture is similar in relation to the size of enterprises. The decline since 1980 in the extent of union recognition was more severe in small enterprises than in large ones. Single-establishment enterprises also showed a sharper fall in recognition than workplaces that belonged to larger organizations.

Two other enterprise characteristics appeared to have become salient since 1990. First, workplaces belonging to foreign-based companies became less likely than workplaces owned by indigenous firms to recognize unions. This difference was observed in company-level research in the early 1990s (Marginson *et al.*, 1993). Second, those belonging to firms without an employment relations specialist on the board of directors became less likely to recognize unions than those with one. This association may well be an indicator of an emerging divergence of approaches to the management of labour among company boards.

Recognition also varied over time in relation to four characteristics of work-force composition. First, whereas in the 1980s male-dominated workplaces in the private sector were nearly twice as likely to have recognized unions as female-dominated workplaces, by 1998 there was no discernible difference between them. Second, from 1980 until 1990 workplaces with a wholly full-time workforce were more likely to have recognition than those with substantial proportions of part-time employees, but in 1998 there was no difference. Third, there was a difference between workplaces with a predominantly manual workforce and those with a predominantly white-collar workforce in 1980; from 1990 onwards no clear difference was apparent. These changes reflect to a certain extent the changes we noted earlier with respect to union presence: the decline of male-dominated, largely manual workplaces as the bedrock of union representation. The fourth characteristic of workforces we looked at was the proportion who belonged to ethnic minorities. Workplaces with high concentrations of ethnic minority workers had experienced a particularly sharp decline in union recognition in the late 1980s, but this trend was not maintained in the 1990s.

A final characteristic of workplaces that we examined in relation to union recognition in our time-series data was their age. Initial analyses of the 1990 survey data identified establishment age as a significant variable in explaining the declining incidence of recognition during the course of the 1980s (Millward *et al.*, 1992: 73; Millward, 1994a: 21–32) and the underlying basis for this was greatly illuminated by subsequent econometric analyses (Disney *et al.*, 1995). The last two sections of Table 4.6 update the cross-tabular results, using two alternative ways of classifying the age of the workplace. Both sets of results indicate a further strengthening of the effect in the 1990s in the private sector. Workplaces that were less than five years old in 1998 were almost half as likely to have recognized unions as workplaces that were twenty-five or more years old, in contrast to the situation in the early 1980s when recognition was commonplace and workplace age had much less bearing on the likelihood of recognition.

While the above results show how recognition changed in relation to a range of characteristics commonly used to describe how workplaces differ from each other, they make no attempt to see whether differences in relation to one particular characteristic are independent of differences with respect to another.

For example, part of the reason why younger workplaces are less likely to recognize unions could be because they were smaller than more mature establishments. To overcome this limitation we turned to multivariate regression analysis, using the logit form of regression with union recognition as the dependent variable.[14] Our specification is similar to that used by Disney *et al.* (1995) when analysing union recognition for the whole economy up to 1990. Because of the difficulties in defining a consistent age variable across the whole time series, we omit the 1990 survey from the analyses reported in Table 4.7. Data from 1990 are included in a subsequent comparison of the two most recent surveys, however.

The first three columns of the table summarize the results of logit regressions for the private sector for 1980, 1984 and 1998, with establishment age measured on a consistent basis. The results confirm the significance of many of the characteristics discussed in the earlier analysis and pinpoint some changes in significance which did not emerge from the tabular results. First, while service sector workplaces had significantly lower rates of recognition in 1980 than manufacturing plants, controlling for other variables, there were no such differences from 1984 onwards. Recognition in services was, of course, lower than in manufacturing throughout the series, but since 1984 these differences were accounted for by other variables lower down in the table. In other words, the distinctiveness of manufacturing as the most fertile ground for union recognition in the private sector disappeared soon after 1980.

The crucial role played by workplace size in affecting the chance of union recognition is well testified by the results and, as suggested by Table 4.6, the gap between small and medium-sized establishments grew over the series. There continues to be a highly significant positive relationship between enterprise size and union recognition in the private sector. However, the effect in 1980 extended down to organizations of 100 or more employees, whereas in 1998 it was confined to those with 1,000 or more. Foreign ownership, which was not found to be associated with recognition in either 1980 or 1984 after controlling for other factors, did become significant in 1998.

Both measures of workforce composition – the proportion of employees in white-collar occupations and the proportion employed part-time – were negatively related to recognition in a highly significant way in the early 1980s. But, as the tabular results suggested, their separate independent influence on union recognition had either decreased or disappeared entirely by 1998.

On workplace age, the results show that, in 1980, older workplaces had a greater likelihood of recognition than young workplaces. However, this association disappeared after 1980. This suggests that there may have been a cohort effect, with workplaces that were set up in the mid-1950s or earlier being more likely to recognize unions than workplaces set up in later years. To test this hypothesis, we constructed a variable representing the year in which workplaces were first established. This was only possible for the 1980 and 1998 surveys and the results are reported in the fourth and fifth columns of Table 4.7. They show

Table 4.7   Logit analysis of trade union recognition in the private sector, 1980, 1984 and 1998

	1980	1984	1998	1980	1998
Industry sector					
Services	– – –	o	o	– – –	o
(Ref. Manufacturing)					
Size of establishment					
50–99 employees	o	o	o	o	o
100–199	o	+ +	+ + +	o	+ + +
200–499	+	+	+ + +	+	+ + +
500–999	+ + +	+ + +	+ + +	+ + +	+ + +
1,000 or more	+ + +	+ + +	+ + +	+ + +	+ + +
(Ref. 25–49 employees)					
Size of organization					
100–999 employees	+ + +	o	o	+ + +	o
1,000–9,999	+ + +	+ + +	o	+ + +	o
10,000 or more	+ + +	+ + +	+ + +	+ + +	+ + +
(Ref. 25–99 employees)					
Ownership					
Foreign owned	o	o	– –	o	–
(Ref. Domestically owned)					
Workforce composition					
Proportion of employees that are non-manual	– – –	– – –	– –	– – –	o
Proportion of employees that work part-time	– – –	– – –	o	– – –	o
Age of workplace					
5–9 years	o	o	o	..	..
10–24 years	o	o	o	..	..
25 years or more	+ +	o	o	..	..
(Ref. Less than 5 years)					
Year workplace established					
1971–76	..	..	..	o	o
1956–70	..	..	..	o	o
1955 or earlier	..	..	..	+ +	+ + +
(Ref. 1977 onwards)					
Number of observations	1,211	1,056	1,036	1,211	955

Base: all private sector establishments with 25 or more employees.

Note: reference categories indicated in parentheses.

Key for significance:
o   Not significantly different from the reference category.
+ (–)   Positive (negative) association, significant at the 90 per cent level of confidence.
+ + (– –) Positive (negative) association, significant at the 95 per cent level of confidence.
+ + + (– – –) Positive (negative) association, significant at the 99 per cent level of confidence.

a significant positive coefficient for workplaces established in 1955 or earlier, but the lack of any association with being established in the 1960s or 1970s. This implies that the golden age for union recognition was earlier than is often supposed and was probably during the Second World War and the years immediately following it. Unions' difficulties in obtaining recognition through voluntary means are clearly of very long standing.

Focusing on the more recent period covered by the latest two surveys, we report in Table 4.8 some further logit analyses using much the same specification. There are two changes. First, because of the large number of missing values on this variable in the 1990 dataset, we had to replace organizational size with a less precise indicator which identifies workplaces that were part of a larger organization. Second, because of changes in question wording, we use a somewhat different age variable: the number of years at the current address. These changes ensure comparability between the variables in the 1990 and 1998 analyses. Table 4.8 contains similar results to those in Table 4.7 except that, on the alternative measure of workplace age, the oldest workplaces have a very significantly greater incidence of union recognition, controlling for other characteristics in the analysis. The clear positive association with being in the oldest age category is apparent in both 1990 and 1998. The negative association with being five to nine years old in the 1990 survey is surprising and implies that the likelihood of recognition increased for workplaces established between 1985 and 1990, this being the base period for the comparisons in the regressions. A pooled analysis for the two years shows a highly negative coefficient on the 1998 indicator, implying that the likelihood of recognition was substantially less in 1998 than in 1990, even controlling for other characteristics.

Changes in recognition, 1990–98

The results from our cross-sectional surveys, discussed above, tell us only part of the story of the changing extent and pattern of union recognition. We are able to enhance this considerably by using some of the other elements of WERS98, particularly the panel survey, where we were able to include questions about changes that had happened between 1990 and 1998 – and the reasons for any changes that had occurred. For the present, we use the term 'derecognition' to refer to situations where a workplace had recognized one or more unions in 1990 for the purpose of pay bargaining, but recognized none in 1998. 'New recognition' refers to the opposite case.

The overall panel results show that derecognitions outweighed new recognitions between 1990 and 1998, but not such as to explain much of the large drop in the time-series results. Of all continuing workplaces, 6 per cent derecognized unions between 1990 and 1998. New recognition cases amounted to 4 per cent of all continuing workplaces. Comparing the panel sample at the two points in time, 56 per cent recognized unions in 1990 and 55 per cent of the same workplaces did so in 1998.

Table 4.8 Logit analysis of trade union recognition in the private sector, 1990 and 1998

	1990	1998	Pooled, 1990 and 1998
Industry sector			
Services	o	o	o
(Ref. Manufacturing)			
Size of establishment			
50–99 employees	o	o	+
100–199	+ +	+ + +	+ + +
200–499	+ + +	+ + +	+ + +
500–999	+ + +	+ + +	+ + +
1,000 or more	+ + +	+ + +	+ + +
(Ref. 25–49 employees)			
Ownership			
Part of a larger organization	+ + +	+ + +	+ + +
(Ref. Independent establishment)			
Foreign owned	o	– – –	– – –
(Ref. Domestically owned)			
Workforce composition			
Proportion of employees that are non-manual	–	o	–
Proportion of employees that work part-time	– –	o	o
Years at current address			
5–9 years	– –	o	o
10–20 years	o	+	o
21 years or more	+ + +	+ + +	+ + +
(Ref. Less than 5 years)			
1998 survey	..	..	– – –
(Ref. 1990 survey)			
Number of observations	1,317	1,259	2,576

Base: all private sector establishments with 25 or more employees.

Note: reference categories indicated in parentheses.

Key for significance:
o	Not significantly different from the reference category.
+ (–)	Positive (negative) association, significant at the 90 per cent level of confidence.
+ + (– –)	Positive (negative) association, significant at the 95 per cent level of confidence.
+ + + (– – –)	Positive (negative) association, significant at the 99 per cent level of confidence.

Derecognition occurred across most industries and types of workplace, although our sample contained none in the banking, finance and business services sector and hardly any in energy and water supply or transport and communications. There was no clear concentration in either the public or the private sector or in workplaces of a particular size or workforce composition, judging by their characteristics in 1990. Perhaps surprisingly, we found no cases of complete derecognition among the small number of workplaces in our panel that had been privatized between 1990 and 1998. More generally, derecognition was not associated with ownership changes in the panel.

Managers gave three main reasons for derecognition in response to our panel interview question on how the change came about.[15] The most common was a change in management policy, mentioned by a half. About a third mentioned a decline in union membership among the workforce and about a quarter mentioned lack of union activity.[16] Taken together, these last two indicators of employee lack of interest in union representation amounted to just under a half of respondents. On balance, then, managers were split roughly equally between those who saw derecognition as arising from a decline in employees' interest in union representation and those who saw it as the outcome of a change in management policy.

New recognition in continuing workplaces occurred in only 4 per cent of our panel cases and in some of those our respondent did not give a usable answer to our question on how the new recognition came about. Where they did, the most common type of answer, given by around a half, referred to recognition being extended from elsewhere in the organization. This was commonly associated with changes of ownership. A few respondents mentioned conformity with other organizations in their industry and even fewer explained that recognition was granted after discussions or negotiations between management and unions. None mentioned actual or threatened industrial action, workplace ballots or the involvement of third parties such as ACAS. This picture is very different from the one we obtained in 1980, when we asked managers where recognition agreements with manual unions had been signed in the preceding five years how recognition had been brought about. Then, the clear majority of cases arose from pressure from employees or unions, sometimes involving ballots or strikes; only a fifth were because management extended arrangements from elsewhere in the organization (Daniel and Millward, 1983: 31–2). The small absolute number of new recognition cases in our panel of continuing workplaces in the 1990s appears to be largely due to a reduced demand for union representation on the part of employees when compared with the situation in the late 1970s.

However, continuing workplaces are only one portion of the population of workplaces. Around one third of workplaces in 1998 were ones that had joined the population since 1990, either through growth or initial establishment. Among these joiners only 30 per cent recognized trade unions by 1998, according to our 1998 cross-section survey results. The proportion was 27 per cent among new workplaces and 35 per cent among those that had grown into the scope of the survey. The overall figure of 30 per cent among joiners was much lower than the figure of 55 per cent found among continuing workplaces that recognized unions in 1998. However, leavers between 1990 and 1998 were similar to those that remained in operation over the period. Overall, 51 per cent of leavers had recognition; the proportion was 50 per cent among workplaces that closed down and 53 per cent among those that fell out of the scope of the survey. This compared with 56 per cent of those that continued. Since continuing workplaces changed little between the two years, it is the very sharp contrast between joiners and leavers that lies at the heart of the decline in union recognition in the 1990s.

We looked at a number of workplace and organizational characteristics to see if any were associated with a particularly low rate of recognition among joiners as compared with leavers with similar characteristics. We found the most illuminating to be the broad sector of employment and the proportion of the workforce who were part-time employees. Both are characteristics that have changed in relation to the composition of workplaces in the economy and are related to union recognition. The results are given in the lower portion of Table 4.9. (The upper portion, for continuing workplaces, is given for completeness and confirms the general continuity of recognition arrangements, mentioned earlier.)

Comparing the incidence of recognition of joiners with that of leavers, public sector workplaces showed a relatively small difference (89 per cent compared with 99 per cent) when compared with the private sector. Among the four private sector categories, those with the biggest difference were private services workplaces with relatively few part-time employees; here leavers with a recognition rate of 47 per cent were replaced by joiners with only 15 per cent recognition. Second, in terms of differences, were manufacturing workplaces with some part-timers; here leavers with 40 per cent recognition contrasted with joiners with only 10 per cent recognition. It is these two types of workplace where joiners behaved very differently from leavers with regard to recognition; in the remaining types the differences were not so marked.

Table 4.9 also suggests that there were compositional changes, but some worked to exacerbate the decline in recognition while others served to moderate it. In order to quantify the relative importance of compositional change in comparison with changes in behaviour among similar types of workplace, discussed above, we used shift-share analysis on the data presented in Table 4.9. In essence, we calculated what the overall rate of recognition among joiners would have been if they had been distributed among the five types of workplace in the same proportions as the leavers were, but with their rate of recognition as it was in 1998. This generated an overall value of 27 per cent, representing a drop in recognition of 24 percentage points. Similarly we calculated what the overall rate of recognition among joiners would have been if each of the five types had had the same rate of recognition as the leavers but had been distributed among the five types as in 1990. This generated a value of 48 per cent, representing a drop in recognition of 3 percentage points. Over nine tenths

Table 4.9 Trade union recognition in continuing workplaces, leavers and joiners, 1990 and 1998, by sector and part-time employment

	Cell percentages			
	Continuing workplaces			
	1990		*1998*	
	Population share	*Percentage with recognition*	*Population share*	*Percentage with recognition*
All workplaces	100	56	100	55
Manufacturing, no part-timers	4	60	4	59
Manufacturing, some part-timers	14	45	14	42
Private services, part-timers less than 25 per cent	28	30	27	35
Private services, part-timers 25 per cent or more	16	24	19	27
Public sector	39	92	36	89
	Leavers 1990–98		*Joiners 1990–98*	
	Population share	*Percentage with recognition*	*Population share*	*Percentage with recognition*
All workplaces	100	51	100	30
Manufacturing, no part-timers	5	(26)	7	#
Manufacturing, some part-timers	24	40	7	(10)
Private services, part-timers less than 25 per cent	41	47	35	15
Private services, part-timers 25 per cent or more	13	(23)	30	17
Public sector	18	99	20	89

Base: all continuing workplaces, leavers and joiners, as specified in column headings, 1990 to 1998.

of the drop in recognition is accounted for by differences between joiners and leavers, and less than one tenth is due to the change in composition.[17] Hence the change in behaviour of joiners compared with similar leavers in the private sector was palpably the overriding reason for the large drop in recognition between 1990 and 1998. Employers in new and growing workplaces appear to have little sympathy with joint regulation with trade unions, while, as noted earlier, their employees appear to have less appetite for union membership and representation.

Other channels for collective employee voice

Historically, trade unions have constituted the most established mechanism of employee 'voice' at the workplace. However, the continued decline in the incidence of union recognition in the 1980s and 1990s has meant that attention has often turned to other forms of collective representation and expression. These include indirect forms of participation such as consultative committees or works councils and employee representatives, as well as direct forms such as workforce meetings and briefing groups. In the 1980s, discussions about new forms of industrial relations included references to such forms of representation and participation as being appropriate alternatives to a trade union presence at the workplace. However, there was clear evidence of limited growth in alternative mechanisms for voicing employees' interests or views. Instead, it became evident from our surveys that many of the so-called alternatives were much less common in non-union workplaces than in unionized ones. Having witnessed a further decline in union representation in the 1990s, it is now even more pertinent to examine the incidence of other forms of employee voice in the workplace. We begin by looking at the incidence of consultative committees.

Consultative committees

Each of the surveys in the WIRS series has asked managers whether their workplace had a formal joint consultative committee of managers and employees. The survey questions have focused on committees that were primarily concerned with consultation, rather than negotiation, and those covering a range of topics rather than a single issue such as health and safety. Such committees were the principal channel of employee voice during the Second World War and the years immediately afterwards (Kessler and Bayliss, 1998: 124). Our first survey in 1980 showed that one third (34 per cent) of all workplaces had a joint consultative committee. There had been no change by the time of our second survey in 1984, but our third survey in 1990 showed a slight drop to 29 per cent. The fall seen in the second half of the 1980s was not repeated in the 1990s, however, with the proportion remaining at 29 per cent in 1998 (Table 4.10).

The above results take the reports of managers at face value and include some committees that meet rarely and thus provide only very limited opportunity for employees to communicate with management. Following the practice adopted by Millward (1994a), we define 'functioning consultative committees' by excluding those that met less often than once every three months.[18] This definition excluded under 10 per cent of workplaces that reported committees in our first three surveys, but it excluded nearly 20 per cent of those that reported them in 1998.[19] The incidence of functioning committees thus showed a further

Table 4.10 Incidence of workplace joint consultative committees, by broad sector and union recognition, 1980 to 1998

	Cell percentages			
	1980	1984	1990	1998
Any consultative committee				
All establishments	34	34	29	29
Functioning consultative committee				
All establishments	30	31	26	23
Size of establishment				
25–49 employees	21	21	18	14
50–99	29	32	31	25
100–199	39	47	37	32
200–499	60	54	43	49
500 or more	66	70	61	58
Private sector	26	24	18	20
Private manufacturing and extraction	32	26	21	24
Private services	22	23	17	18
Public sector	39	42	45	32
Unions recognized	37	36	34	30
No recognized unions	17	20	17	18
Private sector only				
Unions recognized	35	29	21	24
No recognized unions	16	20	17	18

Base: all establishments with 25 or more employees.

decline since 1990, falling to 23 per cent of all workplaces in 1998, compared with 31 per cent in 1984. The proportion of employees in workplaces with a functioning consultative committee fell from 50 per cent in 1984 to 43 per cent in 1998.

The decline in the incidence of functioning consultative committees since 1984 affected all sizes of workplace. For the smallest workplaces (25–49 employees) it fell from 21 per cent in 1984 to 14 per cent in 1998, while for the largest workplaces (500 or more employees) it fell from 70 to 58 per cent over the same period (Table 4.10). However, the decline was confined to the private sector between 1984 and 1990 and to the public sector after 1990. Even so, in 1998 the public sector still remained the sector where consultative committees were most prevalent, while the private services sector remained the one where they were least common.

There has been considerable discussion about the relationship between consultative committees and trade union representation – part of the broader debate about HRM and trade unions. The WIRS results have shown the two types of representative arrangement to be broadly complementary, rather than alternatives. Throughout the 1980s functioning consultative committees were at least twice as common in workplaces with recognized trade unions as they were in workplaces without unions, yet this association appears to have weakened more recently. Between 1990 and 1998, the incidence of consultative committees fell among all workplaces with recognized unions, from 34 to 30 per cent, but remained steady at around 17 per cent among establishments without recognition (Table 4.10). This was the result of the declining incidence of consultative committees in the public sector, where most workplaces have recognized unions. In the private sector the extent of consultative committees rose, if anything, among those workplaces that recognized trade unions.[20]

The period from 1990 onward saw a number of significant changes in the incidence of functioning committees within individual industries. In private sector transport and communications they became more common, while in the public sector significant declines were evident in health services, in the remainder of the energy sector under public ownership, and in 'other services'.

Within the private sector the proportion of workplaces with consultative committees hardly changed between 1990 and 1998 (18 and 20 per cent respectively). Within the public sector, however, there was a substantial fall from 45 to 32 per cent and this was due entirely to the changing population of workplaces. Among continuing workplaces that remained in the public sector, the incidence of functioning consultative committees did not change, standing at 49 per cent in both 1990 and 1998. Yet, whilst 45 per cent of public sector workplaces that left the population had such committees, they were present in only 31 per cent of workplaces that were created, or rose above our twenty-five employee size threshold, in the public sector over the period.

The panel results for all continuing workplaces suggest that many consultative committees are not enduring institutions of employee representation. Between 1990 and 1998 12 per cent of continuing workplaces discontinued their functioning consultative committee whilst 17 per cent established one. Only 18 per cent had a committee at both points in time. Of course, even among these 18 per cent, the committee reported in 1998 might not be the same one as that reported in 1990; we only know that there was at least one at each of the two dates. If we relax our definition to include all committees, however infrequently they met, the pattern of results is very similar, with 22 per cent having a committee in both 1990 and 1998.

Among panel workplaces that had discontinued having any consultative committee between 1990 and 1998, a half of managers explaining the change said it had happened because there had been a change in management's policy or approach, often associated with a change of ownership. Around a quarter of these respondents said that management had centralized consultation arrangements higher in the organization. Around a quarter said that the committee had been disbanded because of improved communications with employees, presumably rendering the committee unnecessary. Fewer than

10 per cent of respondents mentioned other reasons such as lack of interest by employees, the derecognition of unions, the committee becoming a negotiating body and lack of need. Broadly speaking, it appeared that consultative committees were discontinued when management judged it appropriate to do so.

The introduction of a consultative committee where none had previously existed was similarly explained by managers in panel workplaces as generally being a managerial decision. A half said it arose from a change in management's policy or approach, again sometimes arising from a change of ownership. About a third saw it manifesting a more consultative approach with employees, or as an aid to communication with them. Fewer than 10 per cent said it followed an agreement with employees or trade unions. Fewer than 5 per cent said it happened at the request of staff.

Two final pieces of evidence about the growth and decline of functioning consultative committees concern their co-existence with trade union representation. First, we wanted to examine the notion that consultative machinery could act as a springboard for union representation and we did so by looking at our panel data on changes in the presence of functioning consultative committees and of recognized unions in 1990 and 1998. We compared the proportion of workplaces gaining recognition between 1990 and 1998 among those that had a functioning committee in 1990 and those that did not. Both figures were around 5 per cent, leading us to conclude that a functioning consultative committee at a workplace did not increase the likelihood of trade unions gaining recognition there.

Second, we wanted to see whether workplaces that derecognized trade unions retained or created a consultative committee as an alternative channel of employee representation. Our panel evidence showed us that workplaces that derecognized trade unions between 1990 and 1998 were no more likely to retain a functioning consultative committee in 1998 than those that continued to recognize trade unions. Furthermore, panel workplaces that derecognized trade unions were less likely to introduce a functioning consultative committee between 1990 and 1998 than other workplaces. On this evidence, the decline in employee voice brought about by the drop in union recognition is not being offset by the introduction of consultative committees as alternative channels of representation.

The operation of workplace consultative committees

Consultative arrangements at workplace level may vary in terms of their complexity, their effectiveness and many other attributes. Each of our surveys has asked about the number of committees as a measure of the complexity of the arrangements and more recent ones have provided an indicator of the perceived influence of the principal, or only, committee. The trend identified during the 1980s of increasing numbers of committees among workplaces that had them continued through the 1990s. Those with four or more committees constituted only 4 per cent of workplaces with functioning committees in 1980; by 1990 this figure had reached 10 per cent. In 1998 it increased further to 15 per cent. Over the period as a whole, those with a single committee declined from 77 per cent to 57 per cent.

In the 1990 survey we introduced a question asking managers to assess the amount of influence that their workplace's principal consultative committee had on managerial decisions affecting the workforce. A similar question in 1998 produced an almost identical distribution of answers, with about a third of managers in each year rating their consultative committee as very influential. However, employee representatives' views of the influence of these committees were not generally correlated with those of management; there was no significant correlation between them in 1998, while in 1990 the correlation was confined to manual worker representatives. Thus, even if there had been an increase since 1990 in the proportion of managers reporting that their consultative committees were very influential, it would have been unwise to take this increase at face value. Functioning consultative committees appear to be no more influential than they were in 1990 – and there are fewer of them.

We mentioned in the previous section the degree to which workplaces had a dual system of employee representation – through trade unions and through formal consultative machinery. But where they co-exist there may be no link between the two. Early in the survey series we sought to explore this link directly through a question which asked whether any of the employee representatives on consultative committees were nominated by trade unions. The proportion of workplaces with functioning consultative committees that had representatives nominated by unions remained at just over one half from 1980 to 1990.

In 1998 the form of the question was changed to gain a broader idea of how employee representatives on consultative committees were appointed, the question being an open one with 'nomination by trade unions' being only one of several possible responses. Using this form of question, the proportion mentioning nomination by trade unions was only a quarter of cases with a functioning consultative committee. It is very likely that much of this apparent drop from one half to one quarter arose from the question change, because the panel data tell a different story. Here, with identical questions asked in 1990 and 1998, the proportion of continuing workplaces whose consultative committee had employee representatives that were nominated by trade unions was 54 per cent in 1990 and 50 per cent in 1998. These figures are for panel workplaces that had union members in both years, as well as a functioning committee in both years. Other workplaces that existed in 1998 had somewhat lower levels of trade union nomination – including workplaces that joined the population, where we estimate it at around 40 per cent. After consideration of a number of detailed analyses of the different datasets we believe that the proportion given by the cross-section data would have been nearer 40 per cent than 25 per cent if the question had been unaltered. In short, trade union nomination to functioning consultative committees in workplaces with union members declined somewhat in the 1990s, after remaining stable in the 1980s. It remained a more common practice in the public sector than in private sector workplaces with union members.

Higher-level consultative committees

Managements in organizations with a number of different establishments may prefer to consult with employees on a multi-site basis, rather than have a consultative committee for each establishment. We have asked about the existence of such higher-level committees since 1984. Consultative machinery of this kind has been encouraged in recent years by the European Works Council Directive. It comes as no surprise, therefore, that more higher-level committees were reported in 1998 than in previous surveys. In 1998, 56 per cent of workplaces belonging to a larger organization reported a higher-level committee in their organization, compared with 48 per cent in 1990 and 50 per cent in 1984. The increase since 1990 was entirely within the private sector, where the proportion rose from 35 to 48 per cent. Our panel of continuing workplaces also showed a modest increase between 1990 and 1998; 54 per cent of workplaces belonging to larger organizations in both years reported a higher committee in 1998, compared with 47 per cent of the same workplaces in 1990.

A higher-level committee may be so remote from an individual workplace that employees there have no effective voice to management through the committee. In earlier surveys we therefore asked whether our sampled workplace had a representative on the higher-level committee, where a committee was reported. Around two fifths of cases had a local representative in 1990, a similar level to that reported in 1984. Unfortunately, there was no space for a similar question in the 1998 cross-section survey, but we did find room for it in the panel interview. The results indicate no change in the propensity for workplaces to have representatives on higher-level committees – the proportion stayed steady at around two fifths.

A broad indicator of the extent to which employees have access to consultative machinery is whether their workplace has a functioning consultative committee or a representative on a higher-level committee. The proportion of workplaces with such consultative machinery declined between 1984 and 1990, from 39 to 34 per cent. For reasons explained above, we can only construct this indicator for the most recent period for our panel sample. This showed an increase among continuing workplaces, from 37 per cent in 1990 to 43 per cent in 1998. Again the change was confined to the private sector, where the corresponding figures were 27 and 33 per cent. In broad terms, the increase from 1990 onwards did no more than restore the position to what it was in 1984. If legislative developments at the European level in the 1990s were expected to have a pervasive influence on the extent of consultative arrangements in Britain, such an expectation has yet to be fulfilled.

Workplace representatives

While some of the forms of collective representation that we have discussed above clearly entail the existence of on-site representatives, not all of them do so. In particular, some workplaces with recognized trade unions may not have an on-site representative, relying instead on the services of a lay representative at another workplace of the same employer or a local full-time officer of the union. On the other hand, there may be employee representatives who are appointed neither through union channels nor as members of a consultative committee or works council; these, as Terry (1999) points out, are highly unlikely to be granted rights of bargaining by management, but are restricted to consultation and information sharing.

In this section we set out such comparable information as is available from management respondents in the WIRS series on the changing incidence of on-site employee representatives of various types. We restrict our attention here to on-site representatives because their presence is a clear indicator of the immediate availability of assistance from a representative when an employee needs one. 'Voice' at the workplace is our focus here. The comparisons are restricted to 1980 and 1998, since the changes in question design and wording making it impractical to create comparable variables covering all types of establishment for the two intervening surveys.

The available data for 1980 and 1998 allow us to characterize establishments as one of four types regarding the existence of an on-site representative. There are those with the following: one or more union representatives; one or more representatives, but it is unclear whether they are union-based or not; no union representative, but at least one non-union representative; no representative of any kind. The categories are mutually exclusive and prioritize union over non-union representation, a procedure we justify in terms of the historically greater involvement of trade unions in bargaining as against weaker forms of representation. Table 4.11 gives the overall results and a breakdown by the type of employee representation. The second category in the table, where there are representatives but it is not known whether they are union or non-union, is unfortunate but the changes are so marked in the adjacent categories that it does not hinder interpretation. There is no such doubt with the last category in the table; workplaces can be categorized unambiguously as to whether or not they have any representatives.

Two important findings emerge from the aggregate results: there was a dramatic shift from union to non-union representatives between 1980 and 1998; and there was an increase in the incidence of workplaces with no form of on-site representative whatsoever. At a minimum, the drop in the proportion of workplaces with one or more on-site union representatives was from 53 per cent in 1980 to 33 per cent in 1998. (The initial figure could have been as high as 65 per cent, if all the doubtful cases were ones with union representatives.) Mostly the increasing scarcity of union representatives was matched by an increase in the incidence of cases where a non-union representative was present.

Table 4.11 Incidence of on-site representatives, by type of union presence, 1980 and 1998

| | *Column percentages* | | | | | | | |
| | *All workplaces* | | *Unions recognized* | | *Union members, no recognition* | | *No union members present* | |
	1980	*1998*	*1980*	*1998*	*1980*	*1998*	*1980*	*1998*
Type of representative present								
Union representative	53	33	80	74	25	15	0	0
Representative, but status unknown	12	*	13	*	46	2	0	0
Non-union representative (where no union representative)	16	41	2	15	4	62	50	58
None	19	26	5	11	25	20	50	42
Weighted base	*1,978*	*1,999*	*1,265*	*843*	*171*	*232*	*541*	*923*
Unweighted base	*2,021*	*1,927*	*1,563*	*1,114*	*130*	*216*	*328*	*597*

Base: all establishments with 25 or more employees.

At a minimum the increase was from 28 to 41 per cent of all workplaces, but the initial figure could have been as low as 16 per cent, if all the doubtful cases in 1980 were non-union.

Much of the fall in the overall incidence of workplaces with local union representatives arose because the population of workplaces with recognized unions had contracted by about a third, as we saw earlier in the chapter. However, even in workplaces with recognized unions, union representatives were less common in 1998 than 1980, a point discussed further in Chapter 5. There may have been more that had non-union representatives, but it is clear also that more of them had no on-site representative at all.

In the modest number of workplaces with union members but no recognition, around 10 per cent of workplaces in both 1980 and 1998, union representatives became less common while non-union representatives became more common. Complete absence of representatives remained stable, at around a quarter of cases, in this type of workplace. In the greatly expanded part of the population with no union members present, workplaces remained roughly evenly split between those that had some type of non-union representative and those that had none.

Broadly speaking, fewer workplaces in 1998 had any form of employee representative than in 1980 because the decline in union representation was not fully offset by the modest increase in non-union representation. Further analysis of the changes in the presence and types of representative revealed that the above conclusion held for workplaces in both the public and private sectors of the economy. It generally applied in workplaces within the five broad size-bands that we examined, although not all the changes were statistically robust. In terms of broad sectors, the increase in the proportion of workplaces with no representatives was evident in manufacturing (from 10 to 19 per cent of workplaces) and in public sector services (from 3 to 10 per cent); but there was no change in private sector services, where over a third of workplaces had no representative in both 1980 and 1998. When we repeated the analysis on the basis of employees, rather than workplaces, the broad conclusion was similar. Fewer employees in 1998 than in 1980 worked in an establishment that had any form of employee representative because the decline in union representation was not fully offset by the modest increase in non-union representation.

Health and safety representation

In all of the above material we have been examining general mechanisms through which employees may make their views and concerns known to management, irrespective of the topic or issue. Here we briefly sharpen our focus to a single set of issues – health and safety at work. Questions in the survey series on health and safety have always been kept separate from the questions about general consultation mechanisms. Part of the special interest of the topic is that health and safety is one of the areas of working life in which there has been statutory support for employee representation throughout our survey series. This support has been strongest for representation by recognized trade unions and previous surveys have consistently shown much higher levels of employee representation on health and safety matters in unionized workplaces than in those without unions.

While there have been some changes in question wording and format from one survey to another, we do have broadly comparable data from the four surveys on three types of representation: health and safety committees; joint committees of managers and employees dealing with health and safety and other matters; and individual workforce health and safety representatives where there was no committee. In the absence of any of these, we classify the workplace as having no employee representation for health and safety matters, and hence no formal voice, even though management may discuss these matters with employees on some occasions. The results from each of the four surveys are given in Figure 4.1.

In broad terms, around two thirds of workplaces have had one of these three forms of employee representation on health and safety matters throughout the past twenty years. The proportion increased from 66 per cent to 72 per cent from 1980 to 1984, fell to 57 per cent in 1990 and recovered to 68 per cent in 1998. In the most recent period, the increase was barely significant in the public sector, but substantial in both private manufacturing (from 62 per cent in 1990 to 78 per cent in 1998) and private services (42 to 58 per cent).

Each of the three types of health and safety representation became somewhat more common in the most recent period: workplaces with joint health and

Figure 4.1 Health and safety representation, 1980 to 1998

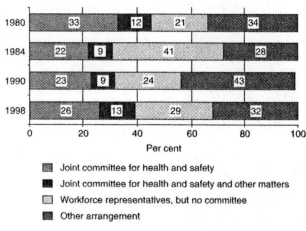

Joint committee for health and safety
Joint committee for health and safety and other matters
Workforce representatives, but no committee
Other arrangement

Base: all establishments with 25 or more employees.

safety committees rose from 23 to 26 per cent; those with joint committees that included health and safety on their agendas rose from 9 to 13 per cent; and those with individual health and safety representatives increased from 24 to 29 per cent. In private sector manufacturing it was joint health and safety committees that increased most markedly (from 32 to 41 per cent of workplaces); in private sector services the increase in health and safety representation was almost wholly a matter of individual representatives becoming more common (from 16 to 28 per cent). In the private sector as a whole, it was smaller workplaces and those without union recognition that showed the clearest increases in health and safety representation. This may well reflect the introduction of regulations in 1996,[21] which placed a new obligation on employers to consult employees directly or through elected representatives on health and safety matters affecting groups of employees not covered by trade union safety representatives.

Whatever the cause of recent changes, the stability that is evident since 1980 in the overall incidence of health and safety representation stands in contrast to the decline in our broader measure of employee representation over the same period.

Direct communication methods

So far in this chapter we have focused on methods of communication between employees and management which rely on employee representatives acting as intermediaries, methods often referred to as 'indirect participation'. We turn now to direct methods of communication between employees and management, but again concentrating on methods whereby employees, at least in principle, can make their concerns heard by management. Three arrangements, first asked about in our 1984 survey, provide the possibility of upward communication, from employees to management. These are as follows: regular meetings between senior managers and all sections of the workforce; regular meetings for teams or work-groups to discuss performance; and regular meetings between junior managers or supervisors and all the workers for whom they are responsible. Communication channels that essentially provide only for downward communication were discussed in Chapter 3.

Regular meetings between senior management and the workforce

The first of the three methods of upward communication we asked about was regular meetings, at least once a year, between senior managers and all sections of the workforce. Such meetings may, of course, offer little opportunity for genuine two-way communication, particularly when large numbers of employees are present, but we cannot rule it out on principle. They were reported in 34 per cent of workplaces in 1984 and 41 per cent in 1990 (Table 4.12). A somewhat similar question asked in the 1998 cross-section survey yielded a figure of 37 per cent, but the question was different in a number of respects and we decided that it was not a robust basis for comparisons. We therefore considered the evidence from our panel survey, where identical questions were asked in 1990 and 1998. Here the comparable figures for all continuing workplaces were 41 per cent in 1990 and 48 per cent in 1998. But before concluding that the use of these meetings had increased after 1990 we first checked to see whether workplaces that had joined the population between 1990 and 1998 had a different incidence of such meetings from other workplaces in the 1998 population on the basis of the rather different question

Table 4.12 Direct communication methods, 1984 to 1998

	Column percentages		
	1984	*1990*	*1998*
Regular meetings between management and workforce	34	41	48[a]
Problem-solving groups	..	35	49[a]
Briefing groups	36	48	65[b]
Weighted base	*1,999*	*1,997*	*1,995*
Unweighted base	*2,015*	*2,057*	*1,922*

Base: all establishments with 25 or more employees.

Notes
a 1998 estimate based on panel data. See text for further details.
b 1998 estimate based on combination of cross-section and panel data. See text for further details.

used in the 1998 cross-section survey. We found no overall differences (although new workplaces reported such meetings much more commonly than those that had grown above our twenty-five employee threshold). It therefore seemed reasonable to use the panel results as a proxy for the time series and conclude that meetings between senior managers and the whole of the workforce continued to become more widespread as a method of direct communication in the 1990s.

Looking at the results in more detail, it appeared that the increase since 1990 was predominantly a private sector phenomenon and was equally apparent whether there were recognized unions at the workplace or not. There was clearly an increase in workplaces without a functioning consultative committee or a workplace representative on a higher-level committee. However, in 1998 meetings of this kind were still more common where there was formal consultative machinery of this kind and where there was union representation.

Problem-solving groups

The second method of employee–management communication that we enquired about was regular meetings for work-groups or teams, at least once a month, to discuss aspects of performance, sometimes referred to as problem-solving groups or quality circles. Although such meetings are designed to be task-oriented, we presume that managements may find it difficult to maintain that restriction and that the meetings will often discuss matters of more general concern. The relevant question was first included in the survey in 1990 as part of a multi-response question with a showcard; in the 1998 cross-section survey it was the subject of an individual question and no mention was made of the frequency of meetings. Both these changes would tend to increase the proportion of positive responses. We therefore had some doubts about whether the recorded increase from 35 to 42 per cent of workplaces represented a real increase in this method of communication between 1990 and 1998. However, our panel survey, which used identical questioning in both years, showed a more substantial increase, from 36 to 49 per cent of continuing workplaces. Since leavers differed little from continuing workplaces in 1990 and joiners differed little from other workplaces in 1998 we judged that, here also, the estimate from our panel survey provided a more reliable comparison with the 1990 figure.

Based on the time-series results, the pattern of change was similar to that noted above for meetings involving the whole workforce. It was predominantly a private sector phenomenon and was equally apparent whether there were recognized unions at the workplace or not. There was clearly an increase in workplaces without a functioning consultative committee or a workplace representative on a higher-level committee. Yet in 1998, as in 1990, regular work-group meetings were more common where there was formal consultative machinery and where there was union representation.

Briefing groups

The third method of direct communication we asked about was regular meetings, at least once a month, between junior managers or supervisors and all the workers for whom they are responsible, sometimes known as 'briefing groups' or 'team briefing'. The question was identical between 1984 and 1990, but revamped in 1998; the focus of the 1998 question was more clearly about briefings than about meetings (which more clearly imply the possibility of upward communication). Nevertheless it is reasonable to infer, from the same combination of analyses that we performed for the previously mentioned method of communication, that the use of team briefing continued to become more widespread in the 1990s, as it had done in the late 1980s. The time-series results, with their uncertainties about question-wording changes between 1990 and 1998, showed overall proportions of 36 per cent in 1984, 48 per cent in 1990 and 53 per cent in 1998. In continuing workplaces, using identical questions, the proportion rose from 51 per cent in 1990 to 60 per cent in 1998. Joiners, both new workplaces and those rising above our twenty-five employee threshold, had notably high proportions at around 75 per cent. These figures suggest that the overall incidence of briefing groups in 1998 was nearer two thirds (Table 4.12).[22] This reinforces the conclusion that the practice of using briefing groups was spreading during the 1990s.

However, unlike the methods of communication discussed previously, the increase was entirely confined to private sector workplaces. The increase was also confined to workplaces without union representation and those without a functioning consultative committee.

In summary, we found that each of the three types of direct communication had become more prevalent over the 1990s. In each case, increases were most apparent in the private sector. However, it was notable that the incidence of two of the three types of communication – regular workforce meetings and problem-solving groups – had risen in the unionized sector as well as in non-union workplaces. In a later section, we shall examine the extent to which the growth of direct communication may have been used to circumvent union channels in such workplaces. We shall also examine the degree to which the growth of direct communication in the non-union sector served to enhance employees' access to voice across the whole economy. Before moving on, however, we look briefly at the durability of direct communication arrangements.

The durability of direct communication arrangements

The three methods of 'direct participation' discussed above are essentially practices that management may introduce or abandon at will. They may only be considered to provide repeated opportunities for employees to voice their views and concerns to management if they have some longevity. We tested this with our panel data by seeing what proportion of continuing workplaces that had each arrangement in 1990 also had it in 1998. The results showed that direct methods of participation were as durable as consultative committees. Three fifths (61 per cent) of workplaces that had workplace-wide meetings with management in 1990 also had them in 1998. The figures were a little higher for problem-solving groups (64 per cent) and for briefing groups (67 per cent). For functioning consultative committees the proportion was 60 per cent. But none of these practices provided as durable a channel of employee voice as trade union representation. For recognized trade unions the equivalent figure was 89 per cent. If direct participation has partially replaced trade union representation as a dominant form of employee voice, it has also involved the replacement of a durable form of voice with a less durable one.

An overall view of employee voice

In this final section we try to capture the essence of the foregoing analysis and provide an initial answer to the question we posed at the beginning of the chapter – have employees lost their voice? We do this by looking at summary variables that categorize workplaces according to the voice mechanisms available to employees. Naturally there are many ways of doing this, but we have chosen two which encapsulate the key distinctions made in policy debates and the research literature. The first distinguishes union from non-union voice mechanisms. The second distinguishes representative or collective voice (indirect participation) from individual voice (direct participation). The summary variables draw on information collected from all workplaces on the existence or non-existence of the following:

1 one or more recognized trade unions;
2 a functioning consultative committee with representatives chosen through union channels;
3 a functioning consultative committee with representatives not chosen through union channels;
4 regular meetings between senior management and the workforce;[23]
5 briefing groups;
6 problem-solving groups;
7 non-union employee representatives.

The surveys contain information on items 1 to 5 from 1984 onwards, but items 6 and 7 in 1990 and 1998 only. We look first at the longer-term changes in the incidence of union and non-union voice mechanisms using the first five items, categorizing items 1 and 2 as 'union voice' and items 3, 4 and 5 as 'non-union voice'.

Union versus non-union voice

The upper half of Table 4.13 shows the variation from 1984 to 1998 in the incidence of workplaces with union-only voice, union and non-union voice,

Table 4.13 Summary of union and non-union voice arrangements, 1984 to 1998

	Column percentages		
	1984	*1990*	*1998*
Type of voice arrangement (5 items)			
Union only	24	14	9
Union and non-union	42	39	33
Non-union only	16	28	40
Voice, but nature not reported	2	*	*
No voice	16	19	17
Weighted base	2,000	1,997	1,991
Unweighted base	2,019	2,059	1,920
Type of voice arrangement (7 items)			
Union only	..	11	6
Union and non-union	..	42	37
Non-union only	..	33	46
Voice, but nature not reported	..	*	*
No voice	..	14	11
Weighted base		1,996	1,995
Unweighted base		2,058	1,923

Base: all establishments with 25 or more employees.

solely non-union voice and no voice. Clearly the most marked change over the whole period was the steep decline in voice arrangements where trade unions formed the single channel of communication (union-only voice). In 1984, 24 per cent of workplaces had union-only voice arrangements, but this declined to 14 per cent in 1990 and to 9 per cent in 1998. There was also a less marked decline in 'dual channel' arrangements, where union and non-union channels existed alongside each other at the same workplaces. These two changes were offset, in numerical terms, by a steep increase in the incidence of voice arrangements that did not involve trade unions; the proportion of workplaces with such non-union voice rose from 16 per cent in 1984 to 40 per cent in 1998. Over the period as a whole, there was no significant change in the proportion of workplaces that had none of these arrangements, the figure remaining at about one in every six.[24]

We examined the changes within the three broad sectors of the economy and found that some were ubiquitous while others were not. The decline in union-only voice occurred in the public sector, private manufacturing and private services. The decline in dual-channel arrangements was confined to private services. The increase in solely non-union arrangements occurred in all three sectors. Workplaces with no employee voice arrangements showed the most variation across the sectors between 1984 and 1998: they remained negligible in the public sector; declined from 26 to 19 per cent of workplaces in private services; and increased from 21 to 35 per cent of workplaces in private manufacturing over the period. All these changes were clear trends, with 1990 having values intermediate between those for 1984 and 1998.

Besides broad sector we looked at the results in relation to size of workplace, size of organization, foreign ownership and various aspects of workforce composition. Each of these analyses showed that the decline in union-only voice affected all types of workplace. Similarly, the increase in non-union voice was evident in every type of workplace. The decline in dual-channel arrangements showed some variation, however. It appeared to be limited to the smallest workplaces and those that had male-dominated workforces. The decline was also greater among foreign-owned workplaces than among those under domestic ownership.

Workplaces without any employee voice arrangement, using this definition, were more common in 1998 in manufacturing than in services (especially the public sector), among smaller workplaces than larger ones, among single independent workplaces than among those that belonged to larger organizations, and in male-dominated than in female-dominated ones. Given the association with size of workplace, it is natural that the proportion of employees in workplaces without any voice arrangement was lower than the proportion of workplaces thus classified. In fact, 10 per cent of employees in 1998 were employed where there was no voice arrangement, a figure that was unchanged from the two previous surveys.

Our second and broader measure of the existence of voice arrangements encompassed all seven of the items listed earlier, adding problem-solving groups and non-union representatives to the non-union elements discussed in the foregoing paragraphs. As the lower half of Table 4.13 shows, the levels and changes for the period 1990 to 1998 are similar to those for the more restricted summary variable. Naturally it shows fewer workplaces having no voice mechanism – around one in ten workplaces. The change in the proportion with no voice mechanism, from 14 to 11 per cent, is on the borderline of statistical significance.

On this broader measure, the decline in union-only voice affected most sizes of workplace, those with male-dominated workforces and those without ethnic minority employees. Private manufacturing was more affected than private services or the public sector. The increase in solely non-union voice was confined to the private sector and mainly to small organizations, but it affected all sizes of workplace and both UK- and foreign-owned establishments alike. The decline in dual-channel arrangements was again apparent only in private services, but there were no clear patterns in relation to other workplace characteristics. Workplaces with no voice arrangements remained negligible in the public sector, declined from 20 to 13 per cent in private services and remained uncommon in manufacturing. Workplaces belonging to small organizations and UK-based companies were the ones that showed a clear fall in the proportion making no provision for employee voice.

Earlier in the chapter we spent some time examining how workplaces created at different historical periods had different propensities to recognize trade unions. Those contrasts are naturally reflected in the summary variable used here. But our summary variable on the different types of employee voice arrangement shows that the change was not simply a lower propensity to institute union-based channels of voice by recently created workplaces compared with their predecessors. A major shift to purely non-union forms of voice is equally apparent. Among workplaces in our 1990 survey that had been at their current address since before 1970, 14 per cent had union-only voice arrangements, 50 per cent had dual-channel, 25 per cent had solely non-union and 11 per cent had no voice arrangements. Among workplaces in our 1998 survey that had been operating at their current address since 1993 or later, only 2 per cent had union-only voice, 25 per cent had dual channel and 66 per cent had solely non-union arrangements. The proportion with no voice arrangements was similar. These figures suggest that the major switch from union to non-union voice involved stark differences between workplaces entering the population and those leaving it. We cannot assess this over the whole period of the WIRS series, but we can do so for the period 1990 to 1998 using our panel datasets.

The only significant difference between workplaces that left the population after 1990 and those that continued in existence through to 1998 was that leavers were more likely than continuing workplaces to have no voice arrangements (18 per cent compared with 11 per cent) (Table 4.14). Among the leavers, workplaces that closed down were indistinguishable from those that shrank to below our twenty-five employee threshold. Around a tenth of continuing workplaces had no voice arrangements in both years; and joiners were similar. So the slight drop between 1990 and 1998 in the extent of workplaces having no voice arrangements was due to the departure of workplaces, through closure or shrinkage, where this situation was more common.

The drop in the extent of union-only voice was largely because the majority of continuing workplaces with union-only voice in 1990 had switched from single-channel union representation to dual-channel voice arrangements in 1998. (Virtually none switched from dual-channel to union-only arrangements.) Otherwise, continuing workplaces maintained their voice arrangements within the four main categories identified in the table.

Workplaces entering the population between 1990 and 1998 differed markedly in two respects from continuing workplaces in 1998. They were much less likely to have dual-channel voice arrangements (and indeed any union voice); and they were much more likely to have solely non-union voice. So it was the different behaviour of joiners, and new workplaces in particular, that accounted for the overall increase in solely non-union voice arrangements between 1990 and 1998.

What specific types of arrangement had replaced union representation? We first examined our cross-section results to see which of the five types of non-union voice mechanism were used by the increasing number of workplaces with

Table 4.14 Summary of union and non-union voice arrangements in continuing
workplaces, leavers and joiners, 1990 and 1998

	Column percentages	
	Continuing workplaces	
	1990	*1998*
Type of voice arrangement (7 items)		
Union voice only	12	5
Union and non-union voice	45	51
Non-union voice only	33	34
Voice, but nature not reported	*	*
No voice	11	9
Weighted base	*881*	*881*
Unweighted base	*846*	*846*
	Leavers 1990–98	*Joiners 1990–98*
Type of voice arrangement (7 items)		
Union voice only	9	3
Union and non-union voice	42	28
Non-union voice only	31	56
Voice, but nature not reported	*	0
No voice	18	13
Weighted base	*560*	*604*
Unweighted base	*382*	*388*

Base: all continuing workplaces, leavers and joiners, as specified in column headings, 1990 to
1998.

solely non-union voice. Similar proportions in 1990 and 1998 had functioning
consultative committees (around a fifth), problem-solving groups (around two
fifths) and non-union employee representatives (around one tenth). However,
the proportion using workplace-wide meetings fell (from 55 to 43 per cent)
and the proportion using briefing groups increased (from 52 to 61 per cent).
Dual-channel arrangements also changed over this period. Among the minority
of workplaces with dual-channel voice arrangements there was a large shift
away from union-based representation on consultative committees to non-union
employee representatives on the committee. In this type of workplace, both
briefing groups and workplace-wide meetings became less common while
problem-solving groups became more common. But our clearest indicator
of how managements were changing the provisions they made for informing
and consulting employees came from our panel of continuing workplaces. Here
the most numerous group to have radically changed their arrangements were
the 8 per cent who had switched from union-only voice to having dual-channel
voice arrangements. Among these, about half had adopted workplace meetings,

half had adopted problem-solving groups and three quarters had adopted briefing groups.[25] By contrast, only a fifth had adopted joint consultative committees with representatives chosen independently of trade unions. Thus newly adopted voice arrangements among these workplaces were overwhelmingly forms of 'direct participation', rather than based on collective representation, or 'indirect participation'.

One might speculate whether, in some cases, the new methods of direct participation were principally brought in by management as a means of undermining union influence. We have no information on the reason for introducing direct arrangements alongside union channels. However, we found that, among continuing workplaces with union-only voice in 1990, the addition of direct forms of participation was just as likely among workplaces where management actively encouraged union membership as it was among those workplaces in which management gave no active encouragement to unionism. In 1998, around one third of the employers who had added direct forms of participation alongside union channels still actively encouraged employees to be union members. Hence, the undermining of union influence may have been a motive for some employers, but it was clearly not in many cases.

Here we have moved away from our categorization of union and non-union voice by introducing a different formulation that highlights direct participation. This is distinguished from collective forms of representation, which is broadly defined to include both union and non-union forms. It is to examine how voice arrangements have changed on this dimension that we now turn.

Representative versus direct participation

Our second broad way of characterizing employee voice arrangements distinguishes 'indirect participation' (representation by recognized unions or the existence of a functioning consultative committee in 1984, 1990 and 1998) from 'direct participation' (workplace-wide meetings or briefing groups for the same three surveys). For 1990 and 1998 comparisons we add in non-union representatives to the 'indirect' category and problem-solving groups to the 'direct' category. Since the alternative classification only involves regrouping the various forms of voice discussed above, the identification of workplaces with no voice mechanism whatsoever is identical and the changes in their incidence require no further comment. Table 4.15 categorizes workplaces according to whether they have the following: representative voice mechanisms only; both representative and direct voice; solely direct voice; or no voice mechanisms.

The overall picture is clearly of a major shift from representative to direct forms of voice. Between 1984 and 1998 the proportion of workplaces with only representative voice arrangements halved, while those with solely direct voice mechanisms more than doubled (upper half of Table 4.15). Workplaces with both forms of voice declined a little.[26]

Examining these changes by various establishment characteristics, we found that the decline in representative-only voice, occurring particularly between

Table 4.15 Summary of indirect and direct voice arrangements, 1984 to 1998

	1984	1990	1998
Type of voice arrangement (5 items)			
Representative only	29	18	14
Representative and direct	45	43	39
Direct only	11	20	30
Voice, but nature not reported	0	*	*
No voice	16	19	17
Weighted base	2,000	1,997	1,991
Unweighted base	2,019	2,059	1,920
Type of voice arrangement (7 items)			
Representative only	..	15	10
Representative and direct	..	48	46
Direct only	..	23	33
Voice, but nature not reported	..	*	*
No voice	..	14	11
Weighted base		1,996	1,995
Unweighted base		2,058	1,923

Base: all establishments with 25 or more employees.

1984 and 1990, affected both private and public sectors, all sizes of workplace and most types of workforce. However, it affected UK-rather than foreign-owned establishments. A notable exception to the general decline between 1990 and 1998 was workplaces with a tenth or more of their employees belonging to ethnic minorities; these had an increase in representative-only voice arrangements after a similar decline in the late 1980s. The increase in direct-only voice arrangements was confined to the services sector, was most apparent in smaller workplaces and occurred among most types of workforce.

Using our more comprehensive measure for 1990 to 1998, representative-only voice decreased, while direct-only voice increased substantially. Workplaces with both forms remained the most common, at just under half of all workplaces (lower half of Table 4.15). Most of the shift from indirect to direct participation took place in the private sector, with manufacturing establishments greatly reducing their use of representative-only voice and service sector workplaces increasing their use of direct-only voice. This shift was most apparent in workplaces belonging to small organizations and those with a UK parent company.

What specific practices were involved in these changing patterns of indirect and direct employee participation? We looked first at our cross-section results. These showed that the marked drop in representative-only arrangements was not simply a result of the fall in union recognition. Representative-only arrangements had also become less dependent on the presence of recognized trade unions and more dependent upon non-union representatives; the presence of these latter had increased from 6 per cent of workplaces with representative-only voice in 1990 to 19 per cent in 1998. The nature of direct-only voice had also changed. Workplace-wide meetings became less common, while briefing groups increased to become the most widely used of the three forms of direct participation that we asked about.

As with our earlier analysis, it was of interest to see how all these changes had occurred – particularly whether they involved changes in the practices used by continuing workplaces and the adoption of particular practices by new workplaces. Our panel of continuing workplaces certainly mirrored the time-series results by showing a drop in the use of representative-only voice. It also revealed that most cases where representative-only voice had disappeared had moved to dual-channel arrangements. Surprisingly, nearly a tenth of continuing workplaces had switched from having direct-only to dual-channel arrangements; the adoption of non-union representatives was the most common innovation for these cases. As with our earlier analysis, leavers were distinguished only in being less likely to have any voice arrangements. Joiners were very different from continuing workplaces in 1998. They were much less likely to have both representative and direct voice arrangements and much more likely to have solely direct participation.

The significance of all these changes depends, in part, on whether one subscribes to pluralist or unitarist social values. Many people regard representation at work to be a fundamental right and among them many believe that independent trade unions are the only legitimate channel of representation. Many others believe it is management's responsibility to choose what forms of information-sharing and consultation, if any, are appropriate to their circumstances. But the pragmatist might ask, does it make a difference? Do different voice arrangements make a difference to how employees view management, in terms of their responsiveness to employees' suggestions, dealing with work problems and at least giving them the chance to comment on proposed changes? We examine these relationships in the following section, drawing on the employee survey in WERS98.

Voice and employees' perceptions of management responsiveness and fairness

The 1998 survey of employees included a bank of questions that asked each employee to provide a rating, on a five-point scale from 'very poor' to 'very good', of how managers at their workplace were on five items relating to information provision, consultation and fair treatment. By combining the establishment-level indicators of the type of voice arrangements present in each workplace in 1998 with this employee data from the same establishments, we were able to investigate, using ordered probit analysis, whether employees' ratings were in any way related to the different types of voice available to them.[27]

Our analyses controlled for the size of the establishment, and of any wider organization of which it was part, in order to avoid any spurious relationship between particular types of voice and employee ratings that merely reflected the intervening effect of employees' distance from management.[28] Similarly, our analyses controlled for the climate of management–employee relations in each establishment, since a positive (or negative) relationship between a specific type of voice and employee ratings might simply reflect the fact that both commonly occurred in workplaces with good (poor) management–employee relations. Managers were excluded from the analyses and, in view of the relationships uncovered in our companion volume (Cully *et al.*, 1999: 175–80), we also took account of a variety of individual and job characteristics, such as the sex, age and normal weekly working hours of each employee.

The first of the five questions asked employees to rate how good managers at their workplace were at keeping the workforce up to date about proposed changes at the establishment. The associations between our dependent variable and our comprehensive categorization of union and non-union voice (that using seven items) are shown in the first column of Table 4.16. In this first analysis, we found that those arrangements which included some form of non-union voice yielded higher ratings than the reference category, 'no voice'. In other words, in establishments of the same size and with the same employee relations climate, similar employees with some type of non-union voice arrangement generally felt that managers were better at keeping them up to date with proposed changes at the establishment than did those employees in workplaces without any formal voice mechanism. This was true whether non-union arrangements were found in isolation or together with union channels of voice. Union-only arrangements did not hold the same association, however. In our analyses, employees working in establishments with solely union forms of voice rated managers no better at keeping the workforce up to date than did employees in workplaces without any formal voice mechanism.

The associations between this first dependent variable and our comprehensive categorization of representative and direct voice were identical to those shown for the union/non-union categorization. After controlling for establishment and employee characteristics, those arrangements incorporating some form of direct voice mechanism yielded higher ratings than the reference category, 'no voice', whilst the ratings among employees in workplaces with solely representative arrangements were no different.[29]

The second question in the bank of five asked employees to rate how good managers at their workplace were at providing everyone with the chance to comment on proposed changes. The same types of analyses were conducted, with identical results. Employees with some type of non-union voice arrangement gave managers a better rating than employees in workplaces with no voice mechanisms in place, whilst the ratings of employees in workplaces with solely union arrangements were no different. Exactly the same pattern emerged when the union/non-union categorization was replaced with that identifying representative and direct voice mechanisms.

Table 4.16 Type of voice arrangement and employees' perceptions of management's responsiveness and fairness, 1998

	How good would you say managers here are at:				
	Keeping everyone up to date about proposed changes	*Providing everyone with the chance to comment on proposed changes*	*Responding to suggestions from employees*	*Dealing with work problems you or others may have*	*Treating employees fairly*
Type of union/non-union voice arrangement (7 items)					
Union only	o	o	o	o	o
Union and non-union	+ + +	+ + +	+	o	+
Non-union only	+ + +	+ + +	+	o	o
(Ref. No voice)					
Number of observations	*19,157*	*18,876*	*18,524*	*18,916*	*19,014*

Base: non-managerial employees, in establishments with 25 or more employees overall.

Notes
Analysis conducted using ordered probit model. Each dependent variable coded on a five-point scale (very poor; poor; neither good nor poor; good; very good).
Control variables not shown in table: employee's rating of the quality of management–employee relations at the establishment (scale as per dependent variables); establishment size and organization size (number of employees); sex; hours worked per week; length of service at establishment; union membership status; broad occupational group; and age.
Reference category for voice variables is 'No voice' in each case.

Key for significance:
o   Not significantly different from the reference category.
+ (–)   Positive (negative) association, significant at the 90 per cent level of confidence.
++ (– –)   Positive (negative) association, significant at the 95 per cent level of confidence.
+++ (– – –) Positive (negative) association, significant at the 99 per cent level of confidence.

The results of these first two analyses suggest that managers were more likely to be perceived as proactive in consulting employees where there were non-union or direct voice arrangements in place. This may be because these arrangements are more likely to bring employees face to face with managers than representative structures, and so provide employees with more direct experience of managerial activity. It might also reflect differences across workplaces in the expectations that employees have of their managers. However, the differences may also say something about the nature of management in such workplaces. Since the responsibility for organizing and maintaining all of the direct arrangements we identify, and most of the non-union ones, lies primarily with management, the presence of such arrangements is an indication that management at the workplace are positively interested in communicating with their employees. That employees should then also perceive them as such is perhaps not surprising. Correspondingly, in workplaces with representative or union-only arrangements, the mechanisms of voice are more likely to have been initiated and organized by employees than by management. Managers in these workplaces may be less keen on extensive communication, tolerating the arrangements that exist but doing little to actively promote or respond to organized forms of expression from their workforce. This may help to explain why employees in such workplaces did not rate managers any higher on these first two questions than managers in workplaces where no voice mechanisms existed at all.

Whilst it is significant that managers in workplaces with non-union or direct voice arrangements were perceived to be relatively effective at informing and consulting employees, these first two questions tell us nothing about the subsequent reaction of the employer. It is arguably more important for the individual employee that managers respond in some way to issues that are raised. To examine this aspect of voice we turned to two more questions in the employee survey that more directly addressed the responsiveness of management. The third question asked employees to rate how good managers were at responding to employee suggestions. The fourth asked them to rate how good managers were at dealing with work problems.

In respect of the third question, concerning managers' responses to suggestions from employees, those mechanisms incorporating some non-union element were again shown to be associated with higher employee ratings than no voice, but at a lower level of statistical significance than was the case for the two earlier questions (90 per cent, compared with 99 per cent). We are therefore slightly less confident that this association would be found in the population as a whole. The associations with the representative/direct categorization were the same, except that dual-channel arrangements showed a positive association that was significant at the 95 per cent level.

These results showed that managers in workplaces with non-union and direct forms of voice were not only seen as more proactive in consulting employees, but were also seen to be more responsive to proposals from the workforce. However, in our analysis of the fourth question, relating to how well managers deal with work problems, none of the three formulations of union and non-union voice were found to be associated with better ratings than those given by employees in workplaces without any of the voice mechanisms included in our measures. Across our two categorizations of voice, the ratings given by employees with some form of voice were only higher than those given by 'voiceless' employees (at a 90 per cent level of significance) in workplaces with a combination of representative and direct participation.

This is the first sign that, when it comes to addressing problems, it may actually be the combination of arrangements that is important, rather than the simple presence of one type of voice or another. But what of the actual nature of the outcomes? Does the ability to speak out, or the channel that is used to do it, mean not only that managers hear issues and respond to them but also that their responses are more likely to be acceptable to the workforce?

For employees, the crucial test of 'voice' must surely be whether, overall, it helps to make their establishment a better place in which to work. There are many factors that could be included in any such investigation: pay; conditions of work; the quality of social relationships in the workplace. However, from the point of view of the workforce as a whole, one general measure is whether the expression of employee voice is associated with a greater degree of fairness on the part of management. As Hyman notes, a vital aspect of collective forms of representation is to limit employers' arbitrary authority (1997: 319). The fifth and final question that we consider examined precisely this issue, asking employees to rate how good managers at their workplace were at treating employees fairly.

The associations with our categorizations of voice were intriguing. On both categorizations of voice, we found that employees in workplaces with only one type of voice, whether union or non-union, representative or direct, rated managers no higher in terms of fairness than employees in workplaces without any of the specified voice mechanisms. Only those employees in workplaces with dual-channel arrangements gave higher ratings than 'voiceless' employees.[30]

The fact that both forms of dual-channel arrangement were found to be important in promoting fair treatment in the workplace is notable in itself. However, this result raised the further question of what lay behind this association. Was it the fact of having a combination of union and non-union, or representative and direct, voice that was critical? Or, alternatively, was the number of arrangements present in the workplace the significant factor, since investigation showed that those workplaces with dual-channel arrangements had a higher number of voice mechanisms, on average, than workplaces with only one type of arrangement?

In order to address this question, we repeated the analyses discussed above but, in each case, replaced the familiar categorizations of voice with variables that indicated the number of each type of practice present in the workplace. A third variable identified workplaces with dual-channel arrangements. As above, the union/non-union and representative/direct formulations were investigated separately.

The results of the analysis concerning union and non-union voice arrangements are presented in Table 4.17. The reader should note that in almost all cases (99 per cent), the presence of a single union arrangement equated to the presence of recognized unions, whilst the presence of two arrangements equated to the combined presence of recognized unions and union representation on a joint consultative committee. The first two rows of Table 4.17 will therefore be referred to in this way in the text that follows.

On the first two items, concerning the provision of information and consultation over changes at the workplace, our reformulated analyses of union and non-union arrangements confirmed that it was the presence of non-union

Table 4.17 Number and type of voice arrangements and employees' perceptions of management's responsiveness and fairness, 1998

	How good would you say managers here are at:				
	Keeping everyone up to date about proposed changes	*Providing everyone with the chance to comment on proposed changes*	*Responding to suggestions from employees*	*Dealing with work problems you or others may have*	*Treating employees fairly*
Number and type of voice arrangements					
One union arrangement	o	o	o	o	o
Two	o	+	o	o	+
(Ref. No union arrangements)					
One non-union arrangement	+ +	+ +	o	o	o
Two	+ + +	+ + +	+ +	+ +	o
Three	+ + +	+ + +	+ +	+	o
Four	+ + +	+ + +	o	o	o
Five	+ + +	+ + +	+ +	o	o
(Ref. No non-union arrangements)					
Combination of union and non-union arrangements	o	o	o	o	o
(Ref. Only one type of arrangement)					
Number of observations	*18,781*	*18,502*	*18,161*	*18,547*	*18,641*

Base: non-managerial employees, in establishments with 25 or more employees overall.

Notes
Analysis conducted using ordered probit model. Each dependent variable coded on a five-point scale (very poor; poor; neither good nor poor; good; very good).
Control variables not shown in table: employee's rating of the quality of management–employee relations at the establishment (scale as per dependent variables); establishment size and organization size (number of employees); sex; hours worked per week; length of service at establishment; union membership status; broad occupational group; and age.

Key for significance:
o   Not significantly different from the reference category.
+ (–)   Positive (negative) association, significant at the 90 per cent level of confidence.
+ + (– –)   Positive (negative) association, significant at the 95 per cent level of confidence.
+ + + (– – –)   Positive (negative) association, significant at the 99 per cent level of confidence.

and direct forms of voice that were associated with more favourable ratings from employees. Employees in workplaces with non-union arrangements gave higher ratings of their managers than employees in workplaces without such arrangements, irrespective of the number of non-union arrangements present. However, ratings were generally no higher among employees in workplaces with either type of union arrangement than among employees in workplaces without such mechanisms. The single exception was the positive association between the combined presence of recognized unions with union representation on a consultative committee and the ratings of management's provision of the opportunity to comment on change. The combined presence of union and non-union arrangements showed no independent association with the ratings given by employees.

The patterns that emerged from the analysis of representative and direct arrangements were generally the same, except that the number of representative arrangements was not significant in either analysis whilst the combination of representative and direct mechanisms did prove to be associated with higher ratings on the second item concerning consultation over proposed changes at the workplace.

There were fewer significant associations between our voice variables and employee ratings on the third and fourth items in Table 4.17. Yet, again, the number of non-union or direct forms of voice was found to have a significant, independent association with the ratings given by employees of their managers, whilst the number of union or representative arrangements had no such association. The only combination of arrangements to be independently associated with the ratings given was the combination of representative and direct mechanisms, and then only in respect of item three: responding to suggestions from employees.

The general pattern that emerged from our analyses of the first four items did not persist in our analysis of the fifth question, however. In relation to this fifth item, concerning the degree of fair treatment accorded by management at their workplace, the only type of arrangement found to be independently associated with the ratings of fair treatment given by employees, after controlling for other factors, was the combined presence of a recognized union and union representation on a consultative committee. None of the other types of voice, whether the presence of a recognized union or any number of non-union arrangements, representative arrangements or direct methods, or indeed the presence of dual-channel arrangements, were found to be significant.

It would therefore appear that it is the particular combination of union arrangements that lies behind the association shown in Table 4.16, rather than the presence of a high number of arrangements *per se* or of dual channels of voice. Moreover, the nature of the combination – union recognition and union representation on a consultative committee – suggests that the degree of union influence may well be the critical factor. Further research would be needed to confirm this. Nevertheless, whatever lies behind the association that has emerged here, the steady decline in the proportion of workplaces where employees have such an extensive form of union-oriented voice (13 per cent in 1980 and 1984, 10 per cent in 1990 and just 4 per cent in 1998) is significant. In comparison with the early 1980s and the beginning of the 1990s, fewer employees are now working in establishments where there are formal arrangements for the expression of employee voice that are positively associated with the degree of fairness exhibited by management.

Given that non-union forms of voice have become more common as workplace unionism has waned, it is particularly notable that even those employees in workplaces with high numbers of non-union arrangements rated managers no more favourably in terms of fairness than did employees in workplaces without any such arrangements. In his recent assessment of collective forms of representation in non-union firms, Terry remarked upon the apparent powerlessness of collective non-union representation (Terry, 1999: 28). He pointed, in particular, to the lack of legal protection afforded to non-union representatives when organizing opposition to their employer, suggesting that this must sometimes tempt non-union representatives into caution when their union counterparts might feel less inhibited. This argument would appear to gain support from our analyses.

In conclusion, this analysis of employee data suggests that formal voice mechanisms do help to promote communication in the workplace, as one might expect. However, the various forms of voice that we have identified seem to differ in their effectiveness. In particular, non-union or direct voice mechanisms may be more effective than union-related or representative forms of voice in enhancing the responsiveness (or apparent responsiveness) of management to specific employee issues. Yet, they appear to be less effective at promoting fair treatment for the workforce. Instead, it is the influence of the trade union that appears to be decisive in this regard.

Conclusions

We set out in this chapter to answer the question, 'have employees lost their voice?' The answer must be 'no' – but with important qualifications. The great majority of workplaces in 1998 had some form of communication channel between employees and managers through which employees could, at least in principle, express their views and concerns to management. This was also the case at the time of our earlier surveys in 1990 and 1984. But the nature of these channels of communication changed a great deal. There was a major shift from channels involving representatives, usually able to call upon the information and resources of independent trade unions, to channels where employees communicated directly with management, largely on occasions and on terms set by management themselves.

Comparing the results from 1998 with those of earlier surveys we saw a continuation of the widespread falls in trade union presence and aggregate membership density that had occurred during the 1980s. Membership declines in the private sector were particularly severe where there had been closed shops or very high density, but they were not confined to such circumstances. Fewer managements gave strong support to union membership, but, even where such support remained, fewer employees were members. There appeared to be a general withering of enthusiasm for union membership within continuing workplaces, especially in the private sector, and a lack of recruitment among new workplaces in both private and public sectors.

Our analysis of the extent of trade union recognition showed that it continued to be very widespread in the public sector and concentrated among large employers and workplaces in the private sector. But recognition in the private sector continued to fall in the 1990s, as it had done since 1984, reaching only 25 per cent of workplaces in 1998 – only half the level of 1980. Our analysis suggested that the propensity of employers to recognize trade unions had been in decline for a very long time, since well before the change of government in 1979.

By 1998, factors that had been strongly associated with union recognition at the start of our series – manufacturing rather than services, full-time work and manual employment – had ceased to be so. But few employers actively derecognized all existing unions at workplaces that continued in existence in the 1990s. It was the persistently lower rate of recognition among new workplaces (and those that grew from being very small) that fuelled the continuing decline in the proportion of workplaces with recognition.

We found that the other main channel for collective or representative voice – functioning joint consultative committees at workplace level – had also shown a further decline in the 1990s. Among continuing workplaces there was no tendency to substitute consultative committees for trade union representation. There was an increase in workplaces with non-union representatives over the period 1980 to 1998, but in overall terms the decline in collective voice was pervasive, involving union and non-union forms alike. Between 1984 and 1998 the proportion of workplaces with some union-based employee voice fell from 66 to 42 per cent; over the same period the proportion with (more broadly defined) collective voice fell from 74 to 53 per cent. Union-only arrangements experienced the sharpest decline.

Over this same period employers and managers substantially increased their use of communication channels that provided some opportunity for employees to express their views and concerns to management directly. Periodic meetings between managers and all employees and briefing groups were both methods of 'direct participation' which were more common in 1998 than in 1984, notably in the private sector. Briefing groups grew only where there was no collective representation.

Broadly these changes were such that similar numbers of workplaces in 1998 as in 1984 had some form of employee voice mechanism. Many workplaces continued to have dual arrangements. But there had been a major shift from collective, representative, indirect and union-based voice, to direct, non-union channels.

We made a preliminary assessment of the impact of these changes by analysing the relationships between the different types of voice arrangement available to employees at their workplace and employees' assessments of how managers responded to their suggestions and concerns. These analyses generally showed that having some form of voice mechanism increased the likelihood of employees giving high ratings to their management on keeping them up to date, giving them the chance to comment on changes, responding to their suggestions and dealing with work problems.

The ratings that were most relevant to managerial responsiveness were positively associated with having either non-union or direct voice mechanisms. However, we viewed managers' responsiveness to employees' suggestions as a partial indicator of the effectiveness of voice mechanisms. A clearer measure of at least one aspect of effectiveness was whether the resulting decisions were viewed as fair. On this criterion our analysis showed that the combined presence of a recognized trade union and union representation on a formal consultative committee was the only formulation to be independently associated with employees' perceptions of fair treatment by their managers. No other form of participation produced this effect.

Workplaces with this combination of arrangements became rarer over the course of our survey series, implying that, in some respects, employees in 1998 had a weaker voice than they did in earlier times.

We now move, in Chapter 5, to examine the strength of employee voice within the context of union representation, and return to the issue on a broader canvas in our final chapter.

5 Union recognition: a 'hollow shell'?

For two decades, British trade unions have been in decline. As we saw in the previous chapter, their membership has dropped continuously since the early 1980s and, since the mid-1980s, the number of employers recognizing them for collective bargaining has also fallen rapidly. Unions have thus generally lost influence, not only within the workplace, but also in the political domain (Smith and Morton, 1997). Within their traditional habitat – workplaces where managers accorded them recognition for collective bargaining – unions were suffering reductions in their bargaining agendas in the early 1980s (Millward and Stevens, 1986: 249–53). Whilst this did not persist in the second half of the decade (Millward et al., 1992), other issues became less subject to union influence. Most notably there was a fall in union wage differentials, reductions in bargaining power translating into a reduced share of available rents going to union members (Stewart, 1995). Other survey evidence spanning the period 1986 to 1992 showed that unions were having diminishing control over 'the pace of work, the internal deployment of labour, and recruitment' (Gallie and Rose, 1996: 47). Since then, union membership density has continued to fall where employers recognize unions, reflecting further decline in union organizational capacity (Cully and Woodland, 1998).

One commentator has gone as far as to say that collective bargaining 'may at times constitute a hollow shell' (Hyman, 1997: 318). Hyman argues that unions are increasingly 'dominated by the employer, with no independent represen-tation of workers' interests' (Hyman, 1997: 314). This situation, according to Hyman, reflects 'labour markets pervaded by insecurity, a restructured workforce and a profoundly hostile legal environment'. The implication is that employers are choosing to use the shift in bargaining power resulting from these changes to refashion their relationship with organized labour in the hope of regaining managerial prerogatives. There is evidence to support this contention. Gallie and colleagues (Gallie et al., 1998: 107) identify a 'hardening of employer attitudes to unions since the mid-1980s' in their survey data, and case studies have uncovered instances in which recognized unions are bypassed in managerial decision-making (Marchington and Parker, 1990; Darlington, 1994). The 1998 WERS results in our companion volume show more generally that managers in workplaces with recognized unions often prefer to deal directly with employees (Cully et al., 1999: 88).

Others, however, argue that unions can and do maintain substantial influence in the workplace, even in a neo-liberal climate. Employees still perceive unions as having an influence over pay, hours of work, and changes in working practices (Gallie *et al.*, 1998), despite a growing perception that they have 'too little power' (Bryson, 1999: 77). A closer look at existing evidence suggests that, within the overall picture of union decline, there is substantial variation in the degree to which unions have maintained influence in particular circumstances. Survey evidence indicates that, by 1990, unions' influence on workplace economic outcomes had become more conditional on their degree of organizational strength (Machin and Stewart, 1996), while recent case-study evidence from New Zealand suggests that union influence varies with the strategic choices unions make when engaging with employers (Boxall and Haynes, 1997).

Weakened unions are not necessarily in employers' best interests. The relationship between employer and union may be viewed as a pseudo-contractual one in which the employer (the 'principal' in the contract) engages with the union as its agent in reducing the cost of maintaining co-operation from the workforce and enforcing desired levels of worker effort. From this perspective, it makes little sense for employers to render unions ineffectual, since unions require influence if they are to deliver the co-operation of workers.

It is against this background that we consider the 'strength' of trade unions within workplaces continuing to recognize them for pay bargaining purposes. We begin with an analysis of union density in workplaces with recognized unions (which we shall refer to as 'unionized workplaces'). This section includes consideration of management support for unions through the closed shop and management recommendations of membership, as well as the incidence of 'check-off' arrangements for the payment of union dues. We turn to the worker side of the relationship with a consideration of the nature and number of union representatives. The second half of the chapter assesses a range of measures by which we can gauge the changing influence of unions in unionized workplaces over time. We begin this by considering some indicators of the way in which recognized unions participate in the joint regulation of the workplace through agreement to procedures and the appointment of employee representatives to consultative committees and health and safety committees. Next we review what has happened to the proportion of employees covered by collective agreements, and the scope of bargaining. Finally, we briefly consider the incidence of industrial action over time, before concluding.

Workplace union density

In the last chapter we spent some time analysing aggregate union density across workplaces, establishing how it had varied over time and across sectors, as a way of examining what has happened to employees' 'voice' since 1980. Here we consider workplace-level union membership density as a measure of union strength in workplaces recognizing unions. The influence the union wields in the workplace is likely to depend, in part, on the proportion of employees it can count among its members. An employer is more likely to listen to the union if the majority of employees back it than if the union represents only a minority voice – even if the employer has chosen to recognize the union (Cully *et al.*, 1999: 105–6). The proportion of employees it has in membership may also influence employees' perceptions of a union's legitimacy in representing their interests. A new employee may be more inclined to join the union if it already boasts majority membership.

A workplace's union density is the proportion of its employees who belong to a trade union. To obtain the average (mean) workplace union density among a given set of workplaces, we sum the percentage of employees in membership for each workplace, then divide by the number of workplaces. This is a different measure from the one we used in Chapter 4, aggregate union density, where we summed the members across a set of workplaces and then divided by the total number of employees in those same workplaces. Aggregate union density gives greater weight to larger workplaces because they contribute more employees. *Workplace* union density, on the other hand, gives equal weight to each workplace, regardless of size, and is therefore a more appropriate measure of union strength at the workplace level.

Mean union density declined markedly in workplaces with recognized unions over the 1980s and 1990s, but there was a sharp increase in the rate of decline in the 1990s (Table 5.1). Between 1984 and 1990, mean workplace union density fell from 72 to 68 per cent.[1] This is a small but statistically significant decline of 0.8 per cent per annum. By 1998 it had fallen to 56 per cent, the rate

Table 5.1 Workplace union membership density in workplaces with recognized unions, 1980 to 1998

| | *Column percentages* | | | |
	1980[a]	*1984*	*1990*	*1998*
0–24 per cent	6	8	9	18
25–49 per cent	8	14	14	21
50–74 per cent	19	22	29	29
75–89 per cent	20	18	20	16
90–99 per cent	19	19	16	11
100 per cent	28	19	13	4
Mean percentage	78	72	68	56
Weighted base	*1,129*	*1,129*	*934*	*818*
Unweighted base	*1,360*	*1,291*	*1,229*	*1,066*

Base: establishments with 25 or more employees where one or more unions recognized and where number of union members reported.

Note
a In 1980, figures refer to full-time employees only.

of decline trebling to 2.3 per cent per annum (Table 5.2, first row). Thus unionized workplaces typically experienced an accelerating loss of union membership.

Besides averages, another way of looking at union density is to examine how the proportion of workplaces with a given level of density has changed over time. This shows that the proportion with a low membership level increased in the 1990s after a period of stability. Between 1984 and 1990 the proportion of unionized workplaces with fewer than half the employees in union membership was roughly constant at just under a quarter. By 1998 it had risen to almost four in ten (39 per cent). At the other end of the scale, 100 per cent union membership fell in the late 1980s (from 19 to 13 per cent), and then collapsed in the 1990s when it fell to just 4 per cent of unionized workplaces.

Returning to mean density, in Table 5.2 we show how the trends in mean density differed across different types of workplace. (We discuss how they differed by types of union representation in later sections.) Across all seven industries for which we have statistically reliable figures, mean workplace union membership declined over the period of the survey series. In all but two (energy and water supply, and metal goods) the rate of decline was faster in the 1990s than in the 1980s.[2] Distribution, hotels and catering – traditionally the industry with the lowest union membership density – witnessed the biggest decline, with mean workplace union density halving between 1984 and 1998.

As well as being much more likely to recognize unions, public sector workplaces have had higher union density than workplaces in the private sector since 1984. Within the private sector, manufacturing workplaces have been more likely to recognize unions than service sector workplaces. They also have higher membership density where they do recognize unions. Furthermore, membership density rates declined much more rapidly in private services during the 1990s, when compared to rates of decline in unionized workplaces in private manufacturing and the public sector, thus widening the difference that existed earlier. In fact, the mean union density rate in private service workplaces declined by a third between 1990 and 1998, from 62 to 42 per cent. The equivalent 1998 figures for the public sector and private manufacturing were 64 per cent and 55 per cent respectively.

However, the relatively small change in mean density in private manu-facturing during the 1990s disguises very significant shifts in the distribution, not least among highly unionized workplaces. The proportion of private manufacturing workplaces that recognized unions and had union membership rates of 90 per cent or more declined from 17 per cent in 1990 to 6 per cent in 1998. Low density rates affected an increasing proportion of private service sector workplaces. Whereas under a third (29 per cent) of unionized private service workplaces had membership density rates below a half in 1990, this had doubled by 1998 to 62 per cent.

More detailed analysis showed that patterns of change differed significantly within the unionized public sector. In the second half of the 1980s, mean workplace union density dropped markedly in central and local government,

Table 5.2 Mean workplace union membership density in workplaces with recognized unions, 1980 to 1998

	Mean percentage				Percentage	
	Workplace union membership density				Average annual percentage change	
	1980[a]	1984	1990	1998	1984–90	1990–98
All workplaces	78	72	68	56	–0.8	–2.3
Industry (SIC 1980)						
Energy and water supply	89	92	79	75	–2.3	–0.7
Extraction of minerals/ores; manufacture of metals, minerals and chemicals	68	68	62	(69)	–1.4	(1.4)
Metal goods, engineering and vehicles industries	69	67	62	58	–1.3	–0.9
Other manufacturing industries	70	63	63	50	–0.1	–2.6
Construction	67	(42)	(71)	(42)	(11.6)	(–5.5)
Distribution, hotels and catering, repairs	76	60	48	31	–3.5	–4.6
Transport and communications	94	86	83	73	–0.6	–1.6
Banking, finance, insurance, business services and leasing	79	73	75	56	0.4	–3.4
Other services	83	76	71	60	–1.0	–2.1
Sector						
Public sector	86	80	75	64	–0.9	–1.9
Private manufacturing	69	65	62	55	–0.7	–1.4
Private services	74	60	62	42	0.5	–4.4
Ownership						
Single independent	63	55	60	33	1.5	–6.0
Part of larger organization	80	74	69	60	–1.0	–1.8
UK owned	71	63	63	45	–0.1	–1.8
Foreign owned	75	56	55	56	–0.2	0.3
Size of establishment						
25–49	80	72	68	56	–0.9	–2.3
50–99	75	69	67	60	–0.6	–1.4
100–199	76	71	69	54	–0.3	–3.0
200–499	80	77	70	55	–1.4	–3.0
500 or more	81	79	71	53	–1.7	–3.3
Proportion of employees that work part-time						
None	80	75	79	63	0.9	–2.7
1–24 per cent	75	71	67	59	–0.9	–1.6
25 per cent or more	83	71	66	53	–1.3	–2.6

Table 5.2 continued

	Mean percentage				Percentage	
	Workplace union membership density				Average annual percentage change	
	1980[a]	1984	1990	1998	1984–90	1990–98
Proportion of employees that are female						
0–24 per cent	79	74	73	64	–0.1	–1.6
25–74 per cent	72	70	64	51	–1.5	–2.6
75 per cent or more	86	69	69	57	–0.1	–2.4
Proportion of employees that are non-manual						
0–24 per cent	81	74	72	61	–0.6	–2.0
25–74 per cent	75	69	64	54	–1.1	–2.2
75 per cent or more	79	73	69	56	–1.0	–2.4

Base: establishments with 25 or more employees where one or more unions recognized and where number of union members reported.

Note

a In 1980, figures refer to full time employees only.

at an annual rate of 2.6 percentage points. Over the same time, it increased in the health sector at an annual rate of 1.6 percentage points. In the 1990s, the situation stabilized in central and local government, but the other parts of the public sector all experienced falling membership rates. It was in the health sector, which has undergone considerable organizational change in the 1990s following the introduction of NHS Trusts, that membership decline was most rapid. Its annual rate of membership decline of 4.5 per cent between 1990 and 1998 puts it on a par with the decline in private services.

Mean workplace membership density remained stable in unionized single independent workplaces between 1984 and 1990, at a time when it was falling among unionized workplaces belonging to larger organizations. However, this was followed by a seven-to-eight-year period in which mean union density almost halved among single independent workplaces recognizing unions. The fall from 60 per cent to 33 per cent is equivalent to a 6 per cent drop per annum – over three times the rate experienced by unionized workplaces belonging to larger organizations. It is also notable that the decline in the 1990s was wholly confined to UK-owned workplaces (which include those owned 50/50 with foreign organizations). These findings suggest that ownership became a more influential factor in determining union membership rates in the 1990s.

Traditionally, unions have found recruitment more difficult in workplaces with large proportions of part-time workers. This is reflected in the persistently lower mean union density rates presented in Table 5.2 in workplaces where at least a quarter of the workforce were part-timers. However, there was no association between the proportion of part-timers in the workplace and the rate of decline in membership density.

Workplaces have also tended to have lower membership rates where they employ a high proportion of non-manual workers and high proportions of women. Membership density has fallen less sharply in unionized workplaces with higher proportions of male employees, particularly in the 1990s. However, although rates of decline in union membership appear lower in workplaces with fewer non-manual workers, the difference is not statistically significant.

This analysis suggests that workplaces where unions were already weak (private services generally and distribution, hotels and catering in particular, and single independent workplaces) experienced the greatest declines in workplace union density since 1984. But what lies behind these changes? Do they reflect the changing composition of workplaces, or changed behaviour among continuing workplaces? To answer this question we turn to our panel.

Panel analysis

To understand what lies behind the cross-sectional change in union density among workplaces recognizing unions, it is worth noting the relative incidence of continuing workplaces, 'joiners' and 'leavers' within the sample of unionized workplaces. In 1990, continuing workplaces made up almost two thirds (63 per cent) of workplaces that recognized unions. The remainder were workplaces that were to leave the survey population before 1998, either because they had closed down or fallen below our twenty-five employee threshold. In 1998, continuing workplaces accounted for almost three quarters (73 per cent) of unionized workplaces. Joiners, which were either new workplaces or those growing above the twenty-five employee threshold, made up the remainder.

In 1990, there was a close correspondence between mean workplace union density in the cross-sectional data and union density in the sub-sample of continuing workplaces (Table 5.3). By 1998, although the mean membership rate had fallen among continuing workplaces, mean density in the 1998 cross-section was much lower (56 per cent compared to 66 per cent among continuous workplaces). There were two reasons for this. First, there was a substantial decline in union density among continuing workplaces in the unionized private sector (falling from 62 per cent to 56 per cent). Second, mean membership rates were much lower among unionized workplaces joining both the public and private sectors in 1998. In the public sector joiners had somewhat lower mean density than continuing workplaces in 1998 (63 per cent compared with 73 per cent). In the private sector the contrast was greater (41 per cent compared with 56 per cent). So the decline in workplace union density among unionized workplaces can be attributed to a decline in membership rates among continuing workplaces in the private sector, coupled with lower membership rates among joiners to both the public and private sectors.

Table 5.3 Comparison of union density in workplaces with recognized unions, using cross-section and panel data, 1990 and 1998

	Cell percentages			
	Cross-section	Continuing workplaces	Joiners	Leavers
All establishments				
1990	68	70	..	67
1998	56	66	54	..
Public sector				
1990	75	75	..	75
1998	64	73	63	..
Private sector				
1990	62	62	..	63
1998	46	56	41	..

Base: all establishments with 25 or more employees where recognized trade unions and number of union members reported.

In both the public and private sectors leavers were no different from workplaces that had continued in operation, so compositional change arose purely from the fact that joiners had lower densities.

In summary, union strength, as measured by the mean membership density among workplaces with recognized unions, fell significantly between 1990 and 1998. In the public sector this arose almost entirely through compositional change because joiners had lower density than leavers. In the private sector it occurred through that same source, but also because mean density fell substantially among continuing workplaces.

Management support for unions

Where employers are at liberty to choose whether they recognize trade unions, unions are heavily reliant on the support, or at least the acquiescence, of management, to conduct their business in representing members. A statutory recognition procedure will replace this 'voluntarist' framework for the first time since the 1970s when the provisions of the Employment Relations Act come into force (Wood and Godard, 1999). However, the 'voluntarist' framework has been in place throughout our survey series.

Employees in workplaces with recognized unions perceive their managers to be less supportive of union membership than they were a decade ago (Bryson, 1999). Some commentators have suspected for some time that this apparent change in management's attitudes towards union membership has been responsible for the demise of trade unions and declining membership rates where unions continue to be recognized. They have argued that many employers have taken advantage of a perceived shift in power at the workplace from workers to managers to refashion their relationship with organized labour (Poole and Mansfield, 1993: 30). We briefly examine, therefore, the WIRS evidence on managerial support for unions to see what bearing this has on the falls in membership density discussed above.

Throughout the survey series we have asked managers whether any employees have to be members of a union to get or keep their jobs and whether new recruits have to be union members before they start work: such workplaces are said to operate a 'closed shop'. Since 1984, we have also asked whether management strongly recommends that all or some of their workers should be union members. Although the format of the questions has altered somewhat during the course of the series, we do not think that this affects the trends presented in Table 5.4.[3] The closed shop has been in decline in the unionized sector since the beginning of the 1980s, partly due to successive legal restrictions imposed on the practice over the period.[4] Between 1980 and 1990, the proportion of unionized workplaces with a closed shop fell from 36 to 8 per cent. However, despite the final legislative moves that made the closed shop unlawful from 1991 onwards, 2 per cent of workplaces recognizing unions were maintaining a closed shop in 1998. They were most in evidence in private manufacturing, where 7 per cent of workplaces recognizing unions had a closed shop. The only industry with a sizeable closed shop presence was the metal goods, engineering and vehicle manufacturing industry: in 1998, 13 per cent of managers in unionized workplaces in this sector said a closed shop operated for at least some of the workers. The pre-entry closed shop had virtually disappeared: they were reported in fewer than 1 per cent of unionized workplaces in 1998.

It was not quite the same story when it came to management strongly recommending union membership. Between 1984 and 1990 there was a marginal increase in the proportion of unionized workplaces in which management strongly recommended union membership, an increase discernible in all three broad sectors of the economy. As noted elsewhere (Wright, 1996), such endorsement may not differ substantially in practice from closed shop arrangements, although closed shop arrangements are more likely to appear in written agreements. It is possible that, in anticipating the anti-closed shop legislation of 1990, some managements matched their abolition of a formal closed shop with continuing strong support for union membership. In fact, Wright (1996: 508) presents WIRS panel evidence for the period 1984–90 that is consistent with this hypothesis. This change of form was not apparent in the 1990s. The further decline in the closed shop after 1990 accompanied a fall in the proportion of workplaces where management strongly recommended union membership. Between 1990 and 1998 the proportion of private sector unionized workplaces where management gave such a recommendation to their staff fell by almost three quarters, from 25 per cent to just 7 per cent. The fall of a quarter in the public sector was less dramatic. By 1998, a third of public sector unionized workplaces still strongly recommended union membership. So, whereas public sector workplaces made up 60 per cent of

Table 5.4 Incidence of the closed shop and management endorsement of union membership in workplaces with recognized unions, by broad sector, 1980 to 1998

	Cell percentages			
	1980[a]	1984	1990[b]	1998
All establishments				
Closed shop	36	28	8	2
Strong recommendation	..	30	34	21
Weighted base	1,271	1,320	1,013	842
Unweighted base	1,570	1,585	1,368	1,113
Private manufacturing				
Closed shop	46	33	15	7
Strong recommendation	..	22	29	7
Weighted base	327	235	183	102
Unweighted base	605	469	436	158
Private services				
Closed shop	38	27	7	1
Strong recommendation	..	22	25	7
Weighted base	351	368	340	253
Unweighted base	288	297	360	396
Public sector				
Closed shop	29	26	5	1
Strong recommendation	..	37	42	32
Weighted base	594	717	490	488
Unweighted base	677	819	572	559

Base: all establishments with 25 or more employees where recognized trade unions.

Notes
a Information on whether management strongly recommended union membership was not collected in 1980.
b Missing data only affected a small number of cases in all years except 1990 when, due to a design fault in the questionnaire, 102 unweighted cases were inadvertently not asked the question. In 1990 a further 34 cases did not answer the question.

unionized workplaces strongly recommending union membership in 1990, this had risen to 86 per cent in 1998.

Further investigation revealed that the collapse in management support for unions did not apply to all types of workplace recognizing unions. Among workplaces recognizing four or more unions, the proportion strongly recommending union membership rose from 42 per cent in 1990 to 47 per cent in 1998. This offset the decline in the incidence of closed shops among these workplaces, which fell from 9 per cent to 3 per cent. Both types of support for unions declined among workplaces recognizing up to three unions. The difference was maintained when controlling for the relationship between size of workplace and number of recognized unions. In fact, perhaps surprisingly, the biggest collapse in management support came in larger unionized workplaces. Between 1990 and 1998, the proportion of unionized workplaces with at least 500 employees in which management gave a strong recommendation of union membership fell from 45 per cent to 8 per cent. This reversed the increase from 33 per cent to 45 per cent between 1984 and 1990. By contrast, such support of union membership remained constant among the smallest unionized workplaces (with fewer than 50 employees): 30 per cent strongly recommended union membership in 1998, compared with 34 per cent in 1990, and 31 per cent in 1984.

The decline in the incidence of the closed shop among continuing workplaces was similar to that shown by our cross-section results. Seven per cent of continuing workplaces recognizing unions in 1990 had a closed shop; this fell to 3 per cent by 1998. But part of the closed shop's demise was also due to the turnover of workplaces in our sample. The incidence of the closed shop was relatively high among unionized leavers at 10 per cent, whereas only 2 per cent of joiners recognizing unions had a closed shop. Among new workplaces, the figure was 1 per cent. However, since continuing workplaces dominated the population of unionized workplaces during the period, the major source of change was the withdrawal of closed shop arrangements in continuing workplaces.

Not all the changes observed in continuing workplaces were in the same direction, however. Two per cent of unionized continuing workplaces had actually introduced a closed shop since 1990. Nearly all were branches of larger organizations. But more common was the situation where closed shops had ceased to operate. This occurred in 6 per cent of continuing unionized workplaces. In these cases, managers were asked the reason for the change; half cited a change of management approach or policy, while four in ten referred to changes in legislation. Equally interesting are the very few cases, all in the private sector, where a closed shop continued to operate. Asked why they had kept their closed shops, their answers included 'we've never thought of taking the union on to change it' and 'we see no reason to change it'. Others simply said 'it's still the union rules'. These responses illustrate that, in rare circumstances, workplace trade union organization may still be sufficiently strong to maintain a *de facto* closed shop, despite the lack of legal underpinning for the arrangement.

Turning to the strong recommendation of union membership among continuing workplaces, the proportion of unionized workplaces where management gave such support to membership fell from 37 per cent in 1990 to 30 per cent in 1998. In the majority of cases (67 per cent) where closed shops ceased to operate, management was not recommending union membership either. So, management support for unions in the form of a closed shop or a strong recommendation fell from 44 per cent of continuing unionized workplaces in 1990 to 33 per cent in 1998.

Among joiners, the figure was 26 per cent in 1998, but only 9 per cent among new workplaces compared to 41 per cent among 'growers'. Where joiners

did recommend union membership, they were almost invariably p
sector workplaces: only 5 per cent of the unionized workplaces recommending
union membership among joiners in 1998 were private sector workplaces. So
behavioural change among continuing unionized workplaces and the practices
of new and growing workplaces both contributed to dwindling managerial
support for unions where they continued to operate during the 1990s.

Managerial attitudes to unions and workplace union density

What, then, are the implications of these changes for union strength at the
workplace? To establish this, we consider patterns of workplace union density
across unionized workplaces, differentiating between workplaces with a closed
shop, those in which management strongly recommended union membership,
and those with no such support for unions.

In both 1984 and 1990, there was a clear ranking of workplace union
membership rates across these three types of unionized workplace (Table
5.5). Workplace union density was highest in workplaces with closed shops,
followed by those where management strongly recommended union membership. Unionized workplaces with no management support on these measures
had the lowest union density rates in this period. Mean union density declined
marginally where management supported unions, and there was actually an
increase in mean density where there was no closed shop or management
recommendation. Between 1990 and 1998 a great deal changed. Workplace
union density declined markedly across all three types of unionized workplace
in the 1990s. The sharp decline in membership among workplaces in which
managers recommended union membership is another reminder of what

Table 5.5 Workplace union density by union membership arrangements in
workplaces with recognized unions, 1984 to 1998

| | *Column percentages and mean percentages* | | | | | | | | |
| | *Closed shop* | | | *Strong recommendation* | | | *Neither* | | |
	1984	*1990*	*1998*	*1984*	*1990*	*1998*	*1984*	*1990*	*1998*
0–49 per cent	7	6	(23)	10	13	24	44	30	44
50–89 per cent	30	45	(71)	47	47	58	42	50	41
90–99 per cent	24	19	(3)	25	21	14	11	12	11
100 per cent	39	30	(2)	19	18	5	4	8	4
Mean	87	84	(61)	79	77	68	55	62	53
Weighted base	*337*	*68*	*(17)*	*331*	*321*	*176*	*458*	*514*	*623*
Unweighted base	*494*	*86*	*(23)*	*392*	*488*	*138*	*402*	*615*	*903*

Base: all establishments with 25 or more employees where recognized trade unions.

we learned in Chapter 4, namely that even in this environment, employees appeared to have lost their appetite for unionism. Where management strongly recommended membership, the proportion of workplaces with 90 per cent or more of their employees in membership halved from 39 per cent to 19 per cent.

As we showed in Table 5.1, the proportion of unionized workplaces with 100 per cent membership declined throughout the survey series. However, Table 5.5 shows that, with the demise of the closed shop, the association between the presence of the closed shop and 100 per cent membership diminished over the period. Whereas closed shop workplaces accounted for 61 per cent of unionized workplaces with 100 per cent membership in 1984, this fell to 17 per cent in 1990, and just 1 per cent in 1998.

We used shift-share analysis to quantify the relative importance for the overall level of union density of change in the incidence of closed shops and management recommendation of membership and changes in density where different levels of support for membership were present. First, we calculated what the overall mean union density would have been in 1990 if the incidence of the closed shop and management recommendation had remained at its 1984 level, but mean union density had changed within these categories. The change in mean union density within these categories would, alone, have resulted in an *increase* in mean union density of 2 percentage points, from 72 per cent to 74 per cent. This is because of the rise in mean density among unionized workplaces without either a closed shop or strong management endorsement of union membership. We then calculated what the overall mean union density would have been in 1990 if mean density across these types of workplace had remained constant at its 1984 level, but changes in the incidence of closed shops and strong managerial encouragement had occurred. The changing composition of the unionized population would have resulted in a mean union density of 66 per cent, some 6 percentage points lower than the actual mean observed in 1984. Mean union density among unionized workplaces actually fell from 72 per cent in 1984 to 68 per cent in 1990. This indicates that the decline in the closed shop and strong management endorsement of membership were the main reasons for the fall in mean union density in unionized workplaces between 1984 and 1990, with the effect being ameliorated somewhat by changes in mean union density within these categories over the period.

However, it does not appear that the fall in density came about as a result of progressive restrictions on the closed shop acting to free large numbers of employees from involuntary union membership. Evidence from the 1984–90 panel of trading sector workplaces showed that, in 1984, the mean density among manual workers in workplaces with a closed shop was 99 per cent. In 1990, by which time such arrangements had been largely abandoned, the mean density in these same workplaces was still very high, at 93 per cent (Millward *et al.*, 1992: 98–101). More important in the late 1980s, it seems, was the broader effect of the closed shop legislation and other reforms in dissuading management from giving encouragement to union membership.

The picture was quite different for the period 1990 to 1998. Shift-share analysis revealed that about three quarters of the decline in mean union density in this period arose from changes in density *within* the three types of unionized workplaces (those that operated a closed shop, those in which management gave strong endorsement and those where neither type of support was present). Only around a quarter arose from changes in the incidence of the closed shop and strong recommendation by management. Thus, around 10 percentage points of the 12–13 percentage point drop in mean union density over the period 1990–98 can be attributed to a reduced propensity among employees to join trade unions, even when encouraged to do so. Unions had not only lost the support of managers but, as stated above, it was clear that, in the 1990s, they had also lost the support of many employees.

The check-off system

Our second measure of how management might support workplace union membership was their operation of check-off arrangements, deducting union subscriptions from pay. This practice became increasingly common in the 1980s among workplaces recognizing unions. In 1980, three quarters (73 per cent) had such an arrangement. This rose to four fifths (80 per cent) in 1984 and 86 per cent in 1990. However, the trend was reversed in the 1990s so that, by 1998, 75 per cent of workplaces with recognized unions had check-off. The decline in check-off in the 1990s was not a universal phenomenon. Although it was apparent in private services and the public sector, check-off actually became much more common in private manufacturing. Whereas 77 per cent of manufacturing workplaces with recognized unions had check-off in 1990, this rose to 93 per cent in 1998.

In 1993, check-off arrangements became subject to individual authorization by union members every three years.[5] This legislative change may have contributed to the overall decline in check-off between 1990 and 1998, since joiners with recognized unions were much less likely to have check-off arrangements: 73 per cent had them. Analysis of the panel suggests that behavioural change within continuing workplaces did not contribute to the decline significantly. Check-off was present in 88 per cent of continuing workplaces in 1990,[6] and in 86 per cent in 1998. Ninety-one per cent of those who had it in 1990 still had it in 1998, confirming some academics' expectations that the legislation would only have a modest impact on established check-off practices (Atkinson and Hillage, 1994). Although the numbers are small, the panel suggests that those unionized workplaces losing check-off between 1990 and 1998 were more likely to suffer a reduction in union density. Union density fell by at least 10 percentage points among half those who lost check-off between 1990 and 1998, compared to a third of those with check-off in both years, and a quarter among those newly acquiring check-off.

This section clearly shows that union density has been falling in unionized workplaces since 1984, and that this decline accelerated in the 1990s. Workplaces where unions were already weak experienced the greatest declines. The reasons for the decline changed over the period. During the 1980s, the fall in union membership density was largely attributable to the decline in management support for union membership. However, in the 1990s, the continued decline in management support played only a minor role in the accelerating decline in union density. Instead, three quarters of the decline in mean union density in the 1990s is attributable to behavioural shifts in unionized workplaces. A reduced appetite for union membership among employees appears to us the most likely explanation for the more recent period.

The nature of union representation

The decline in union density since 1984 is strong evidence in support of the 'hollow shell' hypothesis. Now we turn to our second main indicator for assessing the 'hollow shell' thesis – the presence of a trade union representative at a workplace, a clearly visible indicator of trade union organizational strength on the ground. Union representatives operate as a channel for communication between local membership and management, assisting in the resolution of disputes and grievances (Cully *et al.*, 1999: 201–3). They may assist in the joint regulation of the workplace through negotiation over the form and content of formal procedures (an issue discussed in the next section). As we saw in the last chapter, their presence ensures more effective worker 'voice'. They can also form the basis for more complex forms of union organization such as committees of representatives. So what has happened to union representation in unionized workplaces over the course of the series gives an indication of the organizational capacity or organizational strength of unions at grassroots level.

As we noted in Chapter 4, on-site representation by shop stewards or other lay union representatives became less common in unionized workplaces over the course of our survey series. This decline occurred during the latter half of the 1980s (Table 5.6). Between 1984 and 1990 the proportion of unionized workplaces with on-site representatives fell from 82 per cent to 71 per cent, but there was no further fall in the 1990s. Although the incidence of union representatives varied markedly across the three broad sectors of the economy, each sector experienced this same pattern of change. Analysis by size of workplace reveals that the decline in the incidence of on-site union representatives arose almost exclusively from the lower incidence of union representatives among smaller workplaces with fewer than 100 employees. The incidence of on-site union representatives has remained roughly constant among larger workplaces since the beginning of the series in 1980.

Although there was stability in the incidence of local union representation during the 1990s in the unionized sector as a whole, the decline in union representation continued into the 1990s in some workplaces where unions were traditionally strong. The decline was particularly sharp among workplaces

Table 5.6 Presence of union representatives in workplaces with recognized unions, 1980 to 1998

	Cell percentages			
	1980[a][b]	1984[b]	1990	1998
Any on-site union representatives	78	82	71	72
Full-time union representatives	3	3	2	4
Presence of on-site representatives:				
Broad sector				
Private manufacturing	85	98	90	93
Private services	68	67	57	58
Public sector	81	84	73	74
Ownership				
Single independent establishment	73	82	66	62
Branch of larger organization	79	82	71	73
Workplace size				
25–49 employees	67	75	59	60
50–99 employees	81	83	70	70
100–199 employees	87	89	87	85
200–499 employees	97	95	92	91
500+ employees	97	93	94	94
Number of recognized unions				
1–3	..	..	66	70
4 or more	..	..	88	78
Management support				
Closed shop	83	85	74	(93)
Strong management recommendation of union membership	..	87	82	73
No support	..	76	65	70

Base: all establishments with 25 or more employees where recognized trade unions.

Notes
a Information on whether management strongly recommended union membership was not collected in 1980.
b In 1980 and 1984 information on manual and non-manual unions was collected in separate sections of the questionnaire. Combining these data may result in 'double counting' some unions. Since we cannot estimate the extent of this problem we have not presented figures for these two years.

recognizing four or more unions, and in workplaces where management strongly recommended union membership.

Full-time lay union representatives (not to be confused with full-time union officials) are a strong indication that management regards the role of the union as of central importance. As Table 5.6 shows, full-time representatives were always rare among workplaces with recognized unions and have remained so. The change between 1990 and 1998 from 2 to 4 per cent is on the margin of statistical significance. This result may best be interpreted as showing that full-time lay representatives became no rarer in the 1990s in unionized workplaces than they were in the 1980s.

Our panel data confirmed the relative stability in the incidence of on-site union representatives among unionized workplaces between 1990 and 1998. In 1998, 79 per cent of such continuing workplaces had on-site union representatives, compared to 80 per cent in 1990.[7] In 70 per cent of cases, unionized panel workplaces had on-site representatives in both 1990 and 1998. In a further 11 per cent of cases they had no representation in each year. In only one fifth of cases had they switched status, with 11 per cent losing a representative by 1998, and 9 per cent gaining one.

Examination of the leavers and joiners in our panel datasets suggested that on-site union representation was rarer among workplaces whose workforce has recently grown above or shrunk below our twenty-five employee threshold. We investigated this possible association further by looking at change in union representation by changes in workforce size among the continuing workplaces that recognized unions in both 1990 and 1998. We found a significant association between increases (decreases) in the number of employees and an increased (decreased) likelihood of union representation. Unionized workplaces that had grown were much more likely to have acquired an on-site union representative than other workplaces. Conversely, those that had shrunk were much more likely to have lost on-site union representatives than other unionized workplaces.

If unions were losing their organizational strength in the 1990s, then we might have anticipated a continuation in the decline of on-site representation that had begun in the latter half of the 1980s. In fact, evidence from the 1998 cross-section and our 1990–98 panel clearly indicates that on-site representation stabilized in the 1990s.

The number of union representatives at the workplace

The extent to which union members can be organized depends not just on whether there is a union representative, but also 'on the numbers of representatives available in relation to the size of the local membership' (Millward *et al.*, 1992: 115–16). On this measure, there appears to have been little change in union strength in unionized workplaces during the period 1984 to 1990 (Millward *et al.*, 1992: 116).

Since the 1990s there has been little change in the numbers of union representatives that unionized workplaces have on-site (Table 5.7). Twenty-nine per cent of unionized workplaces had a single union representative on-site in 1998, as was the case in 1990. Around four in ten had more than one on-site union representative. Although there appears to be a small increase in the percentage of workplaces with four or more on-site union representatives, it is likely that the 1990 figure is an underestimate.[8]

Table 5.7 Number of union representatives on site in workplaces with recognized unions, 1990 and 1998

	Column percentages and means	
	1990	*1998*
None	28	27
One	29	29
Two	16	13
Three	8	7
Four or more	19	23
Don't know	2	1
Mean	2.5	2.7
Weighted base	*1,053*	*845*
Unweighted base	*1,416*	*1,116*

Base: all establishments with 25 or more employees where recognized trade unions.

We have calculated the number of union members per union representative, which is an inverse measure of union strength. If we focus on those unionized workplaces with on-site representatives, we find that the number of union members to each union representative has declined marginally in the 1990s. In 1990, there were thirty-two members per on-site union representative. By 1998, there were twenty-nine.[9] On this measure, then, there was a slight increase in union strength, since representatives had fewer members to service.

Of course, union members are union representatives' immediate constituency. But a union's ability to mobilize a whole workforce in pressing its concerns and interests, and its ability to recruit new members, depend in part on the ability of the union to respond to the needs of all employees. Again, focusing on those unionized workplaces with on-site representatives, we can establish the number of employees at the workplace for each representative. In fact, there was possibly a slight increase in the number of employees per representative in the 1990s, the figure rising from forty-nine in 1990 to fifty-five in 1998. On this basis, union strength diminished, since representatives were spread over more employees.

The fact that on-site representatives were dealing with roughly the same number of members in 1998 as they were in 1990, but more employees, reflects the decline in workplace union density discussed earlier. However, union representatives have a clearer responsibility to service members than non-members and the number of members per representative is a more salient indicator of union strength. That changed little and provides no support for the notion that recognized unions were becoming a 'hollow shell'.

Procedural involvement and the appointment of committee representatives

The general picture arising from the analysis so far is relatively mixed with respect to union strength. It is clear than union density declined markedly over the course of the survey series, and that the rate of decline speeded up in the 1990s. The demise of the closed shop began in the 1980s and continued in the 1990s such that, by 1998, it had virtually disappeared. Strong recommendations to join the union by management also became less common, with most of the change occurring in the 1990s. On the other hand, after a fall in the proportion of unionized workplaces with on-site representatives in the period 1984–90, the incidence of on-site union representatives has remained constant in the 1990s. Furthermore, the ratio of members to representatives has remained stable since the mid-1980s, suggesting that recognized unions were maintaining their organizational strength where they continued to be recognized by employers.

As noted in our introduction, some commentators have suspected that, even where unions continue to have a presence, they have lost influence in the last two decades and hence effectively become 'hollow shells'. However, we have found signs that, during the 1990s, union representation held up in workplaces continuing to recognize unions. It may be that, after the change of the 1980s, only the fittest survived. If such a process of selection did occur, then perhaps those unions that remained in place – the 'rump' of the grassroots union movement – were the 'strongest'. If so, it is also conceivable that they may have retained their influence in the workplace. The best way to test this proposition is to consider the extent to which unions were involved alongside management in the joint regulation of the workplace. In this section we focus on two facets of joint regulation. These are as follows: union agreement to procedures and union representation of workers under those procedures; and union involvement in the appointment of employee representatives on joint consultative committees and on health and safety committees.

Union agreement to procedures and union representation of workers

Since 1980, the WIRS series has collected information on the incidence of formal procedures for dealing with discipline and dismissals, other than redundancies. Between 1980 and 1984 the proportion of unionized workplaces with such a procedure increased from 86 per cent to 94 per cent. In 1990 and 1998, 97 per cent of unionized workplaces had such a procedure.[10] Between 1980 and 1990, these procedures were agreed with recognized unions in nine tenths of cases. In nearly all cases, trade unions represented workers covered by the agreement. We do not know what happened to workplaces as a whole after 1990 since the involvement of trade unions in this type of procedure was not covered in WERS 1998. However, in our panel survey we did ask whether formal discipline and dismissal procedures existed and, if so, whether those covered were represented by unions. In 1990, such a procedure existed in 99 per cent of continuing unionized workplaces, and unions represented the workers covered in 99 per cent of cases. In 1998, the figures were 98 per cent and 97 per cent respectively. So there was little sign of change among continuing unionized workplaces in terms of union involvement in agreeing discipline and dismissal procedures, and in representing workers under those procedures.

In the panel survey we also asked whether there was a formal procedure for dealing with disputes over the pay and conditions of any group of employees, another matter on which we have data from the earlier surveys but not in the 1998 cross-section survey. If there was such a procedure, we asked respondents if the procedure was agreed with unions and if employees covered by the procedure were represented by unions. Again, the picture is one of little change. In 1998, four fifths (80 per cent) of workplaces with recognized unions had a pay and conditions disputes procedure, compared to 77 per cent in 1990. In both years, 94 per cent of unionized workplaces with such a procedure had agreed it with unions. In nearly all cases (97 per cent in 1998 and 100 per cent in 1990) unions represented the workers covered by the agreement.

Union involvement in the appointment of committee representatives

Another way in which unions can be involved in the joint regulation of the workplace is through their involvement in appointing employee representatives to workplace committees. Our series contains data on union involvement in the appointment of two types of employee representative: those sitting on joint consultative committees, and those sitting on health and safety committees.

The proportion of unionized workplaces with a joint consultative committee has remained remarkably constant during the series. In 1998, 38 per cent had a consultative committee, compared to 41 per cent in 1980. During the 1980s, the proportion of unionized workplaces where unions were involved in appointing employee representatives to consultative committees also remained roughly constant. This seemed to change dramatically in the 1990s. Whereas unions were involved in appointing employee representatives to consultative committees in 58 per cent of unionized workplaces with a consultative committee in 1990, this had halved to 29 per cent in 1998. Although, as discussed in Chapter 4, this drop may be attributable in part to changes in the question format and wording in the 1998 survey, it is reasonable to conclude that union involvement in consultative committees diminished in the 1990s. The decline was apparent in the public and private sectors, but it was particularly marked in the private service sector. In 1998, where unions were recognized they were half as likely to be involved in the appointment of consultative committee representatives in private services as they were in private manufacturing and the public sector. The loss of influence was greater where there was no on-site representative and where workplace union density was below 25 per cent. Patterns were similar, whether or not the employer supported the union through a closed shop or by strongly recommending union membership. These findings are consistent with this loss of influence arising from unions' weaker organizational capacity, rather than a change in management attitudes towards union involvement.

Our panel provides further evidence of a diminution in union involvement in appointing employee representatives to consultative committees. Among workplaces with recognized unions and a joint consultative committee in 1990 and 1998, unions were involved in the appointment of employee representatives in 60 per cent of cases in 1990. By 1998, this had fallen to 47 per cent. The decline was most marked (58 to 39 per cent) where union density had fallen by at least 10 percentage points. The comparable figures for workplaces experiencing a 10 percentage point rise in density were 59 and 51 per cent. Where density was stable, the fall was from 61 to 47 per cent. So the loss of influence over appointments was greatest where density had fallen, but it was not restricted to these cases.

Another way of measuring the influence of unions is to establish how influential managers viewed consultative committees to be where unions were present and where they had influence over appointments. In our 1990 and 1998 cross-sectional surveys, we asked respondents how influential they thought the consultative committee was in relation to 'management's decisions affecting the workforce'. Among workplaces that did not recognize unions, the proportion responding 'very influential' or 'fairly influential' fell from 91 per cent to 86 per cent. However, where joint consultative committees operated in unionized workplaces the proportion viewing them as influential rose from 74 per cent to 84 per cent. Their perceived influence also rose among the dwindling number where unions appointed employee representatives. Three quarters (73 per cent) of managers viewed these committees as influential in 1998 compared to two thirds (65 per cent) in 1990. So, although, by these measures, unions appeared to have influence in a diminishing number of unionized workplaces during the 1990s, the perceived influence of consultative committees increased where unions continued to operate and where unions appointed employee representatives.

Our series also contains information on the role of unions in appointing to health and safety committees. Since 1984, we have asked management respondents whether unions have chosen employee representatives on health and safety committees. In 1984 and 1990 around four fifths said 'yes'. In the 1990s, the incidence of these committees rose in the unionized sector (from 43 per cent to 48 per cent).[11] However, unions' role in appointing employee representatives to them appears to have declined sharply. By 1998 unions were able to appoint in only one third (34 per cent) of cases. Again, changes in question format and wording in 1998 may explain part of the decline, but it is unlikely to explain such a marked fall.[12] As in the case of the appointment of employee representatives to joint consultative committees, the waning of union influence was most evident where union density was low and where there were no on-site union representatives. Where a union representative was present, unions were involved in appointing employee representatives to health and safety committees in 83 per cent of cases in 1990 and 37 per cent in 1998. However, where union representatives were absent, the fall was from 78 per cent to 4 per cent. Perhaps the absence of an on-site union representative means that unions simply do not have any obvious mechanism by which they can choose an employee representative. Alternatively, the lack of a union representative may indicate unwillingness on the part of the workforce to assist in the joint regulation of the workplace.

There was a strong association between unions' involvement in appointments to joint consultative committees and health and safety committees. Where unions appointed employee representatives to joint consultative committees they were much more likely to appoint employee representatives to health and safety committees. This association strengthened during the 1990s. In 82 per cent of unionized workplaces where unions appointed employee representatives to a joint consultative committee in 1998, they also appointed employee representatives to a health and safety committee. Eighty-nine per cent of those who did not appoint to a joint consultative committee did not appoint to a health and safety committee either. This suggests that either measure might act as an indicator of general union influence in the joint regulation of the workplace. On both measures the decline in the 1990s appears to have been substantial.

No clear trend emerges about union involvement in the joint regulation of the workplace. On the one hand, the influence of recognized unions appears to have waned if measured in terms of their ability to appoint employee representatives to joint consultative committees and health and safety committees. On the other hand, evidence from continuing unionized workplaces indicated that recognized unions continued to be very involved in the agreement of formal industrial relations procedures and in representing workers under those procedures.

Collective bargaining

Ever since the birth of the union movement in Britain in the early nineteenth century, workers have turned to unions for three reasons. First, to protect them against the unfair and arbitrary actions of employers. Second, to provide them with a 'voice' at the workplace to express collective views on matters of common interest with employers. Third, they have turned to unions to bargain on their behalf with employers over pay and conditions. In this section, we consider this third function, focusing on the coverage and scope of collective bargaining.

The coverage of collective bargaining in unionized workplaces

Although one or more unions may be recognized for bargaining purposes, this does not mean that the collective-bargaining arrangements cover all employees within the workplace. A union may represent only a small section of a workforce, perhaps bargaining on behalf of a single occupation at the workplace. Often collective agreements do not cover managers and senior professional staff. Whether a workplace's union or unions can improve the workforce's terms and conditions of employment depends, as a starting point, on the proportion of those workers covered by collective bargaining. Where a high proportion of workers are covered, the union is likely to have greater influence in the workplace as a whole than if it bargains only for a minority of workers. In addition, its bargaining position may be stronger *vis-à-vis* the employer if, for example, the union wishes to tackle an issue affecting the conditions of all workers at the workplace.[13]

Collective-bargaining coverage has fallen steadily since 1984, when we first asked survey respondents about it. At that time, collective agreements fixed pay rates for an average of almost nine out of ten workers in unionized workplaces (Table 5.8).[14] This fell to three quarters (75 per cent) in 1990 and then again to two thirds (67 per cent) in 1998. Although they highlight the decline in collective bargaining within unionized workplaces, these average figures hide significant changes in coverage that are apparent when we look at the distribution of coverage across workplaces.

Perhaps the most striking development is the sudden appearance in 1998 of a large proportion of workplaces where unions were recognized but no workers were covered by collective bargaining. This was the case in one in seven unionized workplaces in 1998, having been virtually unheard of in 1984 and 1990.[15] Further investigation revealed that one third (34 per cent) of workplaces with union density below 25 per cent had no workers covered by collective bargaining. This suggests an association between weak or poorly organized unions on the ground and low coverage. It may be that workers leave a union when management has unilaterally set pay, despite still formally

Table 5.8 Proportion of employees covered by collective bargaining in workplaces with recognized unions, 1984 to 1998

	1984	*1990*	*1998*
None	*	*	14
1–19 per cent	2	7	5
20–49 per cent	7	12	10
50–79 per cent	16	20	18
80–99 per cent	20	25	13
100 per cent	55	35	40
Mean	86	75	67
Weighted base	*1,289*	*1,044*	*777*
Unweighted base	*1,546*	*1,394*	*1,036*

Base: all establishments with 25 or more employees where recognized trade unions.

recognizing the union. Alternatively, employers may respond to low or falling union density by unilaterally setting pay, treating the recognition agreement as a 'dead letter'. (We discuss this further when we come to our panel results, below.) Unionized workplaces with no covered workers were disproportionately found among small organizations of under 100 employees (42 per cent), in the private 'other services' sector (51 per cent) and among single independent workplaces (35 per cent). These are sectors and conditions in which unions have always found it difficult to organize and recruit. It seems likely that some employers took advantage of that relative weakness in the 1990s to unilaterally set pay, despite formally recognizing unions. Whether they sought to take this 'opportunity' seems to have depended, in part, on their attitudes towards union membership. In only 7 per cent of unionized workplaces where management strongly recommended union membership were none of the employees covered by collective bargaining. Among the very small number with a closed shop in 1998, the figure was 5 per cent. By contrast, 16 per cent of the unionized workplaces without either a closed shop or a management recommending union membership had zero coverage.

Employers appeared to be in a better position to take this 'opportunity' where they were not party to multi-employer agreements. Although the abrogation of multiple-employer collective agreements has occasioned much comment (Brown and Walsh, 1991), zero coverage was most common where pay was determined at enterprise or establishment level. Zero coverage affected workers in over half (56 per cent) of single independent unionized workplaces where, nominally, the principal method of pay determination was workplace-level bargaining. This compared to only 6 per cent among those whose pay was determined outside the organization, for example through multi-employer agreements. Among branches of larger organizations, one sixth (18 per cent) of those with pay determined at enterprise level had zero coverage in 1998. This compared to 12 per cent where pay was determined at establishment level and 5 per cent among those whose pay was determined outside the organization.

Declining coverage, plus the emergence of unionized workplaces with no coverage, are trends that are consistent with recognized unions becoming 'hollow shells'. The fall in the proportion of unionized workplaces with high coverage (80 per cent or more) over the period points in the same direction. However, it was not all one-way traffic. Indeed, between 1990 and 1998, the proportion of unionized workplaces with 100 per cent coverage rose, from 35 to 40 per cent. The increase in the proportion of workplaces with complete coverage actually raised mean coverage in the 1990s in some sectors. In public services other than health and education, the proportion of unionized work-places with complete coverage rose from 50 to 83 per cent, increasing mean coverage from 85 to 89 per cent. In distribution, hotels and catering the proportion of unionized workplaces with complete coverage rose from 10 to 41 per cent, raising mean coverage from 57 to 65 per cent. Among single-union workplaces, the proportion with complete coverage rose from 19 to 43 per cent, raising mean coverage from 61 to 67 per cent. However, these were exceptional circumstances, running counter to the general decline in coverage.

From the mid-1980s, collective-bargaining coverage fell in all three broad sectors of the economy. However, the fall was modest in private manufacturing, with mean coverage falling from 75 per cent in 1984 to 70 per cent in 1998. In private services, by contrast, coverage plummeted by 20 percentage points since 1984, from 79 per cent to 59 per cent in 1998. Most of the decline came in the 1990s when the annual rate of decline was 2.8 per cent, compared to 0.8 per cent in the period 1984 to 1990. Private service sector workplaces also accounted for 59 per cent of all the unionized workplaces with no coverage in 1998.

Workplace collective-bargaining coverage has traditionally been higher in the public sector than in the private sector, but during the 1980s that began to change. Mean workplace coverage fell from 94 per cent in 1984 to 78 per cent in 1990. It fell further to 70 per cent by 1998, putting it on a par with private manufacturing. Yet half (48 per cent) of the unionized workplaces in the public sector retained complete coverage in 1998, so that it accounted for over two thirds (70 per cent) of all unionized workplaces with 100 per cent coverage. A closer look reveals marked differences in the rate of coverage decline across sections of the public sector. In public education, coverage fell by a third between 1984 and 1990, from 90 to 60 per cent, following the removal of bargaining rights from teachers in England and Wales. Since then, there has been a further small decline in mean coverage, from 60 to 53 per cent. The demise of collective bargaining has been even more dramatic in the public health sector, coverage falling by over a half between 1984 and 1998, from 97 per cent to 46 per cent. In contrast to the education sector, most of the change occurred after 1990, at which time mean coverage was still relatively high at 84 per cent. Change in the public health sector may reflect the reorganization of the National Health Service into local trusts, many of which pursue their own policies for pay setting (Seifert, 1992: 378–88). Mean collective-bargaining coverage has also fallen among unionized workplaces in central and local government, from 96 per cent in 1984 to 84 per cent in 1990 and 79 per cent in 1998. These trends may be accounted for in part by the changes to pay determination ushered in by the contracting-out of local government services and the inauguration of semi-autonomous agencies to run large parts of government administration.

One might assume that where a union is strong according to one of our measures, it will be strong on others. In fact, our indicators of union strength are not always directly linked to one another. Thus the relationship between collective-bargaining coverage and union density shifted during the 1990s. In 1984 and 1990, there was a strong association between high union density and high collective-bargaining coverage. Since 1990, however, coverage has risen sharply in unionized workplaces with low union density, reversing the decline that occurred in the period 1984 to 1990 so that, by 1998, it stood at its 1984 level. Coverage rose from 27 to 50 per cent in workplaces with union density of under 25 per cent, and from 53 to 71 per cent in workplaces with union density between 25 and 49 per cent. At the same time, it fell among workplaces with union density of 50 per cent or more (from 85 per cent to 70 per cent), continuing a decline that had begun in 1984. By 1998, workplaces with union densities of less than 25 per cent were still associated with lower collective-bargaining coverage than unionized workplaces with higher union density. However, there was no significant difference between the mean coverage in workplaces with 25–49 per cent density compared to workplaces with density of 50 per cent or more.

There was no clear evidence of a link between higher bargaining coverage and another measure of union strength, union on-site representation. Among unionized workplaces with an on-site union representative, mean bargaining coverage fell from 87 per cent in 1984 to 79 per cent in 1990, and then again to 68 per cent in 1998. This decline was mirrored in unionized establishments without on-site union representatives, where coverage fell from 84 per cent in 1984 to 65 per cent in 1998. The difference was that, whereas decline has been relatively steady throughout the period in workplaces with union representatives, most of the decline in unionized workplaces without an on-site union representative occurred in the 1980s. By 1990, mean coverage had already fallen to 66 per cent where there was no on-site representative. It may be that union representatives had a part to play in limiting the fall in coverage in the period through to 1990. In any event, the presence of an on-site representative made no difference to coverage by 1998. Unless, that is, the representative was a full-time representative. Among this small subset of unionized establishments, coverage had been over 90 per cent in the 1980s. It was still higher than other unionized workplaces in 1998, at 75 per cent. It may be that coverage is high because of the organizing efforts of full-time lay representatives. Alternatively, full-time union representatives may continue to operate because coverage remains high. It is not possible to establish from our cross-sectional data how much weight should be attached to these propositions.

Panel analysis of collective-bargaining coverage

Table 5.9 is a replica of Table 5.8, except that this time we are presenting results for our panel of continuing workplaces that were unionized in both 1990 and 1998, plus unionized leavers and unionized joiners. For ease of reference, we have included the cross-section results again in the table. A comparison of columns two and three with columns five and six of the table indicates that the changes evident in the time-series data are mirrored in the panel of work-places recognizing unions in 1990 and 1998.[16] The proportion of continuing unionized establishments with no workers covered by collective bargaining moved from 1 per cent in 1990 to 20 per cent in 1998, a slightly higher figure than the one obtained from the 1998 cross-section.[17] The proportion with complete coverage rose from 37 to 45 per cent in the panel, again a bigger increase than the one observed in the cross-sectional data. The bifurcation of

Table 5.9 Percentage of employees covered by collective bargaining in workplaces with recognized unions, cross-section and panel results, 1990 and 1998

Column percentages and mean percentages

	1990 Cross-section	Continuing workplaces[a]	Leavers	1998 Cross-section	Continuing workplaces[a]	Joiners
None	0	1	0	14	20	16
1–19	7	7	7	5	2	2
20–49	12	16	16	10	6	7
50–79	20	19	16	18	12	25
80–99	25	21	25	13	15	11
100	35	37	37	40	45	39
Mean	75	78	75	67	69	68
Weighted base	*1,044*	*419*	*279*	*777*	*390*	*171*
Unweighted base	*1,394*	*589*	*237*	*1,036*	*535*	*174*

Base: all establishments with 25 or more employees where recognized trade unions.

Note
a Panel data based on those continuing workplaces recognizing unions in 1990 and 1998.

bargaining coverage in the 1990s, apparent in our cross-sectional data, is therefore evident and still more pronounced in our panel, indicating substantial shifts in behaviour among continuing establishments. The net result was a reduction in mean bargaining coverage among continuing unionized work-places from 78 per cent in 1990 to 69 per cent in 1998.

A comparison of the leavers and joiners columns shows that compositional change in unionized establishments also had a part to play in the decline of bargaining coverage in the 1990s. Although joiners were just as likely as leavers to have complete coverage, zero coverage was non-existent among leavers, whereas 16 per cent of joiners had no workers covered by collective bargaining. Consequently, whereas mean coverage was three quarters (75 per cent) among leavers in 1990, it was two thirds (68 per cent) among joiners.

When we compare continuing establishments' bargaining coverage in 1990 with their coverage in 1998, we find that among those with complete coverage in 1990, just over half (56 per cent) still had complete coverage in 1998. A further 13 per cent had coverage of 80–99 per cent, so that two thirds (68 per cent) of those with complete coverage in 1990 still had very high coverage in 1998. However, one quarter (24 per cent) reported having no workers covered in 1998. They made up almost half (48 per cent) of all unionized continuing workplaces reporting no bargaining coverage in 1998.

When respondents informed us that there was no bargaining unit currently operating, we asked them: 'What proportion of the total workforce would have their pay and conditions negotiated by [the bargaining unit/the largest bargaining unit] if you were bargaining?' Intriguingly, half (47 per cent) said 100 per cent,[18] and the mean coverage figure given was 77 per cent. It seems that unionized workplaces with no coverage in 1998 had previously had high proportions of workers covered by collective bargaining. Furthermore, in only a few cases was the respondent unable to answer the hypothetical question about what coverage would be if they were bargaining, suggesting that nearly all had a clear idea of who was in the settlement group. However, none of this negates the finding that, in substantial numbers of cases with formal union recognition, management had taken control of pay and no longer regarded it as routinely dealt with by joint regulation.

Collective bargaining coverage remained roughly stable in half (50 per cent) of unionized public sector workplaces, while coverage rose by at least 10 percentage points among a quarter, and fell by at least 10 percentage points in the remaining quarter. However, coverage increases were generally smaller than coverage decreases, so that mean coverage fell by 10 percentage points from 81 to 71 per cent between 1990 and 1998. This is similar to the 1990–98 decline in the cross-sectional data. In private manufacturing, coverage remained stable in 41 per cent of unionized establishments, but among the remainder those experiencing a decline in coverage outnumbered those experiencing increases by a ratio of two to one. Even so, the decline in mean coverage was no more pronounced than the decline in the public sector, falling 10 percentage points from 74 to 64 per cent. The pattern in private services was similar to that in private manufacturing, with four in every ten unionized establishments having stable bargaining coverage. A further third experienced a decline in coverage, and a quarter experienced an increase. Mean coverage declined from 76 to 67 per cent. The mean figure for 1998 is well above the 59 per cent mean arising from the cross-sectional data. This suggests that some of the decline in coverage in the private service sector arose due to low bargaining coverage among unionized workplaces joining the sector. This proved to be the case: mean coverage among joiners to the private service sector was 53 per cent. This low figure was due to particularly low coverage among establishments that had operated since before 1990 but had only exceeded the twenty-five employee threshold since then, rather than low coverage among new private sector establishments.

Our cross-sectional data pointed to an association between low union density and low collective-bargaining coverage. Our panel data indicate a strong association between changes in union density and changes in collective bargaining coverage among unionized workplaces. As anticipated earlier, coverage rose where density rose, and fell where density fell. Where union density rose by at least 10 percentage points between 1990 and 1998, coverage increased from 60 to 67 per cent. Coverage fell from 81 to 66 per cent among unionized workplaces where density fell by at least 10 percentage points. These findings are consistent with the proposition that managements have reduced coverage where support for unions has diminished. Since those with falling density outnumbered those with rising density by a ratio of three to two, this explains some of the decline in mean coverage among continuing unionized establishments. However, coverage also fell from 81 to 71 per cent among unionized workplaces where density remained stable, suggesting that other factors must have been at play.

We explored associations between changes in coverage and other measures of within-establishment change. Two are particularly worthy of note: change in workplace size, and change in the number of recognized unions. Where the workforce grew by at least 50 per cent between 1990 and 1998, bargaining coverage fell from 77 per cent to 60 per cent. This might happen if the expansion had occurred among occupations new to the workplace that the existing unions would not represent. Coverage fell at a similar rate among unionized workplaces with shrinking workforces. Among those with workforces shrinking by at least 20 per cent, coverage fell from 78 to 58 per cent. This could happen where workforce losses were disproportionately concentrated among union members within a workplace. Alternatively, it might indicate that employers were taking advantage of structural change to alter their methods of pay determination. The association could also arise where employers facing financial difficulties have cut their workforces and dispensed with collective bargaining in favour of unilateral managerial decision-making. It was only among those with stable workforces – namely, those with workforces that had grown or shrunk by less than 20 per cent – that bargaining coverage remained stable (76 per cent in 1990 and 74 per cent in 1998).

One third (34 per cent) of continuing workplaces recognizing unions in 1990 and 1998 experienced a decline in the number of unions recognized at the workplace. In these cases, mean bargaining coverage fell from 80 per cent in 1990 to 65 per cent in 1998, somewhat faster than the panel as a whole (from 78 to 69 per cent). Some of the reasons given by respondents for the reduction in the number of recognized unions give us some insight into why it may have resulted in lower coverage. The second most cited reason for a reduction in the number of recognized unions was the disappearance of jobs (cited by 25 per cent). The main reason cited was union mergers and amalgamations, cited by 69 per cent of respondents. It is not immediately obvious why this should result in lower bargaining coverage, unless the merger resulted in the new union no longer being a party to an existing agreement. In only 2 per cent of cases was the reduction in the number of recognized unions due to derecognition by management, so this is not an important reason for lower coverage among unionized workplaces.

In 13 per cent of workplaces unionized in 1990 and 1998 there had been an increase in the number of recognized unions. The main reason given for this increase, given in 39 per cent of cases, was gaining recognition for new jobs or occupations. Although this is likely to have increased bargaining coverage, the increase in mean coverage from 80 to 85 per cent was not statistically significant.

In more than half (55 per cent) of workplaces unionized in 1990 and 1998, there was no change in the number of recognized unions. These workplaces saw a small but significant decline in union coverage over the period, from 77 per cent in 1990 to 68 per cent in 1998. Broadly speaking, then, reductions in coverage were associated with reductions in the numbers of recognized unions, but overt derecognition was not the principal mechanism.

As we found with the cross-sectional data, there was no clear association in the panel between on-site union representation and bargaining coverage. In 1990, those unionized workplaces with on-site union representation had higher coverage than those with no on-site union representative (80 per cent versus 70 per cent). By 1998, there was no significant difference: those with an on-site representative had a mean coverage of 70 per cent, compared to 69 per cent among those without representatives. This was because coverage actually rose (from 64 to 73 per cent) among unionized workplaces that had no representation in either year. Coverage fell among those workplaces that had representation in 1990, 1998 or both years.

We have seen a marked decline in collective-bargaining coverage in unionized workplaces since 1984 that affected all three broad sectors of the economy. In the 1990s, the decline in coverage was due to changes in the behaviour of continuing workplaces, combined with compositional change in the unionized sector. Although there were some associations between measures of union strength and the maintenance of higher coverage, the relationship was weak and, in some cases, non-existent. The decline in bargaining coverage directly contributes to a decline in unions' influence within unionized workplaces, since it limits their ability to determine terms and conditions for their members (and 'free-riders'). The rate of decline, and the emergence of many unionized establishments with no effective bargaining, may mark a qualitatively different phase in the development of unionism. By the late 1990s, then, unions in most workplaces had lost a good deal of influence over joint regulation, despite being formally recognized for pay bargaining.

The scope of collective bargaining

The scope of negotiations between management and unions usually extends beyond pay to other basic conditions of employment. Some have argued that 'the scope of bargaining may be the clearest indicator of the depth of recognition offered by an employer to a trade union', because the number of aspects of work constrained by collectively bargained rules 'depends heavily upon the power relationship between the employer and the employees' trade union organization' (Brown *et al.*, 1998: 8–10).

Throughout our survey series we have traced the scope of bargaining by asking management respondents whether each of a small number of issues were the subject of negotiation. We found that the number of non-pay issues subject to negotiation declined in unionized workplaces in the early 1980s, but that there was little change over the period 1984–90 (Millward *et al.*, 1992: 249–53). Evidence from case-study research conducted in 1996 and 1997 indicated that 'the scope of bargaining has narrowed substantially in companies that continue to recognize unions'; in some cases, the scope of bargaining has been curtailed so much that the authors suggest 'there has been a measure of implicit or partial derecognition' (Brown *et al.*, 1998: iii).

In our earlier surveys data on non-pay bargaining were collected for the largest bargaining units representing manual and non-manual workers respectively, covering negotiation both at the workplace and beyond the workplace. The 1998 survey departed from this practice. Instead, we asked managers whether management at the workplace negotiated with union representatives over nine issues. Consequently, the data are not comparable with earlier years. However, at the end of this section of the chapter we use the data to show that workplaces joining the population were little different in terms of their bargaining scope from existing workplaces and so the panel results that we now discuss can be broadly extrapolated to all workplaces in 1990 and 1998. In 1998, we asked management respondents in our panel survey to tell us whether negotiations took place with unions or staff associations on six key aspects of work. If so, we asked them at what level the negotiations took place.[19] The questions were identical to those asked at the same workplaces in 1990. The responses allowed us to see whether the scope of bargaining changed over the period and, if so, whether these changes were associated with other union strength indicators and other workplace characteristics.

In fact, there was relatively little change in the scope of bargaining among continuing establishments recognizing unions in 1990 and 1998 (Table 5.10). Whereas in the last section we identified a substantial increase in the proportion of unionized workplaces where pay bargaining was not taking place, no such trend was apparent in relation to non-pay issues. The proportion of unionized

Table 5.10 Scope of bargaining in continuing workplaces with recognized unions, 1990 and 1998

	Cell percentages and means	
	1990	*1998*
Items subject to negotiation		
Physical working conditions	80	79
Staffing levels	57	51
Recruitment	44	34
Redeployment within the establishment	70	66
Size of redundancy payments	46	57
Reorganization of working hours	88	75
None of these	5	7
Mean number of items	3.8	3.6
Weighted base	*359*	*359*
Unweighted base	*524*	*524*

Base: all continuing workplaces with 25 or more employees where recognized trade unions in both 1990 and 1998.

workplaces that bargained over none of the six items appearing on our show-card remained small (5 per cent in 1990 and 7 per cent in 1998). The mean number of items subject to negotiation went from 3.8 to 3.6, a fall which is not statistically significant. There was some movement on particular issues, with reductions in the number of workplaces where recruitment and working hours appeared on the bargaining agenda and an increase in the proportion bargaining over the size of redundancy payments.

The picture appears to be more fluid when we consider change across broad sectors, and within unionized workplaces. We used our panel data to investigate the degree to which the bargaining agenda grew or shrank within unionized workplaces between 1990 and 1998, in respect of the six items covered in Table 5.10. At one extreme were the small minority (1 per cent) of all unionized establishments that shifted from bargaining on all six items in 1990 to none in 1998. At the other extreme were the minority (again, 1 per cent of all unionized establishments) that bargained on six items in 1998, having bargained on none in 1990. In one fifth (21 per cent) of unionized workplaces, there was no change in the number of items subject to bargaining. There was also virtually no change in the mean number of items that were subject to negotiation because the 39 per cent of unionized workplaces with an expanded bargaining agenda in 1998 offset the 41 per cent in which the agenda had shrunk.

Within-establishment change differed across the broad sectors of the economy. The scope of bargaining on non-pay issues declined in private manufacturing, with half (53 per cent) of unionized manufacturing workplaces bargaining over fewer items, compared to a quarter (28 per cent) bargaining over more. The mean number of items subject to negotiation decreased from 3.7 to 3.0: a statistically significant fall. In contrast, one third (32 per cent) of unionized workplaces in private services reduced the scope of their bargaining agenda, while a half (48 per cent) expanded it. The mean increase from 2.9 to 3.3 items was, however, on the borders of statistical significance. Despite the organizational change engulfing the public sector in the 1990s, there was less change in the scope of bargaining here than in other sectors. In 1998, one quarter (23 per cent) of public sector unionized workplaces bargained over the same number of items they had bargained over in 1990. The mean number of items changed only marginally, from 4.3 to 4.1.

We decided to use the panel interview to find out why bargaining had begun or ceased on two items which are likely to recur regularly in negotiations, regardless of the business cycle: physical working conditions and staffing levels. If a change had occurred, we asked an open-ended question: 'How did this come about?' We focused these questions on workplaces where the largest bargaining unit in 1990 was still operating in 1998. Thus, the changes picked up relate to the same bargaining unit as the one identified in 1990. In fact, in only half of unionized workplaces was the 1990 largest bargaining unit still in operation in 1998. However, where it was in operation, there was little change in the arrangements governing bargaining over physical working conditions or staffing levels.

In 71 per cent of the workplaces where the largest 1990 bargaining unit continued to operate, there was no change in the practice of whether or not management bargained with unions over physical working conditions. In 13 per cent of cases bargaining over working conditions had ceased. In a quarter of these cases, managerial respondents said they had ceased to negotiate over physical conditions because they felt that union agreement to change was no longer necessary. Clearly, this is an indication of diminished union influence in this small number of cases. In another fifth of cases working conditions had not been an issue recently, which is why they were not under negotiation. In another 17 per cent of cases, management was negotiating over working conditions when they had not done so in 1990. The main reason cited for working conditions coming on to the agenda, given in a quarter of these cases, was that there was now closer involvement with unions over such matters.

In a fifth of unionized workplaces where the largest bargaining unit in 1990 was still operating in 1998, negotiation over staffing levels had stopped. The main reasons given for this were management-related: a fifth cited a change of management policy or approach. In a tenth of cases respondents said union agreement to change was no longer necessary. In another fifth of cases staffing levels had come on to the bargaining agenda. In a sixth of these cases respondents said they had begun to negotiate on staffing levels following devolution of responsibilities to local level. One in seven cited closer involvement with unions, and one in seven cited changes in management policy or approach.

This evidence suggests that managerial perceptions of the changing influence and power of unions played some part in determining the scope of bargaining. However, the number of instances in which waning power resulted in the narrowing of bargaining scope were offset by a similar number of instances in which a reappraisal of the union role had resulted in widening the scope of bargaining.

There were associations between other indicators of union strength and the scope of bargaining among our panel workplaces. Most notably, the mean number of items for bargaining fell significantly (from 3.7 to 3.2) in unionized workplaces experiencing a decline in union density of 10 percentage points or more. Where union density had increased or remained stable the number of items negotiated with unions did not change significantly. It moved from a mean of 4.0 to 3.8 among those with stable density and from 3.9 to 4.0 among those with a density increase of 10 percentage points or more. It is possible that, in the small number of workplaces where union density increased substantially, unions were able to use their stronger mandate to maintain or extend slightly the scope of bargaining.

Bargaining scope was also associated with bargaining coverage. Where bargaining coverage had fallen by 10 percentage points or more, the mean number of items negotiated with unions fell from 3.8 to 3.1. Where coverage remained stable, the mean number of items for bargaining also fell, from 4.1 to 3.7. But where coverage increased by 10 percentage points or more, the mean number of bargained items rose from 3.6 to 4.3. It may be that workers with new rights to bargain collectively over pay bring with them a different set of non-pay issues they wish to raise with management. Alternatively, managements predisposed to extending bargaining coverage may also perceive advantages in broadening the scope of issues dealt with collectively with unions.

We might have expected the scope of bargaining to be greater where unions had an on-site representative with whom management could negotiate. In fact, there was no simple association between the incidence of on-site union representation and the scope of collective bargaining. Where unions had on-site representatives in 1990, unions negotiated over more items than in unionized workplaces without on-site representatives (a mean of 3.9, compared to 3.5). But there was no significant difference in 1998 (the respective means being 3.6 and 3.7). In fact, the only unionized workplaces where there was a significant decline in the scope of bargaining between 1990 and 1998 were those with on-site representation in both years. Among these workplaces, the mean number of items for negotiation fell from 4.0 to 3.5. The loss or acquisition of an on-site representative made no difference to changes in the scope of bargaining. The picture was similar among unionized workplaces belonging to larger organizations, whether the union representative was on-site or not.[20]

As intimated earlier, changes in management policies and approaches to unions and bargaining, and to the needs of the business more generally, may have an impact on the nature of bargaining. In both 1990 and 1998, there was a link between management support for unions and a more extensive bargaining agenda. Where management required union membership for at least some of its employees, or where they strongly endorsed union membership, the mean number of items bargained over was higher than in other unionized workplaces. The figures for 1990 were 4.3 items and 3.5 respectively; in 1998, they were 4.1 and 3.5. However, there was no association between changes in attitudes towards union membership and changes in the scope of collective bargaining. The maintenance and extension of bargaining rights is not explicable simply in terms of management sponsorship of unionism.

Changes in bargaining scope were associated with ownership changes, and workplace splits and amalgamations. Where any of these had occurred since 1990, we asked whether it affected certain aspects of the business or work processes. We found bargaining scope declined where ownership change had affected a range of workplace characteristics. These were as follows: the type of products made or services provided; the way work was done; management structure; management's approach to employee relations; and, not surprisingly, the way pay and conditions were determined. This is strong evidence that managements have taken the opportunities arising from structural change to challenge union influence.

A further issue that we can address on possible changes in bargaining is the following: where unions' rights to bargain over non-pay issues are removed, is the effect ameliorated by an increase in the extent to which management consults or informs the workforce about change? We focus on the only issue for which we have information on negotiation, consultation and information,

Table 5.11 Links between negotiation, consultation and information over staffing levels in continuing workplaces with recognized unions, 1990 and 1998

| | Negotiation both years | | Negotiation in 1990 | | Negotiation in 1998 | | No negotiation | |
	1990	1998	1990	1998	1990	1998	1990	1998
Consultation and information	60	58	79	27	56	31	37	39
Consultation only	9	30	3	27	*	46	3	19
Information only	15	2	4	6	12	10	32	7
Neither	15	9	13	40	32	13	28	36
Weighted base	*112*	*112*	*78*	*78*	*54*	*54*	*78*	*78*
Unweighted base	*150*	*150*	*112*	*112*	*70*	*70*	*113*	*113*

Base: all continuing workplaces with 25 or more employees where recognized trade unions in 1990 and 1998.

namely staffing levels. In 1990 and 1998 we asked whether management gave their employees or their representatives information about staffing or manpower plans before the implementation of any changes. We also asked whether management consulted with employees or their representatives over staffing or manpower plans. In Table 5.11 we show whether management negotiated over the issue in 1990, 1998 or both years, and how this related to consulting and informing employees.

Where there were negotiations with unions over staffing levels in both years, nine in ten workplaces consulted staff and their representatives on the subject in 1998, an increase of over a quarter since 1990. Management either ignored staff or simply informed them of change in fewer cases than before.

A shift away from negotiation resulted in a decline in the number of cases where employees or their representatives were consulted, from 82 per cent in 1990 to 54 per cent in 1998. There was also a threefold increase in the proportion of cases where employees and their representatives were neither consulted nor informed. The acquisition of negotiation rights boosted the extent to which employees and their representatives were consulted (from 56 to 77 per cent of cases). It also reduced by threefold the instances in which they were neither consulted nor informed. So the maintenance or acquisition of negotiation rights brought greater access to information and consultation with them, while the loss of those rights limited consultation and information.

Where unions did not negotiate over staffing levels in 1990 and 1998, there nevertheless appeared to be a small increase in the extent to which employees and their representatives were consulted over the matter. However, the number of cases in which they were ignored also rose from 28 to 36 per cent. Taken together, these findings on the links between negotiation, consultation and information indicate two things. First, they show that, where unions retained negotiating rights over staffing levels their influence extended beyond negotiation into consultation and information access. This was even more the case in 1998 than in 1990. This is an indication of how negotiation rights continue to give unions real influence. Second, unions needed to maintain bargaining rights to maintain any sort of influence over staffing levels. The likelihood of management consulting and informing staff depended largely on whether the union had bargaining rights over an issue. Where bargaining rights were lost, management did not tend to replace them with consultation rights or access to information.

For our final piece of evidence on the scope of bargaining we turn from our panel of continuing workplaces to the rather different questions in the 1998 main survey. By comparing workplaces that had joined the survey population after 1990 with the remainder we can judge whether the panel results can be more broadly interpreted as applying to the population as a whole – in effect as a proxy for the time-series results. We did this for the five issues that resembled those for which we had panel data: these were pay and conditions of employment; recruitment or selection of employees; systems of payment; staffing or manpower planning; and health and safety. On each of these, respondents were asked whether workplace managers normally negotiated with, consulted, informed or did not involve local union representatives on these matters. We found that, on three of them, joiners were no different from other workplaces. On the other two, staffing and health and safety, there was weak evidence that joiners were less likely to report negotiations than other workplaces. From this we infer that joiners were little different from more established workplaces in 1998 in terms of the scope of their bargaining with recognized unions and that therefore our panel results on the subject can reasonably be read more broadly as applying to the whole population.

What conclusions can we draw from this investigation of the scope of collective bargaining? Certainly, it is not the picture of decline in the scope of bargaining that we might have expected from other evidence on the declining influence of unions in the 1990s, nor the evidence presented earlier in the chapter on the decline in bargaining coverage. Rather, there has been little net change and, in this respect at least, there is no support for the hollow shell hypothesis for the period 1990 to 1998.

Limits on management's ability to organize work

The formal right to negotiate collectively over aspects of work offers unions the opportunity to influence workplace outcomes. The degree to which unions can actually affect the terms and conditions of members depends upon the effectiveness with which they can capitalize on such opportunities. It may be that, in practice, despite 'formal' recognition rights, the ambit of union influence has diminished over time. In fact, there has been mounting empirical evidence to support this contention, some of which we presented in the introduction to this chapter. In 1998, 19 per cent of employees in workplaces with recognized unions agreed with the statement that 'the trade unions at my workplace are usually ignored by management' (Bryson, 1999: 86).

Our penultimate test of the proposition that unions have lost influence in the workplace in recent years comes from assessing the extent to which unions are able to limit management's ability to organize work. In 1990 we asked respondents: 'In practice is management here able to organize work as it wishes among non-managerial employees, or are there limits to the way it can organize work?' If they said there were limits they were then asked what limited the way management could organize work.[21]

Roughly half of unionized continuing workplaces faced limits to the way they organized work in both 1990 and 1998 (Table 5.12). The biggest single limitation in both years was formal agreements with trade unions. Respondents

Table 5.12 Limits on management's ability to organize work in continuing workplaces with recognized unions, 1990 and 1998

	Column percentages	
	1990	*1998*
Union constraints		
Formal agreements with unions	25	28
Opposition from representatives	6	11
Opposition from ordinary union members	8	13
Workforce-related constraints		
Availability of staff	3	*
Lack of management expertise	4	8
Lack of skills among workforce	14	23
Opposition from non-union members	3	8
Agreement of supervisors	*	0
Workplace-related constraints		
Lack of suitable premises or equipment	8	15
Limits from higher management	4	2
External co-ordination requirements	4	1
Restrictions from professional body	1	*
Workflow requirements	3	*
Other limits	5	14
No limits	53	49
Weighted base	444	444
Unweighted base	566	566

Base: all continuing workplaces with 25 or more employees where recognized trade unions in 1990 and 1998.

Note: column percentages add to more than 100 since multiple responses were permitted.

cited formal agreements as a limitation in 25 per cent of cases in 1990 and 28 per cent in 1998. There was a small increase in opposition from union members, from 8 to 13 per cent. Opposition from union representatives almost doubled from 6 to 11 per cent.

It appears that, if anything, union-related constraints on management's ability to organize work increased during the 1990s among continuing unionized workplaces. Producing an index based on the three union constraints, with workplaces scoring '1' for each one they refer to, we found that those citing no union constraints fell from 72 to 67 per cent between 1990 and 1998. Furthermore, the mean score rose significantly from 0.40 to 0.52.

In 1990, around 30 per cent of managers in unionized workplaces in the private service sector and the public sector said their ability to organize work was constrained by unions, compared to only 21 per cent in private manufacturing (Table 5.13). Little changed in the private service sector during the 1990s, whereas the proportion of managers citing union constraints rose in the public sector to 36 per cent. It also rose marginally in private manufacturing, but most of the change was in the public sector.

An increased awareness of union constraints may indicate growing union influence in the workplace. However, managers pressing for change in work organization may feel union constraints more than those who are not introducing change. Managers in the public sector may be increasingly aware of union constraints because the public sector was undergoing so much change during the 1990s. That managers involved in making changes in work organization may have felt the presence of unions more keenly is supported by

Table 5.13 Union-related constraints on management's ability to organize work in continuing workplaces with recognized unions, by broad sector, 1990 and 1998

| | *Column percentages* | | | | | |
| | *Private manufacturing* | | *Private services* | | *Public sector* | |
	1990	*1998*	*1990*	*1998*	*1990*	*1998*
Formal agreement	16	18	26	25	28	31
Opposition from union representatives	10	11	6	5	6	11
Opposition from union members	9	11	7	9	10	13
No union limits	79	75	69	72	70	64
Weighted base	60	60	94	94	267	267
Unweighted base	168	170	122	122	246	246

Base: all continuing workplaces with 25 or more employees where recognized trade unions in 1990 and 1998.

Note: column percentages add to more than 100 since multiple responses were permitted.

indirect evidence from unionized workplaces whose workforce had shrunk by at least 50 per cent since 1990. Among these workplaces, the proportion of managers reporting opposition from union members to work reorganization rose fourfold to 21 per cent. Opposition from union representatives rose threefold to 14 per cent. The proportion reporting limitations due to formal agreements rose from 17 per cent to 32 per cent.

Nevertheless, there are indications that limitations on management's ability to organize work were associated with union strength. There was a significant association between unions constraining management's ability to organize work and the number of items subject to collective bargaining in both 1990 and 1998. This suggests that collective bargaining was continuing to 'bite'. There is further evidence of this from the small number of workplaces where the number of recognized unions had risen since 1990 and where the number of bargaining units had risen.[22] Where the number of recognized unions had increased, the proportion of managers reporting union constraints rose from 22 per cent to 67 per cent. By 1998, half (51 per cent) said formal agreements with unions constrained their ability to organize work, compared to 21 per cent in 1990. Where the number of bargaining units had increased, the proportion reporting union constraints rose from 20 per cent to 42 per cent.

Those reporting union constraints had higher workplace union density than those without union constraints in both 1990 and 1998: 83 per cent against 71 per cent in 1990 and 75 per cent against 68 per cent in 1998. Increases in union density since 1990 were also associated with increases in union constraints. Where union density had risen by 10 percentage points or more between 1990 and 1998, the proportion reporting opposition from union members rose from 3 to 18 per cent. Those reporting opposition from union representatives rose from 2 to 12 per cent, and those reporting constraints from formal agreements rose from 14 to 33 per cent. Whereas only 16 per cent had reported any union constraints in 1990, this rose to 40 per cent by 1998.

However, there is certainly evidence to suggest that, where unions' organizational base was being eroded, managers continued to find that unions constrained their ability to organize work. Thus, union constraints were also more likely to be reported in 1998 than 1990 where union density had *fallen* by at least 10 percentage points. Those reporting union constraints rose from 24 to 33 per cent. Union constraints were more likely to be reported where unions had lost on-site representation during the 1990s, and in cases where there was no on-site representation in either 1990 or 1998. In contrast, union constraints were reported at similar levels in 1990 and 1998 where there was representation in both years. In the small number of cases where unions had gained on-site representation there was a decline in reported union constraints on management.

Managers in 13 per cent of workplaces recognizing unions in 1990 and 1998 said that their ability to organize work was now constrained by a formal agreement with a union, whereas it had not been in 1990. In most of these cases, respondents reported that this was due to a change in management policy or approach, or followed negotiations with unions. In 28 per cent of cases, managers said they had been constrained by a formal agreement in 1990, but this was no longer the case in 1998. Again, in most of these cases, managers cited managerial policy or approach as the reason for the change. In 25 per cent of these cases, managers cited the restructuring of activities within the organization. In a minority of them the change had come about as a result of changing relations with unions and employees. In 14 per cent of these cases, respondents said relations with staff and unions had improved. In 4 per cent of cases, management had negotiated for the change with unions. In only 4 per cent of cases was the removal of the limitation attributed to a decline in union influence. In only 1 per cent of cases had the change resulted from union derecognition.

It seems from the evidence of our panel that unions continued to play an important role in limiting managerial prerogatives in 1998. However, when changes occurred, they were not usually the direct result of a strengthening or weakening in the union's position *vis-à-vis* the employer. In most instances, they were due to changes in managerial policy or approach, or a restructuring of activities within the organization.

Industrial action

Industrial action is the most direct, albeit negative, means by which unions can exert influence over management's ability to run the workplace. We may view unions' ability to deploy this ultimate sanction in the face of employer intransigence as a measure of union strength. Furthermore, to organize industrial action, a union must command substantial support among its members for the action. To sustain industrial action over a period, a union must have sufficient organizational strength and influence over its membership to ensure workers continue to operate in concert. For these reasons too, we may view industrial action as a measure of union strength. However, industrial action is an imperfect indicator of union strength. Unions with strong negotiating power should never have to resort to industrial action to obtain concessions from employers. If they have been unsuccessful in negotiation, resorting to industrial action instead, this may indicate that unions have not been strong enough to win over management with simply the threat of action. In addition, industrial action may only betoken union organizational strength when the action is official, that is, it has been sanctioned by the union. However, industrial action is often unofficial, prompted by what union members perceive to be the limitations of their own unions (Gall and McKay, 1997). So unofficial action may actually be an indicator of relative union weakness *vis-à-vis* its membership.

The WIRS series was launched at a time when industrial action was prevalent, but official information was limited to strikes. Throughout the series we have collected data on the incidence of various forms of collective industrial action from our management respondents, as well as worker representatives. We have not collected data on the impact of industrial action, or whether it was official,[23] so that what we can say about the links between industrial action and union strength is necessarily limited. We therefore limit ourselves to some observations regarding the incidence of the different forms of industrial action and their relationships with other measures of union strength.

The proportion of managers reporting industrial action in their unionized workplaces has been shrinking since the beginning of our survey series (Table 5.14).[24] Between 1980 and 1990, this decline was due to a reduction in non-strike action. Strike action was as prevalent in 1990 as it had been in 1980. In the 1990s, non-strike action continued to decline: it affected 3 per cent of

Table 5.14 Industrial action in workplaces with recognized unions, 1980 to 1998

| | Cell percentages | | | |
	1980	1984	1990	1998
Private sector manufacturing				
None	62	70	88	95
Non-strike action only	11	14	10	5
Strike action only	15	9	*	0
Both strike and non-strike action	12	7	3	0
Weighted base	327	235	169	102
Unweighted base	605	469	397	158
Private sector services				
None	89	85	93	97
Non-strike action only	5	4	1	1
Strike action only	5	8	1	2
Both strike and non-strike action	1	3	5	1
Weighted base	352	369	329	253
Unweighted base	289	300	350	396
Public sector				
None	73	61	67	95
Non-strike action only	12	7	4	2
Strike action only	8	14	23	2
Both strike and non-strike action	8	17	6	*
Weighted base	599	723	450	490
Unweighted base	681	824	535	562
All workplaces				
None	75	69	80	96
Non-strike action only	10	8	4	2
Strike action only	9	11	11	2
Both strike and non-strike action	7	11	5	*
Weighted base	1,277	1,327	948	845
Unweighted base	1,575	1,593	1,282	1,116

Base: all workplaces with 25 or more employees where recognized trade unions.

unionized workplaces in 1998, compared with 9 per cent in 1990. However, strike action also declined rapidly in the 1990s. It affected only 2 per cent of unionized workplaces in 1998, compared with 16 per cent in 1990. Fewer than 1 per cent of unionized workplaces were affected by strike action *and* non-strike action over the previous twelve months.

Throughout the course of the survey series, industrial action has been more prevalent in the public than the private sector. Within the private sector, it was far more prevalent in manufacturing than services. However, by 1998, industrial action was rare in all three broad sectors: each had witnessed a major decline in industrial action.

Although collective industrial action had disappeared in all but a very few unionized workplaces by 1998, it was more in evidence where unions were organizationally strong. It affected only 1 per cent of unionized workplaces with union density below 25 per cent. This compared with 8 per cent of workplaces with density between 90 and 99 per cent, and 6 per cent of workplaces with density between 75 and 89 per cent. Industrial action was also associated with on-site representation. One per cent of unionized workplaces with no union representative were affected by industrial action in 1998, compared with 5 per cent with an on-site representative who was not full-time and 11 per cent where there was an on-site full-time lay representative. That said, the rate of decline in industrial action in the 1990s was faster in unionized workplaces with a representative than in ones without.

Thus, although the link between union strength and industrial action, commented on in the past (Millward *et al.*, 1992: 282), remained apparent, the decline in industrial action in the 1990s throughout the unionized sector was very steep indeed, affecting strong and weak unions alike. It may be that legislative change has made unions more likely to threaten action, often backed by majority support in a ballot, to strengthen their bargaining position, without having to resort to industrial action (Elgar and Simpson, 1993).[25] If this is so, then we would have to qualify the conclusion that the demise of industrial action betokens a more general decline in the strength of unions.

Conclusions

In this chapter we have marshalled wide-ranging evidence to test the 'hollow shell' hypothesis, that in the declining portion of the British economy where trade unions were recognized by management they had little influence in 1998 compared with earlier years. In a period in which unions had suffered a general loss of influence both within the national polity and within the world of work, the argument was that where managements had continued to deal with unions it was largely a matter of form. Unions were reduced to the role of legitimizing to the workforce the changes that management wished to make (Brown *et al.*, 1998). An alternative possibility was that it was the weakest examples of workplace unionism that had disappeared; in this case, the unions' 'batting average' would have improved, since a higher proportion of the surviving ones would be 'strong'. To assess these alternatives explicitly we summarize the evidence of the chapter on our various measures and produce a composite index of strength from our time-series measures to help give an overall judgement.

Our most compelling evidence comes from features of union representation where we have complete and comparable information from our time-series and panel datasets. The time series allows us to track the changes from the 1980s, while the panel reinforces the analysis from 1990 to 1998. The three features where we have full information are union membership density, local union representatives and the coverage of collective bargaining.

Union membership density was the first measure of union strength that we examined. Average density in workplaces with recognized unions declined steadily from 1984 onwards, but the rate of decline accelerated sharply after 1990. The proportion of unionized workplaces with low density rose in the 1990s, after remaining stable in the 1980s, while the proportion with very high density continued to decline. These trends were universal, but those experiencing the greatest declines in union density were workplaces where unions were already weak. Our results showed that the sources of declining union density changed over the period. In the 1980s, the decline in management support for union membership accounted for much of the fall in union density, but in the 1990s three quarters of the fall was accounted for by shifts in workplace behaviour, irrespective of management encouragement for union membership. Reduced support for union membership among employees appeared to be the main source of the decline.

Turning to on-site union representation, our second measure of union strength, the changes are less clear-cut. After a fall in the proportion of unionized workplaces with on-site representatives in the period 1984–90, this measure remained constant in the 1990s. Furthermore, the ratio of members to representatives remained stable from the mid-1980s onwards, suggesting that recognized unions were maintaining their organizational strength where they continued to be recognized by employers.

Collective-bargaining coverage was our third key measure of union strength. Declining coverage since 1984, plus the emergence of unionized workplaces with no coverage in the 1990s, provided strong evidence in support of the 'hollow shell' hypothesis. Reductions in coverage in continuing unionized workplaces were the key to the change in the 1990s, with management presiding over steeper declines in coverage where unions weakened on other measures. Workplaces joining the population between 1990 and 1998 were also more likely to have no workers affected by negotiated pay settlements, even though their unions were formally recognized by management for this purpose.

To quantify the decline in union strength indicated by the three measures just discussed, we created a simple index based on union density, on-site representation and collective-bargaining coverage. Workplaces scored a point for each of the following indicators:

- union density of 75 per cent or more;
- having an on-site union representative; and
- collective-bargaining coverage of 80 per cent or more.

The index gives a clear gauge of the decline in union strength between 1984 and 1998, with the mean score for all unionized workplaces falling from 2.1 to 1.6 (Table 5.15, top left portion). Of equal interest is the changing distribution of union strength. Almost half (47 per cent) of all unionized workplaces scored the maximum of 3 points on the index in 1984. This fell to a third (34 per cent) in 1990 and a sixth (17 per cent) in 1998. The proportion scoring zero doubled between 1984 and 1990, but remained constant in the 1990s. The main feature of the 1990s was the stark fall in the proportion scoring highly on the index.

Table 5.15 Index of union strength within workplaces with recognized unions, 1984 to 1998

	Means and column percentages					
	All unionized workplaces			Public sector		
	1984	1990	1998	1984	1990	1998
Mean strength score	2.1	1.8	1.6	2.4	2.0	1.6
Strength score						
0	5	12	12	2	10	10
1	25	30	38	13	21	37
2	23	24	34	25	26	36
3	47	34	17	60	42	17
Weighted base	1,110	918	753	600	440	432
Unweighted base	1,265	1,204	990	625	483	475
	Private manufacturing			Private services		
	1984	1990	1998	1984	1990	1998
Mean strength score	1.8	1.7	1.7	1.8	1.5	1.4
Strength score						
0	1	9	3	12	16	18
1	49	38	42	33	38	38
2	20	22	36	22	23	29
3	30	31	19	34	23	15
Weighted base	217	171	100	293	307	221
Unweighted base	405	410	154	235	311	361

Base: all workplaces with 25 or more employees where recognized trade unions.

The remainder of the table also shows clear differences in the trends in union strength within the three broad sectors of the economy. Mean union strength hardly changed over the period in private manufacturing, whereas it declined significantly in private services and the public sector. Unions were most severely weakened in public sector workplaces. By 1998, based on this index, we would judge that there was little difference in the strength of unions across the three broad sectors of the economy.

When we look at the distribution of unionized workplaces by union strength within sectors, the most notable change is the declining proportion of workplaces with unions scoring the maximum on the index. In private manufacturing, it fell from 31 per cent in 1990 to 19 per cent in 1998, having remained constant in the second half of the 1980s. In private services, the decline was continuous, from 34 per cent in 1984 to 23 per cent in 1990 and 15 per cent in 1998. The public sector had the sharpest falls, the respective figures being 60, 42 and 17 per cent. On this evidence, there is considerable support for the 'hollow shell' hypothesis, particularly in the public sector, where strong local union organization had been most widespread in the 1980s.

We also assessed evidence on three measures of influence for which we were wholly or largely reliant on our panel data: the scope of collective bargaining, limits on managerial discretion on the organization of work, and joint regulation over procedures and appointments. In the unionized sector as a whole, there was no evidence of a general reduction in the scope of bargaining between 1990 and 1998 within our panel of continuing workplaces. Nor, when we compared joiners with longer-established workplaces in the 1998 cross-section on the basis of broadly similar questions could we detect differences in the scope of bargaining that implied that our panel results could not be generalized to the whole population represented by the cross-section surveys. On bargaining scope, then, the results do not support the 'hollow shell' hypothesis.

Our panel of continuing unionized workplaces also showed that there was no reduction in the extent to which unions could limit management's ability to organize work. If anything, unions' influence on this measure rose in the 1990s. Lastly, the evidence on joint regulation over appointments and procedures was mixed. Unions appeared to have maintained their influence in agreeing procedures and representing staff under those procedures. But they appeared to have lost influence over appointments of employee representatives to consultative committees and health and safety committees.

Finally, we presented some evidence on the decline in industrial action over the course of the series. This may also be interpreted as consistent with a decline in unions' organizational capacity, but the measure is an imperfect one for our current purpose, as we acknowledge.

We summarize the evidence on the 'hollow shell' hypothesis in Table 5.16. It is mixed, with strong supporting evidence coming from the time-series and panel data on union density and bargaining coverage. However, there is considerable contrary evidence from the panel on unions limiting management

Table 5.16 Summary of evidence for the 'hollow shell' hypothesis

	Time series, 1984–98	*Panel, 1990–98*
Union density	Yes	Yes
Union representation	Mixed	No
Bargaining coverage	Yes	Yes
Scope of bargaining	NA	No
Industrial action	Yes	Not presented
Limiting managerial action	NA	No
Joint regulation, procedures	NA	No
Joint regulation, appointments	Yes	Yes

discretion over the organization of work, on the scope of bargaining and on the presence and numbers of on-site representatives.

We conclude that, although the influence of recognized unions declined markedly from the mid-1980s onwards, unions continued to have a significant influence over management and workplace outcomes in 1998. This is at odds with a strict interpretation of the 'hollow shell' hypothesis. However, we qualify that conclusion to the extent that there is evidence that the strongest examples of union organization at workplace level, as captured by our index, became less common in the 1990s, especially in the public sector.

6 Pay determination and reward systems

Pay is one of the central concerns of all who work and of those that employ and manage them, as well as being a topic of considerable interest for trade unionists and policy-makers. Liberating the determination of pay from the perceived rigidities of collective bargaining – and increasing the use of performance-based pay – became increasingly articulated as explicit policy aims of Conservative governments during the 1980s (Kessler and Bayliss, 1998: 222–4). At the same time, 'pay flexibility' joined the labour market lexicon, while 'wage-push' inflation and 'leap-frogging pay settlements' diminished as sources of concern. Many aspects of pay continued to be widely debated in the 1990s, including the decentralization of bargaining, the complexity of bargaining arrangements, the impact of unions on pay levels and inequalities, and the merits of various payment systems.

Pay determination arrangements have been a core topic of the WIRS series since it began and the industrial relations and management literature has made extensive use of the results, particularly as the series progressed (Brown and Walsh, 1994; Brown et al., 1995; Kessler and Bayliss, 1998). The surveys have also addressed some questions about the composition of pay, such as incentive elements (Beatson, 1993; Heywood et al., 1995; Pendleton, 1997). But perhaps the most widely analysed data in the surveys have been those on pay levels and pay dispersion. These, in combination with data on the structures and arrangements for pay setting, have revealed important connections that have contributed much to both policy and academic debates (Blanchflower, 1986; Blanchflower and Oswald, 1995; Blanchflower et al., 1990; Gosling and Machin, 1995; Machin et al., 1993; Metcalf and Stewart, 1991; Millward and Woodland, 1995; Stewart, 1995). We hope the material in this chapter will take many of these discussions forward.[1]

In Chapter 4 we showed that the shrinkage in the extent of the joint regulation of pay which had occurred in the 1980s continued in the 1990s. But we did so in a crude fashion, merely classifying workplaces as either having or not having recognized trade unions that bargained about the pay of some employees. In Chapter 5 we added part of the detail, showing how the proportion of employees covered by collective bargaining had changed within the shrinking sector where unions were recognized. We also showed the ways in which the depth and scope of bargaining had changed within workplaces where pay was collectively determined. Our purpose in this chapter is to both broaden and sharpen these inquiries. We begin by giving an overview of pay determination over the course of the WIRS series.

The overall pattern of pay determination

To provide this overall picture we have characterized workplaces according to their main wage-setting arrangement, that is the arrangement that applies to the majority of employees at the establishment. The WIRS series provides information on whether the most recent pay settlement was negotiated, and also on the remoteness of the process from the workplace itself. By combining these pieces of information, we are able to illustrate how the nature and locus of pay determination at workplace level has changed over recent years.[2]

In order to identify the main type of wage-setting arrangement in each establishment, we subdivided workplaces according to the proportion of all employees that have their pay determined by collective bargaining. This is not possible for 1980, and so we concentrate on the period 1984–98. In workplaces with at least 50 per cent coverage, it follows that collective bargaining is the most common form of pay determination for employees at that workplace. This categorization forms a break with that used in previous sourcebooks, where the practice was to accord primacy to collective bargaining, however small the proportion covered by it in a particular workplace. In practice the two different approaches give similar results for the earlier surveys, since in the great majority of cases where unions were recognized the majority of employees were covered by bargaining. This was less commonly the case in 1998, as we showed in Chapter 5 (Table 5.8). We therefore feel that the earlier approach can no longer be justified, since collective bargaining covers fewer employees within workplaces where it exists and also because collective bargaining has ceased to be the dominant form of pay determination in the economy as a whole.

Within those workplaces in which the majority of employees were covered by collective bargaining, we examined the available information on the conduct of pay bargaining and identified which type of negotiations were said to be the most important in reaching the latest settlement for covered employees: multi-employer bargaining; bargaining at a higher level within the organization; or local, workplace-level bargaining. Where separate bargaining groups within the same workplace negotiated at different levels, the more remote level was given priority.[3] This provides an indication of how the degree of organization or establishment-level autonomy in collective bargaining has changed over time.

In workplaces where the majority of employees had their pay set by some means other than collective bargaining, we examined information on where the decision over the level of pay was taken. Workplaces were then characterized according to whether decisions about the level of pay were made outside the organization (for example by a statutory wages council or pay review body), at a higher level within the same organization, or at the establishment itself. Again, priority was given to the more remote level of decision-making.[4]

The changes in the overall pattern of pay determination since 1984 are shown in Table 6.1. The first row of the table shows that the percentage of workplaces in which collective bargaining was the dominant mode of pay determination fell by a half in the space of fourteen years, from 60 per cent in 1984 to 42 per cent in 1990 and just 29 per cent in 1998. There was also a substantial change in the nature of bargaining in such workplaces, shown by the decline in the influence of national, regional or industry-wide agreements. In 1984, multi-employer agreements were a feature of pay determination in over two thirds (69 per cent) of workplaces where most employees' pay was set by joint regulation. By 1998, the proportion had fallen to less than half (46 per cent). At the aggregate level, this meant that the proportion of all workplaces in which multi-employer agreements formed some part of the dominant arrangements for pay determination fell by around two thirds, from 41 per cent in 1984 to 13 per cent in 1998.

Among the rising proportion of workplaces in which pay was generally not subject to collective bargaining, the late 1980s saw little change in the levels at which such decisions were taken. In both 1984 and 1990, around one fifth of workplaces saw decisions over the pay of their employees taken at a level

Table 6.1 Locus of decision-making within main type of pay determination, 1984 to 1998

	Column percentages[a]		
	1984	*1990*	*1998*
Collective bargaining	**60**	**42**	**29**
Most distant level of negotiations			
Multi-employer bargaining	41	23	13
Multi-site, single-employer bargaining	12	14	12
Workplace bargaining	5	4	3
Don't know	1	1	*
Not collective bargaining	**40**	**58**	**71**
Most distant level of decision-making			
External to organization	7	9	14
Management at a higher level in organization	11	16	25
Management at workplace level	21	30	30
Don't know	1	3	2
Weighted base	*1,977*	*1,990*	*1,939*
Unweighted base	*1,990*	*2,039*	*1,866*

Base: all workplaces with 25 or more employees.

Note
a Subtotals in bold.

beyond the organization. A further three tenths saw some decisions taken at a higher level within the same organization, whilst one half decided pay solely at workplace level. The incidence of each of these forms of pay determination therefore rose in line with the overall proportion of workplaces where pay was generally not negotiated.

Between 1990 and 1998, however, the balance shifted slightly. Among workplaces where most employees' pay was not subject to negotiation, pay levels became more likely to be decided by those higher up in the organization (36 per cent, compared with 28 per cent in 1990) and less likely to be solely under the control of workplace management (43 per cent of workplaces, compared with 52 per cent in 1990). This was despite an increase in the incidence of single independent establishments. As a result, the proportion of all workplaces in which pay was primarily unilateral, and influenced by higher-level management to some degree, rose substantially from 16 per cent to 25 per cent between 1990 and 1998. In contrast, the proportion of all workplaces in which pay determination was principally the domain of establishment-level management, which had risen from 21 per cent to 30 per cent between 1984 and 1990, remained static in the most recent period.

In order to understand the causes of these various changes in the nature and level of pay determination more clearly, it is helpful to examine each of the three broad sectors of the economy in turn. In doing so, it becomes much easier to identify the influence of numerous factors such as the collapse of particular industry-level agreements, the abolition of the wages councils and the establishment of pay review bodies. We look first at private manufacturing industries.

Private sector manufacturing and extraction

In keeping with the overall pattern seen among all establishments, the percentage of private manufacturing plants in which pay was principally subject to collective bargaining fell by around one half between 1984 and 1998. In 1984, collective bargaining dominated pay determination arrangements in exactly half of all establishments in private manufacturing (Table 6.2). By 1990, this had fallen to exactly one third, and by 1998 it was down to less than one quarter (23 per cent).

Among those workplaces where pay was principally subject to joint regulation, both periods saw a decline in the influence of multi-employer agreements. In 1984, multi-employer agreements featured in pay determination within two fifths (41 per cent) of such workplaces. This fell to 36 per cent in 1990 and 27 per cent in 1998. At the aggregate level, among all work-places engaged in private sector manufacturing, these changes had the effect of reducing the proportion of establishments in which multi-employer agreements formed some part of the dominant arrangements for pay determination from 21 per cent in 1984 to just 6 per cent in 1998. What is more, the influence of multi-employer agreements fell in all types of manufacturing industry and

Table 6.2 Locus of decision-making within main type of pay determination in private sector manufacturing, 1984 to 1998

	Column percentages[a]		
	1984	1990	1998
Collective bargaining	**50**	**33**	**23**
Most distant level of negotiations			
Multi-employer bargaining	21	12	6
Multi-site, single-employer bargaining	11	6	5
Workplace bargaining	17	14	12
Don't know	2	1	*
Not collective bargaining	**50**	**67**	**77**
Most distant level of decision-making			
External to organization (e.g. wages council or industry body)	4	7	3
Management at a higher level in organization	11	11	24
Management at workplace level	33	47	48
Don't know	1	2	2
Weighted base	*423*	*425*	*354*
Unweighted base	*588*	*627*	*282*

Base: all private sector manufacturing workplaces with 25 or more employees.

Note
a Subtotals in bold.

among establishments of all sizes. The declining importance of multi-employer bargaining over this period reflects the demise of national agreements in industries such as engineering, textiles and cement manufacture; it represents the continuation of trends that began soon after the Second World War and which have been attributed largely to increases in the degree of international competition (Brown and Walsh, 1991: 48–9).

Returning to those workplaces where collective bargaining dominated pay determination, the decline in the influence of multi-employer agreements was accompanied by a broadly equivalent rise in establishment-level bargaining. In 1984, one third (34 per cent) of such workplaces bargained solely at the workplace. By 1998 the figure stood at 53 per cent. Notably, the rise in workplace bargaining was greater among workplaces that formed part of larger organizations than it was among single independent establishments. However, the overall incidence of workplace-only bargaining as the principal means of pay determination still fell in aggregate within private manufacturing, as the dominance of collective bargaining in general declined so dramatically within this sector.

In the latter half of the 1980s, the declining dominance of the various forms of collective bargaining was accompanied by the consolidation of unilateral, workplace-level pay setting as the dominant means of wage determination in private manufacturing. A marginal rise in the level of establishment autonomy among workplaces in which pay was not generally negotiated (from 67 per cent in 1984 to 70 per cent in 1990) was amplified by the increasing prevalence of this type of workplace as a whole. The result was that the overall proportion of private manufacturing workplaces in which pay was predominantly decided by establishment-level managers rose from one third (33 per cent) in 1984 to almost one half (47 per cent) in 1990.

This pattern changed in the 1990s, however. Between 1990 and 1998, the incidence of establishment-level autonomy among workplaces where pay was not generally negotiated fell from 70 per cent to 62 per cent. At the same time, the influence of the wider organization increased. Among the same group of workplaces, decision-making extended beyond the establishment to the wider organization in three tenths (31 per cent) of cases in 1998. This proportion had doubled since 1990 (16 per cent), although the proportion of workplaces that formed part of a larger organization had remained stable over the same period.

In aggregate, these changes meant that unilateral pay-setting by workplace managers remained the dominant form of pay determination in private manufacturing, accounting for just under half (around 48 per cent) of all workplaces in both 1990 and 1998. However, over the same period, the incidence of unilateral employer decision-making that extended to the wider organization had more than doubled, from one tenth (11 per cent) of all workplaces in 1990 to around one quarter (24 per cent) in 1998. This was now the dominant form of pay-setting arrangement among private manufacturing establishments that were part of larger organizations, accounting for 40 per cent of such establishments in 1998, compared with just 18 per cent in 1990. Around one quarter (23 per cent) principally determined pay by unilateral decision at workplace level without any external influence, down from one third (34 per cent) in 1990. Among single independent manufacturing establishments in the private sector, the proportion that principally determined pay by unilateral decision at workplace level rose from 69 per cent in 1990 to 84 per cent in 1998.

Analysis of our panel survey and data on workplaces leaving and joining the population shows that the declining influence of multi-employer agreements between 1990 and 1998 arose through two separate processes. First, the influence of multi-employer agreements fell among private manufacturing plants that remained in operation over the period. In 1990, multi-employer agreements formed some part of the dominant arrangements for pay determination in 14 per cent of such workplaces. Between 1990 and 1998, around one quarter of these moved to a form of collective bargaining that extended no further than the organization or workplace.[5] A further third of such plants switched from multi-employer bargaining to a situation in which pay was principally determined by management alone.[6] Workplaces that began to engage in multi-employer bargaining were very rare indeed. This meant that, by 1998, multi-employer bargaining featured as part of the dominant form of pay determination in only 6 per cent of continuing private manufacturing establishments.

The second reason for the declining influence of multi-employer bargaining among workplaces in manufacturing was that pay determination in workplaces which joined the sector between 1990 and 1998 was very unlikely to be dominated by collective bargaining which featured some element of multi-employer negotiation. The proportion of 'joiners' with this form of main pay determination arrangement was less than one in twenty.

The same analysis showed that the proportion of workplaces in which pay was principally determined as a result of unilateral decision-making involving higher-level management rose almost entirely because of the distinct behaviour of workplaces that joined the population over the period. Unilateral pay setting involving higher-level management predominated in around one tenth of continuing workplaces in manufacturing industry in both 1990 and 1998.[7] The proportion stood at a similar level among 'leavers'. However, it was much higher amongst workplaces joining private manufacturing. Around two fifths of all workplaces that joined this sector between 1990 and 1998 had this as their main form of pay determination.

In summary, by 1998, British manufacturing industry contained only a small proportion of workplaces where collective bargaining was the dominant form of pay setting. In this minority, the workplace was the usual level at which bargaining took place, in contrast to the dominance of multi-employer bargaining in earlier decades. Unilateral determination by management, either at workplace or higher levels, became the dominant mode of pay determination, accounting for three quarters of manufacturing workplaces in 1998.

Private sector services

Pay determination in private sector services has historically differed from pay setting in private manufacturing in two notable respects: first, the lesser use of collective bargaining; second, the greater prevalence of multi-site, as opposed to workplace-level, settlements. The stereotype has generally persisted throughout the period covered by the WIRS series, although there are many nuances in the way that pay determination arrangements have changed in private sector services during this time.

In 1984, collective bargaining dominated pay determination arrangements in slightly more than one third (36 per cent) of all workplaces engaged in private sector service activities (Table 6.3). The proportion fell by around one fifth in the following six years, to stand at around three in ten (29 per cent) in 1990. At this time, the proportion of workplaces in private services that negotiated pay for a majority of their employees was actually quite similar to that seen in private manufacturing (33 per cent), where the late 1980s had seen a substantial move away from collective bargaining. However, in the 1990s it was the service

Table 6.3 Locus of decision-making within main type of pay determination in private sector services, 1984 to 1998

	Column percentages[a]		
	1984	*1990*	*1998*
Collective bargaining	**36**	**29**	**14**
Most distant level of negotiations			
Multi-employer bargaining	17	8	3
Multi-site, single-employer bargaining	14	19	10
Workplace bargaining	3	2	1
Don't know	1	*	*
Not collective bargaining	**64**	**71**	**86**
Most distant level of decision-making			
External to organization (e.g. wages council or industry body)	13	5	10
Management at a higher level in organization	19	24	36
Management at workplace level	31	41	39
Don't know	1	1	2
Weighted base	838	979	1,057
Unweighted base	590	795	1,016

Base: all private sector service workplaces with 25 or more employees.

Note
a Subtotals in bold.

sector that saw the greater decline in the joint regulation of pay. By 1998, only 14 per cent of private service sector workplaces negotiated the pay of a majority of their employees with trade unions, either at the workplace or at a higher level.

Where pay was negotiated for a majority of employees, the influence of multi-employer agreements clearly declined and multi-site bargaining rose in importance. In 1984, multi-employer agreements helped to determine pay in half (49 per cent) of all private service sector workplaces where bargaining was dominant. In 1990, the proportion had fallen to around one quarter (27 per cent) and by 1998 it was just one fifth (19 per cent). Where establishments were members of employers' associations, the incidence of multi-employer agreements dropped from around four fifths of workplaces to around one quarter in the most recent period, whereas among non-members it remained at around one in six. When combined with the fall in bargaining as a whole, these changes meant that, by 1998, multi-employer agreements featured as part of the dominant form of pay determination in only 3 per cent of all private sector workplaces. This compared with 17 per cent in 1984.

Where collective bargaining continued to dominate pay determination, agreements were increasingly made at organization level as the influence of multi-employer negotiations waned. Organization-level bargaining characterized two fifths (40 per cent) of such workplaces in 1984, two thirds (65 per cent) in 1990 and 70 per cent in 1998, although the proportion of establishments that formed part of larger organizations remained about the same. Between 1984 and 1990, when the decline of collective bargaining within private services was not so great, the proportion of all private service sector workplaces for which organization-wide bargaining was the principal means of pay determination rose slightly, from 14 per cent to 19 per cent. However, the demise of bargaining in the sector in the 1990s brought the figure down to 10 per cent by 1998.

The decline in the influence of multi-employer agreements was particularly notable in two sectors: retailing and banking. Multi-employer agreements featured in the dominant pay determination arrangements of almost one third (31 per cent) of private sector banking establishments and one quarter (26 per cent) of private retail establishments in 1984. However, national negotiating bodies were wound up in both industries in the late 1980s (Brown and Walsh, 1991: 49). In banking, the period between 1984 and 1990 thus saw the virtual disappearance of multi-employer agreements (down to 1 per cent by 1990) and a large switch to organization-wide bargaining. This was followed by an increase in unilateral, organization-wide decision-making in the 1990s. In retailing, the proportion of workplaces in which most employees' pay was set by negotiation involving some multi-employer agreement had fallen to 10 per cent by 1990 and was just 6 per cent in 1998. Here the switch was largely to forms of pay determination that did not involve negotiation, with organization-wide pay setting coming to dominate the sector by 1998.

Returning to Table 6.3, one can see that, between 1984 and 1990, there was a fall in the proportion of workplaces in which pay setting was principally decided without negotiation, with some reference to an external body (13 per cent of private service establishments in 1984; 5 per cent in 1990). This could reflect legislative moves to restrict the powers of the wages councils, beginning with the Wages Act of 1986, such as the abandonment of separate rates for skilled workers and of regional differentials (Rubery, 1995: 566). Or perhaps more employers in the wages council sector voluntarily paid above the statutory minimum. It might also reflect, to some small degree, the withdrawal of the practice of 'contract compliance' whereby private sector contractors were required to pay a pre-determined rate to their employees when doing work for certain parts of the public sector (Kessler and Bayliss, 1998: 146). Whatever the explanation, unilateral pay setting by management at establishment or organization-wide level both became more prevalent. The larger rise was in the proportion of establishments at which pay was determined solely by workplace managers. This rose from 31 per cent in 1984 to 41 per cent in 1990, with increases seen among both independent establishments and those that formed a part of larger organizations.

Between 1990 and 1998, the proportion of establishments in which pay was principally set without negotiation, but with some reference to an external body, rose again, from 5 per cent to 10 per cent. This was despite the wages councils having finally been abolished in 1993. However, the 10 per cent in 1998 included cases in the education and health sectors where private sector respondents may have been citing pay review bodies as providing the basis for pay increases, even though they were not bound by their recommendations. It also included cases in construction, where establishments may have been following the industry body's pay agreement, although not bound to do so.

There was no further rise in the prevalence of unilateral, establishment-level pay determination, however. Instead, the 1990s saw a further increase in the proportion of private service sector establishments in which pay was principally set on a unilateral basis with some element of control being held by higher-level management. In 1998, it was by far the dominant form of pay-setting arrangement among private services establishments that were part of larger organizations, accounting for 53 per cent of such establishments, compared with 26 per cent in 1984 and 33 per cent in 1990. As a result, this type of arrangement characterized some 36 per cent of all private sector service establishments in 1998, compared with 24 per cent in 1990.

In summary, the 1990s saw a decline in the influence of multi-employer and multi-site bargaining over pay in private services, and a rise in the influence of unilaterally determined awards covering multiple sites within the same organization. Analysis of our panel survey and data on 'leavers' and 'joiners' suggested that differences in behaviour between workplaces that left the population and those that joined it lay at the heart of these developments. The pattern of pay determination amongst continuing workplaces in our panel survey remained largely unchanged between 1990 and 1998, since the movements that did occur balanced themselves out at the aggregate level. However, one tenth (9 per cent) of private sector service workplaces that either closed down or fell out of scope of the survey had pay determination arrangements that were dominated by collective bargaining featuring at least some multi-employer negotiations; this compared with just 1 per cent among joiners. Similarly, for one quarter (26 per cent) of leavers, pay arrangements were dominated by bargaining where at least some negotiations covered more than one site within the organization. The equivalent proportion among joiners was just one in twenty (6 per cent). Conversely, pay arrangements in workplaces that joined the population were more likely to be characterized by unilateral decision-making at a higher level in the organization (32 per cent, compared with 24 per cent of leavers).

Public sector

The public sector has undergone substantial reorganization since the early 1980s and this reorganization has impinged significantly upon the way that pay is determined in the sector. In particular, the long-standing public sector norm of nationally negotiated pay settlements covering a majority of employees in each workplace – reflected in our earlier surveys – no longer holds true.

Privatization and compulsory competitive tendering have, of course, removed some activities from the public sector altogether. In other areas, such as teaching and health care, central government has initiated widespread reform of pay setting in an attempt to gain greater control over the pay bill. More recently, however, attempts to commercialize much of the public sector have generated pressure towards the decentralization of pay setting. This has led to an unprecedented fragmentation of pay-setting arrangements within the sector.

The changing patterns of pay determination in the public sector are shown in Table 6.4. The degree of homogeneity in pay determination arrangements that was apparent in the early 1980s is striking when compared with the other two sectors, discussed above, and with later years. In 1984, collective bargaining determined the pay of a majority of employees in some 94 per cent of public sector workplaces, and in the vast majority of these (82 per cent of all public sector workplaces), multi-employer negotiations played at least some part in setting pay. However, in the second half of the 1980s, the pattern began to change.

Between 1984 and 1990, the proportion of public sector workplaces where pay was principally determined by collective bargaining fell from 94 per cent to 71 per cent. A number of factors accounted for the decline. First, the

Table 6.4 Locus of decision-making within main type of pay determination in the public sector, 1984 to 1998

	Column percentages[a]		
	1984	*1990*	*1998*
Collective bargaining	**94**	**71**	**63**
Most distant level of negotiations			
Multi-employer bargaining	82	58	39
Multi-site, single-employer bargaining	11	12	23
Workplace bargaining	*	*	1
Don't know	1	1	*
Not collective bargaining	**6**	**29**	**37**
Most distant level of decision-making			
External to organization (e.g. central government via pay review body)	3	16	29
Management at a higher level in organization	1	6	6
Management at workplace level	*	*	2
Don't know	*	6	0
Weighted base	717	587	528
Unweighted base	812	617	568

Base: all public sector workplaces with 25 or more employees.

Note
a Subtotals in bold.

government ended collective bargaining over pay for many health professionals through the introduction of a pay review body which was to make its first recommendation in the pay round that followed our 1984 survey. A similar situation occurred in the education sector in 1987 when, after a prolonged dispute, the government abolished the collective bargaining machinery responsible for negotiating the pay of schoolteachers in England and Wales. A pay review body was finally introduced in 1991. The effect of these various changes was also accentuated by the privatization of many public utilities, which removed from the public sector a number of workplaces with high degrees of coverage of collective bargaining.

Whilst the proportion of public sector workplaces in which pay was primarily determined by collective bargaining fell in the late 1980s, the pattern of bargaining within such workplaces also became slightly less centralized. Multi-employer bargaining had been a feature of negotiations in 87 per cent of these workplaces in 1984; by 1990 it had fallen to 82 per cent, with a consequent rise in the influence of organization-specific negotiations. Moves to organization-specific bargaining were seen particularly in central government, as a result of moves to devolve many civil service functions to semi-autonomous agencies, and in the health service.

At the aggregate level, multi-employer bargaining was still the dominant form of pay determination among public sector workplaces, but this type of arrangement characterized only three fifths (58 per cent) of establishments in 1990, compared with four fifths (82 per cent) in 1984 (Table 6.4). Organization-specific bargaining continued to be the dominant form of pay determination in around one tenth of all public sector workplaces. In contrast, the proportion of public sector workplaces in which pay was principally set without negotiation, but with some reference to an external body (e.g. by central government via a pay review body), rose substantially, from 3 per cent in 1984 to 16 per cent in 1990.[8]

The same broad trends continued in the 1990s. The proportion of workplaces in which pay was principally set by collective bargaining fell again, albeit less sharply, from 71 per cent in 1990 to 63 per cent in 1998. And amongst these workplaces, there were further moves to decentralize negotiations, with the reorganization of many parts of the civil service into semi-autonomous agencies, greater flexibility amongst local authorities and moves towards trust-level pay determination in the NHS. In 1998, multi-employer agreements featured as part of the principal pay-setting arrangements in only two fifths (39 per cent) of public sector workplaces, down from three fifths (58 per cent) in 1990. The proportion in which organization-specific bargaining was dominant doubled from 12 per cent in 1990 to 23 per cent in 1998.

Our time-series data also showed a further increase in the proportion of public sector workplaces in which pay was principally set without negotiation, but with some element of decision-making taking place outside the organization. This proportion rose from 16 per cent in 1990 to 29 per cent in 1998. However, data on continuing public sector workplaces in our panel survey suggested that these figures may have overstated the true increase over the period, and that the use of consistent forms of questioning in our time series may have generated an aggregate figure nearer 20 than 30 per cent in 1998. (Among continuing public sector workplaces, which represent the bulk of the public sector population, the figures were 19 per cent in 1990 and 23 per cent in 1998.) The increase would then be on the borderline of statistical significance. The time series showed little change in the relatively low proportion of workplaces where pay was principally set by unilateral determination involving decisions at organization or workplace level.

In comparison with the private sector, the patterns of change in the public sector were not as easy to discern within our panel survey and data on leavers and joiners.[9] None the less, our panel survey did show a notable fall in the influence of multi-employer bargaining within continuing public sector workplaces between 1990 and 1998. The proportion of continuing workplaces in which pay was principally subject to collective bargaining, with some element of multi-employer negotiation, fell from 60 per cent in 1990 to 47 per cent in 1998. Further investigation showed that this fall appeared to reflect the introduction of a pay review body for schoolteachers in England and Wales, together with the continuing decentralization of pay bargaining in the civil service and the Post Office.

Looking back over the period between 1984 and 1998, it is clear that there have been substantial changes in the way that pay is determined within the public sector. In some respects, the degree of change may have been greater in the private sector – the collapse of multi-employer bargaining being a case in point. However, the changes that have been evident in the public sector since the mid-1980s are at least as remarkable because, as others have already noted elsewhere (Kessler and Bayliss, 1998: 213), they represent a much more significant departure from past practice than in the private sector, where the changes more closely constitute the continuation of trends that were already apparent before our survey series began.

A brief recapitulation may be useful before we move on. By 1998, collective bargaining between employers and trade unions had ceased to be the dominant form of wage determination in a majority of British workplaces. In fact, it was the dominant form in little more than a quarter of workplaces. In fewer of these cases than previously, pay was set by multi-employer agreements. In the growing numbers of workplaces where most employees' pay was set without negotiation – nearly three quarters of all workplaces in 1998 – the most common locus of decision-making on pay was the workplace itself. However, a growing proportion of workplaces had pay principally set by higher-level management.

The overall coverage of collective bargaining

In the previous section we saw that the proportion of workplaces where bargaining was the dominant mode of pay determination fell in all sectors of the economy. We now look at the coverage of collective bargaining in more detail, including those workplaces where it was not the dominant form of pay setting.

Our use of the data here is different from what was done in Chapter 5, where we used the mean level of coverage across establishments with recognized unions as a measure of union strength. Here we consider all workplaces and use an aggregate measure which sums the number of employees covered by bargaining and divides by all employees. We use this measure to summarize briefly the changes in the coverage of collective bargaining over pay in the economy as a whole. These results are necessarily a combination of the changes in coverage within workplaces with recognition and the changes in the extent of recognition, discussed in Chapter 4. For this reason our analysis is brief and serves mainly to provide a more accurate picture of the continuing decline in collective bargaining in Britain than can be inferred from changes in the extent of recognition among workplaces.[10] As previously, our results are confined to the period from 1984 onwards, since no questions about coverage were asked in the 1980 survey. Other sources suggest that coverage declined somewhat between 1980 and 1984, part of a longer-term decline that began in the mid or late 1970s, after a period of rapid expansion in the 1960s (Milner, 1995: 85).

The aggregate level of the coverage of collective bargaining fell from 70 per cent of all employees in 1984 to 54 per cent in 1990 and further still to 40 per cent in 1998[11] (Table 6.5). The fall accelerated somewhat in the 1990s, rising from an annual rate of 2.9 per cent between 1984 and 1990 to an annual rate of 3.3 per cent between 1990 and 1998. However, whereas in the late 1980s the three broad sectors of the economy had experienced similar rates of change, there was a divergence of experience in the 1990s. Private manufacturing experienced a relatively modest fall from 51 per cent of employees to 46 per cent. Bargaining coverage in the public sector fell more rapidly, from 78 to 62 per

Table 6.5 Overall collective-bargaining coverage, by broad sector and union recognition, 1984 to 1998

	Cell percentages			*Percentages*	
	Proportion of employees covered by collective bargaining			*Average annual change*	
	1984	*1990*	*1998*	*1984–90*	*1990–98*
All workplaces	70	54	40	–2.9	–3.3
Broad sector					
Private manufacturing	64	51	46	–2.6	–1.3
Private services	40	33	21	–2.3	–4.7
Public sector	95	78	62	–2.3	–2.6
Any recognized unions	90	81	69	–1.3	–2.1

Base: all workplaces with 25 or more employees.

cent, while private sector services experienced the most rapid fall. Here the proportion of employees covered by collective bargaining fell by over a third, from 33 per cent in 1990 to 21 per cent in 1998, a rate of decline of nearly 5 per cent per year.

Not all industries were affected by the decline in coverage in the 1990s. Of the nine industries which we examined separately, three maintained similar levels of coverage: energy and water supplies, at over 85 per cent; metal goods and engineering, at just under 50 per cent; and distribution, hotels and catering at around 20 per cent. Both of the last two cases were industries where coverage had fallen substantially between 1984 and 1990. Only in the energy and water supply industry was the coverage level similar in 1998 to what it had been in 1984, perhaps a surprising result, given the experience of some other industries where wholesale privatization had occurred. Looking at industry and ownership sector combined, we also noted that in publicly owned transport and communications coverage remained at the same high level while in the privately owned portion of the same industry coverage fell substantially.

Among the many other establishment characteristics, besides industry, that we examined in relation to changes in coverage, only one stood out against the tide of decline. This was nationality of ownership. We found that foreign-owned workplaces maintained their level of coverage at around 40 per cent while in domestically owned workplaces coverage fell from 40 to 28 per cent between 1990 and 1998. This divergence is at odds with the respective trends in recognition, where foreign-owned workplaces manifested a sharper fall. The aggregate level of coverage held up among foreign-owned workplaces because those workplaces that did have recognized unions were larger, and their total coverage was at least as high in 1998 as it was in 1990.

Overall within workplaces with recognized unions, coverage dropped continuously from 1984 onwards. In 1984, 90 per cent of employees who worked in workplaces with at least one recognized union had their pay determined by collective bargaining (Table 6.5). The comparable figure in 1990 was 81 per cent and there was a further and more rapid fall to 69 per cent by 1998. Using shift-share analysis we calculated that the decline in coverage within the unionized sector accounted for about a half of the overall decline in coverage from 54 to 40 per cent between 1990 and 1998. The other half arose from the shrinkage in the size of the unionized sector itself.

Much of the overall decline in coverage within workplaces with recognized unions came about through changes in the composition of the population, but this effect was confined to workplaces joining the population between 1990 and 1998. Leavers were indistinguishable from continuing workplaces in 1990. Their respective coverage figures, where there was recognition, were 79 and 80 per cent; and workplaces that had closed down were very similar to those that shrank below our twenty-five employee threshold. Joiners, on the other hand, had lower coverage than continuing workplaces in 1998: 70 per cent, compared with 75 per cent. And new workplaces had lower coverage, 68 per cent, than those that grew to above the twenty-five employee threshold (76 per cent). So both the lower coverage within new workplaces and the decline in coverage among continuing workplaces (from 80 to 75 per cent) contributed to the net decline after 1990 in coverage across workplaces with recognized unions.

The result of the above changes was to make Britain even more exceptional within Europe in its low coverage of collective pay setting than it was in the mid 1990s, on the basis of which Brown *et al.* (1997) drew attention to Britain's unusual position. Coverage in Britain has fallen more rapidly than union membership density. Our time-series figures between 1984 and 1998 show that coverage fell from 70 per cent to 40 per cent while density fell from 58 per cent to 36 per cent. There seems little likelihood from our analysis that the decline in the coverage of collective bargaining will be reversed in the short term, even if density were to stabilize or increase.

Multi-unionism and bargaining structure

Multi-unionism

Compared with most other industrialized economies, Britain has long been known for its bewildering number of separate trade unions and complex bargaining structures. As evidence accumulated on the economic implications of these arrangements (Blanchflower and Cubbin, 1986; Machin *et al.*, 1993; Metcalf and Stewart, 1992), commentators, government spokespersons and trade union leaders advocated moves to simpler arrangements, particularly single-table bargaining. Such moves were made easier in some cases by union amalgamations and in others by the increased difficulty for trade unions in mounting secondary industrial action in support of separate arrangements. However, before discussing bargaining structures we set the scene by examining the degree of multi-unionism at workplace level.

The measure of multi-unionism most relevant to the question of pay determination is the number of recognized unions at workplaces with collective bargaining, best summarized by distinguishing between single and multi-union workplaces. After little change in the 1980s (Millward *et al.*, 1992), multi-unionism declined thereafter: 64 per cent of workplaces with recognized unions had more than one such union in 1990; 57 per cent did so in 1998. Multi-unionism did not decline in all types of workplace. It did fall in workplaces where collective bargaining was the dominant form of pay determination, from 70 per cent of such workplaces in 1990 to 57 per cent in 1998. But in the smaller number of workplaces where collective bargaining only affected a minority of employees, it increased substantially (from 39 per cent of workplaces in 1990, to 76 per cent in 1998). However, the aggregate pattern was one of simplification.

Did the overall shift away from multi-unionism come about because managements recognized fewer of the unions that had members in 1998, or because there were fewer unions with members anyway? To answer this question we first look at the numbers of unions present. In our 1990 and 1998 surveys

Table 6.6 Numbers of unions present at workplaces, by main type of pay
determination, 1990 and 1998

| | *Cell percentages and means* | |
	1990	*1998*
All establishments		
Number of unions present		
One	34	43
Two	27	19
Three	12	15
Four or more	27	23
Mean	2.7	2.4
Collective bargaining covers 50 per cent or more employees		
Number of unions present		
One	27	40
Two	33	23
Three	15	15
Four or more	25	32
Mean	2.8	·2.4
Collective bargaining covers 1–49 per cent of employees		
Number of unions present		
One	48	22
Two	21	12
Three	3	17
Four or more	28	49
Mean	2.7	3.7
No employees covered by collective bargaining		
Number of unions present		
One	51	57
Two	10	15
Three	10	14
Four or more	29	14
Mean	2.6	2.0

Base: all establishments with 25 or more employees.

we had a simple question that captured this variety.[12] The results are given in
Table 6.6.

Multi-union representation was the most common arrangement in 1990 and
it remained so in 1998, although by a smaller margin. In 1990, 34 per cent of
workplaces with union members had a single union present, 27 per cent had
two unions, 12 per cent had three and over a quarter (27 per cent) had four or
more. This distribution moved towards single union representation during the
1990s such that by 1998 43 per cent of workplaces had a single union. The mean
number of unions at workplaces with union members fell from 2.7 to 2.4.

Although this fall in the number of unions present was a widespread phenomenon, it did not affect all types of workplace. In particular we found that it varied according to the dominant mode of pay determination. For this analysis we used a slight elaboration of our classification set out at the beginning of this chapter, distinguishing within the category of workplaces where collective bargaining was not the dominant mode of pay determination those workplaces where there was a minority of employees affected by bargaining from those where none at all were. We found that the fall in the number of recognized unions did affect workplaces where collective bargaining was the dominant mode of pay determination; and it affected workplaces where unions had members but no employees were covered by collective bargaining. For these two types of case, the most common in both years, the respective mean number of unions fell from 2.8 to 2.4 and from 2.6 to 2.0. However, for the minority of workplaces where a minority of employees was covered by collective bargaining (10 per cent in 1990; 6 per cent in 1998), the number of unions increased substantially. The mean number of unions rose from 2.7 to 3.7. There were four or more unions present in a half of these workplaces in 1998, compared with just over a quarter in 1990.[13]

The shift away from multi-union representation was more apparent in the public sector, where the mean number of unions dropped from 3.9 to 3.2 between 1990 and 1998, than it was in the private sector (comparable figures being 1.7 and 1.5). Within the private sector, foreign-owned workplaces actually showed an increase (from 1.6 to 2.0), another example of their divergence from some of the trends shown by domestically owned employers. Generally it was larger workplaces where the biggest falls occurred; among workplaces with 500 or more employees the mean fell from 5.7 to 3.8.

Our panel data confirmed the change to fewer unions being present. Among continuing workplaces the change was modest: 30 per cent of those with union members in 1990 had a single union while 33 per cent had four or more unions; in 1998, 33 per cent had a single union and 26 per cent had four or more unions. But where changes occurred within continuing workplaces, decreases in the number of unions were more than twice as common as increases. Leavers, both closures and workplaces that shrank below twenty-five employees after 1990, were in fact more likely to have a single union present than workplaces that continued from 1990 to 1998 (43 per cent, compared with 30 per cent). The effect of their leaving the population, on its own, would have been to reduce the extent of single union representation. Thus it was workplaces joining the population that were the main compositional influence in the trend towards single union representation; among these 53 per cent had a single union present, while only 22 per cent had four or more unions.

The fall in the numbers of unions present at workplaces was the proximate cause of the slight drop in the number of recognized unions. Figure 6.1 shows the mean number of recognized unions by the number of unions present. These numbers did not change substantially between 1990 and 1998; we certainly do not see a general tendency for there to be fewer recognized unions for a given

Figure 6.1 Mean number of recognized unions by number of unions present, 1990 and 1998

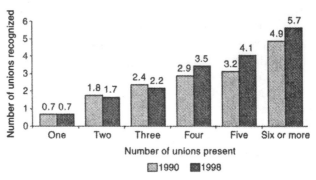

Base: all workplaces with 25 or more employees and union members present.

number of unions present. So the drop in the numbers of recognized unions was largely because fewer unions had members, rather than a lowered propensity for management to recognize those unions with members at a given workplace.

For more detailed explanations of why the number of recognized unions fell in the 1990s we turn to our panel interviews.[14] Panel cases where the number of recognized unions had decreased between 1990 and 1998 outnumbered those where the number had increased by a ratio of 2 to 1. In both types of case, respondents were asked for the reasons. Union mergers or amalgamations were by far the most common explanation for having fewer recognized unions; in 55 per cent of cases this reason was given.[15] The next most common reason, given in 21 per cent of cases, was that the jobs covered by a union that was no longer recognized had declined or disappeared. Members transferring to another recognized union was the explanation given by 9 per cent. A similar proportion mentioned that unions had been derecognized at the establishment following a change in management policy or approach. In the much smaller number of cases where the number of recognized unions had gone up, the most common explanation was that new jobs or occupations had been created and the relevant employees had been granted separate representation. Nearly as common was the fact that an additional union had obtained recognition for jobs already covered by an existing recognized union. The third commonly mentioned reason was that recognition had come about by extension from elsewhere in the same organization.

Compositional changes were also part of the explanation. Leavers were more likely to recognize a single union than workplaces that continued in operation between 1990 and 1998, so this alone would have decreased the extent of single union representation. Again it was workplaces joining the population that contributed to the net decline in multi-unionism. Joiners with union members present were less likely to recognize any unions than continuing workplaces in 1998 (73 per cent did so, compared with 81 per cent). They were also much more likely to recognize a single union where they recognized any; 66 per cent of joiners did so, compared with only 42 per cent of continuing workplaces.

Thus a variety of factors lay behind changes in the number of recognized unions among continuing workplaces. These factors included occupational change, the changing preferences of employees for different unions and employers' withdrawal of recognition. But union mergers, and the greater propensity to recognize a single union among workplaces joining the survey population, were what lay behind the bulk of the changes.

Bargaining structure

Although an individual union may negotiate separately for different groups of workers (especially likely where the union has recently experienced a merger), generally the number of recognized unions at a workplace sets a limit on the number of separate bargaining groups to be found. Of course, separate unions may also negotiate together, and 'single table' bargaining represents the case where all recognized unions negotiate jointly. This type of arrangement became much more common between 1990 and 1998. Amongst workplaces where collective bargaining was the dominant form of pay setting, the proportion with single-table bargaining rose from 40 per cent in 1990 to 77 per cent in 1998 (Table 6.7). This shift, most marked in the public sector, but still very pronounced in the private sector, possibly represents one of the most striking changes in the nature of British industrial relations in the 1990s.

With such a major change in the population generally, it is to be expected that nearly all types of workplace were affected. Of the various separate

Table 6.7 Incidence of single-bargaining units within workplaces where collective bargaining was dominant, by sector and number of recognized unions, 1990 and 1998

	Cell percentages	
	1990	*1998*
All establishments with 50 per cent or more workers covered	40	77
Broad sector		
Private manufacturing	57	80
Private services	57	90
Public sector	23	70
Number of recognized unions		
One	100	100
Two	18	57
Three or more	10	58

Base: all establishments with 25 or more employees, where 50 per cent or more of all employees covered by collective bargaining.

industries that we examined, only the extraction and metal and chemical manufacturing sector showed no move towards single-table bargaining. Foreign-owned workplaces were the other notable exception. But did the change come about from union mergers, partial derecognition or the amalgamation of previously separate bargaining units? We have a number of pieces of evidence with which to address this question.

First of all, as noted earlier, fewer workplaces where collective bargaining predominated were ones with multiple recognized unions. We calculated (using shift-share analysis) that if the same relationship between numbers of bargaining units and multi-unionism had held in 1998 as in 1990, but the incidence of multi-unionism had changed as it did, the proportion of workplaces with single-table bargaining would have moved from 40 per cent to 54 per cent. In fact it moved to 77 per cent. We can infer that the reduction in multi-unionism was not the principal cause of the trend to single-table bargaining. The reduction in multi-unionism played a part, but the principal cause was the change to less complex negotiating structures among those workplaces with multiple unions.

Returning to the principal cause, our panel survey confirmed the major change in behaviour. Among continuing workplaces that had at least 50 per cent coverage in 1990, 36 per cent had single-table bargaining; of those that had 50 per cent coverage in 1998, 57 per cent had single-table bargaining. Among continuing workplaces with at least 50 per cent coverage in both 1990 and 1998, 49 per cent made no change in the number of bargaining units, 40 per cent reduced the number, while only 11 per cent increased the number. Simplification was overwhelmingly the dominant type of change among workplaces that continued to set pay for the majority of their employees through collective bargaining with trade unions.

Changes in the population of workplaces also played a part. Workplaces that joined the population and adopted collective bargaining for the majority of their employees, nearly always did so with a single negotiating forum: 88 per cent of them did so, while only 8 per cent had two bargaining units and a mere 4 per cent had three units. Among these joiners, single-table bargaining was equally common in private and public sector workplaces, whether they were new workplaces or ones that had grown above the twenty-five employee threshold. On the other hand, leavers actually attenuated the change, as more of them (49 per cent) had single-table arrangements in 1990 than the generality of workplaces at the time (36 per cent). But here the public and private sectors differed markedly; few public sector leavers (closures and those shrinking below twenty-five employees) had single-table bargaining arrangements, whereas most private sector ones did. However, private sector leavers were much more numerous than their public sector counterparts and hence dominated the overall results. But it was joiners, with their almost universal adoption of single-table bargaining, that contributed most of the compositional change that reinforced the changes towards simplification of bargaining structures made by continuing workplaces.

As noted earlier, among continuing workplaces with recognized unions in both 1990 and 1998, those reducing the number of negotiating units formed the great majority of those that changed. In these cases our respondents were asked how the change came about, and around a half answered, simply, that previously separate unions or bargaining groups now negotiated jointly. Among those that gave other answers, the most common reply was that jobs previously covered by a separate negotiating group no longer existed at their workplace. A similar number mentioned union mergers or amalgamations. And a similar number said that a union with separate negotiating rights had been derecognized. Our interpretation of this rather insubstantial evidence is that many, if not most, of the moves towards simpler negotiating arrangements were at the instigation of management.

Influences on the size of pay settlements

Policy-makers, labour economists and industrial relations specialists have long had a fascination with the ways in which social and economic forces come to bear upon the levels of pay that employees receive and the ways in which those levels are modified through time. Since 1979 the Confederation of British Industry (CBI) pay databank has been widely used to track changes in the importance of a number of factors bearing upon negotiated wage settlements in private manufacturing industry and, more recently, private services (Ingram *et al.*, 1999). But the databank information – although extensive – is not statistically representative of workplaces, settlement groups or employees. Since 1984 the WIRS series have added some statistically representative information about the factors affecting the pay increases of employees in all sectors of the economy, both for those affected by negotiated settlements and those whose pay was not subject to negotiation. However, changes in coding between 1984 and 1990, plus the redesign of WERS98 and the recasting of many of the questions on pay determination, mean that we cannot present simple time-series data on the influences upon pay settlements. What we can do is present some limited results for 1984 and 1990, together with panel results for 1990 to 1998 using identical questions and coding. Both of these sets of results entail complications which require some initial explanation.

As previous sections of this chapter will have already made clear, many workplaces have complex structures for pay determination affecting different groups of employees. In our initial description of these structures we characterized workplaces according to the arrangement affecting the largest number of employees. We also do that here. Thus where at least 50 per cent of employees had their pay set by joint regulation with trade unions, our description of the factors that managers reported as having influenced the most recent settlement refers to the largest group covered by joint regulation. In 1984 and 1990 there was separate questioning about manual and non-manual employees. In some cases, one or both groups may have been covered by more than one bargaining unit; we selected the largest of these as best representing the establishment as a whole. In workplaces where fewer than 50 per cent of employers were covered by joint regulation we selected the available data on the factors affecting the size of the settlement for the largest group of 'uncovered' employees, manual or non-manual (where a minority were covered by bargaining we ignored this and concentrated on the employees whose pay was not subject to negotiation).

Results for 1984 and 1990 are presented separately for the private and public sectors, with similar items grouped together under broad headings to give a clearer picture of general influences. Table 6.8 gives the results for workplaces where collective bargaining was the dominant mode of pay determination. It

Table 6.8 Factors influencing the size of most recent pay settlements for the largest bargaining units where collective bargaining was dominant, 1984 and 1990

| | *Percentages*[a] | | | |
| | *Private sector* | | *Public sector* | |
	1984	*1990*	*1984*	*1990*
Cost of living	35	54	28	45
Labour market conditions	..	39	..	26
Comparisons with other employers	..	34	..	18
Recruitment or retention	..	6	..	7
Economic factors	..	39	..	7
Ability to pay	..	14	..	6
Performance of workplace or organization	..	19	..	1
General economic conditions	..	5	..	1
Linkage to other settlement	15	13	6	14
Other influences	48	19	56	50
Productivity improvements	..	6	..	6
Limits set by higher authority	..	3	..	15
Individual employee performance	3	2	1	4
Changes in pay systems	..	0	..	3
Industrial action or threat of it, bargaining power	..	2	..	13
Other answers	44	5	55	9
Don't know, not stated	7	8	11	7
Weighted base	*510*	*420*	*662*	*415*
Unweighted base	*679*	*685*	*783*	*510*

Base: all establishments with 25 or more employees, where 50 per cent or more of all employees covered by collective bargaining.

Note
a   Summary totals in italics.

shows that the cost of living was the single most commonly cited factor in both public and private sectors in 1984 and in 1990. In the increased inflationary circumstances of 1990, however, many more managers cited the cost of living than had done so in 1984. Two other factors showed increased importance in the public sector: comparability with other settlements, itself a product of the notable decline in multi-employer bargaining in the sector (see Table 6.4); and individual employee performance. Neither of these increased in private sector workplaces where collective bargaining predominated.

In Table 6.9 we show the comparable results for workplaces where the pay of most employees was not subject to collective bargaining. For technical

Table 6.9 Factors influencing the size of most recent pay settlements for the largest settlement units where collective bargaining was not dominant, 1984 and 1990, private sector only

	Percentages[a]	
	1984	*1990*
Cost of living	30	42
Labour market conditions	..	38
Comparisons with other employers	..	28
Recruitment or retention	..	11
Economic factors	..	32
Ability to pay	..	11
Performance of workplace or organization	..	19
General economic conditions	..	2
Linkage to other settlement	19	15
Other influences	46	34
Productivity improvements	..	2
Limits set by higher authority	..	1
Individual employee performance	24	26
Changes in pay systems	..	1
Industrial action or threat of it, bargaining power	..	0
Other answers	21	3
Don't know, not stated	3	4
Not asked	16	7
Weighted base	*749*	*983*
Unweighted base	*492*	*737*

Base: private sector establishments with 25 or more employees, where less than 50 per cent of all employees covered by collective bargaining.

Note
a Summary totals in italics.

reasons, these are confined to the private sector.[16] The table shows that the cost of living was less commonly mentioned as a factor in determining the size of non-negotiated pay settlements than it was in respect of negotiated settlements. However, the cost of living did become more important in determining the pay of uncovered workers in the latter half of the 1980s (up from 30 per cent to 42 per cent), as it had done for workers whose pay was determined by collective bargaining. The more striking difference between the factors that influenced the pay of covered and uncovered workers, however, was the degree to which individual employee performance affected the size of pay settlements for those not covered by collective bargaining. Around one quarter of private sector respondents mentioned this factor in both 1984 and 1990 (Table 6.9), compared with less than one in twenty where pay settlements were the subject of collective agreement.

Our main source for updating the above results to 1998 is our panel of continuing establishments which we interviewed in 1990 and 1998. Here, in our 1998 interviews, we were able to repeat the earlier questions precisely and then code them in the same way as in 1990, where necessary characterizing the workplace by using data about the largest settlement unit within it. But structural changes within some establishments meant that we might not be talking about the same group of employees on the two occasions. We therefore also mention an alternative analysis of cases where we collected data in 1998 about the largest settlement unit in 1990 – in effect, a panel analysis of bargaining units, rather than workplaces.[17] This is done at the end of the current section.

Using the panel of workplaces as a proxy for unavailable cross-section data, Table 6.10 shows, separately for the private and public sectors, the factors affecting settlements for workplaces where collective bargaining was dominant in 1990 and similarly in 1998. These formed only a minority of private sector panel cases in each year, but a majority of public sector cases. In the private sector, the cost of living retained its position as the principal factor affecting pay settlements, with just over a half of cases citing it in both 1990 and 1998. Labour market conditions became less salient, dropping from 37 to 23 per cent, largely because fewer respondents mentioned comparisons with other employers or 'the going rate'. There was also a slight fall in those citing a link or comparability with other settlements (mostly external ones). Economic factors, on the other hand, were much more frequently cited, increasing from 32 to 63 per cent of cases. The more detailed coding of these responses showed that, in the improved economic conditions of 1998 compared with 1990, many more employers cited general economic conditions while similar numbers cited the firm's ability to pay increases. More respondents, 28 per cent compared with 14 per cent, mentioned the financial performance of the workplace or the larger organization owning it. Some other influences also featured in 1998 that had been very rarely mentioned in 1990: budget limits set by higher management were one such influence, reflecting the reduced autonomy of workplace managers that we noted in Chapter 3. Another was changes in payment systems, a factor prominent only in relation to the private services sector in 1998.

Table 6.10 Factors influencing the size of most recent pay settlements for the largest bargaining units in panel cases where collective bargaining was dominant, 1990 and 1998

| | Percentages[a] | | | |
| | Private sector | | Public sector | |
	1990	1998	1990	1998
Cost of living	60	53	43	40
Labour market conditions	37	23	23	4
Comparisons with other employers	31	22	18	3
Recruitment or retention	6	1	4	0
Economic factors	32	63	6	17
Ability to pay	16	16	2	3
Performance of workplace or organization	14	28	2	11
General economic conditions	3	19	1	2
Linkage to other settlement	11	6	20	18
Other influences	19	31	51	49
Productivity improvements	6	7	5	10
Limits set by higher authority	1	6	16	33
Individual employee performance	3	2	5	3
Changes in pay systems	0	9	6	2
Industrial action or threat of it, bargaining power	2	0	12	0
Other answers	1	6	7	2
Don't know, not stated	8	6	2	11
Weighted base	*140*	*129*	*196*	*164*
Unweighted base	*279*	*244*	*218*	*180*

Base: all continuing establishments with 25 or more employees, where 50 per cent or more employees covered by collective bargaining in the relevant year.

Note
a Summary totals in italics.

Some of these changes were mirrored in the public sector. Here comparisons with other employers became much less common, workplace or organizational performance increased in salience and limits set by higher authority were much more frequently cited. Industrial action or the threat of it completely disappeared as a salient factor between 1990 and 1998.

In workplaces where collective bargaining was not the dominant form of pay determination the picture was less clear. As with our time-series data from 1984 and 1990, we focus solely on the private sector; Table 6.11 gives the results. Fewer employers cited labour market conditions in 1998 than in 1990, but many more cited workplace or organizational performance (up from 19 to 35 per cent). Many fewer (22 per cent down to 6 per cent) mentioned links

Table 6.11 Factors influencing the size of most recent pay settlements for the largest settlement units in panel cases where collective bargaining was not dominant in both 1990 and 1998, private sector only

	Percentages[a]	
	1990	*1998*
Cost of living	34	38
Labour market conditions	46	30
Comparisons with other employers	34	27
Recruitment or retention	12	2
Economic factors	34	47
Ability to pay	15	7
Performance of workplace or organization	19	35
General economic conditions	1	5
Linkage to other settlement	22	6
Other influences	35	49
Productivity improvements	2	4
Limits set by higher authority	2	15
Individual employee performance	21	23
Changes in pay systems	1	1
Industrial action or threat of it, bargaining power	0	0
Other answers	9	6
Don't know, not stated	2	6
Weighted base	*399*	*418*
Unweighted base	*276*	*325*

Base: all continuing private sector establishments with 25 or more employees, where less than 50 per cent of all employees covered by collective bargaining in the relevant year.

Note
a Summary totals in italics.

with other pay settlements, another sign of the weakening of the indirect influence of joint regulation with trade unions. Another notable change was the increasing number who mentioned limits set by higher-level management – corroboration of our results in Chapter 3 on the increasing centralization of decision-making in complex organizations.

Our final piece of evidence on the factors influencing pay settlements uses the panel of continuing workplaces to focus on bargaining units that continued in existence between 1990 and 1998. In the great majority of cases the largest unit in 1990 continued to be the largest in 1998.[18] Where it was not, we asked the panel interview respondent to identify by name what had been the largest unit in 1990; an additional question was then asked on the factors influencing the size of the most recent settlement affecting it. The results for all continuing

Table 6.12 Factors influencing the size of most recent pay settlements for bargaining units existing in both 1990 and 1998, private sector only

	Percentages[a]	
	1990	*1998*
Cost of living	52	51
Labour market conditions	31	23
Comparisons with other employers	27	23
Recruitment or retention	4	0
Economic factors	35	57
Ability to pay	17	14
Performance of workplace or organization	17	30
General economic conditions	1	14
Linkage to other settlement	18	5
Other influences	18	35
Productivity improvements	6	9
Limits set by higher authority	0	8
Individual employee performance	4	3
Changes in pay systems	0	9
Industrial action or threat of it, bargaining power	1	0
Other answers	7	6
Don't know, not stated	8	6
Weighted base	*100*	*100*
Unweighted base	*201*	*201*

Base: all continuing establishments in the private sector in both 1990 and 1998, where the largest bargaining unit in 1990 still existed in 1998.

Note
a Summary totals in italics.

bargaining units in the private sector are shown in Table 6.12. These show the continued importance of the cost of living, the increased importance of economic factors (especially workplace performance) and the declining importance of the labour market and linkages to other settlements. As with the earlier analysis in Table 6.10, other influences that became salient in 1998 were the limits set by a higher authority and changes in payment systems. The latter are what we now turn to for a more broad-ranging discussion.

Payment systems

Systems of payment and reward are among the most complex phenomena that managers and researchers have to deal with. The WIRS series has never attempted to capture their complexity and instead has settled for small groups of questions about specific payment practices, such as payment by results, profit-related pay and employee share ownership. These have been extensively analysed in relation to industrial relations and economic performance variables (Blanchflower and Oswald, 1988; Fernie and Metcalf, 1995; Heywood *et al.*, 1997; McNabb and Whitfield, 1998; Pendleton, 1997; Wood, 1996). One broad conclusion that can be drawn is that the different forms of contingent pay – incentive pay, profit-related pay, employee share ownership and so on – have different sets of determinants and are associated with different outcomes. For this reason we discuss their changing incidence separately.

In the 1998 survey a new attempt was made to grapple with the complexities of payment systems with a raft of new questions on the make-up and levels of pay, as well as on payment-setting arrangements and structures. These new questions have yet to be analysed to give an up-to-date and comprehensive picture of payment systems and pay determination in British workplaces.[19] Unfortunately, only a small selection of them can help us describe and analyse how payment systems have changed since the earlier surveys, most of these being simple questions about the incidence of various forms of contingent pay and employee share ownership. We use them where appropriate in some of the sections that follow. On some other matters we are able to update the results from the previous surveys by using the results from identical questions that were included in our panel interviews.

Incentive pay

The first type of payment system we discuss is incentive pay. In 1990 we asked managers about two forms of incentive payment system: payment by results and merit pay. We distinguished the two by defining payment by results as a system whereby some element of employees' pay was directly linked to an objective measure of their output; merit pay, on the other hand, covered systems where employees' pay depended on the subjective assessment of their work by managers or supervisors. The two questions were asked separately for each of the eight occupational groups distinguished in the 1990 interviews.[20]

The same topics were covered in the 1998 survey, but the structure of the questions was significantly changed from 1990. This reformulation of the questions on incentive pay means that we cannot make direct time-series comparisons between 1990 and 1998 using cross-section data, since investigation has shown that the two sets of questions are not equivalent.[21] Instead, we turn to our panel survey of continuing workplaces to provide an estimate of the overall incidence of incentive pay in 1998 on the basis of an identically constructed summary variable. In doing so, we also compare joiners with the rest of the 1998 cross-section sample (which, by definition, are continuing workplaces), using a summary variable based on the available data. This comparison is done in order to make an assessment of how well the 1998 panel observation might represent the population as a whole. Because of the different occupational groups used in the 1998 survey, plus other complications, our safest course in investigating the changing incidence of incentive pay is to construct a combined measure that looks at the workplace as a whole. This identifies workplaces that used either payment by results or merit pay for any occupational group (with five or more employees), excluding managers.[22]

In 1990, our overall survey calculation was that 63 per cent of workplaces had one or other type of incentive pay. The panel cases selected and surviving from the overall 1990 sample were very close to this: 62 per cent of them had incentive pay in 1990. By 1998, 58 per cent of continuing workplaces in the panel had incentive pay, a statistically insignificant fall. So only if joiners were substantially different from existing workplaces in 1998 would we have grounds for suspecting that the incidence of incentive pay had changed in the population of workplaces as a whole. Investigation of the data available from the 1998 survey, although not strictly comparable, suggested that this was not the case. Joiners had a similar incidence of incentive pay (on this somewhat less comprehensive measure) as existing workplaces: 41 per cent, compared with 45 per cent. Overall, if there was any change in the incidence of incentive pay at workplace level between 1990 and 1998 it is more likely to have been a reduction. But the safest conclusion is that there was no overall change.

In further analysis we did not detect any significant changes among workplaces in the three broad sectors of the economy; under a half of public sector workplaces continued to use incentive pay, compared with two thirds in private services and three quarters in manufacturing. The evidence also suggested that larger workplaces – and those without recognized trade unions – continued to make greater use of incentive pay.

Using the panel data in more detail, we examined continuing workplaces with any form of incentive pay in each year to see if there was a change in the form of pay that they used, or the groups of employee to which it applied.[23] A clear point of continuity was that payment by results remained more commonly based on an individual's performance, rather than on the performance of a larger group. But some changes were apparent. Payment by results was rather more commonly used for non-manual employees than for manuals in 1998, whereas the reverse was true in 1990. (In 1990, 46 per cent had payment by results for manuals, whereas 37 per cent had it for non-manuals; in 1998, the respective figures were 37 per cent and 44 per cent.) There was also an intimation that merit pay for any employees was less commonly used than before. But these findings use the panel sample as a whole, including workplaces that either introduced or withdrew incentive pay between 1990 and 1998. When we considered only the third of panel cases that had any incentive pay in both 1990 and 1998 the changes mentioned above were still apparent.

Profit-related pay schemes

Profit-related pay represents one of the most diffuse forms of contingent pay. It has been a matter of contention between employers and trade unions since it was first introduced in the nineteenth century; the Webbs, for example, 'viewed profit sharing and share-ownership schemes as fundamentally opposed to the principles of collective bargaining and trade unionism' (Poole, 1989: 9). The Conservative governments of the 1980s introduced a series of tax exemptions to encourage specific forms of profit-related pay, as well as share-based schemes, subsequently moving in their last year of office to dismantle the privileges on the former.

Although the precise role of government incentives is uncertain, there is no doubt that profit-related pay became much more widespread during the 1980s. When we first inquired about it in 1984, 19 per cent of workplaces in industry and commerce belonged to enterprises that had a scheme. By 1990 this proportion had risen to 44 per cent. In 1998, however, the figure was little different: 46 per cent (Table 6.13).[24]

Among the significant changes between 1990 and 1998 was an increase in the practice in manufacturing industry (from 33 to 50 per cent) that brought

Table 6.13 The incidence of profit sharing and employee share ownership in industry and commerce, 1984 to 1998, by workplace and enterprise characteristics

	Cell percentages						
	Profit sharing			Employee share ownership			
	1984	1990	1998	1980	1984	1990	1998
All establishments	19	44	46	13	22	30	24
Broad sector							
Private manufacturing	16	33	50	8	14	25	22
Private services	21	50	46	17	27	34	25
Public sector – trading	1	4	17	..	..	..	..
Foreign owned	7	31	51	11	10	13	21
UK owned	21	45	47	14	24	33	25
Size of enterprise							
25–99 employees	12	29	29	3	2	4	3
100–999 employees	15	37	48	7	13	10	14
1,000–9,999 employees	18	50	59	19	33	53	38
10,000 or more employees	31	63	72	27	47	65	58
Employee relations director on board							
Yes	24	53	67	15	33	46	46
No	17	49	51	11	26	41	26
Union recognition							
Yes	23	43	50	16	29	42	33
No	14	44	45	10	14	23	20

Base: all establishments in industry and commerce with 25 or more employees.

it up to the level in private services (46 per cent in 1998). Profit-related pay also grew among the increasing number of foreign-owned workplaces and among the few publicly owned establishments in the commercial sector. Workplaces belonging to UK multinationals continued to be more likely to have profit-related pay than those belonging to purely domestic firms, but the gap narrowed. However, the single most influential characteristic of the extent of profit-related pay in 1998 appeared to be, as it was in earlier years, the size of the enterprise to which workplaces belonged. From 1990 onwards, the majority of workplaces belonging to enterprises with 1,000 or more employees had employees who benefited from a profit-related pay scheme.

We also looked at the extent to which the incidence of profit sharing was associated with the degree of centralization in pay determination within organizations, but no simple patterns emerged. However, we did look more fruitfully at changes in the association between profit sharing and arrangements that encourage non-financial participation from employees, in view of some of the emerging evidence that links combinations of financial and non-financial employee participation to financial performance (McNabb and Whitfield, 1998). We did this by investigating the extent to which profit-sharing schemes were related to the various measures of employee voice that we discussed in Chapter 4. We found that, in 1990 and 1998, those workplaces with some arrangement for non-financial participation, or employee voice, were more likely to also operate a profit-sharing scheme for their employees than those workplaces with no such voice arrangements. Just under a half of workplaces with some form of voice arrangement operated profit-sharing schemes, compared with just over one third of workplaces without any such arrangement. The gap narrowed slightly during the course of the 1990s, however, and in 1998 was on the borderline of statistical significance. With regard to particular types of voice we found that, over the 1990s, private sector workplaces with recognized trade unions became slightly more likely to have profit-related pay than non-union workplaces (50 per cent compared with 45 per cent), in contrast to the situation in 1990 when they were indistinguishable in this respect. Whether this slight difference emerged from a softening of trade union opposition to the practice, we cannot say.

Finally, although the data did not show any substantial change in the overall incidence of profit-related pay schemes between 1990 and 1998, our panel survey did show that a number of workplaces had either introduced or withdrawn profit-sharing schemes over the course of the 1990s. Here, it was interesting to examine the reasons behind these changes. Overall, 40 per cent of continuing workplaces in the trading sector in 1990 operated a profit-related pay scheme. One fifth of these (8 per cent of all continuing workplaces in the trading sector in 1990) withdrew their scheme between 1990 and 1998. However, almost one fifth (17 per cent) of all continuing workplaces that were part of the trading sector in 1998 had introduced a scheme since 1990. This brought the incidence of profit-related pay schemes among continuing trading sector workplaces up to almost one half (48 per cent) in 1998.

Where profit-related pay schemes had either been introduced or withdrawn between 1990 and 1998, we asked respondents why this change had occurred. Up to five reasons were recorded. The most common specific reason given for the withdrawal of a profit-related pay scheme, mentioned in one third of workplaces where a scheme had been withdrawn, was that the workplace had undergone a change of ownership or control. The next most common specific reason, mentioned in one fifth of such workplaces, was that the scheme was too expensive to run or constituted too great an administrative burden.

The most common specific reason given for the introduction of a profit-related pay scheme was also that the workplace had undergone a change of ownership or control. This reason was cited in around one quarter of all workplaces where such a scheme had been introduced since 1990. The aim of increasing incentives for employees was only marginally less common. One tenth of workplaces introducing a scheme cited tax relief amongst its reasons. Tax relief was therefore among the primary motivations for the introduction of profit sharing in some workplaces. However, setting aside those cases in which the introduction of profit sharing came as part of wider organizational changes, attempts to develop more sophisticated incentive and reward systems appeared to be more important in explaining the increased use of profit-sharing amongst continuing workplaces.

Share-ownership schemes

Share-ownership schemes have been the subject of questioning throughout the survey series. In 1980, 13 per cent of all workplaces in industry and commerce had employees who were participating in a share-ownership scheme, reflecting a rapid growth in such schemes in the late 1970s. This figure rose to 22 per cent in 1984 and 30 per cent in 1990. The latest survey, however, shows a drop in the incidence of share-ownership schemes, to 24 per cent (Table 6.13).[25] The recent trend is therefore somewhat different to that seen in respect of profit-related pay.

The incidence of share-ownership schemes in the private sector fell only slightly among manufacturing industries between 1990 and 1998 (from 25 per cent to 22 per cent). A much greater fall was evident within private sector services (from 34 per cent in 1990 to 25 per cent in 1998). As a result, by 1998, the two industry sectors had almost reached a position of parity, having come from a position in 1980 and 1984 in which services were twice as likely to have share ownership schemes as manufacturing. A similar pattern was apparent among domestic and foreign-owned workplaces in the private sector. In the 1980s, foreign-owned workplaces had been less likely to report share-ownership schemes than workplaces owned by UK firms. However, whilst the incidence of schemes among domestically owned workplaces dropped back between 1990 and 1998 (from 33 per cent to 25 per cent), the incidence among those that were foreign owned showed an increase (from 13 per cent to 21 per cent).

Another characteristic that distinguished the type of organization where the fall in share ownership occurred was their top management structure. Where enterprises had a personnel or employee relations director on their top governing body, employee share-ownership schemes remained as common in 1998 as they had done in 1990 (48 per cent of such workplaces reported a scheme). However, where there was no personnel or employee relations director, the incidence of schemes fell sharply, from 41 to 26 per cent of workplaces. We investigated this emerging association between the presence of employee share ownership and the presence of an employee relations director in more detail with our panel survey and, after comparing leavers with joiners, found that the change had largely occurred in continuing workplaces. By comparing those who had changed their arrangements with those who had not, on each of the two variables, we found no single route by which the relationship had emerged. It occurred because those who adopted or abandoned share ownership also adopted or abandoned having a specialist employee relations director. At the same time, most of those who had both arrangements in 1990 continued to do so in 1998.

Looking at the relationship between employee share-ownership schemes and non-financial participation, or employee voice, we found that in 1990 workplaces with some form of voice arrangement were around three times as likely to belong to an enterprise with employee share-ownership (35 per cent) than workplaces without any form of non-financial participation (12 per cent). By 1998, this gap had closed considerably. In our latest survey, employee share-ownership schemes were found in one quarter (24 per cent) of workplaces with some form of voice and in one fifth (21 per cent) of workplaces without. We also found that, in both 1990 and 1998, workplaces with a combination of union and non-union voice mechanisms were more likely to belong to enterprises with employee share ownership than those with a single-voice channel or none at all. Whether the combination of financial and non-financial employee participation continued to have a favourable impact on financial performance, as earlier research has suggested (McNabb and Whitfield, 1998), is one of the many questions that we hope future research will address.

The patterns seen in Table 6.13, which shows that the increases seen in the overall incidence of profit sharing and employee share-ownership schemes in the 1980s have either tailed off or reversed in the 1990s, beg the question of quite how the overall incidence of financial participation schemes has changed in recent years. To investigate this, we compiled a measure that indicated whether a workplace operated either a profit-sharing scheme or an employee share-ownership scheme. In 1984, three in ten workplaces (30 per cent) operated either one of these forms of financial participation. The rise of both types of scheme in the second half of the 1980s meant that, by 1990, the figure stood at 54 per cent. In 1998 it was largely unchanged, at 50 per cent.

The proportion of workplaces with both types of scheme followed a similar pattern, rising from 10 per cent in 1984 to 20 per cent in 1990 and 1998. In 1984, around half of these workplaces were located in the banking, finance and insurance industries, but by 1998 these industries accounted for only one fifth. Instead, between 1984 and 1998, there was a substantial increase in the prominence of workplaces engaged in distribution, hotels and catering. In 1984, around one quarter of those workplaces with both types of financial participation could be found in distribution, hotels and catering. By 1998, the proportion had risen to more than two fifths.

The dispersion of pay within workplaces

If we were to examine how the changing nature of workplace employee relations had fed through into salient outcomes over the whole course of the WIRS series, pay levels would be an obvious outcome to choose. Such an assessment has already been made for the first three surveys in terms of the changing effects of trade unions (Stewart, 1995). Unfortunately, changes in question format and wording in the 1998 cross-section and panel prevent us from making direct comparisons with previous surveys on the levels of pay across workplaces. However, we can examine changes in the dispersion of pay over time. The 1990 survey contained, for the first time in the series, two questions about the dispersion of pay within establishments. One question asked managers to estimate the proportion of full-time employees that earned half or less than the average full-time employee in that workplace; the second question asked what proportion earned twice or more than the average. The initial results (Millward *et al.*, 1992) highlighted the strong association between the coverage of collective bargaining with trade unions and low dispersion of pay within establishments; subsequent analysis confirmed this, using union recognition as the independent variable (Gosling and Machin, 1995). The relevant questions were repeated in our 1998 panel interviews, allowing the possibility of re-examining the union effect on wage dispersion in the circumstances of greatly reduced union influence in 1998, at least within continuing establishments. The comparative figures are given in Table 6.14.

The first point of interest in the table is that the dispersion of pay within establishments was reduced within continuing workplaces between 1990 and 1998. Our overall measure, the mean proportion of full-time employees whose pay was either less than half or more than twice their workplace average, fell from 17 per cent in 1990 to 8 per cent in 1998. This trend is contrary to the general trend towards greater inequality in pay when individuals are compared (Leslie and Pu, 1996) and suggests that, if that trend continued through the 1990s for full-time workers, it arose through an increase in the dispersion between workplaces, rather than within them.[26]

The drop in dispersion came largely from a reduction in the mean proportion of full-time employees paid less than half the average for their workplace (from 12 to 4 per cent). This applied to both public and private sectors. One possible general explanation would be that this arose because employers were disproportionately increasing the pay of their lowest-paid full-time workers in anticipation of the forthcoming statutory minimum wage. We examined how

Table 6.14 Pay dispersion of full-time employees in panel workplaces, 1990 and 1998

	Mean proportion of full-time employees earning:					
	Less than half the average		*More than twice the average*		*Either less than half or more than twice the average*	
	1990	*1998*	*1990*	*1998*	*1990*	*1998*
All continuing workplaces	12	4	5	4	18	8
Public sector, 1990 and 1998	9	4	5	4	13	7
Private sector, 1990 and 1998	14	4	6	4	20	8
Collective-bargaining coverage in the private sector						
80 per cent or more	11	7	4	2	15	9
50–79 per cent	17	(6)	5	(4)	21	(10)
Less than 50 per cent	14	4	7	4	21	8

Base: all continuing workplaces where both proportions reported in 1990 and 1998.

the changes varied by region and found that there was no tendency for regions with lower general pay levels to be less likely to have fewer full-time employees below half their workplace average in 1998 than in 1990. An alternative might be that employers were making adjustments in the composition of their in-house workforce in such a way that fewer of the lowest-paid workers were employed full-time in 1998 than earlier. Besides this we also looked at other variables characterizing changes that workplaces might have made in their workforces between 1990 and 1998, as well as their size and industry sector. It appeared that the reduction in pay dispersion was widespread and occurred in all industries and sectors, among all sizes of workforce and so on. The only clear relationship we found was that workplaces that had shrunk in size were more likely than other workplaces to have a lower pay dispersion in 1998 than they had in 1990. This hardly provides an explanation and we leave the matter for further investigation.

Of course, continuing workplaces are only a part (although the major part) of the population of workplaces, so the decrease in dispersion could have come about from compositional change. We found that workplaces leaving the population from 1990 onwards generally had somewhat lower pay dispersion than continuing workplaces; the respective mean figures on our overall measure were 13 per cent and 17 per cent. The effect of leavers alone, therefore, would have been to slightly increase the dispersion of pay within workplaces by 1998. To examine the impact of workplaces joining the population we constructed a crude measure of pay dispersion among full-time employees in 1998, using the revised questions on pay levels in WERS98 – the main cross-section interview having no comparable questions to those in the panel.[27] When we compared joiners with workplaces that had existed since 1990 we found no tendency for joiners to have greater or lesser pay dispersion than other workplaces. The impact of compositional change from both leavers and joiners would have been a small increase in dispersion, but not enough to outweigh the large drop among continuing workplaces. We conclude that workplaces with twenty-five or more employees had lower pay dispersion among full-time employees in 1998 than was the case in 1990.

From the reduction in union presence and influence documented in earlier chapters, plus the well-established tendency for unions to reduce wage dispersion, we would not necessarily have expected the dispersion of pay within workplaces to have narrowed during the 1990s; yet it clearly did. In the lower half of Table 6.14 we address the question of union influence on pay dispersion directly, by separating workplaces with a large majority of employees covered by collective bargaining from those with fewer or none being covered. The results show that, in 1990, workplaces with a high proportion of employees covered by collective bargaining had fewer full-time employees on less than half the average pay than workplaces with lower or no coverage (14 per cent, compared with 21 per cent). However, by 1998 there were no differences between workplaces according to their collective-bargaining coverage. Thus the results suggest that pay dispersion narrowed, *despite* the fact that the effect of unions in reducing differentials disappeared altogether.

Conclusions

The 1980s and 1990s saw major changes in the structures through which pay was determined, but far less change in the types of payment systems that fixed the details of individuals' pay packets.

As presaged by our analysis of employers' association membership in Chapter 3 and of trade union recognition in Chapter 4, the system of pay determination in Britain changed over the course of our survey series from one of predominantly joint regulation to one of unilateral determination by employers or managers. The shift was most marked in the private sector, but also evident on a lesser scale in public services. Much of the change occurred through newly established workplaces setting the pace in the direction of change. And while the preferences of successive Conservative governments for a less collectivist and centralized system of pay determination were broadly met, the routes through which these changes occurred were by no means uniform and the pace of change varied from sector to sector.

Manufacturing industry was the part of the private sector where collective bargaining had thrived in the 1970s, although the stereotype was often exaggerated on the basis of information confined to large plants. From the mid-1980s to the late 1990s the proportion of manufacturing workplaces where collective bargaining was the major method of setting pay fell from a half to less than a quarter. Bargaining on a multi-employer basis shrank even more dramatically, becoming a rarity by 1998. Most manufacturing workplaces by this time were setting pay without reference to trade unions or collective agreements, let alone those agreed jointly with other employers. Increasingly they were doing so in a centralized way, although pay setting by workplace management remained the most common practice.

In private service industries, unilateral forms of pay determination by management were already dominant in the early 1980s, but their importance grew steadily so that by 1998 nearly nine in every ten workplaces had their pay set without reference to trade unions. Multi-employer agreements all but disappeared. Enterprise-level pay setting largely replaced joint regulation.

In the public sector the degree of change was smaller than in the private sector, but no less significant. Collective bargaining, hitherto almost universal, remained the most common form of pay setting, but other arrangements became more prevalent. In substantial areas of public sector employment, multi-employer agreements were replaced by review body recommendations sent to the ultimate public sector authority – central government.

The impact of these changes, in terms of employees, was that the coverage of collective bargaining fell from 70 per cent in 1984 to 40 per cent in 1998. The pace of change accelerated in the 1990s, notably in private services. During this latter period around half of the fall arose from lower coverage in workplaces with recognized unions, the other half coming from the shrinkage in the unionized sector itself.

A dwindling membership base precipitated a number of union mergers (Waddington and Whitson, 1995: 177) and this was one of the principal reasons for a substantial shift towards single-union representation at workplace level in the 1990s – a change that was hardly detectable in the 1980s. Outright derecognition was not a major contributor to this change. More important was that newer workplaces in the private sector favoured single-union representation, if they had union representation at all.

The decline in representation by multiple unions contributed to an even more marked trend towards single-table bargaining in the contracting unionized sector. Among workplaces where collective bargaining affected a majority of employees, single-table bargaining nearly doubled between 1990 and 1998, after changing little in the 1980s. But the drop in multi-union representation was not the principal reason for this change. Continuing workplaces shifted from complex to single-table arrangements where multiple unions continued to be recognized, while newer workplaces that recognized trade unions almost invariably adopted a single forum for negotiating pay.

Turning from the structures to the processes of pay determination, we examined changes in the considerations taken into account by management negotiators or decision-makers. The cost of living was the single most commonly cited factor where pay was negotiated for most employees. It became more frequently cited in 1990 than in 1984 as inflation increased, but did not become less so as inflation subsided towards the end of the decade. In the 1990s, negotiated settlements became more frequently influenced by economic conditions and financial considerations such as the employer's ability to pay or recent financial results. Fewer referred to labour market considerations, 'the going rate' or comparability – considerations that reflected the concerns of trade unions.

In workplaces where most employees' pay was not the subject of collective bargaining, reference to the cost of living also increased in the late 1980s and held steady thereafter – but throughout the series it was less frequently cited than in negotiated settlements. Non-negotiated settlements took more account of individual employee performance in 1990 than before, but there was no change in this respect by 1998. Otherwise the changes generally mirrored those where pay was negotiated.

On payment systems, we found no clear shift in the 1990s towards types of payment that were contingent upon the performance of the individual; if there was a change, it was away from such schemes. Similarly, profit-related pay spread no further than it had done in the 1980s. Employee share ownership contracted somewhat in the 1990s, also after expansion in the 1980s; such schemes remained more common where employees had a combination of union representation and other channels of communication with management.

Finally, we examined how the dispersion of pay within workplaces had changed between 1990 and 1998. We found that it had narrowed, largely because fewer workplaces had full-time employees earning less than half the average for their workplace. This was despite the declining influence of unions, who apparently no longer helped to narrow differentials. This was symptomatic of the overall decline in the involvement and influence of trade unions in pay setting.

7   Verdict and prospect

> The 1980s was a period of revolution, with rapid changes in industrial relations
> . . . and . . . action to completely dismantle the system, reflecting the fact that
> the essential ideas on which the system was based (which might be termed
> 'egalitarian') were being reconsidered and replaced with a more decentralized,
> 'free market' orientation. Clearly the [new] industrial relations system . . .
> represents a sea change, and the period . . . witnessed both rapid change relative
> to the past and increased experimentation.
>
> (Erickson and Kuruvilla, 1998: 15–16)

Thus a learned journal article summarized the last twenty years in – not Britain
– but New Zealand. Yet could this description also be fairly applied to what
happened in Britain over the same period? Were industrial relations, or indeed
employment relations, transformed during the eighteen years of Conservative
government? Was government policy at the heart of the transformation? What
is the new 'system', if any? What are its implications?

No earlier period of British history could have been assessed with the
resources that we have had available for the period 1980 to 1998. Scholars,
policy-makers and commentators had to rely – in the dark ages before the
large-scale survey series and high-speed computers – on expert testimony,
unrepresentative case studies and single reports of one-off surveys. Valuable as
such sources were, and continue to be, they never provided the generalizable,
transparent information that the modern survey series can provide. The four
surveys that began with the 1980 Workplace Industrial Relations Survey give
us large-scale, generalizable and verifiable information about management–
employee relations over that period. We have been privileged to use it – and
help create some of it – to give initial answers to the questions posed in the
previous paragraph.

In addressing those questions we have drawn widely upon the resources of
the WIRS series. We have created and analysed a time-series dataset that enables
us to compare consistently defined variables for 1998 and at least one of the
preceding surveys, generally two or all of them. We have also drawn extensively
upon the panel of continuing workplaces interviewed in both 1990 and 1998.

This – supplemented with data about 'leavers' and 'joiners' – has given us further insights into how change came about. But our data do have drawbacks. They generally rely solely on management accounts, because we have no earlier data comparable to the employee survey of WERS98 and because worker representatives were selected in different ways in the two most recent surveys. We regard this drawback as a minor one because most of the questions that we have analysed are of a factual nature. Outweighing this are the enormous benefits of having high-quality data from nationally representative surveys of workplaces in all sectors of the economy. The fact that they neatly straddle the eighteen years of Conservative government is particularly advantageous for our purpose.

The changing context of employment relations

It is salutary to recall what Britain was like when the first survey in our series was conducted. After the post-war consensus of the 1950s and 1960s, the 1970s were years of political instability, high inflation and increasing industrial conflict. Matters came to a head in the 'winter of discontent' in 1978/79, when the public's sympathy with striking workers in the public sector was tried to the limit. This led to the general election of 1979 in which Mrs Thatcher was brought to power, heading a Conservative government that was committed to radical reform. The government's aim – highly controversial at the time – was to weaken the power of the trade unions, deregulate the labour market and dismantle many of the tripartite institutions of corporatism in which the trade unions played a major part. Subduing inflation was to be given priority over maintaining low unemployment. Reducing the role of government and levels of public expenditure were policy goals. The free play of market forces was to replace the search for consensus between government and the 'two sides' of industry.

Over the ensuing eighteen years the legal and political contexts of employment relations were transformed. Successive Acts of Parliament restricted the activities of trade unions at all levels. Union power was attacked directly by numerous restrictions and sanctions upon industrial action, as well as the progressive outlawing of action in support of the closed shop. The framework of statutory employment protection was weakened where European Union directives did not inhibit this. Union strongholds in the public sector were undermined by privatization, contracting out and competitive tendering. All these moves were designed to wrest power from organized labour and vest it in management.

At the same time much of the British economy was being opened up to the forces of international competition. Inflation came down, initially at the expense of higher unemployment. But by 1998, both of these crucial measures of labour market performance were low, compared with their levels in 1980. The economic downturns of the early 1980s and early 1990s hastened incipient shifts in the composition of the economy, notably the decline of manufacturing and large-scale manual employment. More employees were women, many working part-time, while many employers increasingly hired workers on a temporary basis.

How, then, did all this impact on the actual conduct of employee relations at workplace level? We plan to reach an answer in the following way. First, we take three themes – the nature of management, local autonomy and joint regulation – to summarize and interpret the empirical material presented in Chapters 3 to 6. We then reassess the material to identify as best we can the main sources of change. This puts us in a position to reach verdicts on our two main questions: were industrial relations transformed during the period, and was government policy primarily responsible? We finish the chapter by drawing out some of the implications of the changes.

The nature of employee relations management

Workplace employee relations were dealt with in 1998 by different sorts of managers from those responsible in 1980. For a start, more of them were women. Whether this simply reflects the increasing employment of women in managerial jobs (see Chapter 2), or a deliberate attempt by employers to respond to the increasing calls for 'family friendly' employment, we leave the reader to judge. Probably a more important change was that employee relations were less likely to be handled by generalist managers and more likely to be handled by employee relations specialists or line managers. The increase in the use of employee relations specialists was particularly noticeable in the 1990s and was a feature of new and growing workplaces. These specialists came to be dominated by those with professional qualifications; and such qualifications were clearly being obtained by specialists with long experience, as well as those entering the occupation. These changes may be pointers to a greater need for knowledge on matters such as employment law; or they may hint at increasing sophistication in management's approach to employee relations.

A more direct signal of increasing sophistication was the adoption of job titles that convey an engagement with modern conceptions of a sophisticated approach to employee relations. 'Human resource management' was heralded as such a conception during the late 1980s and widely adopted as the paradigm for what, in some respects, was previously thought of as good personnel management. Of course, human resource management meant many different things, but it was the banner under which increasing numbers of employee relations specialists marched. Those using the title 'human resources manager' accounted for a third of specialists in 1998; they were particularly common in foreign-owned workplaces and in new workplaces, both being indications of a more sophisticated approach to employee relations and suggesting that the numbers of such specialists will continue to rise.

But surely we are on firmer ground if we examine what employee relations managers actually deal with? Judging by what they said they were responsible for, specialists and non-specialists alike were dealing in 1998 with much the same set of issues as they, or their predecessors, were dealing with in the early 1980s. Where we did identify changes, they were in the roles of non-specialists, who increasingly had responsibility for pay, grievance handling, training and manpower planning. But the most striking finding was that 'human resource managers' were dealing with very much the same set of issues as other employee relations specialists – indeed they were indistinguishable in terms of their responsibilities.

There are other changes that we can infer. Clearly in the early 1980s, when one in every six workplaces experienced industrial action[1] (strikes, overtime bans and working to rule being the most common), many employee relations managers must have spent time coping with the events and the aftermath of collective industrial conflict. In 1998, when managers reported industrial action in a mere 2 per cent of all workplaces, hardly any of them will have done so. On the other hand, they may have spent more time dealing with individual grievances, particularly those that had the potential to involve legal proceedings – or actually did so. The doubling of the number of workplaces seeking advice from ACAS during the 1990s, and the doubling of those consulting lawyers over the same period, are strong indications that this was so. The growth in the number of workplaces subject to claims at an industrial tribunal (Millward et al., 1999a: 245) also points in the same direction. It is hard to avoid the conclusion that employee relations managers switched their attention from dealing with collective conflict to dealing with its individualized alternatives.

A final shift that we can clearly detect in our results is the increasing involvement of workplace managers in collecting and disseminating information. In an age when 'information overload' has become a staple for magazine writers, this may be no surprise. Nevertheless, both our cross-section comparisons and our panel results indicate that substantially more workplace managers were collecting information to review performance and policies. The increase in the 1990s occurred on each of the eleven items inquired about, so it cannot be dismissed as a partial picture. On the dissemination of information to employees our measures are less comprehensive, covering only four topics, but they include important ones like recent workplace performance and future development plans. Here too our results showed a tendency for more workplaces to disseminate information to employees, a trend that excluded manufacturing industry. But the broad picture of increasing collection and dissemination of information to employees surely represented a real change in behaviour by managers. It came across clearly in our panel of continuing workplaces and was not just a feature of new workplaces, which might be expected to have more widespread information technology through which to reach employees.[2]

Decentralization and workplace autonomy

Joint action by employers within the same industry or region was one of the hallmarks of the 'industrial relations system' that characterized the post-war period. Affiliation to an employers' association is one indicator of the degree of co-ordination among employers and our survey series showed that this continued to contract in the 1980s and, more slowly, in the 1990s. Pay determination was the issue on which the most binding forms of multi-employer co-ordination hinged. The declining extent to which workplaces were affected by multi-employer agreements is therefore a potent measure of decentralization. Our results in Chapter 6 showed this to be a very clear and continuing trend. Multi-employer agreements affected one third of the number of workplaces in 1998 that they had in the early 1980s. In parallel with this continuing trend in the 1990s we saw that fewer employers were having regard to the pay increases of other employers or industries when reviewing pay for their own employees.

This is not to say that there was necessarily a progressive shift in the locus of decision-making from industry level all the way down to individual workplaces. On the issue of pay, multi-employer agreements were more likely to have been replaced by unilateral management determination at the level of the employer than at the workplace itself. In the public sector, workplace managers reported greatly increased involvement on pay and conditions matters during the 1990s; this reflected the broader reorganization of many public services, although pay settlements were increasingly subject to limits set by higher authorities (in some cases via review bodies). In the private sector more pay settlements were subject to budgetary limits set by higher-level management. The increasing number of private sector settlements that were influenced by organizational or workplace performance was also symptomatic of the loosening of institutional ties and the greater salience of product and service markets in pay determination.

There were clear indications of control on other matters becoming more centralized within employing organizations during the 1990s. In continuing workplaces in industry and commerce, decisions on senior appointments, on union recognition or derecognition, and on the use of budgetary surpluses were all decreasingly a matter for workplace managers and increasingly decided at higher levels. On the other hand, there was a decline in the extent to which workplaces in multi-site enterprises had a personnel or employee relations specialist on their board of directors, a decline concentrated in smaller, non-union firms. This could signify a move towards regarding employee relations matters as operational, rather than strategic, in a segment of the private sector.

Joint regulation of the employment relationship

In the first three decades of the post-war period, relationships between employers and employees were characterized by extensive involvement of trade unions. These voluntary collective arrangements were supported by a shared commitment to joint regulation and bolstered by high levels of institutional membership on both sides. Our four surveys show a progressive disintegration of this institutional structure, facilitated by the weakening of both sides' commitment to both the structures and the values of joint regulation.

In the absence of alternative structures prescribed by law, as in many other European countries, trade union membership provided – and still provides – the bedrock for the collective representation of employees in Britain. But that foundation shrank: unions lost members throughout the 1980s and continued to do so in the 1990s. Membership declines were apparent in all types of workplace, including those where management continued to subscribe to the principle of joint regulation. Membership renewal failed to materialize as newer workplaces with no or few members replaced those with high density. Employee support for union representation was clearly on the wane. But declining support from management accentuated the fall in the 1980s as the closed shop was progressively curtailed by legislation and fewer managements strongly encouraged membership; by the 1990s the legislative assault on the closed shop was complete, but declining management support for union membership remained a minor influence upon the persistent loss of membership.

Within a 'voluntarist' framework, as in Britain since 1980 (and for most earlier decades), union membership and recognition are mutually reinforcing: high membership levels both encourage continuing recognition by management and are a product of it. Our panel results showed that declining membership precipitated derecognition in some cases; derecognition commonly led to membership loss. But derecognition was only a minor contributor to the stark and continuing decline in recognition that we observed from 1984 onwards. In the 1990s, as in the earlier period, the principal source of this decline was the low rate of recognition among new workplaces. Low or no membership in these workplaces meant that the issue of recognition was rarely raised. Where recognition was newly granted, few cases in 1998 resulted from union pressure, a sharp contrast with the evidence from our 1980 survey.

The fall in the proportion of workplaces with recognized unions naturally meant that fewer employees had their pay and conditions of employment fixed by collective bargaining. But this was accentuated in the 1990s by a further twist of the spiral as collective-bargaining coverage declined within those remaining workplaces with recognition. Although pervasive, the fall in coverage was especially marked in the private services sector, where coverage was already lower than elsewhere. But the fall in coverage in the public sector was also significant because coverage was nearly universal there at the start of the period. The accumulated result of the continuing falls in the 1990s was that collective bargaining had become something of a rarity by 1998, affecting a minority of workplaces and employees – a far cry from its centrality to the system of joint regulation that existed at the start of the 1980s.

If pay was no longer generally a negotiated issue, was it nevertheless still a matter of consultation and discussion with unions? The evidence of WERS98 suggests that this was rarely the case.[3] Moreover, the impact of unions on pay levels declined over the course of the 1980s. By 1990, workplaces with a demonstrable premium were confined to those with strong unions and weak product-market competition (Stewart, 1995). Our analysis in Chapter 5 points to a further thinning out of workplaces with strong unions. Evidence of increasing product-market competition is more plentiful than the opposite. Putting these two together, it would be reasonable to expect that the impact of unions on wage levels had decreased further during the 1990s. And our analysis of wage dispersion in Chapter 6 indicated that the impact of unions in terms of narrowing differentials, evident in 1990, had evaporated.

While better pay may not have remained the issue of overwhelming importance for trade unions that it had been, perhaps they continued to have an impact on other issues? Here our evidence is more mixed. The scope of bargaining on non-pay issues declined in the early 1980s, but remained stable thereafter. Union restraints on managements' ability to organize work remained intact in continuing workplaces in the 1990s. And union involvement in disputes procedures also remained at a high level. On the other hand, unions lost their hold over joint consultative committees and health and safety representation. But the overall picture of union influence on all these matters must be one of decline, since so many fewer workplaces in 1998 had union representation than in the early 1980s.

As evidence accumulated during the 1980s and 1990s of the progressive shrinkage of the unionized sector, some commentators looked for signs of an emergence or revitalization of alternative forms of collective employee voice at workplace level. Joint consultative committees were the most common form of this, but they did not grow to even partially fill the gap left by declining unionism. In fact, they became less common during the 1980s and have become no more common since then. Indeed, 'functioning committees', as we defined them in Chapter 4, became even less common in 1998 than in 1990. Part of the reason was that they have always been strongly associated with a union presence, and that had become rarer. The only structures for collective employee voice that we found to be as common in 1998 as they had been in 1980 were health and safety committees. These became less common in the 1980s, but returned to similar levels by 1998. We attribute this to the introduction of new legal requirements, rather than a spontaneous resurgence of interest in the joint regulation of these matters on the part of both employees and employers. Broadly speaking, then, alternative collective representation structures did not grow to replace those based on trade unions. If they had, questions about the comparative effectiveness of union and non-union forms of collective representation would have become more salient.

What did grow as collective representation declined were management-initiated methods of direct communication with employees. Regular meetings between senior managers and the workforce and briefing groups showed continued growth from the mid-1980s onwards and problem-solving groups grew during the 1990s. Only in the case of briefing groups was the growth evident in non-union workplaces but not union ones. This would be flimsy evidence on which to argue that consultation and communication channels have switched from joint arrangements to direct forms of communication which are equally effective in making employees' voice heard. We addressed the question more broadly at the end of Chapter 4, examining the whole range of consultation and communication arrangements for which we have data over time and distinguishing between union-based and non-union (largely direct) methods. We then looked at whether employees' assessments in 1998 of how managers responded to their concerns and suggestions were associated with the different arrangements in place at their workplace, controlling for a number of other factors. These assessments were positively associated with having some formal voice mechanism, but only with non-union or direct communication channels. However, only union-based channels, and those indicating a well-established union presence, were positively associated with greater perceptions of fair treatment by management. No form of direct participation produced this effect. If 'fairness at work' is to remain one of the criteria by which labour market policy is judged (Department of Trade and Industry, 1998), then the continuing decline of union representation must be a cause for concern. No amount of 'direct participation' – management-dominated arrangements which we showed to be less durable than union representation – can be expected to encourage fair treatment for employees at work.

Sources of change

Clearly, much changed in the way that industrial relations were conducted in Britain during the 1980s and 1990s. But what lay behind these changes? This is what we now address. In doing so, we pay particular attention to the role played by successive Conservative governments, in power for almost the entirety of the period covered by our survey series.

The Conservatives' approach to industrial relations, outlined in Chapter 1, was both distinctive in its nature and particular in its aims. Previous state support for collective organization and voluntary collective bargaining was reversed as successive Conservative administrations set about dismantling the props to joint regulation and restricting the power of trade unions. To this end, a substantial legislative programme was implemented in an attempt to control the activities of organized labour. At the same time, concerns that minimum labour standards represented a 'burden' on business and impaired competitiveness led to the weakening or dismantling of certain individual rights, such as those governing unfair dismissal and minimum rates of pay. The conduct of industrial relations in the public sector also came under particular scrutiny as concerns over the efficiency of many activities and lack of control over the public sector pay bill led to a substantial programme of reform involving gradual marketization and, in some cases, the wholesale privatization of particular activities.

Yet, although the government made an explicit link between its programme of reform and changes in the behaviour of those that were party to industrial relations during its time in office (Department of Employment, 1991), the period also witnessed broader changes in the nature of the economy and the labour market which might also have been expected to have had an impact. Increasing competition in product markets, rising unemployment and changes in the composition of the labour force are just some. The task of assessing the particular contribution of government policy and legislative reform is, therefore, far from straightforward. Assessments were made as the programme unfolded (Blanchflower and Freeman, 1994; Freeman and Pelletier, 1990), but even the more recent ones (Brown *et al.*, 1997; Dunn and Metcalf, 1996) were too early to be able to call upon the wealth of time-series data that is at our disposal. So, having presented and discussed a great deal of information on the changes that have occurred in the conduct of industrial relations in Britain over the past two decades, it is appropriate to return once again to the question of what was the contribution of government policy to those changes.

One of the first legislative actions of the Conservative government was to restrict the enforceability of the closed shop, first in 1980 and then again in 1982. However, not until 1988 was action in support of a post-entry closed shop actually made unlawful. The same treatment was extended to the pre-entry variant in 1990. In view of the nature and timing of these developments, we see no reason to contest earlier judgements that the slight decline in the closed shop evident in the first half of the 1980s came about primarily as a result of structural changes in the manufacturing sector (Millward and Stevens, 1986: 306), rather than early legislative restrictions. The legislation was more likely to have played a role in the dramatic decline that was seen in the latter half of the decade and which continued in the 1990s. It is notable that, having abandoned the closed shop, many public sector employers still make a strong recommendation that employees join a trade union. Some of these workplaces might have operated closed shops in the 1990s, had they felt less pressure to comply with the law. Yet, at the same time, management encouragement for union membership in the private sector, whether enforced or not, has largely fallen away. This suggests that the law is not the only factor at work and that management's changing view of the appropriateness of strong unionism has also been important. In this respect, other parts of the Conservative programme may have been significant in changing attitudes. However, it is difficult to argue that the incidence of the closed shop would have undergone such a dramatic decline had the promotion of involuntary union membership not been outlawed.

To what extent did the progressive restriction and subsequent outlawing of the closed shop contribute to the decline in trade union membership between 1980 and 1998? Union density has certainly fallen and it would be tempting to say that the virtual disappearance of the closed shop was a major reason. But density fell in all sectors of the economy and in many workplaces where there had never been a closed shop. Moreover, in the late 1980s when the closed shop was contracting most rapidly, our earlier panel survey (1984–90) showed that density contracted only slightly in workplaces that had had a closed shop in 1984. The closed shop legislation was only part of a broader set of influences which can be summarized as the withdrawal of state support for union membership and collective bargaining. This withdrawal led to managements in far fewer workplaces providing strong support for union membership as the

1990s progressed. In consequence, workplaces with high density became rarer. By the start of the 1990s the closed shop was already a rarity and its further demise had little impact on density.

Another legislative intervention that might have had a detectable effect on union membership density was the requirement, introduced in 1994, for check-off arrangements to be subject to prior written consent, renewable every three years. Our evidence indicated that these restrictions did not have a very significant effect on density in the late 1990s. Membership did decline rather more quickly in workplaces that withdrew check-off, but such cases were rare. The legislation may have played a part in the fact that newer workplaces with recognized unions were somewhat less likely to have check-off, but it is more likely that it was not sought in many of these cases.

When we turn to union recognition itself, a direct influence of the legislative programme is also hard to detect. The one specific measure affecting union recognition was the repeal in 1980 of the limited legal provisions, introduced in 1975, for unions to obtain recognition where the employer resisted a voluntary request. The restrictions on secondary industrial action, which had sometimes been used in support of recognition claims, may also have had a bearing on claims for new recognition. The generally declining incidence of recognition among new workplaces, which was the main driving force behind the sharp and continuing decline in recognition over the period after 1984, can be put down to reduced enthusiasm for union representation by employees and a general withdrawal of the earlier presumption by large employers that joint regulation was the norm – rather than any specific effect of the withdrawal of the statutory procedure. Nor can the modest scale of derecognition from the early 1980s onwards be attributed directly to the lack of a statutory procedure for retaining recognition against an employer's wishes. Yet another part of the Conservatives' policy programme, privatization and deregulation, might also be a candidate as a cause for reducing union recognition. However, the survey evidence is that privatization did not lead to derecognition in the late 1980s (Millward *et al.*, 1992: 359) and we noted in Chapter 6 that collective-bargaining coverage had maintained its high levels in the previously state-owned utilities.

Besides its extent, other features of collective bargaining were the target of government hostility during the period of our study, notably the structures used to conduct it and the scope of issues covered. In terms of structures, both the demise of multi-employer bargaining and the less dramatic decline of multiple bargaining units can be seen as moves in the direction that the government advocated. In the public sector, however, there were direct and clear consequences of the government's policy. The abolition of multi-employer collective-bargaining machinery for teachers and nurses manifestly reduced the number of workplaces affected by such arrangements in the late 1980s. In the public health sector, the government's reorganization of services into local trusts coincided with a halving of collective-bargaining coverage in the sector in the 1990s.

If collective bargaining and union representation were clear targets of the Conservatives' programme, so was industrial action. Legal requirements for the calling of industrial action were progressively introduced between 1980 and 1993. Research on the balloting requirements before industrial action has returned an 'ambivalent' verdict (Martin *et al.*, 1991). But the more specific legislation outlawing secondary industrial action reached its targets: secondary industrial action and picketing in support of it virtually disappeared, with a declining incidence that was far steeper than for industrial action in general (Millward *et al.*, 1992: 309).

Other evidence of the effectiveness of the legislative attack on industrial action comes from our analysis of the factors that managers took account of in pay negotiations. Industrial action or the threat of it completely disappeared as a salient factor between 1990 and 1998 in both the public and private sectors. Over the same period fewer managers cited comparability with other settlement groups while more cited economic performance and product-market circumstances – shifts in the direction favoured by the government, though possibly more influenced by competition policy than the employment legislation or related policies. Another feature of pay in which we saw government industrial relations policy as influential was its dispersion. Here we noted the apparent disappearance after 1990 of the tendency for unionized workplaces to have a lower pay dispersion than non-union workplaces. This can surely be seen as due in part to the broad attack on trade union power and influence.

There are two further areas where a direct link between government policy and workplace practices may be noted. The rapid growth of profit sharing and employee share-ownership schemes in the 1980s must owe something to the financial incentives that the government introduced during that period. Second, the increasing prevalence of health and safety representatives after 1990 can be seen as a response to the legal requirements for consultation in this area, introduced in 1996 to provide representation where unions were absent; the growth was greatest in small workplaces and those without union recognition.

Broadly speaking, then, government policy was an important source of change in employment relations over the eighteen years of the Conservative administrations, but on only a few specific matters could we clearly isolate it as the principal agent of change.

Finally, in this brief discussion of the nature of change, we wish to highlight how our analysis has, on occasions, been able to distinguish two different routes through which overall changes may occur – compositional change and change within continuing workplaces. From our time-series data we documented the continuing fall in union recognition from the mid-1980s onwards and isolated the effect of when workplaces were first established – young workplaces had a progressively smaller likelihood of union recognition in the private sector as time progressed. But only our panel data could show that the main source of change in the overall results during the 1990s was the radically different incidences of union recognition among joiners and leavers. The latter had similar rates of recognition to continuing workplaces and so their departure did not affect the overall results. It was the much lower rate of recognition among joiners (new workplaces and those growing above our sample threshold) that produced the major change. Of course, if the rate of recognition had increased with workplace age then the overall incidence would have dropped more slowly, or even remained stable. In fact, recognition remained at virtually the same level in continuing workplaces, with derecognitions almost balanced by cases of new recognition. In this example, then, it was the distinctive behaviour of management in new workplaces, rather than a change in behaviour among continuing workplaces, that was at the heart of the decline in this crucial indicator of joint regulation.

A transformation – but to what?

Our broad conclusion is that the changes we have documented in this volume in the structures and conduct of British industrial relations can reasonably be regarded as a transformation. The Conservative government that came to power in 1979 confronted a system of collective employment relations that was dominant, though not universal. It pervaded the whole of the public sector, including the then extensive nationalized industries, and it covered large parts of the private sector, especially manufacturing industry and large employers generally. That system of collective relations, based on the shared values of the legitimacy of representation by independent trade unions and of joint regulation, crumbled in the intervening eighteen years to such an extent that it no longer represents a dominant model. True, the substantially reduced public sector still operates that model to a large degree. But in the far larger private sector of the economy, joint regulation is very much a minority activity.

This change is almost wholly in the direction in which public policy was directed. The Conservatives aimed to 'curb the power of the unions' – and overall union influence, on most of the measures available to us, has diminished. On some matters the direct impact of legislation can be discerned – the closed shop and industrial action are two clear examples. On other matters, government action through legislation or exhortation made a contribution to the change. Often such influences were indirect and were reinforced by changes in the economic or societal context over which the government had no direct sway. One example is the decentralization of bargaining structures, where changes in the private sector were part of the more pervasive attack on collective bargaining. Another was the increasing recognition of workplace and organizational performance in deciding the size of pay increases – a change that was probably more a consequence of economic pressures than the government's exhortation in this direction. But, in our view, the government's programme had a more pervasive and deeper impact. This was to undermine the foundation of the system of collective representation and joint regulation.

Clearly the institutional fabric of collective relations was destroyed to a large extent. But equally important was that the widespread assumption that voluntary joint regulation was the desirable basis for employment relationships was abandoned by swathes of managers and employees. If this change had not occurred, the crumbling of the institutional structure could not have happened on the scale that it did.

The new Labour government elected in 1997 has not sought to restore the system of collective representation and joint regulation that existed at the beginning of the 1980s. Nor has it sought to reinstate fully the collectivist philosophy that underpinned it. Many of the legal changes introduced by the Conservatives are to be retained. The new government has extended some existing individual employment rights and introduced a number of new ones. However, its introduction of a statutory minimum wage can be seen as an overt recognition that collective bargaining in the British tradition cannot be relied upon to eliminate poverty wages in all sectors of the economy. The Employment Relations Act 1999 will provide a mechanism for establishing collective representation where a majority of the workforce wills it. But although it is too early to judge the effects of this provision it is, in our view, inconceivable that the procedures, however widely and vigorously used, will lead to the restoration of collective bargaining to the extent that it existed in 1980.

What is more, our analyses of the changes in continuing workplaces – and of the comparisons between new workplaces and those that they replaced – broadly suggest to us that collective bargaining will continue to contract in extent and effectiveness. In parallel with this, we expect that representative and union-supported methods of communicating employees' concerns to management will continue to be replaced by direct methods of communication which have their timing, agendas and very existence controlled by management.

We consider, therefore, that the prospect is for a further disintegration of what remains of the system of joint regulation and employee voice based on trade union representation. This is, of course, not just a matter of government policy. There have been many changes in product markets, both in Britain and globally, that have heightened the incentives for employers to abandon co-operation with fellow employers and 'undertake the risks of challenging the pay levels, working practices and controls, which their predecessors in easier times had allowed the trade unions to build up' (Brown *et al.*, 1998: 15). These changes have reinforced, and been reinforced by, a more widespread adoption of the values of 'acquisitive individualism' (Phelps Brown, 1990: 1) amongst managers and employees. All these changes militate against the restoration of the conditions in which the former, predominantly collectivist, system of employment relations grew and survived.

What has replaced, and will continue to replace, the former system? Here it is more difficult to give answers. Our companion volume (Cully *et al.*, 1999) provides the most up-to-date picture of employee relations in Britain from which new patterns might be discerned. But the authors do not claim to have identified a new, dominant 'model' of employee relations that has displaced the formerly dominant model based upon collective representation. Nor, from what we know of work in progress by other researchers using the WERS98 data, have others yet identified sizeable and distinct new groupings that might become such a model or models.

Such efforts may yet bear fruit. But our most likely expectation is that the economy will continue to generate more workplaces in which the nature of employment relationships is almost exclusively a matter for managerial choice. In some cases, managerial regimes may approximate to versions of enlightened 'human resource management'; in others, there will be authoritarian regimes which give little opportunity for employee voice. However, we consider that neither of these alternatives to joint regulation are likely to produce the incentive to fairness which we have seen is associated with, although by no means guaranteed by, trade union representation. Should the current reforms also prove insufficient, we see a yet more extensive floor of employee rights, rigorously enforced by state agencies, as the most feasible method of preventing the more extreme forms of exploitation that an unregulated labour market can produce in the increasingly competitive world in which Britain operates.

Whether any particular model will come to dominate employment relations in Britain depends upon a range of influences, including Government policy and the preferences and actions of the parties to the employment relationship. But we confidently expect that the debates about the directions to be taken, and the outcomes of past choices, will continue to be enlightened by research and analysis that is based on the kinds of evidence that we have used in this volume.

Technical appendix

This appendix describes the design and execution of each of the elements of the Workplace Industrial Relations Survey (WIRS) series used in the preparation of this volume. It also describes the compilation of each of the datasets used in our analysis, provides information on the statistical reliability of our results, and gives details of how to gain access to the data. Further details of each of the surveys in the WIRS series are included in the technical appendices to each of the four sourcebooks (Daniel and Millward, 1983; Millward and Stevens, 1986; Millward *et al*., 1992; Cully *et al*., 1999) and in technical reports compiled by the National Centre for Social Research (formerly SCPR) who were responsible for conducting the fieldwork for each survey in the series (Airey and Potts, 1983; Airey *et al*., 1992, 1999).

The Workplace Industrial Relations Survey series

The WIRS series comprises a set of four national surveys of workplaces in Britain, in which key role-holders provide information on the nature of employment relations at their place of work. The four surveys took place in 1980, 1984, 1990 and 1998.

In each of the surveys in the series, the establishment or workplace constitutes the principal unit of analysis. A workplace is defined as comprising the activities of a single employer at a single set of premises; examples might include a single branch of a bank, a car factory, a department store or a school. The central focus of the survey series has been the formal and structured relations that take place between management and employees at the workplace although, as stated in Chapter 1, this focus softened in the 1998 survey.

The principal component of each survey in the WIRS series is a face-to-face interview at the establishment with the senior person dealing with industrial relations, employee relations or personnel matters. Interviews are also sought with worker representatives, where present. Individual surveys have also included interviews with production managers (1984), and with financial managers (1990) and a survey of employees (1998). Together, these elements constitute the four cross-section surveys in the series. Panel surveys of continuing workplaces included in the previous cross-section have also taken place in 1984, 1990 and 1998. The various elements of the WIRS series are shown in Figure 1.1 of Chapter 1. Those parts of the series that have been focused upon in the preparation of this volume, which have been highlighted in Figure 1.1, are described in more detail below.

The 1980–98 time series

The 1980–98 time series is formed from the main management interviews in each of the four cross-section surveys. In Figure 1.1 these interviews are represented by the four large, highlighted cells labelled 'Senior person dealing with employee relations'. In each case, the cell also contains the total number of achieved interviews that form our sample. The time series contains a selection of data items from the 1998 main management interview for which there are also comparable items in at least one earlier survey in the series, plus a range of derived variables. None of the information obtained from cross-section interviews with other role-holders is used, except for those elements of the 1990 survey of financial managers in which selected questions from the main interview were asked of this respondent instead of the personnel manager.[1]

Sampling frames and samples

The samples for each of the four cross-section surveys have been taken from frames considered to be the best available at the time, namely the Censuses of Employment of 1977, 1981 and 1987 and the Inter Departmental Business Register (IDBR) of 1997. In each of the first three surveys, the sampling universe comprised all workplaces in Britain with twenty-five or more employees, except those in Division 0 (Agriculture, Forestry and Fishing) of the 1980 *Standard Industrial Classification* (SIC). In the fourth survey, the sample was extended to include workplaces with between ten and twenty-four employees, although we have only used those workplaces with twenty-five or more employees in our analysis. The 1998 sample excluded workplaces in major groups A to C (Agriculture, Hunting and Forestry; Fishing; and Mining and Quarrying), P (Private households with employed persons) and Q (Extra-territorial bodies) of the 1992 SIC. The industrial scope of the first three surveys is therefore very slightly wider than that of the fourth in the series, but the proportion of workplaces involved in the variation of scope is not greater than 1 per cent in any one year. We have found very few results to be affected by excluding these cases from the whole of the survey series and have retained them in the results presented in this volume. A final set of exclusions from the sampling frame for the fourth survey consisted of all eligible addresses from the 1990 survey for which a match could be found between the IDBR and the 1987 Census of Employment records. This was done in order to avoid duplication between the 1998 cross-section and 1990–98 panel survey samples.

In each of the four surveys, a stratified random sample was drawn from the file of eligible records. This sample totalled 2,994 units in 1980, 3,217 in 1984,

3,215 in 1990 and 2,830 in 1998 (excluding those units in the 1998 sample with between ten and twenty-four employees). A 'reserve pool' of units was also selected from each of the sampling frames. This reserve pool numbered 1,000 units in 1980, 513 in 1984, 357 in 1990 and 500 in 1998. Units from the reserve were issued in 1980 and 1984. The combined number of units in the selected sample and reserve pool became smaller in each successive survey as experience bred confidence in a smaller reserve pool and as less priority was attached, in 1998, to producing separate estimates for those workplaces with 500–999 employees and those with 1,000 or more employees.

The sample for the first three surveys was selected by, first, stratifying the sampling frame by workplace employment size and then employing differential sampling fractions within each stratum. In 1990, a second stage of sampling also took place in which units in SIC (1980) Classes 91, 93 and 95 were undersampled by a factor of 1 in 4, leading to the removal of 209 units from the initial sample of 3,217. In 1998, the principle of differential sampling by employment size and industry was extended, but in a one-stage design: units were undersampled in SIC (1992) group D and oversampled in major groups E, F, H, J and O. In each survey, sampling fractions increased with employment size in order to provide sufficient numbers of workplaces within each size-band for separate analysis whilst permitting accurate employee-based estimates to be made. In each year, weights have been used in analysis to compensate for unequal probabilities of selection (see section below on Weighting). The sampling fractions employed and numbers of units drawn within each size stratum in each of the surveys are shown in Table A1. Units with between ten and twenty-four employees in the selected sample for the 1998 survey are excluded from the table for consistency with earlier years.

A number of units were withdrawn from the selected sample before addresses were issued to interviewers. Some were 'aggregate returns', where the census unit or IDBR local unit referred to more than one establishment and the employer was unable or unwilling to provide disaggregated information to enable resampling to take place. Conversely, some sampled units referred to only part of an establishment. If other parts of the establishment featured as separate units on the sampling frame, it was necessary to delete all but one of the units. Further units were removed if they referred entirely to peripatetic employees, such as supply teachers, who could not be allocated to a single establishment. Other reasons for the removal of units from the issued sample included incomplete address information and extreme geographical location. Units engaged in deep coal-mining were also withdrawn from the sample in 1984, because of the industry-wide dispute taking place at the time, and in 1990, for reasons of consistency. The exclusion of SIC (1992) major group C from the 1998 sample ensured that consistency on this matter was preserved in the fourth survey.

Table A1 Sampling fractions and numbers of units drawn for the selected cross-section samples, 1980, 1984, 1990 and 1998

Year of survey Year of sampling frame	1980 1977	1984 1981	1990 1987	1998 1997	1980 1977	1984 1981	1990 1987	1998 1997	1980 1977	1984 1981	1990 1987	1998 1997
	Number of units				*Sampling fractions*				*Sample selected*			
Number of employees recorded at unit												
25–49	66,959	70,000	74,956	76,087	105	107	112	126	636	653	667	603
50–99	33,881	33,288	35,215	36,004	57	60	64	64	599	558	552	566
100–199	18,340	17,625	18,178	18,701	35	33	36	33	525	533	498	562
200–499	10,649	9,880	9,921	9,832	20	19	21	16	524	515	466	626
500–999	3,098	2,796	2,693	⎫	8	7	7	7	374	430	380	⎫
1,000–1,999	1,332a	1,169	960	⎬ 3,249	7	4	2	7	187	309	474	⎬ 473
2,000 or more	571a	484	360	⎭	4	4	2	7	149	129	178	⎭
Total	134,825	135,242	142,283	144,053	45	43	44	51	2,994	3,217	3,215	2,830

Notes

The selected samples exclude the 'reserve pool' of units selected in each year.

The sampling fractions and selected sample given for 1990 are prior to the undersampling of units from SIC (1980) Classes 91, 93 and 95. This removed a further 209 units from the 1990 selected sample. The figures given for 1998 have already taken account of differential sampling by industry.

The sample indicated for the 1998 survey excludes 362 workplaces with between 10 and 24 employees that also formed part of the overall sample in 1998; these are excluded from the table for consistency with earlier years.

a Estimated subdivision.

Questionnaire development and fieldwork

The interview schedules used in each of the four cross-section surveys were carefully developed and piloted before final versions were prepared for use in fieldwork. In 1990 and 1998, the development stages included specific contributions from academics, whilst much was also learnt from the Australian Workplace Industrial Relations Surveys of 1989/90 and 1995. Two pilot surveys were conducted in the preparation of the first survey questionnaire in 1980, and also during the development of the much redesigned 1998 questionnaire. A single pilot was conducted in 1984 and 1990, when the changes that were made to the questionnaire between surveys were, in many ways, less radical.

The conduct of fieldwork has remained broadly the same throughout the series. First, a group of between 120 and 150 experienced interviewers have attended a two-day briefing conducted jointly by the research team and the fieldwork contractor (in each case SCPR, now the National Centre for Social Research). Many interviewers working on the first, second and third surveys have returned to work on later surveys in the series. Following these briefings, an initial approach letter has been sent to respondents from the government department responsible for the survey (the Department of Employment in 1980, 1984 and 1990; the Department of Trade and Industry in 1998). This describes the purposes of the survey, outlines the procedures for ensuring the anonymity of respondents and informs the recipient of the forthcoming request for an interview. In most cases, this letter is sent directly to the sampled establishment. However, from 1984 onwards, certain types of establishment have been subject to a slightly different procedure whereby the initial contact is made at corporate, rather than establishment, level. This procedure is used in cases where head office approval has proved to be particularly crucial in securing establishment-level response to the survey. Such cases include central government, emergency services, the utilities, and particular organizations engaged in telecommunications, postal services, banking and retail.

Following the initial contact, an interviewer has contacted the establishment by telephone and sought the main management respondent's agreement to be interviewed. The interviewer has then sent a letter of confirmation, together with a small pre-interview questionnaire about the composition of the workforce at the sampled workplace.[2] The intention is that this short questionnaire is completed prior to the interview, giving the respondent time to consult workplace records.

The main management interview is conducted face to face. Paper question-naires were used in the first three surveys in the series but, in 1998, Computer Assisted Personal Interviewing (CAPI) was introduced, with favourable outcomes in terms of data quality.[3] Interviews have generally lasted around 100 minutes, on average, albeit with considerable variation around the mean. In total, interviewing on each of the surveys has taken around eight to ten months to complete, with the date of the median interview moving slightly earlier in the year each time. The fieldwork timetable on each survey is shown in Table A2.

Table A2 Fieldwork timetable for main cross-section survey, 1980, 1984, 1990 and
1998

Survey year	Period of interviewing	Median interview date
1980	February 1980–September 1980	June 1980
1984	March 1984–October 1984	May 1984
1990	January 1990–September 1990	March 1990
1998	October 1997–July 1998	February 1998

Fieldwork outcomes

The initial sample has grown smaller for each survey, but has averaged around
3,000 addresses (Table A3). Around one fifth of each sample has proved to be
ineligible for the survey or otherwise out of scope. Addresses are classified as
ineligible or out of scope if, for example, the establishment has closed down
between the last update of the sampling frame and the time of interview, the
number of employees at the workplace has fallen below the survey threshold in
that time, or the premises indicated by the address are found to be derelict,
vacant or demolished.

Around one fifth of the remaining eligible, in-scope addresses have generally
not yielded productive responses. This has commonly been because the
respondent was unwilling to take part, but also, in a small number of cases,
because contact could not be made with the respondent, or they were ill or away
from the establishment for the duration of fieldwork. The response rate to
each survey – the number of cases yielding a satisfactory management interview
and workforce profile questionnaire, expressed as a percentage of eligible and
in-scope addresses – has thus stood at around 80 per cent. It rose from 75 per
cent in 1980, to 77 per cent in 1984 and 83 per cent in 1990, but fell back
slightly to 80 per cent in 1998 (Table A3).[4] Response rates in each of the surveys
have varied by region, industry and size of establishment (as recorded on the
sampling frame). Response rates have consistently been higher among larger
units.

As stated above, the response rate is based on the achievement of a successful
interview with a main management respondent and the satisfactory completion
of the workforce profile questionnaire. However, interviews have not always
been conducted with a manager based at the sampled establishment. This might
occur, for example, in cases where no-one at the sampled establishment has
sufficient knowledge of personnel matters to answer the questions contained in
the survey. In such cases, the interview is conducted at head office, at an
intermediate regional or divisional office or, in some cases, interviewing is split
between two respondents whose combined knowledge permits the completion
of the questionnaire. Together, these types of interviews accounted for between
8 and 10 per cent of the total in 1980, 1984 and 1998. However, the proportion
was higher, at 18 per cent, in 1990.

Table A3 Summary of fieldwork response for cross-section samples, 1980, 1984, 1990 and 1998

	Number of addresses			
	1980	*1984*	*1990*	*1998*
Selected sample with 25 or more employees	2,994	3,217	3,215	2,830
Undersampling by SIC			−209	
Reserve units issued	313	27		
Addresses generated from aggregate returns	25	55	17	
Initial sample	3,332 *(100%)*	3,209 *(100%)*	3,023 *(100%)*	2,830 *(100%)*
Ineligible/Out-of-scope/ Otherwise withdrawn	−606 *(18%)*	−584 *(18%)*	−531 *(18%)*	−456 *(16%)*
Total eligible and in-scope	2,726 *(82%)*	2,625 *(82%)*	2,492 *(82%)*	2,374 *(84%)*
Non-productive addresses	−686 *(21%)*	−606 *(19%)*	−431 *(14%)*	−479 *(17%)*
Interviews achieved from selected sample	2,040 *(61%)*	2,019 *(63%)*	2,061 *(68%)*	1,895 *(67%)*
Response rate	75%	77%	83%	80%
Additional interviews from units with 10–24 employees on IDBR				34
Total interviews	2,040	2,019	2,061	1,929

Coding and editing of the data

Data collected in each of the surveys has been coded and edited by experienced data-processing teams, with substantial involvement from research team members. The process of coding and editing the data was made more efficient in 1998 through the introduction of CAPI. However, in each year, these tasks have been afforded considerable effort in order to ensure that the data is of the highest quality when passed to the research teams for primary analysis.

In each survey, the verbatim answers to all open-ended questions have been coded to detailed frames, whereby similar answers are grouped under a single numeric code. Frames are developed during the first months of fieldwork, but generally kept open and refined during the remainder of the coding period so that the full range of answers can be accounted for.

Rigorous checks are conducted on all of the questionnaires in order to identify inconsistencies and missing data. These include range checks to highlight extreme values and logic checks to examine the internal consistency of answers given throughout the questionnaire. Attention is given, in particular, to the data collected on the workforce profile questionnaire. In cases where major problems are identified, the case may be referred back to an interviewer or direct contact may be made with the respondent by editors in an attempt to resolve the query. In many cases, however, the source of the problem is clear and the data can be edited after referral to the research team. Significant discrepancies in the data, whether resolved at the editing stage or not, are flagged with appropriate codes.

Weighting the data

The sampling procedures employed in each of the surveys mean that workplaces within the same survey none the less have differing probabilities of selection into the survey sample. The data arising from the survey therefore have to be weighted in order to adjust for the fact that, in the unweighted sample, certain types of workplace are either under-represented or over-represented in comparison with their representation in the sampling frame. For each workplace, the weight required to adjust for this is derived as the inverse of the estimated probability of selection of that case from the sampling frame. In most cases, this is simply the inverse of the sampling fraction applied to the sample stratum from which the case originated. However, in a minority of cases where the sampled unit represented more than one workplace, or a subsection of a workplace, it has been necessary to calculate an individual weight to account for the true probability of selection.

Additional weighting was also included for the first three surveys to compensate for the age of the sampling frame and its consequent under-inclusion of smaller workplaces near the threshold of twenty-five employees. In 1998 the new sampling frame was considered sufficiently up to date to make this unnecessary. However, the 1998 weighting scheme was the first to involve the trimming of weights within each sample stratum. The use of inverse probability weights generates unbiased estimates. Even so, substantial differences between the size or SIC of the establishment as recorded on the IDBR and its size or SIC at time of interview can lead to large variation in the weights applying to cases within the same interview-SIC and interview-size groups during analysis. The effect of a large variation in weights within analysis groupings is to considerably increase standard errors, and so extreme weights were trimmed.

All of the results presented in the main text of this volume have been produced using weighted data, unless otherwise specified.

Sampling errors

The use of stratification and subsequent weighting in the design of a survey mean that the standard errors of estimates derived from the survey sample are generally larger than those pertaining to a simple random sample of the same size. The 'design factor' associated with a particular estimate is a measure of the degree to which the survey design may have inflated the standard error of that estimate when compared with the standard error that would have been derived from a simple random sample of equivalent size.

Design factors were calculated for a number of variables in each of the surveys at the time that each survey was conducted, although the number of variables that formed part of the exercise in 1998 was much greater than it had been in earlier years. The average design factor for each of the first three surveys was estimated to be 1.25 (indicating that the average design-based standard error in each survey was 25 per cent higher than the standard error from a simple random sample). The average design factor for the 1998 survey was estimated to be 1.5. Some of the increase may reflect the more complex stratification of the 1998 sample, but it may also partly reflect the more comprehensive nature of the calculations that were carried out to estimate the effect of survey design.

The most common statistical requirement when reading this volume will be to assess the statistical significance of differences between percentages arising from different surveys in the series. For example, if one survey estimates that 20 per cent of workplaces possess a certain characteristic, and the next survey estimates that figure to be 15 per cent, can we be confident that the incidence of the characteristic has actually gone down in the population as a whole? The average design factor for each survey has been used to compile 'rule of thumb' tables that can be used to assess the significance of differences between percentages across surveys. Table A4 gives the approximate standard errors associated with differences between two estimates from the series, when those estimates are based on any two of the surveys from 1980, 1984 and 1990. Table A5 gives the approximate standard errors associated with differences between two estimates, where those estimates are based on the 1998 survey and any one of the surveys from 1980, 1984 and 1990. For simplicity, the tables assume that the sample sizes for any two survey comparisons are the same.

The most common criterion used when comparing results from large-scale social surveys is that differences pass a 95 per cent test of statistical significance. In such cases there is, at most, only a 5 per cent chance that the difference identified by the survey is actually zero within the population as a whole. In order to estimate the 95 per cent confidence interval of a difference between two estimates, one multiplies the approximate standard error in Table A4 or A5 by a factor of two. For example, if the 1980 survey gave an estimate of 20 per cent based on a sample size of 2,000 and the 1990 survey gave an estimate of 15 per cent based on the same sample size, the approximate standard error of the difference of 5 per cent (20 minus 15) would be 1.50. The 95 per cent confidence interval would then be 5 per cent (the difference) plus or minus 3.0 (the confidence interval), i.e. 2.0 per cent to 8.0 per cent. The lower bound of the confidence interval is greater than zero and so we can be confident, at the 95 per cent level, that the difference of 5 per cent identified in our survey samples is not zero in the population as a whole. In other words, we can be confident, at the 95 per cent level, that there has been a real fall in the incidence of the phenomenon in the population.

Table A4 Standard errors of differences between two estimates arising from the 1980, 1984 and 1990 surveys

N = 2,000 Estimate from Survey 2

Estimate from Survey 1	5	10	15	20	25	30	35	40	45	50
5	0.86	1.04	1.17	1.27	1.35	1.42	1.47	1.50	1.52	1.52
10		1.19	1.30	1.40	1.47	1.53	1.57	1.61	1.62	1.63
15			1.41	1.50	1.57	1.62	1.67	1.69	1.71	1.72
20				1.58	1.65	1.70	1.74	1.77	1.78	1.79
25					1.71	1.76	1.80	1.83	1.84	1.85
30						1.81	1.85	1.88	1.89	1.90
35							1.89	1.91	1.93	1.93
40								1.94	1.95	1.96
45									1.97	1.97
50										1.98

N = 1,000 Estimate from Survey 2

Estimate from Survey 1	5	10	15	20	25	30	35	40	45	50
5	1.22	1.47	1.65	1.80	1.92	2.01	2.07	2.12	2.15	2.16
10		1.68	1.84	1.98	2.08	2.17	2.23	2.27	2.30	2.30
15			2.00	2.12	2.22	2.30	2.36	2.40	2.42	2.43
20				2.24	2.33	2.40	2.46	2.50	2.52	2.53
25					2.42	2.49	2.55	2.58	2.61	2.61
30						2.56	2.61	2.65	2.67	2.68
35							2.67	2.70	2.72	2.73
40								2.74	2.76	2.77
45									2.78	2.79
50										2.80

N = 1,500 Estimate from Survey 2

Estimate from Survey 1	5	10	15	20	25	30	35	40	45	50
5	0.99	1.20	1.35	1.47	1.56	1.64	1.69	1.73	1.75	1.76
10		1.37	1.51	1.61	1.70	1.77	1.82	1.85	1.88	1.88
15			1.63	1.73	1.81	1.88	1.92	1.96	1.98	1.98
20				1.83	1.90	1.96	2.01	2.04	2.06	2.07
25					1.98	2.03	2.08	2.11	2.13	2.13
30						2.09	2.13	2.17	2.18	2.19
35							2.18	2.21	2.22	2.23
40								2.24	2.25	2.26
45									2.27	2.28
50										2.28

N = 500 Estimate from Survey 2

Estimate from Survey 1	5	10	15	20	25	30	35	40	45	50
5	1.72	2.07	2.34	2.55	2.71	2.84	2.93	3.00	3.04	3.05
10		2.37	2.61	2.80	2.94	3.06	3.15	3.21	3.25	3.26
15			2.82	3.00	3.14	3.25	3.33	3.39	3.42	3.43
20				3.16	3.30	3.40	3.48	3.54	3.57	3.58
25					3.42	3.52	3.60	3.66	3.69	3.70
30						3.62	3.70	3.75	3.78	3.79
35							3.77	3.82	3.85	3.86
40								3.87	3.90	3.91
45									3.93	3.94
50										3.95

Notes

Table assumes that both estimates are based on samples of equivalent size.

For estimates greater than 50, simply subtract the estimate from 100. For example, if the estimates from Surveys 1 and 2 were 85 per cent and 60 per cent respectively, one would use the row labelled 15 per cent (100 − 85 = 15) and the column labelled 40 per cent (100 − 60 = 40).

Table A5 Standard errors of differences between two estimates arising from the 1998 survey and any one of the 1980, 1984 or 1990 surveys

N = 2,000 — Estimate from 1998 survey

Estimate from Survey 1	5	10	15	20	25	30	35	40	45	50
5	0.95	1.18	1.34	1.47	1.57	1.65	1.71	1.75	1.78	1.78
10	1.11	1.31	1.46	1.58	1.68	1.75	1.81	1.84	1.87	1.88
15	1.24	1.42	1.56	1.67	1.76	1.83	1.89	1.92	1.94	1.95
20	1.34	1.50	1.64	1.75	1.83	1.90	1.95	1.99	2.01	2.02
25	1.41	1.57	1.70	1.81	1.89	1.96	2.01	2.04	2.06	2.07
30	1.47	1.63	1.75	1.85	1.94	2.00	2.05	2.08	2.10	2.11
35	1.52	1.67	1.79	1.89	1.97	2.03	2.08	2.12	2.14	2.14
40	1.55	1.70	1.82	1.92	2.00	2.06	2.11	2.14	2.16	2.17
45	1.57	1.72	1.84	1.93	2.01	2.07	2.12	2.15	2.17	2.18
50	1.58	1.72	1.84	1.94	2.02	2.08	2.12	2.16	2.18	2.18

N = 1,000 — Estimate from 1998 survey

Estimate from Survey 1	5	10	15	20	25	30	35	40	45	50
5	1.35	1.66	1.90	2.08	2.23	2.34	2.42	2.48	2.51	2.52
10	1.57	1.85	2.07	2.24	2.37	2.48	2.55	2.61	2.64	2.65
15	1.75	2.00	2.20	2.36	2.49	2.59	2.67	2.72	2.75	2.76
20	1.89	2.13	2.32	2.47	2.59	2.69	2.76	2.81	2.84	2.85
25	2.00	2.23	2.41	2.56	2.67	2.77	2.84	2.89	2.92	2.92
30	2.09	2.30	2.48	2.62	2.74	2.83	2.90	2.95	2.97	2.98
35	2.15	2.36	2.53	2.67	2.79	2.88	2.95	2.99	3.02	3.03
40	2.20	2.40	2.57	2.71	2.82	2.91	2.98	3.02	3.05	3.06
45	2.22	2.43	2.60	2.73	2.84	2.93	3.00	3.04	3.07	3.08
50	2.23	2.44	2.60	2.74	2.85	2.94	3.00	3.05	3.08	3.09

N = 1,500 — Estimate from 1998 survey

Estimate from Survey 1	5	10	15	20	25	30	35	40	45	50
5	1.10	1.36	1.55	1.70	1.82	1.91	1.98	2.02	2.05	2.06
10	1.28	1.51	1.69	1.83	1.94	2.02	2.09	2.13	2.16	2.17
15	1.43	1.64	1.80	1.93	2.03	2.12	2.18	2.22	2.25	2.25
20	1.54	1.74	1.89	2.02	2.12	2.19	2.25	2.29	2.32	2.33
25	1.63	1.82	1.97	2.09	2.18	2.26	2.32	2.36	2.38	2.39
30	1.70	1.88	2.02	2.14	2.24	2.31	2.37	2.41	2.43	2.44
35	1.76	1.93	2.07	2.18	2.28	2.35	2.40	2.44	2.47	2.47
40	1.79	1.96	2.10	2.21	2.30	2.38	2.43	2.47	2.49	2.50
45	1.81	1.98	2.12	2.23	2.32	2.39	2.45	2.49	2.51	2.52
50	1.82	1.99	2.13	2.24	2.33	2.40	2.45	2.49	2.51	2.52

N = 500 — Estimate from 1998 survey

Estimate from Survey 1	5	10	15	20	25	30	35	40	45	50
5	1.90	2.35	2.69	2.95	3.15	3.31	3.42	3.50	3.55	3.57
10	2.22	2.62	2.92	3.16	3.35	3.50	3.61	3.69	3.73	3.75
15	2.47	2.83	3.12	3.34	3.52	3.67	3.77	3.85	3.89	3.90
20	2.67	3.01	3.28	3.49	3.67	3.80	3.90	3.97	4.02	4.03
25	2.83	3.15	3.41	3.61	3.78	3.91	4.01	4.08	4.12	4.14
30	2.95	3.26	3.51	3.71	3.87	4.00	4.10	4.17	4.21	4.22
35	3.04	3.34	3.58	3.78	3.94	4.07	4.16	4.23	4.27	4.28
40	3.10	3.40	3.64	3.83	3.99	4.12	4.21	4.28	4.32	4.33
45	3.14	3.43	3.67	3.86	4.02	4.15	4.24	4.31	4.34	4.36
50	3.15	3.44	3.68	3.87	4.03	4.15	4.25	4.31	4.35	4.37

Notes

Table assumes that both estimates are based on samples of equivalent s.ze.

For estimates greater than 50, simply subtract the estimate from 100. For example, if the estimates from Surveys 1 and 2 were 85 per cent and 60 per cent respectively, one would use the row labelled 15 per cent (100 − 85 = 15) and the column labelled 40 per cent (100 − 60 = 40).

The 1990–98 panel survey

The 1998 WERS panel survey traced a random selection of workplaces that responded to the cross-section survey of 1990 for re-interview at the same time as the 1998 cross-section survey was taking place. The target was for around 1,000 interviews with the main management respondent in workplaces that had continued in operation between 1990 and 1998, and that employed twenty-five or more employees at the time of both interviews.

The 1990–98 panel survey followed previous panel surveys that were either largely experimental, as in the case of the 1980–84 panel, or restricted to workplaces in industry and commerce, as in 1984–90.[5] Alongside its larger size, the 1990–98 panel survey differed from its predecessors by the use of a specially designed CAPI interview schedule. Panel surveys conducted at earlier points of the series had simply used the questionnaire being employed in the main cross-section survey at the time.

Sampling frame and sample

The sample of workplaces for the 1990–98 panel survey was drawn as a stratified random sample from the 2,061 productive interviews in the 1990 cross-section survey. Workplaces from the 1990 cross-section were first stratified into seven groups according to the number of employees at the establishment at the time of the 1990 interview. A 63 per cent random sample was then taken from within each of the seven groups, giving 1,301 workplaces. An additional reserve sample of 132 workplaces was also drawn in view of uncertainty over the proportion of workplaces that would have survived between 1990 and 1998, but this reserve was not called upon. The coverage of the panel survey was equivalent to that of the cross-section surveys that comprise the time series, namely workplaces from almost all types of industry across Britain, in both private and public sectors.

Questionnaire development and fieldwork

As stated above, earlier panel surveys in the WIRS series had simply utilized the questionnaire that had been designed for the cross-section survey in that year. However, the questionnaire used in the 1998 interview of the 1990–98 panel survey was specifically designed to measure change. The questionnaire included many questions from the 1990 cross-section questionnaire. In addition, through the use of CAPI technology, it was possible to feed data collected in the 1990 survey directly into the 1998 interview. Seventeen items of data were fed forward into the 1998 interview, covering such things as the size of the establishment, the presence of recognized unions and the use of incentive payments at the workplace in 1990. Changes in practice between 1990 and 1998 could then be automatically identified during the interview by comparing this feed-forward data with responses given in the 1998 interview. Consequently, questions were triggered to enquire about the circumstances surrounding a particular change.

The questionnaire was piloted twice before being finalized. Both pilots were conducted using addresses that featured in the 1984–90 panel of trading sector workplaces, so as not to encroach upon the 1990 cross-section sample. As a consequence, no public sector workplaces featured as part of either pilot. In both pilots, the average interview length was in excess of requirements and substantial deletions were made from the questionnaire. In addition, after the second pilot, it was decided that the detail of the occupational grid on the pre-interview questionnaire (the *Basic Workforce Data Sheet* or BWDS) would not be keyed in during the interview, but entered later during data processing.

During fieldwork itself, the 1,301 workplaces in the sample were first subjected to a short telephone inquiry by a small team of experienced interviewers in order to identify continuing establishments. A continuing workplace was defined as one that employed twenty-five or more employees at the time of both the 1990 and 1998 interviews and had continued to operate throughout the intervening period. Changes of activity, ownership or location were not considered to critically impair this concept of continuity, but meticulous checks were made during screening and data editing to ensure that the history of the 1998 unit could be clearly traced back to that surveyed in 1990.

Once the continuing portion of the sample had been identified, fieldwork progressed in much the same way as for the 1998 cross-section survey, as described above. Interviewers were briefed about the panel survey at the same time as they were briefed about the cross-section, and 142 of the 156 interviewers that were briefed on the project worked on both panel and cross-section addresses during the course of fieldwork. The panel addresses were divided into two groups: those necessitating an initial contact at corporate level, and those in which the establishment could be contacted direct in the first instance. Initial approach letters were sent, and interviewers subsequently contacted the establishment by telephone in order to seek the main management respondent's agreement to be interviewed. As in the cross-section surveys, the pre-interview questionnaire (BWDS) was sent in advance of the interview.

The mean interview length was 66 minutes (median 60 minutes), with longer interviews generally taking place in larger establishments. Interviewing began in November 1997 and came to an end in July 1998. The median interview month was January 1998, compared with March 1990 for the earlier cross-section survey that formed the first observation in the panel.

Fieldwork outcomes

Of the 1,301 addresses that formed the initial sample, 261 (20 per cent) proved to be ineligible or otherwise outside the scope of the panel survey. These primarily consisted of establishments that had closed down between 1990 and 1998 and those which, although in operation, employed less than twenty-five employees at the time of the 1998 interview. Of the remaining 1,040 workplaces that were eligible and in scope, 882 yielded a productive interview. However, thirty-six cases were rejected at the editing stage because the 1990 and 1998 units were not consistently defined, making comparisons unreliable. Of these thirty-six workplaces, fourteen were judged to have been incorrectly classified as in-scope for the panel survey. In the remaining twenty-six cases, the 1998 interview was judged to have related to more than one workplace or a subsection of a workplace. Excluding the fourteen from the base of eligible, in-scope addresses and removing the twenty-six from the number of productive interviews brought the effective response rate for the 1998 observation of the panel survey down from 84 per cent (882/1,040) to 82 per cent (846/1,026).

Strenuous efforts were made throughout fieldwork to ensure that the paper copies of the BWDS were retrieved by interviewers and returned to the data-processing office. By the end of fieldwork, the paper copy of the BWDS had been retrieved and filed for 89 per cent of the final sample of 846 workplaces. The detail of the occupational grid, which had not been entered during the interview, was keyed and handed over, unedited, to the research team.

Coding and editing of the data

In common with the data from the cross-section survey, the data from the 1998 interviews in the panel survey were coded and edited by experienced data-processing teams, with substantial involvement from research team members. The verbatim answers to all open-ended questions were coded to detailed frames. In cases where a question had been repeated from the 1990 cross-section questionnaire, the frames were also repeated from that survey. Additional frames were developed for new open-ended questions.

Rigorous checks were conducted to ensure that both the 1990 and 1998 observations were of units that met the definition of a workplace, and that the history of the 1998 unit could be clearly traced back to that surveyed in 1990. These checks included comparisons between the number of employees at the workplace in 1990 and 1998, the industrial activity of the establishment, its workforce composition and its union status. A very large recorded growth or decline in the numbers employed at the workplace might indicate, for example, that one of the interviews in fact referred to the whole organization to which the workplace belonged. All such cases were referred to the research team for further investigation. In the above example, the site may have simply been amalgamated with another workplace and, as long as there was some continuity of employment between the 1990 workplace and the amalgamated unit, the definition of continuity would have been met. However, these checks were invaluable in identifying units that were inconsistently defined across the two observations.

Checks were also conducted on all of the questionnaires in order to identify inconsistencies and missing values within the 1998 interview data. As in the case of the cross-section questionnaires, these include range checks to highlight extreme values and logic checks to examine the internal consistency of answers given throughout the questionnaire.

In total, around two fifths of the 1998 panel interviews were referred to the research team as a result of the various edit checks that were run on the 1998 interview data. Many were swiftly dealt with, but some required detailed investigation. Data were edited where appropriate. Flags (also called 'overcodes') were subsequently added to the data in order to identify cases in which the data had been amended by the research team, and also to identify cases in which further investigation generated continued concerns about the consistency of definition of the establishment.

Weighting the data

The weights to be applied to the panel data were calculated as the inverse of the probability of being selected for *and* agreeing to take part in the survey. This probability can be broken down as follows:

P(in survey and responding) =

P(being in 1990 survey) · P(selected for panel) · P(responding)

and the panel weight is then estimated as:

$$\text{Panel weight} = \frac{1}{P(\text{being in 1990 survey})} \cdot \frac{1}{P(\text{selected for panel})} \cdot \frac{1}{P(\text{responding})}$$

$$= (1990 \text{ weight}) \cdot \frac{2{,}061}{1{,}301} \cdot \frac{1}{P(\text{responding})}$$

To estimate the probability of responding to the panel survey, a logistic regression model was fitted to the data, using a range of independent variables selected from the 1990 establishment questionnaire. Just two of these variables were found to be significant predictors of response: legal status (trading public corporation/nationalized industry) and the presence of union-related limits on the organization of work. Both were associated with a greater likelihood of response to the panel survey. The model-predicted probability of responding was used directly in the calculation of the panel weight.

The single panel weight is used in the analysis of data from both the 1990 and the 1998 observations of the survey. It gives estimates that are intended to be representative of all 'continuing' establishments with twenty-five or more employees in both survey years.

Sampling errors

As with a cross-section survey, the various features of the design of a panel survey, such as sample stratification and weighting, must be taken into account when calculating estimates of standard errors. However, the two observations of a panel survey are based on correlated (paired) rather than independent samples (i.e. the data come from the same set of sampled establishments). The calculation of the standard error for the difference between two given percentages from the two surveys must take this factor into account also. This means that in order to calculate the standard error of the difference between two (paired) percentages, apart from the percentages themselves, the sample size and the design factor, one needs to know the percentage of cases that did not change over time. In other words, one needs to know the percentage of cases that had the same characteristic in both years.

The design-based standard errors associated with a number of differences between point estimates from the 1990 and 1998 panel observation were calculated and compared with the standard errors that would have derived from a survey based on a simple random sample. These calculations were conducted over a range of classification and headline variables. In each case, a design factor was calculated. On the basis of these calculations, the average design factor for differences between estimates from the 1990 panel observation and the 1998 panel observation was estimated to be 1.5.

Using this average design factor, it is possible to present a look-up table (Table A6), which gives the standard error of the difference between various percentages from the 1990 and 1998 panel observations. For simplicity, a sample size of 846 is assumed throughout. As stated above, apart from the 1990 and 1998 point estimates, we also need to know the percentage of cases (rounded to the nearest multiple of 5) that did not change over time, and subtract this percentage from the 1990 and 1998 percentage respectively. For example, suppose that, in 1990, 50 per cent of establishments had a certain characteristic, and that in 1998 this percentage had declined to 30 per cent. Suppose also that 15 per cent of establishments had this characteristic in both years. Then the standard error associated with the difference of 20 per cent (i.e. 50 minus 30) can be found in Table A6 as the cell corresponding to row (or column) '35%' (i.e. 50 minus 15), and column (or row) '15%' (i.e. 30 minus 15). This gives a standard error of 3.50. A 95 per cent confidence interval associated with the difference between 50 per cent in 1990 and 30 per cent in 1998, when 15 per cent stayed the same over time would be 20 per cent plus or minus 7 per cent, in other words between 13 and 27 per cent.

The 1990 dataset of 'leavers'

The 1990 dataset of 'leavers' comprises those establishments from the 1990 cross-section sample that either closed down between 1990 and 1998 or fell out of the scope of the survey. Workplaces that fell out of scope were, essentially, those in which the size of the workforce was below the twenty-five employee

Table A6 Approximate standard errors for various percentages for the difference between estimates from the 1990 panel observation and the 1998 panel observation

Survey % minus % no change (rounded to the nearest multiple of 5)

	Survey 2										
	0	5	10	15	20	25	30	35	40	45	50
0	0.00	1.12	1.55	1.84	2.06	2.23	2.36	2.46	2.53	2.57	2.58
5		1.63	1.98	2.25	2.46	2.63	2.77	2.87	2.95	3.01	3.04
10			2.31	2.57	2.78	2.95	3.10	3.21	3.30	3.37	3.42
15				2.83	3.04	3.22	3.37	3.50	3.60	3.69	3.75
20					3.26	3.45	3.61	3.75	3.86	3.96	4.03
25						3.65	3.82	3.96	4.09	4.19	4.28
30							4.00	4.15	4.29	4.40	4.50
35								4.32	4.46	4.59	4.69
40									4.62	4.75	4.87
45										4.90	5.02
50											5.16

(Row label for the vertical axis: *Survey 1*)

Note: For percentages greater than 50, simply subtract the percentage from 100. For example, if the percentages from 1990 and 1998 were 85 per cent and 60 per cent respectively, one would use the row labelled 15 per cent (100 – 85 = 15) and the column labelled 40 per cent (100 – 60 = 40).

threshold at the time of fieldwork for the 1998 panel survey.[6] Each workplace in the sample of leavers formed part of the 1990 cross-section survey, and so the leavers dataset contains full information on the nature of each workplace in 1990, together with an indicator of why it left the population (whether through closure or through falling outside the scope of the survey).

Sample selection

The survival status of each of the 1,301 workplaces included in the sample for the 1990–98 panel survey was obtained through the initial telephone inquiry mentioned earlier. The same telephone inquiry was also conducted on the 132 workplaces that formed part of the panel reserve sample, and on the remaining 628 workplaces that were not selected from the 1990 cross-section data file. Contact with these 760 workplaces was limited to establishing specific details relating to their survival status.

The details collected in the telephone inquiry enabled each of the 2,061 workplaces that took part in the 1990 cross-section survey to be classified according to whether it continued in existence with twenty-five employees or more (1,679 workplaces), was still in operation with less than twenty-five employees (123 workplaces) or had closed down (259 workplaces). The dataset of leavers therefore contained 382 workplaces.

Table A7 Approximate standard errors for the sample of 'leavers' and the sample of 'joiners'

Survey %	Leavers dataset n = 382	Joiners dataset n = 390
10	1.92	2.28
20	2.56	3.04
30	2.93	3.48
40	3.13	3.72
50	3.20	3.80
60	3.13	3.72
70	2.93	3.48
80	2.56	3.04
90	1.92	2.28

Sampling errors

Since the leavers dataset has been compiled from all relevant productive cases in the 1990 cross-section survey, the dataset can be treated as a subset of the 1990 cross-section data. Therefore, estimates from the leavers dataset are assumed to have an average design factor equal to that of the 1990 cross-section sample, i.e. 1.25. In the second column of Table A7, this average design factor is used to compile a 'rule of thumb' guide for assessing the approximate standard errors associated with various estimates from the sample of leavers.

The 1998 dataset of 'joiners'

The 1998 dataset of 'joiners' comprises those establishments in the 1998 cross-section sample that had joined the population since 1990. There were two groups. The first consisted of new workplaces that had been in operation for less than eight years at the time of the 1998 survey. The second consisted of workplaces that were judged to have grown into the scope of the survey between 1990 and 1998. For reasons of comparison with the other data used in this volume, the sample of joiners was restricted to those cases with twenty-five or more employees at the time of the 1998 cross-section interview.

Sample selection

New workplaces were identified by means of a set of questions giving the age of the workplace. As stated in Chapter 1, these questions gave the total number of years that the establishment had been at its current address and the number of years at a previous address if it had moved within the last ten years. The figures were summed to give an approximation of the total age of the workplace. This measure would underestimate the total age of those workplaces that had moved more than twice during their lifetime. However, this would only compromise the formation of our joiners sample if a workplace had been in existence for more than eight years but had moved more than twice since 1990. Such cases, which must be extremely rare, would be erroneously included in the sample of new workplaces.

In the absence of more suitable data, workplaces that were judged to have grown into the scope of the survey were identified using a retrospective question that gave the number of workers employed five years before (hence at some point between October 1992 and July 1993, depending upon the date of the interview). Since the economy was in recession for much of the period between 1990 and 1993, this solution was felt to be preferable to any estimate of employment size in 1990 that could be produced by linear interpolation through the 1998 and 1993 data points. Linear interpolation would necessarily imply growth in employment within each workplace between 1990 and 1993, whereas the solution that was adopted assumed stability. We believe this approximation does not invalidate the estimates derived from the sample of joiners.

The procedures outlined above yielded 286 new workplaces and 104 work-places that were judged to have grown into the scope of the survey. The sample of joiners therefore comprised a total of 390 workplaces. Some 1,141 workplaces in the 1998 cross-section sample were neither new nor had they grown into scope, and therefore amounted to continuing workplaces. A further 398 workplaces could not be classified.

Sampling errors

Since the joiners dataset was compiled from all relevant cases in the 1998 cross-section survey, the dataset can be treated as a subset of the 1998 cross-section data. Estimates from the joiners dataset are therefore assumed to have an average design factor equal to that of the 1998 cross-section sample, i.e. 1.5. In the third column of Table A7, this average design factor is used to compile a 'rule of thumb' guide for assessing the approximate standard errors associated with various estimates from the sample of joiners.

Accessing the data used in this volume

It is an enduring principle of the WIRS series that the data collected in each of the surveys should be made publicly available to bona fide researchers wishing to conduct their own analyses. To this end, the data from each of the surveys in the WIRS series, together with the derived datasets used in the compilation of this volume, can be obtained at cost from the Data Archive at the University of Essex.

Notes

1 Introduction

1 A bibliography (Millward *et al.*, 1999b) provides details of all known, published research work based on data from the WIRS series.

2 Naturally, such a complex task also brings its own problems and, as in earlier years, the revision of the questionnaire structure and content has generated a break in the continuity of questioning for some key items. These are noted, alongside minor inconsistencies, where relevant.

3 In 1999, Social and Community Planning Research was renamed as the National Centre for Social Research.

4 Occasionally, interviews are not conducted with a respondent at the sampled workplace but with a manager located at a higher level in the organization. This situation may arise because it is not possible to identify a respondent at the workplace who is sufficiently knowledgeable about its system of employment relations to answer the questions contained in the interview, or because the organization is unwilling to place the burden of responding on workplace-level management. The incidence of such cases was lowest (8 per cent) in 1980 and highest (18 per cent) in 1990.

5 The purpose of this was to reduce the burden on personnel managers. In workplaces where the respondent was identified as a personnel specialist and a financial manager could also be identified, certain questions which, elsewhere, were asked of the personnel manager were instead directed to the financial manager. This occurred in 454 workplaces in total.

6 Further details on the conduct of the panel survey are provided in the Technical Appendix to this volume and in the Technical Report of the 1998 WERS (Airey *et al.*, 1999).

7 Results from the 1984–90 panel survey are presented in two dedicated volumes (Millward, 1994b, 1996) and in two volumes covering the whole of the 1990 survey package (Millward *et al.*, 1992; Millward, 1994a). A small number of findings from the 1980–84 panel survey may be found in the second WIRS sourcebook (Millward and Stevens, 1986).

8 Workplaces might also fall out of scope by changing their activity to one not covered by the series (e.g. agriculture) or by relocating to a site outside of Great Britain. However, such cases can be considered to be extremely rare.

9 These questions gave the total number of years that the establishment had been at its current address and the number of years at a previous address if it had moved

within the last ten years. The figures were summed to give an approximation of the total age of the workplace. This measure would underestimate the total age of those workplaces that had moved more than twice during their lifetime. However, this would only compromise the formation of our sample if a workplace had been in existence for more than eight years but had moved more than twice since 1990. Such cases, which must be extremely rare, would be erroneously included in our sample of new workplaces.

10 Since the economy was in recession for much of the period between 1990 and 1993, this solution was felt to be more preferable than any estimate of employment size in 1990 that would be produced by linear interpolation through the 1998 and 1993 data points. Linear interpolation would necessarily imply growth in employment within each workplace between 1990 and 1993, whereas the solution that was adopted assumed stability.

11 Figures are for the United Kingdom, in the absence of published data for Great Britain in 1998. Sources: *Employment Gazette* 90(1) (January 1982): Table 1.1; *Labour Market Trends* 106(8) (August 1998): Table B1.

12 See endnote 11.

13 Figures are for the United Kingdom, in the absence of published data for Great Britain. Sources: Casey (1997); *Labour Market Trends* 106 (8) (August 1998): Table B1.

14 See endnote 13.

2 The dynamic context of workplace employment relations

1 See, for example, Bach and Sisson (2000); Edwards *et al.* (1998); Nolan and Walsh (1995).

2 In his analysis of the decline in aggregate union density in Britain between 1983 and 1989 Green, for example, attributed 17 per cent of the total fall to changes in the composition of industry over that period (Green, 1992).

3 Private manufacturing comprises all private sector establishments in which the main activity lies within Division 2 (Extraction and manufacture of metals, minerals and chemicals), 3 (Manufacture of metal goods and engineering) or 4 (Other manufacturing) of the 1980 *Standard Industrial Classification*.

4 Private sector services comprise all private sector establishments in which the main activity lies within Division 1 (Energy and water supply), 5 (Construction), 6 (Distribution; hotels and catering; and repairs), 7 (Transport and communication), 8 (Banking; finance; insurance; business services; and leasing) or 9 (Other services) of the 1980 *Standard Industrial Classification*. The public sector is defined simply with respect to ownership.

5 A comprehensive list of privatizations between 1982 and 1997 is provided by Kessler and Bayliss (1998: 148).

6 This difference is on the borderline of statistical significance at the 95 per cent level.

7 The number of unweighted cases in these specific sectors, being less than 60 in each case, is too low for precise percentages to be given here.

8 See, for example, Winchester and Bach (1995); Bailey (1996).

9 Unfortunately, it is not possible to identify whether any change in approach came as a result of only one of the phenomena, two or all three in workplaces that experienced a combination of the three over the period in question.

10 The incidence of freelancers and homeworkers is covered later in this chapter.

11 It should be noted that, by definition, continuing establishments employed at least twenty-five employees in both 1990 and 1998.

12 Responses were not detailed enough to ascertain reliably whether the increasing use of part-time work referred to the substitution of full-time workers with employees working part-time hours or the provision of additional employment on part-time (as opposed to full-time) contracts.

13 Marginson and colleagues (Marginson *et al.*, 1988: 214–21) explore some of the reasons for differing degrees of establishment autonomy within organizations citing, among other things, the homogeneity of products or services across establishments and the degree of devolution in profit accountability.

14 In 1990, a clause in the question wording may have resulted in some head offices being coded as branch offices in cases where the head office site engaged in the production of goods or delivery of services alongside its administrative function.

15 There are two possibilities: either the operations of multi-site organizations now tend to be concentrated on fewer sites, or such organizations now have fewer sites that break the twenty-five employee threshold for inclusion in the survey. We are unable to adjudicate between the two.

16 In 1980 and 1998, our survey questions asked respondents to specify the total number of persons employed within the UK by the organization which owned the establishment. In 1984 and 1990, the question wording, instead, referred to the ultimate controlling company in the UK which, in some cases (around one fifth of establishments belonging to larger organizations in 1990), represents a wider entity than the organization which directly owns the establishment. The comparability of the data is therefore questionable. In addition, a routing error in the 1990 questionnaire led to a substantial number of respondents being routed around this question.

17 The WIRS series also covers the issue of outward investment through questions in the 1990 and 1998 surveys that identify British establishments belonging to UK multinationals. However, the 1998 question concerns the activities of the organization that owns the establishment. This organization may itself belong to a larger entity, and it is this ultimate controlling company that is the subject of the question in the 1990 survey. This incomparability between the most recent surveys, together with the absence of a directly comparable observation from one of the earlier surveys, means that the issue is not discussed here.

18 In 1990, the ultimate controlling company differed from the organization that directly owned the establishment in the case of around one quarter of all private sector workplaces that were part of larger organizations.

19 The estimate of the degree of foreign ownership among joiners can be considered an underestimate in comparison with the estimates for continuing workplaces and leavers. This is because the 1998 survey question, used to derive the estimate for joiners, concerns the organization to which the establishment belongs, whereas the 1990 survey question, used to derive the estimate for continuing workplaces and leavers, concerns the ultimate controlling company. In some cases (around one fifth in 1990) the ultimate controlling company represents a wider entity than the organization which directly owns the establishment. This does not impair the general point made within the text.

20 It should be noted that the banding of the oldest category was revised in 1990 in

order to group together all establishments aged twenty-one years or more, rather than all those aged twenty-five years or more as in 1980 and 1984, thereby creating further problems for comparisons between the 1980s and 1990s.

21 The precise links between union recognition and age, and their effect on overall rates of recognition in the economy as a whole, are explored in Chapter 4.

22 Respondents were identified by a direct question, which should not be confused with the detailed information on the establishment's activity used to derive the SIC code for each workplace. The full list of applications comprised: machine control of individual machines; process control of individual items of process plant; centralized machine control of groups of machines; integrated process control of several stages of processes; automated handling of products, materials or components; automated storage and testing or quality control.

23 See, for example, annual issues of *Labour Market and Skill Trends*, published by the Department for Education and Employment.

24 The relative influence of behavioural and compositional changes in bringing about the decline of male-dominated workplaces were much more difficult to discern.

25 Eligible workplaces accounted for 89 per cent of the population in 1984, 90 per cent in 1990 and 93 per cent in 1998. Most of the remainder were excluded as a result of having no employees in middle or senior management positions, rather than as a result of having single-sex workforces. Some eligible cases were also excluded because of missing data.

26 Efforts were made in the second and third surveys to ensure that respondents did not include individuals participating in the Youth Training Scheme or Community Programme scheme, or sandwich students. In the 1984 surveys, the question wording explicitly excluded sandwich students, with the other exclusions being mentioned in a note to interviewers. The 1990 survey included all three exclusions in an interviewer note.

27 The 1998 question asked if there were any employees who worked for the establishment at or from their own homes, but who were not employees. Disaggregating the results by detailed industry shows steep rises in the incidence of such workers between 1990 and 1998 in extraction, heavy manufacturing and construction, together with a substantial fall in light manufacturing. It is possible that the 1998 question has been interpreted by some respondents to cover self-employed contractors.

3 The management of employee relations

1 Some commentators have expressed concern at the reliance placed on survey data collected from workplace-level managers in understanding the management of employee relations in Britain (Purcell, 1983). Although there is clearly a case for supplementing these data with other approaches, data generated through rigorous survey techniques have a unique role to play in depicting the contours of change over time (see Chapter 1).

2 In total, 7,099 of the 8,049 interviews conducted over the four main surveys were conducted entirely on site, as were 700 of the 846 panel interviews in 1990 and 783 of the panel interviews in 1998.

3 Since 1980, specialists have become more prevalent in all sectors of the economy, with the exception of 1980 SIC Division 3 (Manufacture of metal goods and engineering).

4 Specialists have managed employee relations in nine tenths of establishments with 1,000 or more employees since 1980.

5 'Joiners' comprise new workplaces that did not exist in 1990, and those workplaces employing fewer than twenty-five people in 1990 who had reached this threshold by 1998. 'Leavers' were all interviewed in 1990 that had either ceased to operate or employed fewer than twenty-five people by 1998. See Chapter 1.

6 The base is continuing workplaces where the interview was conducted on site in both years.

7 The 1998 survey contains 161 interviews with HRM Managers/Officers, 123 of which were conducted on site. The 1990 sample contained twenty-one cases, including five interviewed on site.

8 In 1980 the question was only asked of those who said they spent a major part of their time on personnel and industrial relations matters, and in 1998 it was only asked of those who said that employee relations was their 'major job responsibility', or equal with other responsibilities. There was no filtering in the 1984 and 1990 surveys. To obtain a consistent time series we have confined our analyses on formal qualifications to those spending at least 25 per cent of their time on employee relations issues. This information was not available for 1980, so 1980 figures should be treated with caution. Unfortunately, 19 per cent of those spending at least 25 per cent of their time on employee relations in 1998 did not consider employee relations to be their main or joint equal responsibility, so they were not asked the qualifications question. Since the proportion with qualifications rises with the time spent on employee relations, the omission of this group from the 1998 figures may upwardly bias the proportion of employee relations managers with qualifications. We therefore reran our analyses on respondents who spent at least 50 per cent of their time on employee relations issues, thus minimizing the 1998 missing data problem (since only 6 per cent of these respondents did not view employee relations as the main or joint equal responsibility). These figures also show a substantial rise in the proportion of qualified managers, from 43 per cent in 1990 to 54 per cent in 1998. This indicates that any upward bias in the 1998 figures is not seriously distorting the trend.

9 In 1980 the question was only asked of those who said they spent a major part of their time on personnel and industrial relations matters, and in 1998 it was only asked of those who said that employee relations was their 'major job responsibility', or equal with other responsibilities. In 1984 it was asked if the respondent identified one of a list of employee relations functions as a job component. In 1990 there was no filtering. To obtain a consistent time series we confined our analyses to those spending at least 25 per cent of their time on employee relations issues. Trends were similar when the analyses were confined to those spending at least 50 per cent of their time on employee relations issues. The 1980 variable is a dummy variable identifying whether or not the respondent had two or more years' experience, so comments are confined to the period 1984–98.

10 In 1984 and 1990 the question refers to 'personnel or industrial relations matters', whereas in 1998 the question refers to 'employee relations matters'.

11 Some academics would consider increasing involvement of line managers in employee relations matters as consistent with a growth in human resource management practices (Storey, 1992). Although there is no evidence here of such a trend among line managers with overall responsibility for employee relations in

the workplace, the WIRS series contains no information on the time other line managers spend on employee relations.

12 Whether the rise of female managers has any implications for the way employee relations is conducted depends, in part, on whether women bring a distinct style of management to organizations, an issue which lies outside the scope of this chapter (see Wajcman, 1996, for a discussion).

13 It is possible that this development is linked to an increasing proportion of female employee relations managers working part-time. However, the series did not collect data on respondents' hours of work, so this is conjecture.

14 The 1980 data are not strictly comparable because respondents were asked which responsibilities formed part of their job, omitting 'or the job of someone responsible to you'. The discussion therefore focuses on the period 1984–98.

15 Equal opportunities, health and safety and performance appraisal were only listed in 1998. Job evaluation/grading was asked for every year except 1998. Staffing or manpower planning was not included in 1980. In 1998 the list included 'handling of grievances', rather than the broader 'grievances, discipline, disputes' which had appeared in previous years.

16 There are no time-series data for health and safety so the figures are not shown in the table. In 1998, it formed part of the job for 68 per cent of specialists and 87 per cent of non-specialists.

17 In 1984, specialists were performing, on average, 5.06 of the six tasks, compared with 4.54 by non-specialists – a difference that is statistically significant at the 1 per cent level. By 1998, specialists were performing 4.96 tasks, compared with the 4.89 performed by non-specialists.

18 Equal opportunities policies covering gender were reported in 94 per cent of public sector workplaces and 67 per cent of private sector workplaces with recognized unions, compared with 45 per cent of private sector non-union workplaces.

19 To retain consistency with the analysis of information collection, we confine ourselves to the period 1990–98 and to workplaces where the survey interview was conducted on site. The data for all respondents and for 1984 are reported on in Chapter 10 of our companion volume (Millward *et al.*, 1999a: 231).

20 Each WIRS has asked about relationships between workplace employee relations managers in multi-site organizations and employee relations managers higher up in the organization. However, the 1980 question refers to 'reporting' to a manager at a higher level, while the 1984 and 1990 questions refer to 'contact' with a higher manager. The 1998 question simply asks if such a person exists. Consequently, it is not possible to establish whether these relationships have changed over time. The lack of comparable data also hamper analysis of the staff support for the employee relations manager. The first three surveys ask an identical question: 'Do you have any staff – apart from clerical and secretarial staff – to assist you in these responsibilities?' The 1998 question asks whether they have 'any staff to assist you', with a prompt to *include* clerical and secretarial staff.

21 The questions and code frames were different each year. In 1990 respondents were asked: 'Thinking now of industrial or employee relations, have any matters, during the last 12 months, caused management here to obtain advice from a person or body outside this organization?' If they had, they were asked to identify which sources from a showcard, and to specify other sources which did not appear on the showcard. Respondents in 1980 were asked an identical question, but were asked to consider advice from outside the *establishment*, rather than the organization. For

the purpose of this analysis we removed sources of advice from within the organization. In 1998 respondents were asked: 'Looking at this card, have you sought advice from any of these bodies on any employee relations issues during the last 12 months?' It is unlikely that the alternative wording affects the comparability of the data. Code frames varied each year, so these have been recoded to create a consistent time series.

22 Note that the table records whether or not the workplace used each advice source, but not the number of times.

23 According to ACAS, 'In 1998 the caseload of actual or potential claims to Employment Tribunals rose by 6 per cent compared with the previous year and, at 113,636, has more than doubled since 1990' (ACAS press release, 5 May 1999).

24 All figures relating to board-level employee relations representation are based on all respondents, as opposed to only those respondents interviewed at the sampled establishment. To retain consistency across years, the time series is confined to workplaces in multi-site organizations in the private sector with a UK head office. Some of the decline may be accounted for by the fact that the 1998 survey question did not include representation on the 'top governing body', but any discrepancy is minimized by confining the time series to workplaces in the private sector.

25 The tendency for organizations to decentralize operating decisions does not necessarily undermine efforts at maintaining a strategic approach to employment matters. However, in practice, the decentralization of operating decisions does result in a 'reduction in the strategic importance of personnel and industrial relations at the corporate level' (Purcell and Ahlstrand, 1989: 402).

26 To retain consistency with the time-series data, the analysis of continuing workplaces and those leaving and joining the series was confined to private sector workplaces in multi-site organizations with a UK head office. Some of the change recorded in the panel may be accounted for by a difference in question wording. In 1998, panel respondents were asked: 'Is there someone on your Board of Directors or top governing body of the organization (in the UK) whose main job is dealing with personnel, human resources or industrial relations?' The word 'main' was not present in the 1990 question.

27 Panel data indicate that employee relations representation on the top governing body is much lower in independent workplaces than in workplaces belonging to a wider organization, and that there has been little aggregate change among continuing workplaces. In 1990 and 1998 panel respondents in independent workplaces were asked: 'Does the most senior management body here include anyone who has specific responsibility for personnel, human resources or industrial relations?' Among those in the trading sector, 48 per cent had such representation in 1998, compared with 47 per cent in 1990. Unfortunately, we do not have comparable data for the 1998 cross-section.

28 In 1990 the question was filtered so that it was only asked of workplaces in the trading sector and excluded establishments which were the sole UK establishment of foreign parent organizations. The 1998 figures are confined to this subgroup to retain consistency. In addition, analyses are confined to workplaces where the survey interview was conducted on site, and excluded head offices. Unfortunately, there are no comparable data for the time series.

29 ($F = 8.122$, sig. 0.005). These figures are based on eighty-three weighted cases with ownership change and 130 without ownership change, all of which were trading sector branch sites with interviews conducted on site in 1990 and 1998.

4 Have employees lost their voice?

1 Throughout our discussion staff associations are included under the heading of trade unions unless otherwise noted.

2 Recognition is used to mean the situation where management recognize trade unions as the agent for negotiating pay and conditions of employment on behalf of an agreed category of workers.

3 In the 1980 and 1984 results, other answers, 'don't know' and 'not answered' were treated as having no members. In both 1990 and 1998 every productive case has a 'yes' or 'no' answer. See Millward *et al.* (1992: 102–3, note 1).

4 Here, as in our analysis in *Britain at Work* and in previous WIRS sourcebooks, aggregate membership density is the number of union members summed across the sample of workplaces, divided by the number of employees in the same workplaces. It is not a mean of the union density for each workplace. All information is obtained from management respondents. Figures for 1980 refer to full-time employees only; union membership numbers were not collected for part-time employees in the 1980 survey. Figures may vary slightly from those in earlier sourcebooks because of different treatment of some missing values and minor computational differences between the present and earlier analyses.

5 On a purely statistical judgement at the 90 per cent confidence level the extraction and metal manufacturing industry cannot confidently be stated as having declined; the unweighted base for this industry was only 50 in 1998.

6 Our surveys did not aim to collect separate union membership data for males and females, full-time and part-time employees. The separate effects of these characteristics on the likelihood of joining a trade union are best understood from analysing data on individuals.

7 For similar analysis based on individual employee data see Cully and Woodland (1998: 353–64).

8 The figure of 27 per cent in 1998 for continuing workplaces includes continuing workplaces that had been transferred from public to private ownership.

9 This is partly a statistical artefact, because our change variable is defined in terms of percentage point changes and membership is generally very low where there is no recognition.

10 Too few workplaces with recognized unions in both 1990 and 1998 recorded more favourable attitudes to unions in 1998 to be included in Table 4.3.

11 The question was also asked where there was a change to or from non-membership. Up to five responses were coded for each respondent.

12 Privatization served to attenuate the drop in union density in the private sector. Aggregate union density among privatized workplaces in the panel only dropped from 91 to 83 per cent between 1990 and 1998.

13 Data from both the 1990 and 1998 surveys have been amended in the course of our analysis for some public sector workplaces engaged in primary or secondary education to remove measurement error arising from the mis-reporting of union recognition. In 1990, 2 per cent of such workplaces reported recognized unions although the only unions present came under the remit of the Pay Review Body for Schoolteachers in England and Wales; these workplaces were therefore not party to collective bargaining over pay. Recoding such workplaces to having no recognized unions lowered the proportion of all public sector primary and secondary schools that had any recognized unions in 1990 from 70 per cent to 67 per cent.

The scale of the adjustment was not sufficient to alter the proportion of recognized workplaces in the public sector as a whole.

In 1998, cases of this type were much more common and amounted to 20 per cent of all workplaces in this sector. Recoding these workplaces to having no recognized unions lowered the proportion with any recognized unions from 93 per cent to 73 per cent. Accordingly, the proportion of recognized workplaces in the public sector was reduced from 94 per cent to 87 per cent, and from 44 per cent to 42 per cent in the sample as a whole.

14 For further explanation of the method the reader is referred to Hosmer and Lemeshow (1989).

15 A relatively high proportion of respondents did not answer the question on the reasons for the change in recognition or gave vague or other unusable answers. In the case of derecognition, these amounted to a third of cases with derecognition, leaving valid results for 33 (unweighted) cases. In the case of new recognition, similar exclusions and the lower initial number who were asked, left us with only 10 unweighted cases.

16 The only other usable reason for derecognition, mentioned by about one tenth of respondents giving usable answers, was that the jobs covered by the former recognized union had disappeared.

17 The sum of the two effects slightly overstates the actual drop in recognition, owing to a small interaction term.

18 The further restriction adopted by Millward (1994a) for earlier surveys, concerning the issues discussed by committees, cannot be implemented for the 1998 survey because the relevant question was asked in a different way.

19 Where managers reported more than one committee at an establishment the first three surveys asked about the frequency of meetings of the 'most important' committee. In 1998 this follow-up question was asked in relation to the committee with the widest range of issues or, if this could not be identified, the most important one. In all surveys the majority of establishments reported a single committee, although the size of this majority has progressively declined. We consider the change in format for the minority of cases in 1998 to have had no impact on the reported results for functioning committees.

20 The difference between 21 per cent and 24 per cent is not statistically significant, given the numbers of observations on which these estimates are based.

21 The Health and Safety (Consultation with Employees) Regulations 1996.

22 This estimate of 65 per cent for 1998 was calculated using the population proportions stated in Figure 1.2 and the estimates of the incidence of briefing groups cited in the text. It comprises the sum of (a) the proportion of all establishments in 1998 that were continuing (64 per cent) multiplied by the incidence of briefing groups among such establishments (60 per cent), and (b) the proportion of all establishments in 1998 that were joiners (36 per cent) multiplied by the incidence of briefing groups among these establishments (74 per cent).

23 It was noted, earlier in the text, that workplace meetings between senior management and the workforce may offer limited opportunity for the expression of employee voice, particularly when large numbers of employees are present. This might weigh against the inclusion of such meetings in our summary variables. However, we found that, in only a small proportion of workplaces with some form of voice (5 to 10 per cent in each year) did such meetings constitute the sole arrangement. Moreover, the vast majority of these workplaces were small in size:

around nine in ten employed less than 100 employees. Workforce meetings may well offer real opportunities for two-way communication in such workplaces.

24 In view of the concerns that were noted above over the comparability of the 1998 cross-section questions on direct communication methods, we used our panel data to investigate the extent of any possible measurement error on this composite variable. It was found to be negligible.

25 The unweighted base for these figures is 80.

26 As with the previous categorization of voice, concerns about the comparability of the 1998 cross-section questions on direct communication methods prompted us to investigate the extent of any possible measurement error on this composite variable. Again, it was found to be negligible.

27 For an explanation of the ordered probit form of multiple regression, the reader is referred to Greene (1990: 703–6).

28 If a particular type of voice was found most commonly in larger organizations, it might naturally be associated with lower employee ratings than other types of voice because of the greater difficulty of communicating with staff in larger workplaces, rather than because of any difference in the effectiveness of different voice mechanisms.

29 In fact, for each of the five dependent variables, the associations identified with the representative/direct categorization of voice were similar to those identified with our union/non-union categorization. The detailed results have therefore been omitted from the table to avoid repetition; the text identifies any differences that did emerge in the course of our analyses.

30 The association was significant at the 90 per cent level in both cases.

5 Union recognition: a 'hollow shell'?

1 We do not have data for 1980 because we did not collect union membership information for part-time workers in that year.

2 Small sample sizes do not permit us to say anything definitive about trends in the extraction and construction industries.

3 Between 1980 and 1990 the questions were asked separately of manual and non-manual workers, and the coding was fairly elaborate (Millward *et al.*, 1992: 96–8). In 1998 the question was split into two simpler questions and referred to 'employees' rather than 'workers' as in previous years. To produce a consistent series we have combined the separate data for manual and non-manual workers collected in earlier years.

4 Actions in support of the post-entry closed shop, whereby employers required union membership of employees taking up their posts, were made unlawful in the Employment Act of 1988 when non-members were protected from dismissal and other sanctions. Since January 1991, the 1990 Employment Act has made it unlawful for employers to refuse employment on the grounds of union membership, effectively outlawing the pre-entry closed shop.

5 Under legislation contained in the 1993 Trade Union Reform and Employment Rights Act. This provision was subsequently repealed in 1998.

6 The figure was similar for unionized leavers, 87 per cent of whom had check-off in 1990.

7 Of the panel workplaces recognizing unions in 1990 and 1998, 6 per cent either did not know or did not answer the question relating to the presence of union

representatives in 1990. This missing data problem affected 14 per cent of these unionized workplaces in 1998. The figures presented here exclude these missing data cases. If it is assumed that these missing cases do not contain on-site union representatives the incidence rate for 1990 is 71 per cent, and the rate for 1998 is 67 per cent. However, an investigation of the missing data problem suggests that in around half these cases the unionized workplace may well have had an on-site union representative. This is possible where the workplace was large, there were multiple recognized unions, or the respondent was not based at the sampled site. It is therefore reasonable to assume that the 'true' figure lies somewhere halfway between the estimates with and without missing data.

8 Precise figures are not available for 1980 and 1984 since union representatives covering manual and non-manual workers may have been double counted in the separate sections on manual and non-manual union representatives. Since we can not establish the amount of 'double counting' there might be in summing these two types of representative we do not present results for those years. However, it is worth noting that Millward *et al.* (1992: 116) say 'there is little doubt that there was decline across the 1984 to 1990 period and that it was substantial'.

Due to the way the data were collected in 1990 we know that in 176 unweighted cases workplaces had at least one union representative on site, but the numbers are not given. In most of these cases we have simply imputed a value of '1' (although, in some cases, we have been able to obtain a more accurate figure). Checks on the nature of workplaces with missing data reveal that they were larger than other unionized workplaces and had more recognized unions. So our imputation is likely to underestimate the number of on-site union representatives in 1990. The omission of cases with missing data makes little difference to the 1990 figures.

9 This difference is on the margins of statistical significance. This is an estimate based on all cases with no missing data. If we include those unionized workplaces where we know there were union representatives, but not how many, imputing the value '1' in most cases, we arrive at an estimate of 45 members per on-site union representative in 1990. This compares to 29 members per on-site union representative in 1998. The difference between these figures and those presented in the main text is due to the large workforces among workplaces with missing data for the number of union representatives.

The difference between our 1990 figures and those presented by Millward *et al.* (1992: 116) arise because the earlier work presents an aggregate member to union representative ratio, whereas we present an establishment-level measure.

10 The figure has not fallen, despite the fact that the 1998 question was confined to agreements covering non-managerial employees.

11 They also became more prevalent in the non-unionized sector, with one third (33 per cent) using them in 1998, compared to one fifth (20 per cent) in 1990.

12 In 1984 and 1990, we asked respondents: 'Are any of the employee representatives on the committee dealing with health and safety chosen by trade unions or staff associations?' In 1998, we asked 'How are employee representatives appointed to the committee?' We did not give respondents a showcard. Rather, they had to say spontaneously that unions or staff associations chose them.

13 If a minority of the workers at a workplace is covered by collective bargaining, the union may still have a powerful bargaining position if the workers it represents are vital to the operation of the workplace.

14 The means reported in this section are the averages of the percentage covered in each

workplace. In Chapter 6 we present aggregate percentages which are obtained by calculating the total number covered and dividing by the total number of employees. The workplace-level means give equal weight to workplaces regardless of the number of employees they employ, whereas the aggregate mean is largely determined by coverage in larger workplaces which contain the majority of workers.

15 In 1984 and 1990 the question asked directly what proportion of employees were covered by negotiations between management and recognized unions or groups of unions. In 1998, there were up to nine questions asking how pay was determined for each major occupational group at the workplace. Responses that referred to collective bargaining have been summed in relation to the number of employees in the relevant occupational group to provide the number covered at each workplace. The absence of cases with no workers covered in earlier years is not the result of format differences in questioning. In 1984 and 1990 respondents were asked how pay was negotiated for workers at their workplace. If the respondent said pay was not negotiated, but was decided by the employer or management, then coverage was set to zero in these cases. The fact that there are so few in earlier years is an indication of their rarity. Similar results for the panel presented below are further evidence that the finding is robust.

16 Workplaces recognizing unions in 1990 and 1998 constituted 92 per cent of all panel establishments recognizing unions in 1998, and 90 per cent of those recognizing unions in 1990.

17 Again, it is worth stressing that this result is not an artefact of the way the data were collected. In 1998 we simply asked for the name of bargaining units. It was at this point that some respondents informed us spontaneously that there was no bargaining unit currently operating.

18 Among unionized workplaces where coverage had been 100 per cent in 1990, the figure was 65 per cent.

19 In 1998, we asked these questions of the largest or only bargaining unit operating at the workplace or, if the largest bargaining unit in 1990 was still operating, we asked them of this bargaining unit. This makes it possible to analyse what happens at the level of the bargaining unit over time. However, this means that we do not have data on the scope of bargaining for the current largest bargaining unit where the 1990 largest unit still exists but is not the largest unit in 1998.

20 Although the sample sizes are small, there were indications that switching from on-site to external representation was associated with a decline in bargaining scope, while moves from external to on-site representation were associated with increases in bargaining scope.

21 The question was only asked of production managers in 1984 and there was insufficient space for its inclusion in 1998, so we have no time-series information. However, we asked identical questions of our panel respondents in 1990 and 1998.

22 The unweighted number where the number of recognized unions had risen was 58. The unweighted number where the number of bargaining units increased was 43.

23 We did identify whether action was official in our 1990 survey.

24 In 1980 to 1990 we asked: 'Have any of the forms of industrial action on this card taken place affecting the [manual/non-manual] workers at this establishment during the last 12 months?' The showcard included strikes, overtime bans, work to rule, go slows, blacking work, work or sit-ins, and other industrial action. It also included lock-outs by the employer but, since we are analysing action by employees, we have omitted this from our analysis. Whereas the figures presented in the 1990

sourcebook (Millward *et al.*, 1992: 279) are based on managers and worker representatives, our figures are based on management respondents. In 1998 we asked: 'Which, if any, of the forms of industrial action on this card have taken place at this establishment during the last twelve months?'

We also asked whether the establishment had been picketed during the last twelve months. This had also declined in the 1990s, from 10 per cent of unionized workplaces in 1990 to 3 per cent in 1998.

25 Certainly, ballots of members to establish support for industrial action were far more prevalent in 1998 than industrial action itself. Such ballots took place in 15 per cent of unionized workplaces in 1998. Unfortunately, we do not have data on balloting for earlier years.

6 Pay determination and reward systems

1 The analysis of pay levels does not feature within this chapter, due to the absence of up-to-date comparable data from the time series or panel survey. However, analysis of pay levels using the 1998 cross-section alone is being undertaken by the authors as part of a project funded by the Joseph Rowntree Foundation.

2 Much of the complexity of pay-setting arrangements within workplaces in 1998 is described in our companion volume (Cully *et al.*, 1999: 106–9), which also describes these arrangements across different types of employee. Comparable questions were not asked in earlier years and so we cannot describe changes in either of these ways.

3 This was necessary for 7 per cent of (weighted) cases with coverage of 50 per cent or more in 1984, and just 3 per cent in 1990 and 1998.

4 Here, the incidence of multiple arrangements was much higher. Priority coding was necessary in 19 per cent of (weighted) cases with less than 50 per cent coverage in 1984, 14 per cent in 1990 and 20 per cent in 1998.

5 For one independent establishment, this followed its merger with a larger organization. For another workplace, it followed trade union pressure to bargain locally in the hope of negotiating more favourable terms. The number of cases moving between these two types of pay determination was too low to provide more detailed or representative information on their motivations.

6 Only one – a printing firm – had formally derecognized its trade unions; the remainder had simply stopped bargaining over pay. Again, the number of cases moving between these two types of pay determination was too low to provide more detailed or representative information on their motivations.

7 Some workplaces did switch to and from this form of pay setting, but the two groups served to balance each other out.

8 The 1990 figure may be a slight underestimate, since around two fifths of those cases where coverage was low but the level of decision-making was not known were state education establishments. The remainder were dispersed throughout the rest of the public sector.

9 This was, in part, because the relatively low degree of churning of establishments generated comparatively small samples of leavers and joiners, making comparisons less secure. It was also the case that the 1998 cross-section picture for the public sector was less accurately disaggregated by the panel survey and data on joiners than was the picture for the private sector.

10 Changes in question structure and wording between the surveys also justify a cautious approach. The variable for 1984 combines data from separate questions for

manual and non-manual workers on the proportion of employees covered by negotiations between management and recognized unions or groups of unions. In 1990 a single question with identical wording was asked in respect of all employees. For both surveys the relevant data have been recoded to zero if a subsequent question on the most recent pay settlement received the spontaneous response that the pay of the group was decided by management; these amounted to less than 1 per cent of the sample in both surveys.

In 1998 there were up to nine questions asking how pay was determined for each major occupational group at the workplace. Responses that referred to collective bargaining have been summed in relation to the number of employees in the relevant occupational group to provide the number covered at each workplace. There were some cases where this measure was inconsistent with the response to the earlier question on union recognition. The inconsistencies have been resolved, as far as possible, by reference to further questions about the manner in which the most recent pay increase or pay cut was determined; but there remain cases with reported recognition but no coverage. The 1998 coverage estimate should therefore be viewed with some caution and probably regarded as a lower bound.

11 This differs from the figure given in Chapter 10 of *Britain at Work* (Cully *et al.*, 1999: 242) because further investigation of discrepant answers within the 1998 data led us to subsequent revisions, as discussed in the earlier note.

12 Earlier surveys asked about unions representing manual workers and unions representing non-manual workers separately. Because some unions represented both, but cannot always be identified, a valid measure of the total number of unions with members at each workplace cannot be constructed.

13 We investigated whether the reform of pay determination arrangements in the National Health Service had made a significant contribution to these changes by bringing a number of establishments with many unions into the group of workplaces with minority bargaining coverage. This explanation was not supported by the data.

14 The information presented here is similar to that discussed in Chapter 5, where the analysis was restricted to continuing workplaces with recognized unions in both 1990 and 1998. Here we also include workplaces that had no recognized unions in any one of the two years.

15 Multiple reasons were catered for, but rarely given.

16 Respondents who reported that the pay of uncovered workers was primarily determined outside their organization, by a wages council or some other body, were not asked about the factors that influenced pay settlements. This served to exclude a large majority of public sector respondents. Those in the public sector were also more commonly unable to answer the question when asked.

17 This type of analysis can only be performed for cases where there was collective bargaining, since 'settlement groups' were not named in the 1990 interview, making it difficult to refer to them in the 1998 interview.

18 There were many more cases where the 1990 bargaining unit had ceased to exist.

19 Work in this vein is currently being undertaken by the authors as part of a project funded by the Joseph Rowntree Foundation.

20 Earlier surveys had asked the questions differently, or omitted some occupational groups, and so no comparisons can be made on an all-establishment basis. The 1990 questions were only asked where five or more employees were present in the group.

21 Specifically, cross-checking between the results from the 1990 and 1998 cross-sections and the 1990–98 panel suggested that the 1998 cross-section questions captured only a subset of the payment by results and merit pay systems captured by the more closely comparable questions used in the 1990 cross-section and 1990–98 panel survey.

22 Managers were excluded from the relevant questioning in 1998. We follow that restriction so as to improve the reconciliation of results presented later in the section.

23 The panel interview also contained questions about the reasons for abandoning or adopting payment by results, but the results are unreliable because substantial numbers of respondents were unable to give usable answers.

24 In 1998, respondents were asked if 'any employees at the workplace received payments or dividends' from a list of five types of arrangement, the first two being 'profit-related payments or bonuses' and a 'deferred profit-sharing scheme' (see Chapter 4). In previous years, the question was broader, asking whether 'the employing organization operated any of the schemes for employees here'. The effect of the change in wording between 1990 and 1998 is likely, if anything, to have led to an understatement of the increase in profit-related pay over the period.

25 As noted above the incidence of such schemes in previous years was derived from a broader question asking whether 'the employing organization operated any of the schemes for employees here'. To promote comparability between years, cases from 1980–90 have been restricted to those where at least some employees at the workplace were actually participating in the scheme. None the less, it should be noted that only the 1984 and 1990 questions made specific reference to share-option schemes. At least some of the observed drop between 1990 and 1998 may result from these changes in question wording.

If public trading organizations are excluded from the overall results (since none of them report share ownership) the respective figures for the four surveys in the private sector are 14, 23, 31 and 24 per cent.

26 Another possibility is that it was particularly pronounced in the smallest workplaces, excluded from our surveys.

27 The data for each workplace consisted of the proportion of full-time employees (male and female) whose annual earnings (including bonuses and overtime) fell into the following bands: less than £9,000; £9,000 to less than £12,000; £12,000 to less than £16,000; £16,000 to less than £22,000; £22,000 to less than £29,000; £29,000 or more. Our measure of dispersion calculated the proportion of employees in the extreme bands at either end, plus an adjacent band, where appropriate. For example, for workplaces whose median pay was within the £12,000 to less than £16,000 per annum band, we summed the proportion in the bottom band and the top two bands. In this particular case, joiners had an average of 11 per cent of employees in the three extreme bands, while workplaces that had existed since 1990 also averaged 11 per cent.

7 Verdict and prospect

1 The figure of 16 per cent for all workplaces is derived from Table 5.14.

2 In fact, new workplaces were no different from continuing workplaces in 1998 in their use of e-mail to communicate or consult with employees.

3 When asked about the most recent pay settlement for the largest occupational group at the workplace, managers reported that negotiations had taken place with

employee representatives in around one fifth of all cases. Employee representatives had been consulted in only a further tenth of all workplaces.

Technical appendix

1 The purpose of this was to reduce the burden on personnel managers. In workplaces where the respondent was identified as a personnel specialist and a financial manager could also be identified, certain questions which, elsewhere, were asked of the personnel manager were instead directed to the financial manager. This occurred in 454 workplaces in total in 1990.
2 In 1980, 1984 and 1990 this was called the *Basic Workforce Data Sheet (BWDS)*. In 1998, the name was changed to the *Employee Profile Questionnaire (EPQ)*.
3 CAPI ensures that routing instructions are not missed in error by interviewers. It also enables edit checks to be incorporated into the interview so that inconsistent answers might be highlighted and dealt with during the interview.
4 One plausible reason for the slight fall in the response rate between 1990 and 1998 is the inclusion of a survey of employees, for the first time, in the 1998 survey.
5 Further details of the 1980–84 panel survey in the WIRS series, and a selection of results, may be found in the second WIRS sourcebook (Millward and Stevens, 1986). The 1984–90 panel survey is discussed in two volumes covering the whole of the 1990 WIRS (Millward *et al.*, 1992; Millward, 1994a) and in two dedicated volumes (Millward, 1994b, 1996).
6 Workplaces might also fall out of scope by changing their activity to one not covered by the series (e.g. agriculture) or by relocating to a site outside of the British Isles. However, such cases can be considered to be extremely rare.

Bibliography

Adams, K. (1991) 'Externalization vs. specialization: what is happening to personnel?', *Human Resource Management Journal* 1(4): 40–54.

Advisory, Conciliation and Arbitration Service (1998) *ACAS Annual Report 1998*, Leicester: ACAS Reader Ltd.

Airey, C. and Potts, A. (1983) *Survey of Employee Relations: Technical Report*, London: Social and Community Planning Research.

Airey, C., Tremlett, N. and Hamilton, R. (1992) *The Workplace Industrial Relations Survey (1990): Technical Report (Main and Panel Surveys)*, London: Social and Community Planning Research.

Airey, C., Hales, J., Hamilton, R., Korovessis, C., McKernan, A. and Purdon, S. (1999) *The Workplace Employee Relations Survey (WERS) 1997–8: Technical Report*, London: National Centre for Social Research.

Atkinson, J. and Hillage, J. (1994) 'Employers' policies and attitudes towards check-off', *Manpower Commentary Series* 271.

Bach, S. and Sisson, K. (2000) 'Personnel management in perspective', in S. Bach and K. Sisson (eds) *Personnel Management: A Comprehensive Guide to Theory and Practice*, 3rd edition, Oxford: Blackwell.

Bailey, R. (1996) 'Public sector industrial relations', in I. Beardwell (ed.) *Contemporary Industrial Relations: A Critical Analysis*, Oxford: Oxford University Press.

Beatson, M. (1993) 'Trends in pay flexibility', *Employment Gazette* 101(9): 405–28.

Blanchflower, D. (1984) 'Union relative wage effects: a cross-section analysis using establishment data', *British Journal of Industrial Relations* 22(4): 311–32.

—— (1986) 'What effect do unions have on relative wages in Great Britain?', *British Journal of Industrial Relations* 24(2): 195–204.

Blanchflower, D. and Cubbin, J. (1986) 'Strike propensities at the British workplace', *Oxford Bulletin of Economics and Statistics* 48(1): 19–39.

Blanchflower, D. and Freeman, R. (1994) 'Did the Thatcher reforms change British labour market performance?', in R. Barrell (ed.) *The UK Labour Market: Comparative Aspects and Institutional Developments*, Cambridge: Cambridge University Press.

Blanchflower, D. and Oswald, A. (1988) 'Profit-related pay: prose discovered?', *Economic Journal* 98(392): 720–30.

—— (1995) 'The British wage curve', in D. Blanchflower and A. Oswald, *The Wage Curve*, Cambridge, MA: MIT Press.

Blanchflower, D., Oswald, A. and Garrett, M. (1990) 'Insider power in wage determination', *Economica* 57(226): 143–70.

Boxall, P. and Haynes, P. (1997) 'Strategy and trade union effectiveness in a neo-liberal environment', *British Journal of Industrial Relations* 35(4): 567–91.

Brown, W. (1993) 'The contraction of collective bargaining in Britain', *British Journal of Industrial Relations* 31(2): 189–201.

Brown, W. and Walsh, J. (1991) 'Pay determination in Britain in the 1980s: the anatomy of decentralization', *Oxford Review of Economic Policy* 7(1): 44–59.

—— (1994) 'Managing pay in Britain', in K. Sisson (ed.) *Personnel Management: A Comprehensive Guide to Theory and Practice in Britain*, Oxford: Blackwell.

Brown, W., Marginson, P. and Walsh, J. (1995) 'Management: pay determination and collective bargaining', in P. Edwards (ed.) *Industrial Relations: Theory and Practice in Britain*, Oxford: Blackwell.

Brown, W., Deakin, S. and Ryan, P. (1997) 'The effects of British industrial relations legislation 1979–97', *National Institute Economic Review* 161: 69–83.

Brown, W., Deakin, S., Hudson, M., Pratten, C. and Ryan, P. (1998) *The Individualization of Employment Contracts in Britain*, Department of Trade and Industry Employment Relations Research Series 4, Department of Trade and Industry: London.

Bryson, A. (1999) 'Are unions good for industrial relations?', in R. Jowell, J. Curtice, A. Park and K. Thomson (eds) *British Social Attitudes: The 16th Report*, Aldershot: Dartmouth.

Casey, B., Metcalf, H. and Millward, N. (1997) *Employers' Use of Flexible Labour*, London: Policy Studies Institute.

Colling, T. and Ferner, A. (1992) 'The limits of autonomy: devolution, line managers and industrial relations in privatized companies', *Journal of Management Studies* 29(2): 209–27.

Cully, M. (1998) *A Survey in Transition: The Design of the 1998 Workplace Employee Relations Survey*, London: Department of Trade and Industry.

Cully, M. and Woodland, S. (1998) 'Trade union membership and recognition 1996–97: an analysis of data from the Certification Officer and the LFS', *Labour Market Trends* 106(7): 353–64.

Cully, M., Woodland, S., O'Reilly, A. and Dix, G. (1999) *Britain at Work: As Depicted by the 1998 Workplace Employee Relations Survey*, London: Routledge.

Daniel, W. W. (1987) *Workplace Industrial Relations and Technical Change*, London: Policy Studies Institute.

Daniel, W. W. and Millward, N. (1983) *Workplace Industrial Relations in Britain: The DE/PSI/SSRC Survey*, London: Heinemann.

Darlington, R. (1994) 'Shop stewards' organization in Ford Halewood: from Beynon to today', *Industrial Relations Journal* 25(2): 136–49.

Department of Employment (1991) *Industrial Relations in the 1990s*, London: HMSO.

Department of Trade and Industry (1998) *Fairness at Work*, White Paper, Cm 3968, London: HMSO.

Dickens, L. and Hall, M. (1995) 'The state: labour law and industrial relations', in P. Edwards (ed.) *Industrial Relations: Theory and Practice in Britain*, Oxford: Blackwell.

Disney, R., Gosling, A. and Machin, S. (1995) 'British unions in decline: determinants of the 1980s fall in union recognition', *Industrial and Labor Relations Review* 48(3): 403–19.

Dunn, S. and Metcalf, D. (1996) 'Trade union law since 1979', in I. Beardwell (ed.) *Contemporary Industrial Relations: A Critical Analysis*, Oxford: Oxford University Press.

Edwards, P., Hall, M., Hyman, R., Marginson, P., Sisson, K., Waddington, J. and Winchester, D. (1998) 'Great Britain: from partial collectivism to neo-liberalism to where?', in A. Ferner and R. Hyman (eds) *Changing Industrial Relations in Europe*, Oxford: Blackwell.

Elgar, J. and Simpson, B. (1993) 'The impact of the law on industrial disputes in the 1980s', in D. Metcalf and S. Milner (eds) *New Perspectives on Industrial Relations*, London: Routledge.

Employment Gazette (1988) 'Ethnic origin and the labour market' 96(3): 164–77.

Enderwick, P. (1985) 'Ownership nationality and industrial relations practices in British non-manufacturing industries', *Industrial Relations Journal* 16(2): 50–9.

Erickson, C. and Kuruvilla, S. (1998) 'Industrial relations system transformation', *Industrial and Labor Relations Review* 52(1): 3–21.

Fernie, S. and Metcalf, D. (1995) 'Participation, contingent pay, representation and performance: evidence from Great Britain', *British Journal of Industrial Relations* 33(3): 379–415.

Freeman, R. and Pelletier, J. (1990) 'The impact of industrial relations legislation on British union density', *British Journal of Industrial Relations* 28(2): 141–64.

Gall, G. and McKay, S. (1997) 'Unofficial strikes in Britain, 1960–1996', Paper presented to the Annual Conference of the British Universities Industrial Relations Association, University of Bath, July.

Gallie, D. and Rose, M. (1996) 'Employer policies and trade union influence', in D. Gallie, R. Penn and M. Rose (eds) *Trade Unionism in Recession*, Oxford: Oxford University Press.

Gallie, D., White, M., Cheng, Y. and Tomlinson, M. (1998) *Restructuring the Employment Relationship*, Oxford: Oxford University Press.

Gennard, J. and Kelly, J. (1997) 'The unimportance of labels: the diffusion of the personnel/HRM function', *Industrial Relations Journal* 28(1): 27–42.

Gooch, L. and Ledwith, S. (1996) 'Women in personnel management: re-visioning of a handmaiden's role?', in S. Ledwith and F. Colgan (eds) *Women in Organizations: Challenging Gender Politics*, London: Macmillan.

Gosling, A. and Machin, S. (1995) 'Trade unions and the dispersion of earnings in British establishments, 1980–90', *Oxford Bulletin of Economics and Statistics* 57(2): 167–84.

Green, F. (1992) 'Recent trends in British trade union density: how much of a compositional effect?', *British Journal of Industrial Relations* 30(3): 445–58.

Greene, W. (1990) *Econometric Analysis*, New York: Macmillan.

Guest, D. (1987) 'Human resource management and industrial relations', *Journal of Management Studies* 24(5): 503–22.

Guest, D. and Hoque, K. (1993) 'The mystery of the missing human resource manager', *Personnel Management* June: 40–1.

Guest, D. and Peccei, R. (1994) 'The nature and causes of effective human resource management', *British Journal of Industrial Relations* 32(2): 219–42.

Hakim, C. (1996) *Key Issues in Women's Work: Female Heterogeneity and the Polarization of Women's Employment*, London: Athlone Press.

Heywood, J., Siebert, W. and Wei, X. (1995) 'Piece rate payment systems: UK evidence', Department of Commerce, University of Birmingham, mimeo.

—— (1997) 'Payment by results systems: British evidence', *British Journal of Industrial Relations* 35(1): 1–22.

Hosmer, D. and Lemeshow, S. (1989) *Applied Logistic Regression*, New York: Wiley.

Hyman, R. (1997) 'The future of employee representation', *British Journal of Industrial Relations* 35(3): 309–36.

Ingram, P., Wadsworth, J. and Brown, D. (1999) 'Free to choose? Dimensions of private-sector wage determination, 1979–1994', *British Journal of Industrial Relations* 37(1): 33–50.

Kessler, S. and Bayliss, F. (1998) *Contemporary British Industrial Relations*, 3rd edition, Basingstoke: Macmillan.

Leslie, D. and Pu, Y. (1996) 'What caused rising earnings inequality in Britain? Evidence from time series, 1970–93', *British Journal of Industrial Relations* 34(1): 111–30.

Lucas, R. (1995) *Managing Employee Relations in the Hotel and Catering Industry*, London: Cassell.

McGovern, P., Hope-Hailey, V. and Stiles, P. (1998) 'The managerial career after downsizing: case studies from the "leading edge"', *Work, Employment and Society* 12(3): 457–77.

Machin, S. and Stewart, M. (1996) 'Trade unions and financial performance', *Oxford Economic Papers* 48: 213–41.

Machin, S., Stewart, M. and Van Reenan, J. (1993) 'The economic effects of multiple unionism: evidence from the 1984 Workplace Industrial Relations Survey', *Scandinavian Journal of Economics* 95(3): 279–96.

McNabb, R. and Whitfield, K. (1998) 'The impact of financial participation and employee involvement on financial performance', *Scottish Journal of Political Economy* 45(2): 171–87.

Mansfield, R. and Poole, M. (1991) *British Management in the Thatcher Years*, Corby: British Institute of Management Foundation.

Marchington, M. and Parker, P. (1990) *Changing Patterns of Employee Relations*, Hemel Hempstead: Harvester Wheatsheaf.

Marginson, P. (1984) 'The distinctive effects of plant and company size on workplace industrial relations', *British Journal of Industrial Relations* 22(1): 1–14.

Marginson, P., Edwards, P., Martin, R., Purcell, J. and Sisson, K. (1988) *Beyond the Workplace: Managing Industrial Relations in the Multi-Establishment Enterprise*, Oxford: Blackwell.

Marginson, P., Armstrong, P., Edwards, P. and Purcell, J. with Hubbard, N. (1993) *The Control of Industrial Relations in Large Companies: An Initial Analysis of the Second Company Level Industrial Relations Survey*, Warwick Papers in Industrial Relations no. 45, Coventry: Industrial Relations Research Unit.

Martin, R., Fosh, P., Morris, H., Smith, P. and Undy, R. (1991) 'The decollectivisation of trade unions?' *Industrial Relations Journal* 22(3): 197–208.

Metcalf, D. and Stewart, M. (1991) 'Unions and pay: does the closed shop thicken the gravy?', Department of Economics, University of Warwick, Working Paper no. 9215.

—— (1992) 'Closed shops and relative pay: institutional arrangements or high density?', *Oxford Bulletin of Economics and Statistics* 54(4): 503–16.

Millward, N. (1994a) *The New Industrial Relations?* London: Policy Studies Institute.

—— (1994b) *Change within the Workplace: Trade Union Organization, Bargaining Arrangements and Payment Systems in the 1984–1990 Workplace Industrial Relations Survey Panel*, London: Policy Studies Institute.

—— (1996) *The 1984–1990 Panel in the Workplace Industrial Relations Survey: Some Substantive Analyses and a Methodological Assessment*, London: Policy Studies Institute.

Millward, N. and Stevens, M. (1986) *British Workplace Industrial Relations 1980–1984: The DE/ESRC/PSI/ACAS Surveys*, Aldershot: Gower.

Millward, N. and Woodland, S. (1995) 'Gender, segregation and male/female wage differences', *Gender Work and Organization* 2(3): 125–39.

Millward, N., Stevens, M., Smart, D. and Hawes, W. R. (1992) *Workplace Industrial Relations in Transition: The ED/ESRC/PSI/ACAS Surveys*, Aldershot: Dartmouth.

Millward, N., Forth, J. and Bryson, A. (1999a) 'Changes in employment relations, 1980–1998', in M. Cully, S. Woodland, A. O'Reilly and G. Dix (1999) *Britain at Work: As Depicted by the 1998 Workplace Employee Relations Survey*, London: Routledge.

Millward, N., Woodland, S., Bryson, A. and Forth, J. (1999b) *A Bibliography of Research Based on WIRS*, London: Policy Studies Institute.

Milner, S. (1995) 'The coverage of collective pay-setting institutions: 1895–1990', *British Journal of Industrial Relations* 33(1): 69–91.

Nolan, P. and Walsh, J. (1995) 'The structure of the economy and labour market', in P. Edwards (ed.) *Industrial Relations: Theory and Practice in Britain*, Oxford: Blackwell.

O'Mahony, M., Oulton, N. and Vass, J. (1998) 'Market services: productivity benchmarks for the UK', *Oxford Bulletin of Economics and Statistics* 60(4): 529–51.

Pendleton, A. (1997) 'Characteristics of workplaces with financial participation: evidence from the Workplace Industrial Relations Survey', *Industrial Relations Journal* 28(2): 103–19.

Peters, T. and Waterman, R. (1982) *In Search of Excellence*, New York: Harper and Row.

Phelps Brown, H. (1990) 'The counter-revolution of our time', *Industrial Relations* 29(1): 1–14.

Plewis, I. (1985) *Analysing Change: Measurement and Explanation Using Longitudinal Data*, Chichester: Wiley.

Poole, M. (1989) *The Origins of Economic Democracy*, London: Routledge.

Poole, M. and Mansfield, R. (1993) 'Patterns of continuity and change in managerial attitudes and behaviour in industrial relations 1980–1990', *British Journal of Industrial Relations* 31(1): 11–35.

Purcell, J. (1983) 'The management of industrial relations in the modern corporation: agenda for research', *British Journal of Industrial Relations* 21(1): 1–16.

—— (1993) 'The end of institutional industrial relations', *Political Quarterly* 64(1): 6–23.

Purcell, J. and Ahlstrand, B. (1989) 'Corporate strategy and the management of employee relations in the multi-divisional company', *British Journal of Industrial Relations* 27(3): 396–417.

Purcell, J. and Gray, A. (1986) 'Corporate personnel departments and the management of industrial relations: two case studies in ambiguity', *Journal of Management Studies* 23(2): 205–23.

Rubery, J. (1995) 'The low paid and the unorganized', in P. Edwards (ed.) *Industrial Relations: Theory and Practice in Britain*, Oxford: Blackwell.

Scarborough, H. (1998) 'The unmaking of management? Change and continuity of British management in the 1990s', *Human Relations* 51(6): 691–716.

Seifert, R. (1992) *Industrial Relations in the NHS*, London: Chapman and Hall.

Sisson, K. (1993) 'In search of HRM', *British Journal of Industrial Relations* 31(2): 201–10.

—— (1994a) 'Personnel management: paradigms, practice and prospects', in K. Sisson (ed.) *Personnel Management: A Comprehensive Guide to Theory and Practice in Britain*, 2nd edition, Oxford: Blackwell.

—— (1994b) 'HRM and the personnel function', in J. Storey (ed.) *Human Resource Management: A Critical Text*, London: Routledge.

Sisson, K. and Marginson, P. (1995) 'Management: systems, structure and strategy', in P. Edwards (ed.) *Industrial Relations: Theory and Practice in Britain*, Oxford: Blackwell.

Sly, F., Thair, T. and Risdon, A. (1998) 'Labour market participation of ethnic minority groups', *Labour Market Trends* 106(12): 601–15.

Smith, P. and Morton, G. (1997) 'Union exclusion: retrospect 1979–97 and prospect', Paper presented to Annual Conference of the British Universities Industrial Relations Association, University of Bath, July.

Stewart, M. (1995) 'Union wage differentials in an era of declining unionization', *Oxford Bulletin of Economics and Statistics* 7(2): 143–66.

Storey, J. (1992) *Developments in the Management of Human Resources*, Oxford: Blackwell.

Storey, J. and Sisson, K. (1993) *Managing Human Resources and Industrial Relations*, Buckingham: Open University Press.

Terry, M. (1999) 'Systems of collective employee representation in non-union firms in the UK', *Industrial Relations Journal* 30(1): 16–30.

Thornley, C. (1998) 'Contesting local pay: the decentralization of collective bargaining in the NHS', *British Journal of Industrial Relations* 36(3): 414–18.

Tyson, S. (1987) 'The management of the personnel function', *Journal of Management Studies* 23(2): 205–23.

UNCTAD (1998) *World Investment Report 1998: Trends and Determinants*, New York: United Nations Conference on Trade and Development.

Waddington, J. and Whitson, C. (1995) 'Trade unions: growth, structure and policy', in P. Edwards (ed.) *Industrial Relations: Theory and Practice in Britain*, Oxford: Blackwell.

Wajcman, J. (1996) 'Desperately seeking differences: is management style gendered?', *British Journal of Industrial Relations* 34(3): 333–49.

Winchester, D. and Bach, S. (1995) 'The state: the public sector', in P. Edwards (ed.) *Industrial Relations: Theory and Practice in Britain*, Oxford: Blackwell.

Wood, S. (1996) 'High commitment management and payment systems', *Journal of Management Studies* 33(1): 53–77.

Wood, S. and Godard, J. (1999) 'The statutory union recognition procedure in the Employment Relations Bill: a comparative analysis', *British Journal of Industrial Relations* 37(2): 203–45.

Wright, M. (1996) 'The collapse of compulsory unionism? Collective organization in highly unionized British companies, 1979–1991', *British Journal of Industrial Relations* 34(4): 497–513.

Index